this book belongs to

_____

date I started this study

_____

CHRISTOS
God's Transforming Touch

Clarity Publishers • Birmingham, AL

Printed in the United States of America.

Life Bible Study
P.O. Box 36040
Birmingham, AL 35236

To order additional copies of this resource, call the publisher at 888.811.9934 or order online at www.lifebiblestudy.com.

Inside images © jupiterimages, BananaStock, Comstock, Photodisc, and Margie Williamson

Editorial and Design Staff

Author
C. Gene Wilkes

Executive Editor
Margie Williamson

General Editor
Jill Puckett Aldridge

Editor
Ginny Bollinger

Copy Editor
Kaci Lane Hindman

Graphic Design
Brandi K. Etheredge

Vice President, Ministry Resources
Paul Kelly

C. Gene Wilkes—Gene is the Pastor of Legacy Church, Plano, Texas, where he has served since 1987. The church has transitioned during his ministry to more effectively carry out its mission "to help people trust Jesus," and to live out its vision as "a mission outpost where every member is a missionary in his or her mission field."

Gene is the author of *Jesus on Leadership: Discovering the Secrets of Servant Leadership from the life of Christ*; *Paul on Leadership: Servant Leadership in a Ministry of Transition*, *My Identity in Christ*; *With All My Soul: God's Design for Spiritual Wellness*, and *Yahweh—Divine Encounters in the Old Testament* (Clarity Publishers). *Community-Based Servant Evangelism* and *An Angel in the Flame: A Tale of Two Saviors* will be released in 2008. He has also written for Student Life, an online Bible study for students.

Gene speaks at national conferences on the topics of spiritual gifts, lay mobilization, disciple making, and servant leadership. He has also led conferences and taught in Canada, China, Albania, Russia, and Cuba.

Gene received his bachelor's degree from Baylor University and his M.Div. and Ph.D. in New Testament Studies from Southwestern Baptist Theological Seminary.

Gene is a Resident Teaching Fellow for B. H. Carroll Theological Institute and an adjunct professor in the Gary Cook Graduate School of Leadership, Dallas Baptist University. He leads peer learning groups, coaches church leaders in the transition ministry, and serves on the Plano Independent School District's Diversity Advocacy Advisory Committee.

Introduction

His-story has two beginnings. The first was when the biblical storyteller wrote, "In the beginning God created the heavens and the earth" (Gen. 1:1). The second was when the Holy Spirit inspired John, one of Jesus' followers, to write, "In the beginning was the Word" (John 1:1). In the first beginning, God created life and established a special relationship with His most favored creatures—people—through a covenant, or agreement. That part of His-story is recorded in the 39 books traditionally called the Old Testament. (We will call it the Old Agreement of God.) We studied this part of His-story in *Yahweh: Divine Encounters in the Old Testament*.

When Adam and Eve chose to be like God through their willful act of disobedience, God separated Himself from them but began a rescue mission to restore that broken relationship.

The centerpiece of God's rescue mission for all people was built upon His agreement with Israel, the Law of Moses, and the Prophets' message. Outward expressions of God's agreement with Israel included priests, sacrifices, festivals, and daily practices. While these rules and rituals kept the agreement between God and Israel, they were incomplete. The relationship was missing someone.

The Bible reveals the "Word" in the first beginning of His-story was the in-flesh presence of God: Jesus—the Rescuer of all people, Second Person of the Trinity, and Creator of all things. The Creator entered His creation to establish a new covenant, or New Testament with those who turned their backs on Him in the first beginning. The second part of the Bible, the New Agreement, is the 27 books that reveal the life, teachings, and purpose of Jesus with His people and through the Church.

Jesus is the *Christos* (Greek for the Jewish Messiah), who was the Deliverer all people, not only one chosen ethnic group.

The name *Christos* declares Jesus was God's Son who came to rescue all people and show that their history is really His-story. He is the fulfillment of the Old Agreement of God. His death, burial, and Resurrection completed the Old Agreement and established the New Agreement of God will all people. Salvation is possible for all through trust in Jesus.

Christos is a walk through Jesus' life as told in evangelistic stories by His apprentices and those who learned from them. They witnessed what Jesus said and did. The four evangelists, Matthew, Mark, Luke, and John, wrote the Gospels so ". . . that you may believe that Jesus is the Christ, the Son of God, and that by believing you may have life in his name" (John 20:31). Guided by the Holy Spirit each writer purposely recorded Jesus' story from his perspective. Combined they give us a complete picture of Jesus, the *Christos.*

Christos will introduce you to the historical Jesus and the exalted *Christos*, leaving you with the decision to trust Him or not.

TABLE OF CONTENTS

STATEMENTS OF FAITH

As Christians, there are some essential truths we believe. We discover these truths in the Bible. At Clarity, we have identified eight truths we believe are essential for every Christian to know and understand. These statements give descriptions of those biblical truths and have been developed to help you talk about your faith. They will help you know what you believe.

GOD IS

Only one true and living God exists. He is the Creator of the universe, eternally existing in three Persons—the Father, Son, and Holy Spirit—each equally deserving of humanity's worship and obedience. He is infinite and perfect in all His attributes.

THE BIBLE IS GOD'S WORD

The Bible is God's written revelation to people, divinely given through human authors who were inspired by the Holy Spirit. It is entirely true. The Bible is totally sufficient and completely authoritative for matters of life and faith. The goal of God's Word is the restoration of humanity into His image.

PEOPLE ARE GOD'S TREASURE

God created people in His image for His glory. They are the crowning work of His creation. Yet every person has willfully disobeyed God—an act known as sin—thus inheriting both physical and spiritual death and the need for salvation. All human beings are born with a sin-nature and into an environment inclined toward sin. Only by the grace of God through Jesus Christ can they experience salvation.

JESUS IS GOD AND SAVIOR

Jesus is both fully God and fully human. He is Christ, the Son of God. Born of a virgin, He lived a sinless life and performed many miracles. He died on the cross to provide people forgiveness of sin and eternal salvation. Jesus rose from the dead, ascended to the right hand of the Father, and will return in power and glory.

THE HOLY SPIRIT IS GOD AND EMPOWERER

The Holy Spirit is supernatural and sovereign, baptizing all believers into the Body of Christ. He lives within all Christians beginning at the moment of salvation and then empowers them for bold witness and effective service as they yield to Him. The Holy Spirit convicts individuals of sin, uses God's Word to mature believers into Christ-likeness, and secures them until Christ returns.

SALVATION IS BY FAITH ALONE

All human beings are born with a sin nature, separated from God, and in need of a Savior. That salvation comes only through a faith relationship with Jesus Christ, the Savior, as a person repents of sin and receives Christ's forgiveness and eternal life. Salvation is instantaneous and accomplished solely by the power of the Holy Spirit through the Word of God. This salvation is wholly of God by grace on the basis of the shed blood of Jesus Christ and not on the basis of human works. All the redeemed are secure in Christ forever.

THE CHURCH IS GOD'S PLAN

The Holy Spirit immediately places all people who put their faith in Jesus Christ into one united spiritual body, the Church, of which Christ is the head. The primary expression of the Church on earth is in autonomous local congregations of baptized believers. The purpose of the Church is to glorify God by taking the gospel to the entire world and by building its members up in Christ-likeness through the instruction of God's Word, fellowship, service, worship, and prayer.

THE FUTURE IS IN GOD'S HANDS

God will bring the world to its appropriate end in His own time and in His own way. At that time, Jesus Christ will return personally and visibly in glory to the earth. Both the saved and unsaved will be resurrected physically to be judged by Christ. Those who have trusted Christ will receive their reward and dwell forever in heaven with the Lord. Those who have refused Christ will spend eternity in hell, the place of everlasting punishment. The certain return of Christ motivates believers to be faithful in their daily lives.

1—Finding Salvation in Christ: Discovering Christ's Identity

Jesus is a central figure in history. Few would dispute that claim. But if you add the title *Christos*, the Christ, to His name, you might have an argument on your hands. In a postmodern world, Christianity's claim that Jesus is the central figure in all human history has fallen under attack. People want to know: "What about the other religious leaders in history? What makes Jesus more significant than Muhammad, Buddha, or Mahatma Gandhi?"

The Christian assertion that Jesus of Nazareth was not only a key person in human history but also the risen Son of God is founded on who He is and what He did to establish that reality. The source of this truth is the Bible. One's trust in Jesus as the *Christos* is based on his or her trust in what the writers recorded and the Church preserved in the Gospels, or evangelistic biographies, that tell us what Jesus did and taught. This chapter will examine what the New Testament (or what I will call the New Agreement of God) tells us about Jesus Christ.

The Memory Verse for this chapter is John 1:14. The mystery of the in-flesh person of *Christos* is the core of Jesus' identity. This verse serves as the basis for the theological truth of the "incarnation" of God in the person of Jesus Christ.

Our question to consider for this chapter is "Which Person of the Trinity created everything?" Other questions may include: "What is the Trinity?" or "Was everything created, or did it just happen?" We will discuss these questions at the end of this chapter.

1.1 Telling the Story

We have four Gospels in the New Agreement of God that tell the story of Jesus: Matthew, Mark, Luke, and John. The Gospel writers each had a unique perspective on who Jesus is and what He did. But they all agreed that He was the Son of God who inaugurated the Kingdom of God on earth, and was crucified on a cross, buried, and raised on the third day according to the Scriptures. They all agreed that Jesus was the Messiah, or the *Christos*, the Promised One told about in the Old Agreement of God with Israel. The Fourth Gospel, John's story of Jesus, is unique in that John was the only one of the inner circle of Jesus' apprentices who lived to an old age. John, unlike the other disciples, lived to reflect upon and write about the significance of Jesus as *Christos* in ways different from the other three.

John began his story of Jesus with "In the beginning." He wanted his readers to know that the One he followed and whose story he told did not enter time like everyone else. This One called the *Christos* was present at the beginning of all time. Before time came the Word who created all things.

Read John 1:1–2. Circle "Word" each time it occurs in these verses. What does this teach us about the "Word"?

John's beginning of Jesus' evangelistic biography with the words "in the beginning" is the second "in the beginning" in the Bible. The first occurs in Genesis 1:1 and tells the origin of all things. This introduction to Jesus links Him back to the Maker and beginning of all things. The concept of the "Word," or *logos*, reflects more the Old Agreement's concept of the "word of God" (which was spoken at creation and from the mouths of prophets) than the Greek idea of a principle as the foundation of reality. Through words spoken in covenant relationship God reveals Himself to people. Jesus, as we will see, came as God's revelation, His Living Word.

Read John 1:3–5. Underline the first phrase in verse 3. Circle the words "life," "light," and "darkness" in verses 4 and 5. Would you confess that Jesus is divine and the resurrected Son of God?

1.2 Jesus' Uniqueness

Write the name of a close friend or loved one here: _____. What qualities make that person unique to you? If asked to write one sentence to describe that uniqueness to others, what would you write? _____
_____

Read John 1:14. Underline the words "flesh" and "dwelling." Rewrite the first sentence in your own words. _____
_____

John confessed that the same Word who was present at the beginning of time "became flesh." We get the word *incarnation* from the Latin translation of the Greek word for *flesh*, or *skin*. The Word of God clothed Himself in a human body. This reality confirms the humanity of Jesus. He was a flesh and blood person who walked the earth like everyone else, and John will point out He was different. The word for "dwelling" in this verse is the same word for the dwelling place of God in the Tabernacle tent in the Old Agreement of God. (See Exodus 25–27 for details of the Tabernacle.) This portable tent represented the presence of God with the Jews as they wandered in the wilderness for 40 years. John confessed Jesus was the "tabernacle," or "dwelling place of God," among people as He lived on earth.

Circle the words "glory," "Father," "grace," and "truth" in John 1:14. What does this part of John's confession tell us about Jesus? Write your answer here:

_____

_____

John added that along with seeing the human Jesus that he and others saw, they also saw His "glory, the glory of the One and Only." "Glory" in Scripture refers to the presence of God (for example, Psalm 24:7–10). John recognized the presence of God in the human person of Jesus. He also added that Jesus "came from the Father," which emphasized His deity as God's only Son. But what about His character? John wrote that He was "full of grace and truth," both significant biblical concepts in our relationship with God. "Grace" is the means by which we are made right with God (Eph. 2:8), and "truth" is the essence of God's character (John 14:6).

The Bible reveals the person of Jesus as both human and divine, the dwelling place of God when He was on earth. Each of these concepts communicated who Jesus is to both the Greek and Jewish readers of John's Gospel about Jesus. They carried powerful images of who Jesus of Nazareth is as God's only Son.

Expand your confession of who Jesus is based on John 14:6. Write this in your own words in the space below.

_____

_____

_____

1.3 The One Who Rescues Us

One Sunday evening we hosted a group of people at our home. Our children were still young, and they loved to mingle among the adults and older children who wandered throughout our house. Our youngest, who loved being around people, followed a group of us outside onto the deck. It was winter, making the weather and water in the spa cold. As we talked, I heard a splash and turned to see my daughter sinking to the bottom of the spa. A friend who stood next to me stepped into the cold water without hesitation, grabbed her by her coat, and pulled her up into his arms. She

sputtered some, and we rushed her into the house for warm clothes and hot chocolate. The friend who rescued my daughter stood in soggy shoes and wet clothes with a towel around his shoulders but a smile on his face. I hugged him, wet clothes and all. Needless to say, my family feels grateful to this day for his quick response to my daughter's misstep.

Has anyone ever rescued you or a loved one? Under what circumstances? What did you do to show your appreciation for that person's act of heroism? Write some of your thoughts here: _____

_____

_____

_____

Every confession that God inspired to describe Jesus centers around His death on the cross. If you have experienced rescue from some danger, either physical or spiritual, you understand.

Read Colossians 1:13–14. A rescue mission frees a person from the danger he or she faces and brings him or her to a safe place. These two verses tell of Jesus' rescue mission for all people. In your own words, describe what He did based on the information in these verses. What was the result of His rescue mission?

_____

_____

Jesus, the *Christos*, has rescued those who have trusted Him from the "dominion of darkness" and brought them into the "kingdom." Through this act we have receievd freedom (redemption) and forgiveness.

Read Colossians 1:15–17. Underline the words "image" and "firstborn" in verse 15, and circle "all things" every time it appears in verses 16 and 17. What do these concepts reveal to you about Jesus?

Paul, the writer of the Colossian letter, concurred with John, the beloved disciple of Jesus, that Jesus was the visible presence of invisible God. We get our English word *icon* from the transliterated Greek word for *image*. Like the icon on your computer desktop that links to the unseen software on your hard drive, Jesus is the visible link to the very person and power of God, the Father. Paul also confirmed that Jesus, the *Christos*, created "all things," not only the physical realities of the universe but also the spiritual realities of the unseen world. He is before and above all that exists. The Bible also states that "in him all things hold together." If energy is the glue that holds matter together, then energy has a name; and that name is Jesus.

Read Colossians 1:18–23. Record in the space below key phrases in this passage that describe Jesus.

v. 18

v. 19

v. 20

v. 21

v. 22

v. 23

Again, add to your confession of who Jesus, the *Christos*, truly is. Take time to meditate on who He is and the fact that He rescued you from darkness.

_____

_____

1.4 Jesus as Servant

Imagine a member of the president's Secret Service calling to say that the president wants to come by and clean your house. After your initial suspicion that this is a prank call, the caller says that the president just arrived in your city and one of the things he likes to do when he has time is choose a house that he and his closest aides could clean. He would not arrive in the presidential motorcade, and he would not come dressed in a suit and tie. The president would wear jeans and a t-shirt and would walk from a certain place with four or five of his coworkers, carrying the mops, brooms, and dusting materials. When he knocks on the door, you must ask, "What is the president doing at my house?" He will answer, "The president is here to serve you." The caller then says the president will show up in about an hour.

How would you first react if such a thing happened? What suspicions and concerns would you have? What emotions would you feel? What would you do?

By instinct and revelation, people know they should respect, revere, and even fear God. If you believe God exists, you understand He is worthy of worship and reverence. The thought of God coming to you to serve your deepest needs seems a foreign concept to many religions, but it forms the heart of the Christian faith.

Read Philippians 2:5–8. Underline the key words that describe Jesus' actions. Do not overlook the words "humbled" and "obedient" in verse 8.

The Bible affirms both the full deity of Jesus (v. 6) and the in-flesh presence of Jesus on earth (v. 7). The unique message of this passage is that Jesus, the *Christos,* willingly limited His divine attributes in order to come in the form of a servant in "human likeness." The Creator comes to His creation as a servant in order to clean house. His humble act of service born out of obedience to His mission resulted in death on the cross and the rescue of all who would believe (v. 8).

Read Philippians 2:9–11. How did God the Father respond to His Son's willful obedience? Circle the word "exalted" in verse 9. What does the Bible say about the name of Jesus?

Eternal exaltation followed Jesus' earthly humiliation on the cross. The name of Jesus exists above every other name. God has exalted Him above all others for His obedient, humble service on the cross for all people, which resulted in their rescue from sin and death. The Suffering Servant-Messiah is the Exalted *Christos* forever.

The story of Jesus' incarnation as an humble and obedient servant who died to save others is the central story of all history. His-story defines our story and reveals to everyone the essence of life as created by God.

How would you describe Jesus' humiliation and exaltation to a friend or one of your children? Write this passage in your own words or write a parable or short story to tell of Jesus' choice to lay aside His divine attributes in order to enter the world of His creation so He could save those He had created and loved so deeply.

1.5 Jesus is Constant

My wife and I have college buddies we meet every other year for a week of vacation. We have done this for over 25 years, and we see one another and our children grow older each time we gather. While much has changed around and about us, one thing has not: who each of us is as a friend. We can count on one another being the same as always every time we get together. While the years and events that we all have experienced have varied, who we are has remained the same.

Do you have a friend or group of friends you have kept in touch with through the years? What aspects of their identity do you like that has always made up part of who they are? What about them allows you to keep trusting them as friends?

The biblical writers we have examined show us three essential things about Jesus' identity and aspects of our relationship with Him that never change and that form the basis of our trust in Him.

The first is that Jesus is God's Son. We know from the Bible that God manifests Himself as Father and Spirit. This has led to the concept of the Trinity, or God as Three in One. The Bible confesses, "The LORD our God, the LORD is one" (Deut. 6:4); but in reading History we see that our one God reveals Himself as Father, Son, and Spirit. Jesus, fully God and fully human, is the Second Person of the Triune God revealed in Scripture.

The second reality we learn about Jesus is that He is Creator. Reread John 1:3–5 and Colossians 1:16–17. What do these verses say about Jesus' role in creation?

We learn from the biblical revelation that "through him all things were made" and that "by him all things were created." *Christos* is Creator, and His entry into His creation in order to rescue it from destruction is the next reality we have learned about Jesus.

Jesus is our Rescuer. Read John 1:4; Colossians 1:13; and Philippians 2:8. We learn that "in him was life," He was "the light of men," "he has rescued us from the dominion of darkness," and He was obedient to a "death on a cross."

Jesus, the Second Person of the Trinity, the Creator of all things, entered His creation to rescue it from destruction. The Eternal Christ humbled Himself and wore the flesh of a man in order to die on the cross so all could find rescue from the eternal consequences of rebellion.

You have now met the central figure of all history. The story of Jesus, the Christ, is the most important story you will ever encounter. As we end this chapter, write the fresh understanding you have of the one called Jesus.

_____

_____

_____

For further study:
- **1 John 4:7–10**
- **John 14:5–7**

2—Trusting Prophecies About Christ: Discovering Christ's Identity

If Jesus is Creator and God-in-flesh whose death on the cross rescued from darkness those who trust Him, then you can suspect that history would provide signs of who He is and of His coming. The central figure of history has remained active from the first nanosecond of creation until now. He has revealed Himself and His purposes to those who look for Him. One piece of evidence that Jesus is the *Christos*, the Promised One, is that people who trusted and listened to God spoke of His coming—His in-flesh arrival—centuries before His birth in the village of Bethlehem in faraway Israel. In this chapter we will examine some of those who spoke what they heard from God in their own historical setting and whose words pointed to the coming of Jesus long before His birth.

The Memory Verse for this chapter is Isaiah 9:6. The words of this verse make up the chorus "For Unto Us a Child is Born" for the "Hallelujah Chorus" in Handel's *Messiah*, arguably the best-known rendition of biblical prophecy about Jesus' birth. Grow familiar with this promise that God would send His Son to free people from the bondage of sin and death.

Our question to consider for this chapter is "What is the oldest prophecy concerning Christ's coming?" The answer to this question provides a historical basis for the reliability of the Old Testament's hints about the coming Christ.

2.1 God's Messenger

I drove up on a head-on collision while going home from a speaking engagement. I pulled over and ran to the car that was in my lane of traffic. Five people were in the car. I asked the three in the back to exit the car and tended to the two in the front. The passenger-side rider had a bump on her head, and one of her friends helped her out of the car. I moved to the driver who was slumped over the steering wheel. He obviously took the brunt of the collision. He was groggy but conscious, and when he lifted his head I knew he was in serious trouble. I took off the camp t-shirt I wore and covered his wound. I did not leave his side until the paramedics arrived. My words to him for the half hour while I sat there consisted of "Help is on the way. Be still. Help is on the way."

Have you ever had to sit with someone in trouble or pain when the only thing you could do was sit there and say, "Help is on the way"? Write your experience on the lines below. If you do not have such an experience, do you know of one? How can you relate to that story?

_____

_____

_____

_____

Israel divided into Judah in the south and Israel in the north after a civil war that followed King Solomon's reign. The tribes of the northern kingdom suffered greatly at the hands of invading Assyrians, a process that eventually culminated in their overthrow in 721 B.C. Through Isaiah, who began his ministry in 740 B.C., God sent them a message that help was on the way. That help would not come immediately, but the humiliation of their affliction would come to an end and honor would come through a great king not yet born. This king from the line of David, whom Christians now know as Jesus Christ, would rule forever in peace, wisdom, justice, and righteousness.

Read Isaiah 9:1–2. Underline words such as "gloom" and "distress" that describe the gravity of the situation. Circle words such as "honor" and "light" that give hope.

Israel faced trouble. Its days were numbered, and the people knew it. Massed troops of foreign enemies stood outside the capitol as tension filled the air. Then in stepped God's messenger, Isaiah, a priest called to prophesy God's judgment and provision for His people.

Compare Isaiah's use of light in his promise (v. 2) and John's description of the Word in his introduction (John 1:4–5).

_____

_____

Read Isaiah 9:3–5. Underline the words that describe the gravity of the situation, and circle the words that give hope. What is the tone of Isaiah's message here?

_____

_____

Isaiah's colorful language points to a time when people would rejoice, like "at the harvest" and or "when dividing the plunder" (v. 3). God would shatter "the yoke," "the bar," and "the rod" of their oppressors (v. 4); and the bloodied clothes and boots of warriors would be burned (v. 5).

Take some time to meditate on God's promise to Israel that it may become God's words to you during trials.

2.2 A Message of Hope

Birth announcements have changed since we had our two girls over 20 years ago. Now people post "I'm pregnant" videos on YouTube and set up a Web site so people can follow the development and birth of the child. My wife and I receive "evites" to join friends at showers and to go online to shop and ship baby gifts. But the results remain the same. When we know our friends or family members have the blessing of taking part in bringing a new life into the world, we rejoice with them and share their hope for the life of the child.

Describe the last birth or pregnancy announcement you received. Who sent it? Did it surprise you? Did it make you sad? Write some of your memories here:

_____

_____

_____

_____

_____

Read Isaiah 9:6. Circle the word "son" and circle the titles He will bear.

The reason for the great joy expressed in verses 1–5 of this chapter is the birth of the coming King announced in verses 6 and 7. God revealed to Isaiah over 700 years before Jesus' birth that He would send Israel a child, "a son." "The government" would rest upon His shoulders, and He would bear divine titles of respect and worship.

We know from the historical record of Jesus that He did not hold any place in the country's government. The reference here refers to spiritual position of leadership as God's Reigning Son over all creation. The titles in verse 6 display His roles and character as the *Christos*.

Read Isaiah 9:7. Circle whose throne He woud reign from and underline the lengths of time Isaiah said He would rule.

God revealed that Jesus would "reign on David's throne." This refers to God's eternal covenant He made with King David that his throne would "be established forever" (2 Sam. 7:8–16). The Promised One would rule forever from the throne of the lineage of David. Again, Jesus never reigned as the earthly king of Israel, but He rose from the dead to sit at the right hand of the Father "far above all rule and authority, power and dominion, and every title that can be given, not only in the present age but also in the one to come" (Eph. 1:21). Physically, Jesus came from the line of David (Matt. 1:1–18); He rules from the eternal throne as the risen King over all creation—spiritual and physical.

God promised He would send a boy child from the lineage of Israel's King David who would grow up and ascend the throne from which He would rule forever. You can imagine what hope and joy such a promise would bring to the suffering Israelites.

What does this promise mean to you? How does it strengthen your trust in God? Write your thoughts here:

_____

_____

_____

Christos—God's Transforming Touch

2.3 Mission Accomplished

Great leaders accomplish a mission or cause that affects many people. Martin Luther King Jr. was a great leader because he gave his life to the vision that all Americans are created equal no matter their race. Margaret Thatcher, England's prime minister from 1979 to 1990, displayed greatness when she served her country's interest in the war over the Falkland Islands. Mayor Rudy Giuliani showed himself a great leader as he led New York City through the attacks of September 11, 2001, and restored that city to its former greatness. Think of a leader you consider great because he or she led well in a situation that he or she chose to address or was forced to face because of the role held at the time.

God sent His Son to accomplish the mission of rescuing a fallen creation from destruction. This is the central plot to His-story. Jesus came as a servant-leader to carry out the mission motivated by God's love for all people.

Read Isaiah 49:5–6. Circle the word "servant" in both verses. Underline those phrases that describe what God's servant would do. What does this tell you about who Jesus is and what He came to do?

God revealed that He formed the Coming One before birth "to be his servant." Those God used mightily who remained faithful to Him were called servants of God. God called King David "my servant David" (2 Sam. 7:8). Moses was known as "the servant of the Lord" (Deut. 34:5). Moses pleaded with God to remember His "servants Abraham, Isaac and Israel" (Ex. 32:13) and to not destroy the people when they built the golden calf. Great people in the Bible humbly wore the title servant.

This Promised One would "bring Jacob back to him" and "restore the tribes of Jacob" (Isa. 49:5–6). God also promised that He would make Him "a light for the Gentiles" so that He would bring God's "salvation to the ends of the earth" (v. 6). This One sent by God had a purpose and intention for His coming.

Read Isaiah 53:11. Underline the words "suffering" and "servant" and the phrase "bear their iniquities." What do these words tell you about the One promised in this prophetic chapter of the Bible?

_____

_____

Jesus came as the Suffering Servant-Savior. He would suffer on the cross and be the Servant to God's purpose for His life. He was the Savior who bore the sins of all people. Through His sacrificial death He justified, or made right, before Holy God those who trusted in Him. When we observe Jesus' ministry and death, we see Him as Servant to this clearly defined mission that God described centuries before He came. (See also Matthew 12:15–21, which quotes Isaiah 42:1–4 and directly connects this prophecy with Jesus.)

Prophecy told not only of Jesus' coming but also the purpose for His coming. Jesus is the Suffering Servant of God who saves those who trust in Him.

What new insight do you have about who Jesus is or what He came to do from these prophetic passages? Write your impressions in the space below. Then, end your time with a prayer of thanks to Jesus for His humble service that resulted in salvation for so many.

_____

_____

2.4 A Word from the Prophet

Few prophecies of Jesus' coming contain such vivid detail as Isaiah 53. In the middle of God's revelation to Israel of its destruction by Assyrian invaders, God showed to His prophet the true nature and work of the *Christos*. While Jesus did not meet the expectations of many who met Him, He faithfully lived out God's description of His role in the grand plan to rescue creation from destruction. Jesus' humble appearance and sacrificial death were God's way of rescuing all who had "gone astray" and each who had "turned to his own way" (v. 6).

Read Isaiah 53:1–5. Circle the word "like" throughout the passage to highlight some of the images Isaiah used to describe the Coming One. Underline the phrases in verse 5 that give us the results of the Messiah's suffering.

The prophet said that the Promised One God would send would have nothing attractive about Him to draw people to Him. Most people say they want charismatic, attractive, and strong people as leaders. However, God's plan was that our trust would not rely on the outward appearance or capabilities of the Sent One but upon what He did. Through His suffering and death He would bring the peace and healing that people desired and God required (Isa. 53:5).

Read Isaiah 53:6–10. How does verse 6 describe the condition of all people, and upon whom did the consequences of our condition fall? List the ways in which the Coming One was treated unjustly and how the passage described His character. Write your answers here:

_____

_____

_____

_____

_____

_____

Everyone has "turned to his own way," or sinned against God; but God placed our "iniquity" on Jesus, who like a sacrificial lamb was led to slaughter on a cross (vv. 6–7). He quietly gave His life for our "transgression" (v. 8). The detail of the prophecy is amazing. The first two phrases of verse 9 were fulfilled as Jesus died with two thieves and was placed in the grave of a wealthy religious leader. Jesus' death served as a "guilt

Christos—God's Transforming Touch

offering" (v. 10), the same concept Moses was instructed to teach for one's atonement in Leviticus 5:14–19.

God would honor the One who sacrificed His life for "the iniquity of us all" (v. 6). Philippians 2:9–11 echoes this exaltation and reveals to us Jesus' exalted place as the *Christos*.

2.5 Markers, Messages, and Signs

One aspect of trusting Jesus as the *Christos* is accepting the reality that God ultimately guides history. This may seem difficult for anyone who sees the evil and suffering in the world. To trust that God is who He says He is, we must come to that place of accepting that God is in control, not us. But this is not a blind faith. As with the other prophecies of Jesus' coming, God embedded into His-story details about Jesus' birth and death. The story of Jesus, the *Christos*, spans the entire history of time. From creation to His coming as a baby in a manger, God placed markers, messages, and signs that pointed to His Son's sacrificial solution to our rebellion against Him. The earliest signal of God's plan to rescue us through Jesus came in the moments of God's judgment on Adam and Eve for their rebellious act against Him.

Read Genesis 3:1–15. Underline the first sentence in verse 6. What did God ask Eve and what was her answer? (v. 13)

The serpent personified the evil one in this passage. He seduced Eve into eating the forbidden fruit in the Garden of Eden. Adam and Eve's eyes were opened (v. 5), and innocence was lost for all time. God knew of their choice and confronted them. Like a loving father, God led them to confess what they had done and then punished them.

God put "enmity" (from the root word for *enemy*) between the evil one and the children of Eve. Satan, personified as the serpent, would be the enemy of people forever, seducing them away from God's way of life to act as their own gods. But that was not the final solution. The second part of verse 15 reads, "he will crush your head, and you will strike his heel." Many believe that this was God's first revelation of His plan to send Jesus as the *Christos* to rescue people from the consequences of their rebellion against God. "He" in the verse is *Christos* who will defeat Satan when Satan gets "thrown into the lake of burning sulfur" (Rev. 20:10). "You" points to Satan's efforts to destroy Jesus through His death on the cross. The irony is that Satan's plan to defeat Jesus was the very plan of God to rescue those Satan deceived into trusting themselves as god.

Jesus did not come to earth as a last-minute reaction of God to human circumstance. From the moment of our rebellion, God instigated an all-out pursuit of people to rescue them from destruction. God purposefully revealed His plans so we would not miss that Jesus was "the Christ, the Son of the living God" (Matt. 16:16).

For further study:
- **Philippians 2:6–11**
- **Hebrews 9:28–10:4**

3—Responding in Humility: Discovering Christ's Identity

My favorite Christmas carol is "O Little Town of Bethlehem." I like it for the peaceful melody and pictures it paints of the town and world where Jesus was born. A preacher wrote it. Philips Brooks, a pastor in Philadelphia in the mid-19th century, wrote the words after a trip to the Holy Land. The church organist then added music for a children's Christmas program. I think I first learned it for a Christmas program as a child. Words written on memories of a trip to Bethlehem and captured in a tune for children's voices created a lasting chorus of God's gracious act of love by Jesus' birth.

Mary's words to God upon her visit to Elizabeth form the first song of Christ-mass that celebrates the coming Child of God. Her praise rises from the heart of a humble girl who realized God's mysterious presence in her life was part of a bigger plan to rescue her people. She did not know the full extent of God's work through her life, but she knew enough from angels' songs and Elizabeth's story to know this was no ordinary child or common situation.

The Memory Verse for this chapter is Luke 1:49. This phrase makes up part of Mary's confession of the greatness and holiness of God for His work in her life.

Our question to consider for this chapter is "Did Mary recognize the full impact of her pregnancy?" Can we fully understand what God is doing in our lives from our limited perspective on things? Write your initial answers in the space below, and then we will revisit them at the end of this chapter.

_____

_____

_____

_____

3.1 Gabriel's News

Have you ever heard about an event that happened to a friend or relative, and you just had to see it for yourself? Maybe a friend got a new car or a college acceptance letter or an engagement ring. Maybe the test results came back bearing bad news, and you wanted to sit with that person for a while. Whatever it is, you want to see and be with your loved one during moments of big news. Friends and family share life together; and in the middle of it all, they discover God's purposeful plan.

When was the last time you went to a friend or relative to see the news you heard? What circumstances surrounded the news? Did it cause joy or pain? Write your description here:

_____

_____

_____

_____

Read Luke 1:39–40. Circle the first three words of verse 39. Underline the proper nouns in the sentence to identify the characters and places in the story.

The phrase "at that time" signals we have stepped into a storyline that started before we began reading. Take a moment to read Luke 1:1–38 to see how this passage connects to the bigger story.

Mary was the engaged spouse of Joseph, and Elizabeth was her relative and the wife of Zechariah. They lived in the "hill country of Judea" (v. 39). At this time in the story, God had announced to both Elizabeth and Mary that their pregnancies were part of God's rescue plan for all people. Elizabeth was barren, and Mary had not yet married. Both situations were not "normal" settings for pregnancy in those days.

The angel Gabriel had come to both Zechariah and Mary to announce the birth of a son to each family. Zechariah's son would "go on before the Lord" (v. 17) who would "be called the Son of the Most High" (v. 32). In the angel's announcement to Mary, he mentioned that her relative Elizabeth was pregnant, too. Mary had to see for herself and tell her relative of the angel's visit that revealed the news to her.

Mary's trip to Elizabeth's home was filled with awe. She stood in awe of her own pregnancy along with that of her barren relative. But even better, an angel had announced this truth to her. She had to go tell her story.

End your time with this part of His-story by praising God for revealing His plan to those who would participate in it. Ask God to reveal anything He would have you do today to serve His greater purposes.

3.2 Sharing the Joy

When my wife was pregnant with our first child, we were most fascinated with how the baby would kick and move in my wife's womb. Kim would say, "Come here, quick. It's doing somersaults in there!" She would place my hand where she thought the baby's feet would push against her stomach again. It felt bizarre to touch the moving foot of a child not yet born. Sometimes while sitting in the car or at a restaurant, she would say, "Whoa! The baby just kicked me." We would laugh and talk about how active the child would be when she was born. And she is an active child just as we had thought.

Have you ever felt the movement of a child in its mother's womb? If you were the father, what emotions did you feel? If you were a friend, what did you tell the mother? If you were the one pregnant, what thoughts and emotions did you have the first time you felt your child move? Write your answers here:

_____

_____

_____

_____

When Mary entered the house of Elizabeth, whom the angel had said was pregnant, something happened that affirmed the angel's word.

Read Luke 1:41. Underline what Luke tells us about Elizabeth when Mary greeted her.

The baby in Elizabeth's womb jumped when he heard Mary's greeting. The one who would announce the Messiah's coming leaped in anticipation when he heard the voice of the one who would bear Him. Luke also noted that "Elizabeth was filled with the Holy Spirit." God's guiding presence rested upon her as the child grew within her.

Read Luke 1:42–45. Circle the words "blessed" and "favored" in these verses. Underline in verse 45 the reason Elizabeth said Mary was blessed.

Elizabeth's response to the baby's movement when Mary greeted her was to acknowledge Mary as "blessed,"

or "favored," because God had chosen her to bear the *Christos*, the Promised One. "Blessed *art* thou among women, and blessed *is* the fruit of thy womb" (KJV) is the scriptural basis for the Roman Catholic prayer "Hail Mary," which venerates the mother of Jesus beyond the intention of Elizabeth's greeting. Elizabeth primarily blessed Mary because of her faith. Mary trusted God's word, and she came to share that joy with the one the angel had said was six months pregnant with a son, too.

Like two relatives today who fill with joy when they first meet after finding out about their pregnancies, Elizabeth and Mary shared the joy of the God-promised life within them. Elizabeth reminded Mary how blessed she was to carry the "Lord" (v. 43). She also acknowledged faith as trusting that God would accomplish what He had said (v. 45).

Christos—God's Transforming Touch

What joys have you shared with a friend that caused you to call him or her "blessed" by God because of what was happening at the time? When have you considered yourself blessed by God because of what He had done for you? Write a prayer of thanks here:

_____

_____

_____

_____

3.3 Words of Praise

Praise is at the heart of our relationship with God. It includes more than a passing "thank you" for service rendered. Praise acknowledges who God is and what He has done for us. It is taking time to put into words what our heart feels about God's kindness shown to us. From Moses (Deut. 32) to David (2 Sam. 22) to almost every psalm sung by Israel (Ps. 113) to the prophet Daniel (Dan. 2:19–23) to Mary, the mother of Jesus, praise has remained core to the worship of God.

Read some of the passages of praise mentioned in the paragraph above. Find ways to include these words of praise into your personal worship of God. Let these words guide your heart to praise God.

As soon as Mary heard what Elizabeth said, she sang her own song of praise to God. Elizabeth's announcement affirmed the words of the angel who said she and her relative were pregnant by the work of the Lord.

Read Luke 1:46–49. Circle the verbs that tell what Mary's soul and spirit do in verses 46 and 47. Underline the word "for" at the beginning of verses 48 and 49 to identify why she praised God. Underline the last phrase of verse 49.

Verses 46–55 compose Mary's song of praise to God for choosing her to bear the *Christos*, the Coming One. In some faith traditions, her lyrical praise is known as The Magnificat after the first word in the Latin translation for "magnify."

Worship is our soulful response to God for who He is and what He has done for us. Praise points to who He is and what He has done, and Mary "glorifies" and "rejoices in" God for His work in her life. The word "for" indicates the reasons behind her praise. God had considered her His humble servant and had done "great things" for her. She concluded her praise by confessing His name as "holy."

What reasons do you have to praise God today? You may not consider what God is doing in your life as praiseworthy as the saints of Scripture did, but God is active in every aspect of your life. Take some time to list reasons why you can praise God today as part of your lifestyle of worship.

_____

_____

_____

_____

_____

_____

_____

_____

_____

_____

3.4 Mary's Song

God seldom works in the way we expect Him to work. We anticipate Almighty God to work with the powerful, and the God who created all things to come alongside the richest. When God sent His Son to establish a new creation, He did not choose a queen like Esther to have the child. He chose a common, humble girl named Mary. We who look to the powerful and rich for our hope to make things better get a hint of God's ways by His choice of who would bear His only Son. God chose the weak and poor, the humble and powerless, to establish His will on earth.

To whom do you look to make things better? Do you trust those in power more than those without power to change the world? Do you expect the wealthy to have a greater impact on changing people's lives than ordinary people without many means? Write some of your thoughts here:

_____

_____

_____

_____

Read Luke 1:50. Circle the word "mercy" and underline "extends to those who fear him."

Mary continued her song of praise to God by confessing His mercy, which He shows to "those who fear him, from generation to generation." Mary sang that she was a recipient of His mercy in her generation. She then continued to confess how God had shown His mercy.

Read Luke 1:51–53. Circle the verbs that describe what God did and underline those who received God's actions. For example, in verse 51, circle "performed" and "scattered" and underline "mighty deeds" and "those who are proud."

God revealed to Mary how He had worked throughout history to bring about His purposes and plans. Her song tells of God choosing the humble and hungry over the proud, rich rulers. Joseph and she were among the humble ones of Israel, and she saw how God's choice of her as the mother of the coming *Christos* was consistent with how God worked throughout history.

Read Luke 1:54–55. Circle those to whom God has shown His mercy as He said He would.

Mary concluded her song by acknowledging that God remained true to His word to Abraham. God had remembered to show mercy to him and his descendants, which included Mary. God faithfully completed His promises, and He chose Mary to bear His Son, Jesus.

You have seen God do things in your life and the lives of your extended family. Maybe you have heard stories of how God has worked in your extended family. Take time to record some of those times in the space below. You may want to write your own song of praise to God to declare how He has shown His mercy. Or, choose your favorite song of praise and sing or listen to it as part of your worship today.

_____

_____

_____

_____

Christos—God's Transforming Touch

3.5 Miracle Babies

Have you ever known a "miracle baby?" I knew a family in our church whose son was 16 when they joined our fellowship. I learned later that he was born at 24 weeks, weighed one pound and seven ounces, and measured only 12 inches long. No one but his mother and father trusted the boy would live, and live he did. He served as a constant reminder to all who know his story how God sustained that baby to live a special life for Him.

Write the story or circumstances of the "miracle baby" you know in the space below. It may be your own story. Share as many of the details as you would like to recall the events surrounding the birth.

_____

_____

_____

_____

Read Luke 1:56. Underline how long Mary stayed with Elizabeth. How many months pregnant was Elizabeth when Mary left? (Refer to verse 26 for a hint.)

Mary stayed with her relative the first three months of her pregnancy and the last three of Elizabeth's. Luke seems to tell us that Mary left in the ninth month of Elizabeth's pregnancy, just before the birth of John (v. 57). Mary may have needed to go home as her pregnancy progressed and left before John's birth. The three months must have comprised of family chores and stories and anticipation of how the lives of the two angel-announced boys would mesh. Remember, they had no medical way of knowing the gender of their children. They depended on the angel's message and their

trust in God to know the sex of their children. They surely rehashed the angel's appearance and promises and most surely how Mary became pregnant without the aid of a man!

Our question to consider for this chapter is "Did Mary recognize the full impact of her pregnancy?" How would you answer this question after observing her worshipful response to God? Write your answer here.

_____

_____

_____

_____

From the words of her song and the reaction of Elizabeth to her presence, Mary knew that the angel's message had merit. We can see that her trust in God gave her reason to sing for joy and acknowledge that God had invited her into His bigger story that would rescue Israel from its bondage. She had no way of knowing the full extent of what went on. She did not know what her child would do, but her trust in God and the affirming events around her pregnancy told her this was something huge and that God had invited her into it.

How will you express your humble worship to Jesus? God has invited you into His-story to play a part of His love story with people through trust in Jesus, the *Christos*. How can you tell others of God's great love for you and His demonstration of love in Jesus?

For further study:

• **Matthew 1:18–25**
• **1 Samuel 2:1–10**

4—Discovering God's Great Gift: Jesus' Birth

Why was Jesus born? What about the Christmas story makes it so important to a third of the world's population today, and why has it been the foundation of Western Civilization for over two millennia? Why has Jesus' birth brought up so much controversy about who He really is?

Jesus, the baby born in a manger to Mary and Joseph of Nazareth, is the Second Person of the Trinity who came in flesh to demonstrate God's love for all people. He came to show us what a life ruled by God looks like and how the Kingdom of God would look among real people who trust God to reign in their lives. God-in-flesh had a name, given to Him by God. Jesus, the *Christos*, came to suffer and die for people whom He had created with a free choice to love Him or not.

Jesus, who was born in Bethlehem, had human ancestors in a lineage of covenant people God chose to reveal Himself to the entire world. Fully God and fully human, Jesus died, was buried, was raised on the third day, and ascended to the right hand of the Father and now reigns as the *Christos*, the Son of God.

The Memory Verse for this chapter is Luke 2:11. Here we read the name *Christos* for the first time. The angel's announcement that the Christ would be born in the city of David delivered a promise the Jews had waited for centuries to hear.

Our question to consider for this chapter is "Why was Jesus born?" The answer may not be as obvious as it seems. Jesus' birth revealed many things about the nature of God and the condition of people. Take a shot at the answer, and we will return to the question later.

Christos—God's Transforming Touch

4.1 Birth Stories

I was born when Dwight D. Eisenhower was president of the United States and Nikita Khrushchev was in power in the Soviet Union. My mother and father were born in the panhandle of Texas but moved to Corpus Christi because my father, a chemist, had found an excellent job there. We lived in this breeze-blown, beach-lined town for the first six years of my life. After a couple of short stays in other Gulf Coast towns, my family settled in Beaumont, Texas, a port city with many refineries and international connections. We lived there until after I graduated from college, when I moved to Dallas. These are the general historical facts of my early years. While they may not sound interesting to anyone but me, they establish my birth with historical markers that others can know and reference.

Take a moment and describe the historical information surrounding your birthplace and early years of life. Google™ your birth year and see what all happened at the time. Write your information here:

_____

_____

_____

_____

Read Luke 2:1–2. Underline the references to historical people and events that mark the time Luke describes. Use a commentary or Bible handbook to find further facts about the reference.

Luke, who wrote one of our four evangelistic stories about Jesus, anchored the birth of Jesus in history. His-story is not a myth or ancient legend contrived by a group to get you to believe what they want you to believe. The story of Jesus makes up part of human history just as your birth story makes up part of history.

Along with the historical references around Jesus' birth, the rule of Rome brought many social and political issues. Rome dominated the known world at that time. It subjugated Israel, the nation of God's chosen people who paid taxes to the occupation government. A powerful emperor ruled his expansive empire, which engulfed the haggard and harassed the people of Israel. Among them was a young couple about to give birth to a son, the Rescuer of all.

End your time by thanking God that while you may not have all the details, you feel grateful for the risk of Him sending Jesus into our world as a gift to demonstrate His love for us.

4.2 God's Plan

How big is your God? How much credit do you give God for the movement of world events? Do things "just happen," or does God play a part in either allowing or orchestrating world events for history? Write some of your initial thoughts here:

_____

_____

_____

The prophet Micah (5:2) prophesied that Bethlehem in Judea, the birthplace of King David with whom God made a covenant to establish an eternal kingship through his lineage, would be the place from which the

Promised One would come. There posed a problem, however. Joseph, the man in the line of King David and the one to whom the angel Gabriel had promised would have a son who would be the Savior of Israel, happened to live kilometers away in Nazareth at the time of his wife's pregnancy. How could God's plan work out?

Read Luke 2:4–5. Underline the names and places Luke provides in his story. Underline the word "because" in verse 4 to mark the reason for this movement. Verse 5 provides us with the rest of the details about Mary and her condition.

Caught up in the movement of world politics, Joseph, a descendant of King David, made his way from his town of Nazareth in northern Israel, Galilee, to Bethlehem in the southern province of Judea. Why? Our storyteller tells us he was forced to go to "the town of David," Bethlehem, the king's birthplace, to register his wife and himself in the Roman census.

Luke tells us Joseph "belonged to the house and line of David," a key detail in the legitimacy of Jesus as the *Christos*. Both Luke and Matthew provide a genealogy to demonstrate evidence for Joseph's lineage (Matt. 1:1–17; Luke 3:23–38).

Read Luke 2:6–7. Underline the verbs "gave birth," "wrapped," and "placed" to follow the action of the events. Underline "because" in verse 7 for why Mary placed Jesus in a manger.

After a long and uncomfortable walk/ride from Nazareth in the north to Bethlehem in the south, Mary gave birth to her first child. As was common in those days, she wrapped the baby in strips of cloth to keep him warm. The next phrase catches our attention: "and placed him in a manger." Wait! The Savior, the Messiah, the *Christos* put in a feeding trough for animals? Luke explains this happened "because there was no room for them in the inn."

Overcrowded conditions forced Joseph and Mary to a barn to have her baby where the only crib was a hay-filled, stone-carved trough. The birth of the King of kings happened outside of any acceptable or expected ways of life. This either then signaled something completely new or a terribly botched plan to make Jesus look like the Messiah. I trust it was the former.

According to Luke's account of Jesus' birth, God moved the world to position Joseph and Mary in Bethlehem so that history would play out as He had promised it would. This would mean that even the Emperor's thought to have a census and then to direct it at this time in world history would have come from God. This, of course, is a matter of faith. So, let us return to the first question of this day's study: How big is your God? Prayerfully make your confession to God. Be honest. Ask for the faith to trust His Word and ways.

4.3 The Angels' Message

If you were God and you wanted to present your Son to those He came to rescue, what circumstances would you have surrounding His birth? Who would have attended His birth? What would you choose for His social, religious, and educational pedigree?

Read Luke 2:8–9. Circle the main characters in this part of the story. What time of day did this event occur? How did the shepherds respond to the angel appearing?

_____

_____

Angels are God's messengers. Whenever they show up, something important related to His-story will soon follow. God sent "an angel of the Lord" to tell of Jesus' birth. This is the expected part of the story. To whom the angel appeared throws us a curve. Shepherds? They belonged to the lower-end, unsophisticated branch of that society. Yes, they were doing what King David did before he became king. They could have been keeping the sheep used as sacrifices in the Temple; but after analyzing everything, these guys were lowlifes who drew the short straw to stay up with the sheep all night.

Read Luke 2:10–12. Underline the first response of the angel to the shepherds. Circle the key words "Savior" and "Christ the Lord." Underline "a sign" to mark the evidence of the angel's words.

The angel felt comfortable at the place and with the people he came to deliver his message to, but the shepherds felt terrified by his presence (v. 9). These out-of-the-mainstream men never expected an angel to appear to them. The messenger calmed them down and began to deliver the message God sent him to give (v. 10). Every Jew waited for the "Savior" or "Christ the Lord" of Israel. Even poor shepherds recognized those titles.

And what "sign" confirmed the angel's words as truth? A sign only a shepherd would understand or could find: a baby lying in a feeding trough. God moved the world

to get Joseph and Mary to a manger. Now He had to get the world to His Son. And He used the shepherds to do so. They not only found the baby but they also knew this Savior came not for the high and mighty but for the common folk like them.

Read Luke 2:13–14. Underline those who joined the single herald of God. Highlight the message of the "heavenly host" in verse 14.

A "host" of angels appeared with the one who spoke. You could interpret the phrase to mean, "a vast host of others—the armies of heaven" (NLT). Why so many angels in one spot? It was not because they needed a choir to sing part of the "Hallelujah Chorus." I like the idea of them waiting in the shadows to ensure the birth of God's Son. The angels could have been there to stand against the army of Satan.

4.4 Shepherds with a Message

When I was in the third grade a tornado almost destroyed our house in Milton, Florida. When my mother heard the winds moving closer to the house, she herded her five children downstairs to a split-level den and behind a couch by the wall. As we turned to go down the stairs I saw daylight between the wall and ceiling. I knew this was serious. When we got downstairs I peaked over the back of the couch to see tree limbs, trash, trashcans, and rain flying horizontally past our sliding glass doors. When the roar ended, we went outside to find a path through the blown-down trees that lined our back yard. We thanked God for our safety, and you can imagine how many times I have told that story over the years!

What fantastic event have you told often to friends and family? What makes it so invigorating to tell? How do others respond to it? Write your thoughts here:

_____

_____

_____

_____

_____

_____

Read Luke 2:15–16. Underline what the shepherds found when they went into town.

The angels faded back into the spiritual realm and left the shepherds holding the sights and sounds of their message. Someone must have broken the silence of awe and said, "Who wants to go see if we can find this child? If God is right, I want to be in on this." The lead shepherd probably left the young and the doubters with the sheep and led the others to the pens and barns to find the baby. They found the Promised One and His parents exactly as the angels had promised.

Read Luke 2:17–18. Underline what the shepherds did after they had seen Jesus (v. 17). Circle the response of those they told about what they saw and heard.

When they witnessed what they had been told about, like fishermen returning from a huge catch, they had to tell their friends what had happened. It is not every day that a company of the angel army shows up over the fields, and then you find a baby child in an animal trough just as the angels had said. And yes, the people who heard their story were "amazed" at what they heard. Would you not be?

The pattern of the shepherds' actions was to hear, trust and see, go and tell. They had no choice in hearing, but they did have to trust the message and verify it as truth. They then had the choice to keep the mystery to themselves or to tell everyone they could find. Even shepherds could be called crazy after telling a story like that, but they did; and people were amazed and faced the same choices the shepherds had before them.

What would you have done in the shepherds' place? Have you had a similar pattern of trusting God's Word about Jesus? Where are you in that journey? Who have you told about what you have heard and seen? Prayerfully reflect on these things.

4.5 Reflections and Praise

A favorite preacher of mine once said, "I believe because certain uncertain things happen." He meant that his trust in God and God's work was based on specific events that happened in ways for which there was no immediate explanation but that God obviously planned to happen that way. For example, you sit down beside a longtime friend on a plane ride back to where you face a tough decision. You had no idea she would take that flight, and she has just gone through the same experience. She gives you firsthand advice of how God helped her decide and get through the hard choices she had to make. That sort of "uncertain thing" can lead to a deeper trust in God's presence in your life.

What "certain uncertain things" have occurred in your life that have caused your trust in God stronger? Write one example here:

_____

_____

_____

Read Luke 2:19–20. Underline the words that describe Mary's response to the shepherds' visit. Circle the shepherds' responses and underline the last phrase as the reason for their responses.

Mary and shepherds gave different reponses to Jesus in the manger. Mary "treasured up" and "pondered" what had happened (v. 19), and the shepherds went back to their sheep "glorifying and praising God" (v. 20).

Mary's quiet reflection came after the shock of intruding shepherds. After they told her how they heard about her baby and where they could find Him, Luke writes that she "treasured up all these things." She had seen a "certain uncertain thing" that she held precious to her trust in God. Our storyteller says she also "pondered them in her heart." Mary must have taken time to connect the dots between Gabriel's visit, her visit to Elizabeth, and now the shepherds sent by angels to see her son. Surely it all was true as she pondered the unlikely possibilities of all this happening the way it had.

The shepherds, on the other hand, danced back to their sheep giving God credit because, having seen the baby in a manger, things "were just as they had been told" by the angel (v. 20). They did not have to ponder anything. Everything happened within a span of hours! They had certain and immediate evidence God was up to something. Their trust in God would never be the same.

Our question to consider for this chapter is "Why was Jesus born?" Luke 2:1–20 tells us Jesus was born because He was the Savior, the *Christos*, the Lord (v. 11). Those titles, along with the circumstances of His birth, tell us Jesus was born to rescue people from their separation with God as the Messiah, or Christ, God Himself.

For further study:
- **Matthew 2:1–12**
- **Luke 2:21–39**

5—Developing Godly Priorities: Jesus' Adolescence

Jesus the baby soon grew into Jesus the boy. As devout Jews, His parents guided Him through the rites of passage every Jewish boy went through growing up. They circumcised Him and gave Him His name in the Temple on the eighth day of His life, as required by the Law (Luke 2:21). When He was 12, the age of adulthood for boys, He went with His family to the annual Passover Feast in Jerusalem. While there, His parents and others saw a special side of Jesus that other boys His age did not exhibit: He was intensely interested in the things of God, and He skillfully engaged the leading religious leaders of His day. As we observe this episode in His-story, we see that Jesus was like young people in many ways and unlike them in others.

Joseph and Mary faced some of the same issues parents today face as they sought to nurture their child into adulthood. How should we discipline? How do we teach this child respect while allowing Him freedom to mature to become uniquely whom God created Him to be? Even Jesus' parents got frustrated with His behavior, but we see His gentle obedience and the results of Him honoring His mother and father.

The Memory Verses for this chapter are Ephesians 6:1–3. Jesus modeled what God's Word commands. This "commandment with a promise" forms the basis for family life and society, and Jesus can serve as our example even at 12 years old.

Our question to consider for this chapter is "Does God call us to sacrifice time with our families?" Obedience sometimes turns into obsession, and in the name of serving God we sometimes neglect our first mission field—our family.

5.1 Rites of Passage

Rites of passage are important for children growing into adulthood. The first day of school and graduation from elementary, junior high, and high school mark stages along the path to maturity in many cultures. In wealthier cultures, gaining a driver's license and going to college are mileposts. Religious rites such as circumcision, baptism, catechism, bar mitzvah, and going to "big church," signal passage from one stage of development to another.

What rites of passage marked your childhood? What events signaled you were growing up, having adults acknowledge your maturing?

_____

_____

Read Luke 2:41–42. Underline the words or phrases that describe the time, and circle places and events. Underline the last word in verse 42.

"Every year" describes the frequency of Joseph and Mary's trip to Jerusalem. The purpose of their visit was to observe the "Feast of the Passover," the annual event when the Jews celebrated God's deliverance from Egypt, and to make a sacrifice at the Temple (see Exodus 12). The couple continued to demonstrate their obedience to the things of God and their participation of the Jewish customs and practices.

When Jesus was 12 years old, His parents took Him with them. He was eligible to participate in the ceremonies and enter the Temple for worship and the observances related to the feast. Luke tells us they "went up" "according to the custom." Jews were required to go to Jerusalem at least once in their lifetime to observe the feast's activities. (Note: Although Jerusalem lies to the south of Nazareth on a map, the Jewish people "went up" to the city where the Temple was located. Its foundations still sit on a hill in the center of Jerusalem.)

Read Luke 2:43. In your own words, describe what happened in this part of the story. Write your description here:

_____

_____

Just like parents today who lose track of their teenagers in crowded places, Joseph and Mary headed home after the festivities, assuming that their Son was somewhere in the group. Families usually traveled in groups for protection and as an opportunity to spend time together when going to and from the festivals. Jesus' parents naturally assumed He was with relatives or friends in the caravan headed north for home.

If you are a parent, what similar experiences have you had in keeping up with your children? Under what circumstances? How did you respond to people who asked you, "How could that happen?"

_____

_____

_____

_____

Thank God for His constant care of your family and you. If you have suffered the loss of a child, spend time sharing your loss with God and listening for His presence and promises.

5.2 Jesus as a Teenager

Our youngest daughter enjoyed shopping with us when she was a child. The only problem was that she did not like to stay in the stroller. She would squirm and ask permission (in verbal and nonverbal ways) to get out. When we finally let her out of her confines and went on about our shopping, she would explore the area around us. One day, we looked up and she was gone. You can imagine our panic as we started calling her name and looking frantically everywhere for her. Just before we called security and had the store shut down, Summer stuck her head out from inside a circular clothing rack of dresses and said with a Cheshire cat grin on her face, "You looking for me?" She had been hiding in the same spot while we ran around trying to find her. If you have had a similar experience with a child, you know the combination of anger, relief, and the "cute factor" that comes in a moment such as that. We disciplined her when we got home, but the story's legend lives on at our family gatherings to this day.

Write a list of the emotions that arose in your heart if you have experienced a similar situation. What have you thought about parents whom you saw running around looking for their lost child?

_____

_____

_____

_____

Read Luke 2:44–45. Underline how long Joseph and Mary traveled without knowing Jesus was missing. Where did they look for Him?

It must have been time to set up camp on the way home after the first day's travel when Jesus' parents realized His absence. The word for "company" can also be translated "caravan" or "group of travelers." We do not know the size of the group, but Joseph and Mary felt comfortable that their Son was safe and among them. They traveled with "their relatives and friends." After a day's travel from Jerusalem, they discovered Jesus was missing; and they headed back to the city to find Him.

Read Luke 2:46–47. Underline how long it took Joseph and Mary to find Jesus and where they found Him. Circle the word "amazed" in verse 47.

It may have taken three days to find Jesus because a place of worship was the last place you would expect to find a 12-year-old boy! Jerusalem had many other places for a young boy to get lost. But they found Him

Christos—God's Transforming Touch

"sitting among the teachers" listening and asking questions (v. 46). The teachers were religious leaders trained in the knowledge and application of the Jewish Law. Jesus wanted to know about the things of God, so He sat with His elders and experts of the Law to learn them. The Greek word for "amazed" literally means "to stand outside [your mind]." (See Matthew 7:28 for another time when Jesus' teaching amazed the people.) The people who heard Jesus interact with the teachers were "amazed at his understanding and his answers" (v. 47).

Summarize what you can apply to your knowledge of Jesus in these verses. What gives evidence of His humanity? What gives evidence of His divinity? How is He like the teenagers you know?

_____

_____

_____

_____

5.3 Obeying the Father

Remember the scene in the animated film *The Incredibles* when the mother scolded her son, Dash, at the dinner table for getting sent to the principal's office? He had supposedly gotten caught on videotape putting a tack in the teacher's chair; but he was so fast that the principal could not see the infraction and had to let him go without reprimand. Dash's mother wanted his father to correct him for the infraction; but dad's response was, "Man, you must have been booking!" Mom felt frustrated because her son was sent to the principal. Dad was just amazed at the speed and agility of his boy.

Have you ever had those two responses to an action of your child? If so, describe it here:

_____

_____

_____

_____

Read Luke 2:48. Underline Jesus' parents' response when they found Him and how His mother described their feelings.

Luke wrote that Joseph and Mary "were astonished" when they found Jesus. This is a similar word for "amazed" in the previous verse and can mean "overwhelmed." (This is the same word used in Matthew 7:28.) Their Son sat in the outer courts of the Temple in dialogue with the recognized experts of the Law! Mary's wonder, however, soon turned to frustration. She scolded her Son by telling Him that she and His father had searched "anxiously" for Him. It is interesting that Luke did not record Joseph's response to Jesus. Could Joseph have responded similar to Dash's father?

Read Luke 2:49–50. Circle the two question marks in verse 49 to mark the questions Jesus asked His parents. How did they respond to Him?

_____

_____

Jesus was not disrespectful to His mother but answered matter-of-factly that they should have expected to find Him in His "Father's house," the Temple. Jesus' confession indicates He had begun to understand what His parents had taught Him about who the angels had reported He would become and what God had revealed to Him about His relationship to God, the Father. We wonder where Jesus slept and ate while away from His parents. Did He befriend one of the teachers? Did He have relatives in the city? He may have felt as anxious about losing his parents as they felt about Him missing.

While Jesus understood His place in the Temple among the teachers of the Law, His parents "did not understand" His response. This had to add one more wonder to all He brought into their faith and lives.

Put yourself in Jesus' parents' place. What emotions would you have experienced when you found Him? What would have gone through your heart and mind when you heard His response? What does this tell you about who He truly is? Prayerfully listen to God's Spirit as you ponder these things.

5.4 Obeying Parents

A child is obedient when he or she does what a parent or other authority figure instructs him or her to do. My child is not obedient if I tell her to clean her room and she simply agrees to do so. But after she has hung up her clothes, made her bed, and straightened her closet, then she is obedient. People often fail as adults when their parents do not teach them obedience as children. In any walk of life, you can pick out those who obeyed as children and those who did not.

How would you assess your children's willingness and ability to obey? How would you rate yourself as a person who can take directions from someone in authority over you? What childhood experiences helped you learn this?

Read Luke 2:51. Underline the words "obedient" and "treasured." These words show how Jesus responded to instructions from His parents and how His mother responded to His actions.

Our storyteller wrote that Jesus returned to Nazareth with His parents and "was obedient to them." The word for "obedient" in the original language of Luke's Gospel has a military background and means "to stand under" the authority of another. This same word is translated "submit" in famous passages such as Ephesians 5:21 and Romans 13:1. Jesus submitted, or stood under, His parents' authority and went home with them. This was a characteristic of His entire life. He obeyed the Father and taught His disciples to obey His teachings (John 15:10). By doing so they would "remain in" His love.

Read Luke 2:52. Circle the three ways Luke said that Jesus matured.

Jesus continued to mature into a young man. He matured in three aspects of life. He grew in "wisdom," or understanding. He grew in "stature," or literally, "years." He matured in "favor" with both "God and men." The wisdom among men and the favor of God that His parents saw in the Temple remained characteristics of His life as He grew in years and maturity.

What characteristics give evidence of maturity in a teenager's life? What characteristics can you point to and know that a teenager is maturing into a godly young adult? What does verse 52 say about the person of Jesus?

5.5 Jesus as Fulfillment of the Law

His-story is consistent in its revelation of God's purposes for all people in all times. The laws in the Old Agreement of God with Israel can be found both in the life and teachings of Jesus and in the instructions of the New Agreement of God. Jesus said He did not come to "abolish" the Law but to "fulfill" it (Matt. 5:17). He did not dismantle the heart of God's instructions to His people for how to live in families and society.

Read Exodus 20:12. This is the fifth command in the Ten Commandments. Underline the word "honor."

One of the foundational laws God gave His people was that children must honor their parents. The Hebrew word for "honor" carries the sense of respect as well as obedience. (Read Deuteronomy 5:16 for another statement on the law of life.) God designed the longevity of the family around the order of children respecting their parents. This law did not change with the New Agreement of God.

Read Ephesians 6:1. Underline the word "obey" and the phrase "in the Lord."

Paul, God's servant to the ethnics, turned to instructions for the home after explaining the nature and person of Jesus. His inspired directions for how to live in the home flows out of his directions for how to live as the *ekklesia*, or "church." This instruction comes from the very nature and person of the *Christos*. Paul explained how husbands and wives should live under the leadership of Jesus, and here he recalls the law of life he learned as a Jewish boy growing up in Tarsus. "In the Lord" designates a relationship "in Christ" (Eph. 1:3–4). The root word for "obey" in this verse means "to hear." Obedience is putting into action what you hear.

In Ephesians 6:2–3, Paul observed this as the first of the laws for life that had a promise attached to it. God said if His people would do this, it would "go well" with them and they would "enjoy long life on the earth." It made sense to the spiritual father of the Christ-followers in Ephesus that they should follow God's instructions and receive the promise He made to those who obeyed.

How do you honor your parents as an adult with your own family? Given the dissolution of the nuclear family, how do you live out "honor your parents?"

Our question to consider for this chapter is "Does God call us to sacrifice time with our families?" Given Jesus' example in the Temple, how would you answer this question?

Spend time in prayer asking God to show you ways to honor your parents and to teach your children to honor you. Thank God for the example of His Son as you seek ways to live out His purposes in your family.

For further study:
- **Exodus 23:14–17**
- **Ephesians 6:1–8**

6—Sacrificing Everything for God: The Example of John the Baptist

God patiently spells out His purposes and plans to help people trust Him. Prophets centuries before and angels on the same night announced Jesus' birth. God had also told everyone He would send a prophet before the *Christos*' life work. John the Baptist was that prophet. Like Jesus' birth on the outskirts of military, religious, and political power, John introduced Jesus' mission far from the day-to-day activities of religion and politics.

John did not enter the priestly work his father performed in the Temple. He apparently began a reform movement that sought to bring revival to the ways and means of relating to God. He dressed like a prophet of the Old Agreement of God, and he introduced the Coming One of Israel to those who came to hear him. He spoke a straightforward message of life-change and called for behavior that was consistent with a person's beliefs. The locust-eating prophet who lived in the desert served as the relay runner who handed off the baton of God's purposes to the Victor, who finished the race of God's rescue mission for the hearts of all people.

The Memory Verse for this chapter is Matthew 11:11. Jesus acknowledged the importance of John's ministry and message. John ranked above all the prophets before him but least among those who joined the ranks of people who trusted Jesus and became Kingdom people.

Our question to consider for this chapter is "Does God call us to do what is uncomfortable?" As you observe the ministry of John the "Baptizer," you will see a difficult life that ended in an unjust death. While we cannot judge all of God's ways by one life, we can see how saying yes to God's call does not always result in popularity and comfort.

6.1 John the Baptist's Message

One Christmas my family spent four days in Colonial Williamsburg, Virginia. It is a living history book of the time in our country's history when British colonialists decided to gain freedom from England's rule. As I walked through the streets, toured the restored buildings and homes, and heard the people's stories, I wondered whose side I would have chosen in those days. As a pastor, I would have been educated, paid by the Church of England, and parson to those who decided to take up arms against the Crown. I wondered how I would have led the people spiritually as they struggled with their loyalties. I wondered if I would have risked my salary and family's place in the community to join the ranks of the revolutionaries. Changes like that are hard to make, and those who call for those changes are brave people.

Put yourself in my place. What would you have done? It seems easy to be a patriot when you are far from the events. What would you have thought about those who spoke against the only way of life you had known and the country that had made it possible for you to live a comfortable life? Write some of your thoughts here:

_____

_____

_____

_____

Read Matthew 3:1 and Luke 3:1–2. Underline the data in the verses that describe the time when John began his public ministry.

Matthew is inexact in his placement of when these events took place. "In those days" was a phrase to move the story along, not mark history like he did with Jesus' birth. Luke, on the other hand, gave historical markers to pinpoint John's emergence into public notice.

John the Baptist was the son of a priest, Zechariah (Luke 1:13). He stood in line to perform the practices of the Levites in the Temple like his father, but somewhere along the way he left his expected career path and concentrated on bringing people back to an authentic relationship with God. Rather than his common name, John ben Zechariah, he gained the title "The Baptist" because of his message and practice of baptism.

His ministry took place "in the Desert of Judea." This was the desolate region outside of Jerusalem. Unlike his father who worked in the ornate halls of the Temple, John chose the wilderness as the place to worship God.

Read Matthew 3:2. Underline John's message.

John called the people who came to him to "repent." This word means to "turn around" or "change your mind." It implied significant change in both heart and mind that resulted in changed behavior. The reason for such a change, John said, was "the kingdom of heaven is near." The Kingdom of Heaven represented the rule of God in people's hearts. John said change was necessary in the face of a new way of life as people ruled by God.

Like the American colonialist who called for a new way of life out from under the rule of the king of England, John called for a new way of life under the rule of the King of the universe. How does Jesus' rule on your life impact the way you live?

6.2 John the Baptist's Mission

T-shirts are today's billboards. My favorite t-shirt message reads, "The older I get, the better I was." Some messages are not so clever, and the wearer has something to say intended to hurt others. I have a collection of t-shirts from the running and cycling events I have participated in as well as shirts that identify me with my college and church. My clothing sends a message about my identity and my message.

What messages and labels do you have on your t-shirts? What do you want others to know about you when you wear them? Write your thoughts here:

_____

_____

_____

_____

Read Matthew 3:3 and Isaiah 40:1–5. Underline "the prophet Isaiah" and highlight the message of this "one."

Matthew wrote that John the Baptist was the "one" whom the prophet Isaiah spoke about when he comforted the people of Israel while in captivity. The prophet encouraged the people by sharing God's revealed Word that He would "make straight" the way of God. The nature of this message, as we have seen with other prophecy, was first to the original listeners and then for those yet to come in history. God inspired Matthew to connect His revealed Word through Isaiah to that of John the Baptist.

Read Matthew 3:4. Underline the phrases that describe John's appearance and diet.

John the Baptist did not look or eat like the typical Jewish religious leader of his day. But he was more than an eccentric person. He adopted the life of a prophet who stood outside the religious ways of God's people in order to stay distinct in his message and life. His lifestyle associated him with the great prophet Elijah, who constantly reminded King Ahab of Israel that God ruled the kingdom, not him (1 Kings 17–18). John wore the signs of the prophet: a camel hair mantle and leather belt (2 Kings 1:8); and many believed him to be Elijah (John 1:19–28). However, John told them he was not Elijah but "the voice of one calling in the desert" (John 1:23). He could have worn this message on his t-shirt—if he had had one.

God guided the Gospel writer to point out how even the details of the one prior to Jesus lined up with history as He promised it would. These details serve as elements that help build a case for faith to those who wonder if Jesus is the *Christos*.

How has learning these details about John increased your faith? What parts of his lifestyle and message help you to see the significance of Jesus? What of his message could you print on a t-shirt and wear boldly?

_____

_____

_____

6.3 Revival in the Land

In 1995 what became known as the "Brownwood Revival" began to make headlines in our state. The story of a student-led revival on the campus of a small

Baptist college, Howard Payne, gained momentum and spread nationwide. People made trips to Coggin Avenue Baptist Church and to the campus in the small West Texas town to experience what some referred to as a fresh awakening of God's presence. Some claimed they received a new fervor and passion for God and a renewed desire to tell others about Jesus. Some people from the church I pastored made the pilgrimage to the town to experience part of God's refreshing presence.

Have you ever seen or heard of a similar phenomenon? How did those inside and outside of the church react? How did you respond to it?

_____

_____

_____

_____

Read Matthew 3:5 and Mark 1:5. Underline the locations mentioned in the verses.

John the Baptist became somewhat of a religious rock star among people who longed for a renewed relationship with God. Matthew tells us people journeyed "from Jerusalem and all Judea and the whole region of the Jordan." They came from the city, province, and region around where John preached. Curiosity as well as a genuine desire to be part of a movement of God drew them to the prophet.

Read Matthew 3:6. Circle the two things our storyteller said the people were doing when they came out to see and hear John.

One sign of revival is willingness for people to confess their sins. "Confessing" literally means "to say the same thing," or "to agree together" (see 1 John 1:8). When we confess our sins or actions that expose our self-centered, God-dishonoring hearts, we agree with God about our spiritual condition and our self-honoring tendencies. To confess to God is to agree with Him that we have done wrong and that He is the only One who can truly help us. John baptized the people as they confessed their need for God.

Baptism was a sign of cleansing among the Jewish people. John did not invent it, but he associated it with confession and repentance of sins. To be baptized by John meant to identify with his message and the movement of God he led. The same purpose lies behind our identification with Jesus and His message when we are baptized.

Have you ever been drawn to a movement of God that led to your confession of sin and subsequent baptism? If not, what reasons have stood in the way of identifying yourself with Jesus through this ancient act of identification with Him? Write your thoughts or experience in the space below. Take time to pray and thank God for sending His prophets to reveal our need for God and how we can join Him on the mission to rescue the hearts of all people.

_____

_____

_____

_____

6.4 John the Baptist's Boldness

One of my core motivations is for people to like me. On the upside of this motivation, I am aware of the feelings and needs of others and can respond to them. On the downside, I find it hard to speak truth to someone for fear of causing that person not to like me. This aspect of who I am has posed a problem for me as I have been called to lead others to trust Jesus and grow more like Him. I have discovered, however, that when I lean more into my calling than into my natural tendencies, I find the boldness to speak and lead like Jesus. The mission call of God on my life outweighs the natural tendency that keeps me from leading and living the way He would want for me.

What are some of your core motivations? How do you respond when you need to tell someone something truthful but fear it could change the dynamics of your relationship? Write some of your thoughts here:

_____

_____

Matthew 3:7–10. Circle who came to see John and underline key phrases of his response to them.

"Pharisees and Sadducees" joined the crowds to see and hear John. Both groups made up part of the religious leadership among the Jews, and they had made alliances with the Romans to keep their way of life intact while ruled by the foreigners. Those who came out to see John may have simply been curious, or sent to spy out the situation for the leaders in Jerusalem, or possibly interested in joining his movement.

John the Baptist had no problem with what people thought about him. He called the religious leaders a "brood of vipers" and called them out for their lack of "fruit in keeping with repentance" (v. 8). He reminded them they could not fall back on their religious heritage to ensure their part in the Kingdom of God. Only actions in line with a new life of repentance were acceptable to God. Judgment would come, and they must prepare themselves for it (v. 10).

John boldly called people to change their lives as a response to their confession and baptism. Salvation has a direct effect on how we live every day, not just on how we feel about the afterlife.

What is the connection between repentance and lifestyle? What of John's message to those who came to repent connects with you today? (See Luke's version of the story, too, in Luke 3:7–9.) Pray that God would allow the truth of His message through John to speak to your heart and that you will seek ways to live it out in what you do today.

Christos—God's Transforming Touch

6.5 A Message of Judgment

They say the hardest chair to fill in an orchestra is second chair. Everyone wants first chair. Who wants to be known as "second" in everything performed? But sometimes number two is important to any endeavor or accomplishment.

How do you feel about playing "second fiddle?" Maybe you have not placed first in many things. How do you feel about those who seem to win all the time? What are some positive things about being second in line behind the leader?

_____

_____

Read Matthew 3:11. Underline how John the Baptist described his baptism and that of Jesus who "will come."

John's baptism was "with water for repentance." Water cleaned the outside of a person and identified him or her with confession of an offense against God and a changed life. John said one much greater than him would come with a baptism of "the Holy Spirit and with fire." This would be a baptism of the heart, one in which God's Holy Spirit entered at the core of a person's being and cleansed and empowered him or her to live for God.

John understood his place in history. He was never meant to be first chair. He always knew that he would prepare the way for Jesus, and he confessed, "He must become greater; I must become less" (John 3:30).

Read Matthew 3:12. Underline the details of the metaphor John used to tell of Jesus' ministry after him.

Jesus came, too, with a message of judgment. John used a common metaphor of harvesting grain to describe Jesus' work. Like someone thrashing grain and then tossing it into the air to separate the husks from the grain, Jesus would work like the "winnowing fork" to separate the true followers from the untrue and gather them into "the barn" of His movement. (Jeremiah also used this image, which linked Jesus to this prophetic tradition in Jeremiah 15:7.)

Our question to consider for this chapter is "Does God call us to do what is uncomfortable?" After viewing John's ministry of preparing the way of Jesus, we can see that God does in fact call us sometimes to do what is outside our comfort zone. To prepare the way for a new way of life always means disrupting the status quo of your present life. To follow Jesus means to change how you live because the Kingdom of Heaven is near. Change brings discomfort and can not only bring a new way of life under the King but can also result in an eternally new life.

As you review the ministry of John, how do you relate to his message and actions? How has his message helped you know more about Jesus, the *Christos*? What must you change in order to join the movement of God? Answer in a spirit of prayerfully listening to God.

For further study:
* **Mark 1:1–8**
* **Luke 3:1–20**
* **John 1:19–34**

7—Following Christ in Baptism: Jesus' Baptism

The universal, visible sign of a Christian is baptism. It is the rite of entrance into the family of God. I have seen people baptized in a bathtub in China, a river in Albania, and a portable pool in the church I pastor. Baptismal fonts and baptisteries can be as basic as a bathtub or as ornate as the most elaborate architecture of any building. Baptism makes up part of every Christian's life with Christ. So how did it come about, and what makes it an essential part of Christian faith and practice?

Since Jesus is our model for all we do in our relationship with God, we will observe His example for us in this matter. At the beginning of His earthly ministry, Jesus went to John to be baptized. John initially hesitated because he felt unworthy to do such a thing for the "Lamb of God, who takes away the sin of the world" (John 1:29), but he eventually baptized Jesus. When Jesus came out of the Jordan River, the Holy Spirit, in the form of a dove, came down upon Him. God's voice proclaimed He was well pleased with His Son. As a result, John professed Jesus as the Son of God who would baptize with the Holy Spirit.

The Memory Verse for this chapter is Acts 2:41. On the day God sent His Holy Spirit into the lives of the first Christ-followers, those closest to Jesus led those who came to identify themselves with the Jesus movement to get baptized. From Jesus to His first followers to now, baptism is the outward sign of belonging to Jesus.

Our question to consider for this chapter is "What is the purpose of baptism?" What thoughts do you have? What answers do you believe others would give? Why have you or have you not gotten baptized? We will return to answer this question at the end of the chapter.

Christos—God's Transforming Touch

7.1 Baptism Stories

I was baptized at age nine. It happened after I became convinced I needed Jesus as my Savior and Lord by trusting Him alone for my salvation and eternal life with God. The associate pastor baptized me on a Sunday night, white robe, waders, and all. My family and some friends went out afterward to celebrate, but life went on pretty much as it had before I was baptized. I soon learned some of my friends were baptized as infants and others at the end of a catechism class. Some wanted to argue that you have to be baptized to be saved, and others were not so sure it was all that important. My tribe of Christ-followers said you have to go under water to make it valid, while other Christian tribes claimed a sprinkle or water poured over the head as sufficient.

As I grew older, I met people who were baptized about the time I was in life but had quit going to church and trusting Christ altogether—except for the certainty of going to heaven. I met others who were baptized as young adults and seemed more in tune than I was with God and His ways. Although baptism was the shared event, yet the impact varied on the lives of people.

What experiences have you had concerning the religious rite of baptism? Describe your beliefs and interactions with others in the space below or on additional paper.

_____

_____

_____

Read Matthew 3:13 and Luke 3:23. Underline the time and geographic markers in the story. Circle how old Jesus was when He got baptized.

Jesus grew up in Nazareth in the northern province of Galilee. John the Baptist lived and served God in the southern province of Judea. He baptized people in the Jordan River. (Use a Bible atlas or Bible handbook to locate these places.) At age 30, Jesus made His way from Galilee to the Jordan River. It was easy to find the popular preacher who had attracted so many.

Read John 1:29. Underline what John called Jesus when he saw his friend and relative.

The biblical storytellers remain silent about the time between Jesus' 12th and 30th years. Sometime later, fanciful writers tried to fill the gaps; but the earliest followers of Jesus deemed them as unauthentic. Jesus chose to go to John because He knew exactly the purpose behind His relative's ministry and message.

When John saw Jesus approaching, he announced to those around him, "Look, the Lamb of God, who takes away the sin of the world!" Lambs were used in Jewish sacrifices to make atonement for sin. John proclaimed Jesus was God's Lamb who would atone for the sin of the entire world. (See Genesis 22:8 for God's promise to Abraham of a sacrificial lamb and Revelation 5:6 as a picture of the "Lamb" who was slain.)

7.2 Jesus' Baptism

My oldest daughter served on the Hospitality Committee at Texas A&M University while she was a student there. She was on the committee when the school chose Robert Gates as its next president. Before the installation ceremony, Dr. Gates and dignitaries, including former President George H. Bush whose presidential library is on the campus, gathered in a small room to put on their academic robes for the event. My daughter was in the room to help, and she saw President Bush for the first time in person. She immediately walked over to him and said, "May I hug you?" Being the gentleman he is, he said, "sure," and she hugged one of her heroes. She stammered to say some things as to why she admired him and sheepishly returned to her place. She wondered if she could feel more embarrassed. She told us later that she wanted to say something else and act more dignified but that is what came out of her mouth when she stood in front of the former president. Protocol flew out the window like a fleeting bird in the excitement of the moment, and all she could say was what came to her childlike heart when she saw the man she admired.

Have you ever said or done something embarrassing when you met someone important? If not, how do you think you would respond?

_____

_____

_____

Read Matthew 3:14–15. Underline "deter" in verse 14 and "consented" in verse 15. Highlight why Jesus said He must be baptized. Also read John 1:30–31.

When John the Baptist saw Jesus approaching him, he responded with respect toward the "Lamb of God." He tried to "deter" Jesus from coming to him for baptism. John had already said he was not even worthy to untie Jesus' sandals (John 1:27). How could he even think of baptizing Jesus? Jesus should baptize him! (v. 14)

Jesus responded to John's hesitation by telling him they must do this in order to "fulfill all righteousness" (v. 15). Righteousness among the Jewish people meant doing what God commanded as well as being right with God. Jesus knew that His baptism meant doing what the Father had sent Him to do. Both John and Jesus had a part to play in history. The act of baptism by the prophet John and the *Christos*, Jesus, signaled the fulfillment of God's work to send Jesus as the Rescuer of all people and Jesus going public with His identity as the Messiah. Jesus identified with John's movement of repentance and the sins of the people when He insisted John baptize Him. John "consented" (v. 15) and "revealed to Israel" the Messiah (John 1:31).

One way to grow familiar with Scripture is to put yourself in the place of the characters in history. Take some time to stand in the sandals of John. Review the passage and ask God to reveal His purposes for you in the story.

Christos—God's Transforming Touch

7.3 God's Blessing of Jesus

After one weekend of spending time together and doing odd jobs around the house, my father, who was 78 at the time, said, "You know your mother and I are proud of you." I was 54 at the time, and those words still meant as much to me then as they did after I brought home my first "A" from elementary school. Every child wants to hear a parent say, "I'm proud of you." My wife, Kim, and I have tried to pass that blessing on to our children. On occasions we go out of our way to let them know how much we love them for who they are as well as for the things they do. It saddens me when I talk to people who have never heard a blessing from their parents or those who cared for them. Too often, those people spend the rest of their lives seeking to receive such a blessing from anyone willing to give it.

Have you heard a parent or someone close to you bless you by saying that you make him or her proud? How did that make you feel? Do you give your children or others a similar blessing for who they are as well as for when they accomplish something?

Read Matthew 3:16. Circle the words "Jesus," "heaven," and "Spirit of God." Underline the verbs "went up," "was opened," and "saw" to mark the event's movement.

John baptized Jesus, and when he had completed the act Jesus "went up out of the water." This phrase has created denominations and caused much debate among Christ-followers about how Jesus was baptized. Some say the phrase suggests immersion under the water while others say the phrase simply described Jesus coming out of the river onto dry land. The English word "baptize"

is a transliteration of the Greek word that means "to dip or plunge." The point of the biblical storytellers is not how Jesus was baptized but that He *was* baptized. When He came out of the water, certain things happened.

Matthew said the sky "was opened," and Jesus "saw the Spirit of God descending like a dove and lighting on him." John the Baptist testified to the same facts (John 1:32–34). The Holy Spirit, in the form of a visible dove, settled on Jesus as certainty that John's prophecy that Jesus would baptize "with the Holy Spirit and with fire" would be fulfilled (Matt. 3:11).

Read Matthew 3:17. Highlight what those present at Jesus' baptism heard.

The voice of God, the Father, announced to everyone present that Jesus was His beloved Son with whom He was "well pleased." God the Father said to the Son, in the presence of the Spirit, "I am proud of You." The people anticipated such words of blessing when the promised Servant of God would appear (see Psalm 2:7; Isaiah 42:1).

Here we see the Father, Son, and Spirit of God revealed at Jesus' baptism by John. All of these signs pointed to who Jesus was and who He would be for those He came to rescue.

Meditate on this scene from His-story. Imagine standing on the side of the river seeing those events. What does this do for your trust in who Jesus is? Why do you believe the storytellers recorded these details in their accounts of Jesus' life?

7.4 Being a Good Leader

Someone once said that the proof of one's leadership was not what happened while he or she was present but what got done when he or she was not there. For example, if I told my church for years that our mission is to "help people trust Jesus" and within a couple of years beyond my departure the church decides their mission is to "help people," then my leadership proved not that effective. You can judge every great leader by those who followed his or her practices long after he or she has left the scene. This is what makes George Washington and Martin Luther King Jr., for example, great American leaders.

Who would you judge as a great leader by how he or she influenced not only those who followed in his or her presence but those who followed the leader's ways after he or she left? What about his or her leadership caused people to follow this leader beyond his or her direct influence?

Read Matthew 28:19–20 and Acts 2:41. Summarize in your own words Jesus' instructions to His disciples before His ascension. What did the disciples do for those who became followers of Jesus at Pentecost?

_____

_____

_____

While we have no record of Jesus baptizing anyone, Jesus told His disciples, or apprentices, to baptize those who became His disciples after He ascended into the presence of the Father. They must follow His example of identifying with the movement of God by being baptized. His followers were to baptize those who publicly identified with Jesus in this way "in the name of the Father and of the Son and of the Holy Spirit" (v. 19). Like the Father, Son, and Spirit who were part of Jesus' baptism, followers of the *Christos* must baptize others in the same way.

After God sent His Holy Spirit on Jesus' followers during the Pentecost festival in Jerusalem (Acts 2:1–4), Peter boldly told the story of Jesus. He called for people to change how they lived and identify themselves with Jesus through baptism because Jesus was the Messiah, the *Christos* (vv. 38–39). The people followed Peter's instructions and were baptized (v. 41).

Acts 2:41 is our Memory Verse for this chapter. It reminds us that from the first followers of Jesus to today, those who trust Jesus as the *Christos* follow His example and teaching by following Him in baptism. This ancient rite of repentance and identification is the way those who trust Jesus show others their commitment to Him.

Take time to grow familiar with or to memorize this verse. Pause and meditate on the fact that millions before you in various cultures and under favorable and unfavorable circumstances have said "I am a follower of Jesus" through this act. What does baptism mean to you? Have you told anyone about your public statement of trust in Jesus lately? Have you invited anyone to take his or her stand for Jesus through baptism?

Christos—God's Transforming Touch

7.5 The Purpose of Baptism

I ride bikes with a friend who has not been baptized. We started riding when I learned of his passion for cycling and thought it would be a way to get to know him. We have ridden for over two years now. Others have joined the group, and we have formed the Legacy Church Cycling Team. We have team rides and outings, and it has evolved into sort of a small group on wheels.

As we ride for hours at a time, our conversation almost always turns to faith and the issues that prevent him from jumping in with all of his heart, soul, mind, and strength. He understands that baptism is one's public identification with Jesus, and he takes that very seriously. He hesitates to be baptized because he has not settled all the discrepancies he perceives as part of the Christian faith. One is "How can an omnipotent, loving God allow such horrible things as the abduction and killing of an innocent child?" He says he trusts Jesus for who he is and what He has done to rescue him from his sins, but he just is not ready to say he's figured it all out by being baptized.

I have tried to explain that baptism is the starting line, not the finish line of a person's public relationship with Jesus. When the disciples said yes to Jesus' call to follow Him, they did not have all the answers. Time and commitment to Him gave them the courage and love to live like Him—even with all the questions they carried around about who Jesus truly is. I still wait for the day my friend feels ready to publicly state his trust in Jesus.

Do you know of someone who has no desire get baptized? What have you told them?

Our question to consider for this chapter is "What is the purpose of baptism?" Some have said it is for salvation. Others say baptism has nothing to do with salvation but is an act of obedience that demonstrates one's salvation. Others have said a specific form of baptism is required for membership in their churches. Still others have insisted that baptism is for infants and children as a sign of association with the church until the child personally chooses to follow Jesus. Denominations and churches have split and formed over the meaning of baptism. In some cultures people lose status, wealth, and even life when they are baptized. In the end, we all have the same information: Jesus' example, His teachings, and His Church's teachings recorded in Scripture.

What core convictions do you have concerning baptism? What does your church or denomination teach about the purpose of baptism? Write your thoughts here:

_____

_____

_____

_____

_____

Spend time in prayer thanking God for Jesus' clear example. Ask for faith to identify with Jesus through baptism if you have not already. Thank God for the expression of baptism as a way to tell others you are a follower of Jesus, the *Christos*.

For further study:

- **Colossians 2:11–12**
- **Ephesians 4:4–6**
- **Romans 6:4**

8—Overcoming Our Temptations: Jesus' Temptations

Temptation is part of every person's life. We usually associate it with sexual sins, lying, or cheating. These are genuine temptations, but a deeper temptation persists in our lives: the temptation to leave God's call on our lives and pursue our own desires. If Jesus is our model for what a life fully devoted to God looks like, then His temptation after His baptism is the kind of temptation we all must overcome. Although Satan's temptation to draw Jesus from His appointed mission of Suffering Servant-Messiah (Isa. 53:11) is unique to Jesus, we all will face a similar temptation to forsake our divine calling and seek to live a life for ourselves. Since Jesus is the pioneer of our faith, we can learn the secret to overcoming all temptations if we follow His example and overcome this temptation. Everything Jesus said and did teaches us how to live as His followers in any and every situation. He taught us how to overcome the temptation to leave God's calling on our lives.

The Memory Verses for this chapter are 2 Timothy 3:16–17. God's Word gives us a source of strength and direction when we feel tempted. Grow familiar with these verses, and you will know where to go in the face of temptation.

Our question to consider for this chapter is "Did Jesus experience every possible temptation?" Since Jesus is fully God and fully human, did He face every temptation we have faced?

Write some of your thoughts in the space below, and we will return to this question later.

_____

_____

_____

_____

_____

Christos—God's Transforming Touch

8.1 Being Obedient

Obedience is turning what we hear into action. Concerning the things of God, it means to do what God has called us to do. However, we too often reduce disobedience to morals. Temptation has to do with breaking a moral rule. As we observe Jesus' life, we see temptation is about staying true to what God rescued you to do in Christ Jesus. Satan, the adversary of God in His-story, would want nothing more than for us to do anything other than what God created and rescued us to do.

Read Luke 4:1. Highlight the phrase "full of the Holy Spirit" and underline who led Him into the desert. (Compare this verse to Mark 1:12 and Matthew 4:1.)

Our storyteller described Jesus as "full of the Holy Spirit." This does not mean Jesus did not have the Holy Spirit prior to His baptism. The phrase meant that after the experience of affirmation of God's voice and the dovelike presence of the Spirit, Jesus became fully aware of who He was and what God had sent Him to do. That same Spirit led Him into the desert to fast and pray. He had much to consider as He began His mission.

Satan wanted to derail Jesus from His appointed mission. So, just as he tested Job, the evil one tempted Jesus to forsake His love for the Father and to take shortcuts to accomplish what God sent Him to do.

Read Luke 4:2. Underline how long Jesus was in the desert. How did He feel at the end of that time? (Compare this verse to Mark 1:13.)

Jesus fasted for 40 days, which is physically possible with water and rest. Physical weakness can lower one's resistance to temptation and resolve. This put Jesus in a perfect place for Satan to attempt to seduce Him from His call as the Suffering Servant-Messiah. Satan's offer for Jesus not to suffer and die would have seemed attractive after suffering so long without food in the heat of the desert.

If you know your life mission statement, write it here:

_____

_____

_____

_____

If you have never stopped to consider it, accept Jesus' clear words for His followers to "love the Lord your God with all your heart and with all your soul and with all your mind and with all your strength" and to "love your neighbor as yourself" (Mark 12:30–31). Or adopt His commandment to "make disciples of all nations" (Matt. 28:19). If you have no mission, you have no direction. To know the mission call of God on your life is to face the evil one's seduction to draw you from it. Prayerfully ask God to begin to reveal His life purpose for you as you observe Jesus' example.

8.2 Power Struggle

My youngest daughter graduated with honors, earning a Bachelors of Science in Education. Her concentration was Special Education, and she teaches children with special learning needs. She spends most of her day teaching children to acquire the basic skills most people take for granted. One learning goal may be to touch the color red or to tell the difference between smooth and rough objects. She could have used her ability to learn and the skills she acquired to make more money or to teach less troublesome children. She believes, however, that God has called her to serve these students in this way. Some days she has felt tempted to use her gifts for different purposes, but each time she returns to this call on her life.

What abilities do you have that you use to serve others? How have you felt tempted to use those things to better your life first? What makes it hard to put the needs of others before our own? Write your thoughts here:

_____

_____

_____

_____

Read Luke 4:3. How did Satan tempt Jesus? Underline his words in your Bible.

The phrase "If you are the Son of God" can be translated "Since you're God's Son" (MSG). Satan knew who Jesus was, and he played on His power as the Son of God to meet His personal need of hunger. Satan tried to seduce Jesus to use His power over creation to "tell this stone to become bread."

What was the heart of this temptation? If Satan sought to distract Jesus away from His mission as the Suffering Servant, the *Christos*, then this temptation was to use His supernatural power as God not to suffer by serving His own needs. He would care for Himself, not the needs of those He came to rescue. Also, if Jesus would

use His divine power to turn stones into bread, people would follow Him without Him having to die on the cross. Was not the goal to get people to trust Him? Why not buy that trust by meeting basic human needs?

Read Luke 4:4. How did Jesus answer Satan? Write out your interpretation of Jesus' answer in your own words in the space below. (Also read Matthew 4:4.)

_____

_____

Jesus answered Satan's offer with a truth from God's Word that taught the reason behind God's leading Israel into the wilderness.

Read Deuteronomy 8:1–5. This passage records Moses' instructions to the Israelites as they wandered through the wilderness waiting for the Lord to lead them into the promised land. Moses explained that God led them through the desert "to humble [them] and to test [them] in order to know what was in [their] heart[s], whether or not [they] would keep his commands" (v. 2) and "to teach [them] that man does not live on bread alone but on every word that comes from the mouth of the LORD" (v. 3). Could the Spirit have led Jesus into the desert for the same reasons God led the Israelites into the wilderness? After the test, Jesus could tell Satan the truth of God's purposes He had learned through suffering.

8.3 Satan's Offer

When Kim and I were first married, we received in the mail an offer of free photo processing for life if we would come down and hear about the offer and receive a free gift. We were young, naïve, and took a lot of pictures; so we went and listened to the sales pitch. The offer was what it had said on the mailer, but to join the photo club cost almost $400. No problem, though, we could finance that over a year and start our free processing immediately. Like a bass on a lure, we bit. About six months later, our film returned unprocessed. We called around and found out that the guy who sold us the deal was no longer in business. We got stuck with paying off the $400 to the bank that had put up the money. We learned our lesson the hard way.

Have you ever accepted an offer from someone that turned out unlike anything the person described? Write your experience here:

_____

_____

_____

Read Luke 4:5–7. Describe Satan's offer to Jesus in your own words. (Also read Matthew 4:8–9.)

_____

_____

Satan led Jesus to a high place and "showed him in an instant all the kingdoms of the world" (v. 5). Satan then offered Jesus "all their authority and splendor" based on his authority to do so. Satan's offer was half true. He is "the prince of this world," according to Jesus (John 12:31; 14:30; 16:11), but he is also condemned and will ultimately be destroyed by Jesus (Rev. 20:7–10). Satan proudly offered to Jesus what he had influence over at the time, but Jesus knew the final fate of His adversary. The offer was empty and temporary. Jesus' mission was complete and eternal.

Satan's offer to Jesus was that He could rule over all the kingdoms of the world. Was not that the goal of His coming? And if Jesus would simply bow down and worship Satan, He could have His kingdom instantly.

Read Luke 4:8. What response did Jesus give to Satan's veiled offer? (Also read Deuteronomy 6:13.)

_____

_____

Jesus answered Satan not with His own reasoning or His own authority but with the truth of God's Word. Jesus quoted the words God gave His servant Moses, "Fear the LORD your God, serve him only" (Deut. 6:13). This command lies at the heart of what is known as the Shema, which means "hear" or "listen" and begins the passage of instructions to Israel (Deut. 6:4–9).

Satan offered Jesus a shortcut to a kingdom by offering Him an earthly kingdom. Jesus knew He did not come to rule the kingdoms of the earth alone. He came to reign over "all rule and authority, power and dominion, and every title that can be given" (Eph. 1:21). Jesus would claim rule over all by following the path the Father had laid out for Him. Jesus refused Satan's offer based on His commitment to the Father and the clarity of His mission.

Take time again to stand with Jesus and Satan on the high place. See what they see. Sense the authority and power that would come with such a position. Ask God to show you Jesus' heart and how He did not flinch in refusing Satan's bogus offer. Pray for God to give you that same resolve to worship and follow Him alone.

8.4 Twisting God's Word

A megalomaniac is someone who is obsessed with extravagant or grandiose things or actions. You would think that anyone who came as the Messiah would be that sort of person, and that any opportunity to gain attention by some great act would help His cause to become known as a hero among the people. In America, people win elections in order to lead the nation; and they win elections by becoming known by the most people. Why not a splash here or there to make headlines and get your name out so people will want to vote for you? The difference between an elected president and the Sent One from God is the former needs recognition and votes to win, but the Sent One needs only the approval of God the Father.

In what ways do people get attention in order to achieve their goals? What ways seem the most outlandish to you? Have you ever tried something spectacular to get attention in order to get what you wanted?

Read Luke 4:9–11. Circle where Satan took Jesus next and underline his offer to Jesus. What did Satan do differently in this temptation of Jesus? (Also read Matthew 4:5–6.)

Satan invited Jesus to prove His identity by jumping from a prominent place in Jerusalem. People would see Him standing above them, silhouetted against the sky; and when they saw angels catch Him before He hit the ground, they would surely believe He was who He claimed to be. A spectacular miracle rather than humiliation on a cross was the offer this time.

Satan quoted God's words to Jesus. He, however, did what so many do. He used the Bible for his own purposes, giving no attention to God's meaning behind the words. Psalm 91:11–12 is a song of praise for those who trust God, not those who test God. Satan twisted the words of the psalm to mean God would come to Jesus' side simply because He was the Son of God. The promise actually comes after the command: "If you make the Most High your dwelling" (Ps. 91:9). To dwell with God as Jesus did meant to know God's protection for God's purposes, not the presumption that God would keep Him from harm.

Rather than showing people He could not be hurt, like a superhero, Jesus knew He would suffer for the people. Angels would watch Him suffer and die at His own command rather than rescue Him from His pain. He came as the Suffering Servant-Messiah. He would fulfill His mission through suffering, not the spectacular.

Read Luke 4:12. Underline Jesus' response to Satan. (Also read Matthew 4:7 and Deuteronomy 6:16.)

Christos—God's Transforming Touch

Jesus returned again to the core commandments of God to His people in His response to Satan. Jesus would not put God to the test as God's Word warned (Deut. 6:16). Although God's promises are true, we must not presume on God's blessings. Suffering, not cheering crowds, may be His plan for us. If it was so for our Servant-Leader, why can it not be true for us, His followers? Jesus identified with the people of Israel in the wilderness and claimed the very words God gave to them there.

Would it have seemed easier to trust Jesus if He had jumped from the Temple rather than dying on the cross? Why was it necessary for Jesus to refuse this temptation of Satan? What do you do to test God?

8.5 Answering with Scripture

You and I face temptation every day. Some temptations are as simple as rolling through a stop sign to as complex and major as cheating on a test or a spouse. Anyone who has lived long enough knows we all face temptation that causes us to sin. But what about Jesus? As the Son of God, was He immune to temptation? Or did He get a pass because He was fully God?

Our question to consider for this chapter is "Did Jesus experience every possible temptation?" After observing this episode in Jesus' life, how would you answer this question? Write your answer here:

_____

_____

_____

Read Hebrews 4:15. Underline the last four words.

The writer to the Hebrews wanted his readers to know Jesus was the final High Priest and the final sacrifice required by the Old Agreement of God to make people right with Holy God. In describing Jesus, God inspired the writer to note that Jesus "has been tempted in every way, just as we are." There is, however, one huge difference: Jesus was without sin. He never allowed temptation to seduce Him away from the Father's call on His life. The Bible says that Jesus experienced every possible temptation we all face, but He never sinned.

We also observe that Jesus answered Satan with Scripture. He did not argue or debate. Jesus simply quoted what God, the Father, had said through His servant-leaders in the Old Agreement. Scripture serves as a powerful tool in the battle with temptation.

Read 2 Timothy 3:16–17. Circle "God-breathed" and underline what the Bible says Scripture is good for.

God inspired Paul to teach his apprentice Timothy to count on the reliability and authority of Scripture because it was "God-breathed" and "useful for teaching, rebuking, correcting and training" people how to live God's way. He should use it to equip or train other Christ-followers to trust Jesus and live like Him. Paul's words to Timothy are God's words to all Christ-followers. Scripture is God's inspired Word that trains us to live like Jesus.

For further study:
Matthew 4:1–11
Mark 1:12–13

9—Following Jesus' Invitation: Jesus Calls His Disciples

After Jesus refused Satan's shortcuts to His Kingdom, He intentionally began to carry out His mission as the *Christos* by recruiting others to learn how to live in His Kingdom. He had the same message as that of John the Baptist: "Repent, for the kingdom of heaven is near" (Matt. 3–4). Jesus introduced a new Kingdom in which He ruled as King and a new way of life for those who trusted Him as their ruling Lord. This meant giving up their old way of life and learning to live as Kingdom people from the King himself. We use the biblical word "repent" to describe this heart change that leads to a new way of life learned from Jesus.

The Kingdom way of life under the King's leadership begins when Jesus invites, or "calls," you to trust Him as your Rescuer and King and you embrace Him as both in your life. Jesus called 12 men to be His closest followers. These men learned how to live as Kingdom people from Jesus as they went about their lives together. His three-year course in Kingdom life took them on an adventure they would have never known without His leadership.

The Memory Verse for this chapter is Matthew 4:19. This is Jesus' call to Peter and Andrew to follow Him. They worked as fishermen, and He used a metaphor they understood to help them know what He wanted them to do. Grow familiar with this verse as you discover Jesus' call to join Him.

Our question to consider for this chapter is "Does Jesus call every Christian?" Some American Christians confuse calling with career. This leaves some feeling that their job is God's call on their lives while others wonder if they are called at all. Observe Jesus' call to His first followers, and we will return to this question later.

Christos—God's Transforming Touch

9.1 Beginning a New Life

Imagine Jesus showed up where you work one day. As you go about your daily duties, He asks you to stop what you are doing and follow Him. He says He wants to show you a new way of life, but you have to be with Him in order to learn from Him. He says time is short; so you do not have much time to put things in order to follow Him. This is not the first time you have heard about Jesus. You know He has told people to change how they live because "the kingdom of heaven is near," but you never expected Him to stand in front of you and ask you to go with Him.

How would you immediately respond if this happened? What would you say? Would you go? Write some of your responses here:

_____

_____

Read Matthew 4:17–18. Highlight Jesus' message in verse 17. Circle the names and places in verse 18. Underline what the men did for a living. (Also read Luke 5:1–10.)

After John baptized Him, Jesus left the area of the Jordan and returned to His home near the Sea of Galilee. (Use a Bible atlas to get your bearings.) There He began to tell others why He had come. Like John, Jesus told people to "Repent [change how you live], for the kingdom of heaven is near" (v. 17). Jesus called people to "repent" from the way they lived because He had come to show them a new way of living, one in which He is King. This change began in the heart and showed itself in daily living. He came to demonstrate what the spiritual Kingdom of the *Christos* looked like on earth. This demanded a whole new way of how people lived and how they treated one another.

Jesus came upon two brothers who worked as fishermen, Peter and Andrew. They were going about their business of casting their nets into the lake when Jesus came up to them. As part of the common people, fishermen went about their lives catching and selling fish to provide for their families. They held no offices nor had any religious status. They lived common lives trusting God and waiting for the Messiah.

Luke provided more details of the event than Matthew. He described how Jesus told Peter to throw the nets into the water and they would catch fish. Peter reminded Jesus they had fished all night but had caught nothing. Still, he would do so because Jesus told him to do it (v. 5). When they did, they caught so many fish they needed help pulling them into the boat. James and John were among those who helped (v. 10).

Jesus stepped into the daily lives of some fishermen and offered them a chance to trust Him and start a new life. Take some time to put yourself in Peter and Andrew's boat. Ask God to show you how you would have responded if you were them. Be honest.

9.2 Accepting Change

Into the Wild is a film that tells the story of Christopher McCandless, who after graduation from college gave away his inheritance, abandoned his car, burned all the money in his wallet, and headed toward the Alaskan wilderness. He died within four months of living in the wilderness, but his story caught the attention of many who are intrigued with leaving everything and seeking a life different from the life they grew up in or that others expected of them.

Such change seems harder for some people than for others. Few abandon everything and pursue an entirely new way of life. Some people can pick up everything and move to another city and start over with ease. Others stay in the same town their entire lives.

If Christopher McCandless stood on one end of the scale and "never move or leave home" stood on the other end of the scale, where would you place your attitude toward change? Write your comments here:

_____

_____

_____

_____

Read Matthew 4:19. This is the Memory Verse for this chapter. Underline the two imperatives Jesus used to call Peter and Andrew. (An imperative is a verb of command.) What did Jesus say He would make them?

Jesus called out to Peter and his brother to "come" and to "follow" Him. He used the metaphor of fishing as a picture to describe what Jesus wanted to teach them. This image of "fishers of men" implied teaching the men skills to catch the hearts of people with the things of God. Jesus did not invite them to join Him in a classroom. He called them to learn from Him life skills that would lead people into the Kingdom of Heaven He came to establish. Fishermen learned how to catch fish

from other fishermen. Now, they would learn how to catch people from the Master Fisherman who knew how to "catch people" and lead them to trust God.

Read Matthew 4:20. Circle the words "at once" and "followed him."

Peter, Andrew, James, and John did not hesitate at Jesus' words. They dropped their nets and joined His mission as the Messiah. How could they do such a risky thing? They had others who worked for them who could continue after they left. This was probably not their first meeting with Jesus. Jesus was 30 years old at the time and had lived around that area His entire life.

What could Jesus say or do that would cause you to drop what you were doing and follow Him? Could He simply say, "Come, follow Me" and you would? Write some of your thoughts here:

_____

_____

_____

_____

Christos—God's Transforming Touch

9.3 Jesus' Call

What skill or hobby have you learned from someone else? This could include anything from creating computer graphics to baking Christmas cookies. But it must have required you to depend on the knowledge and skill of another. You could have learned it in an unstructured (kitchen or garage) or structured (college or trade school) setting.

You chose to learn that skill from someone who knew something you wanted to know, and you committed the time and resources necessary to learn from him or her. You gave up some things to learn it, and most likely you invested your time and money in order to get better at your skill. Describe some of your learning process here:

_____

_____

_____

_____

Following Jesus is like trusting someone to teach you a skill you do not have and knowing that having the skill would completely change your life.

Read Matthew 4:21–22. Underline the names of those Jesus called and circle "immediately" in verse 22.

After Jesus called Peter and Andrew, He went to two other brothers, James and John. They, too, worked as fishermen on the Sea of Galilee and were preparing their nets for the next cast when Jesus walked up. The word for "prepare" in verse 21 is the same one in Ephesians 4:12 "to prepare God's people for works of service."

Ministry is often like preparing a group of Christ-followers for the next "cast" to catch people.

Our storyteller wrote that James and John, like the brothers before them, "immediately" left their boats "and their father" and followed Jesus. They gave up the security of what they knew to trust Jesus and join Him on an adventure they knew nothing about. Peter, James, and John became the followers in whom Jesus invested most of His time. They stayed with Him the longest and learned the most from Him.

Jesus' call was without a doubt the single most transforming event in their lives. From the moment they decided in their hearts to follow Him and dropped what they were doing to go with Him, all else flowed from that decision. The adventure of following Jesus on His mission began when they said yes in their hearts and followed Him with their feet. They literally "repented," or changed how they lived, because "the kingdom of heaven is near." They trusted Jesus' message, heard His call, and then followed Him.

To say you accept Jesus' call on your life holds more importance than just a statement of belief. You trust Jesus to lead you, and you release those things and people you have depended on for security in order to follow Him wherever He may lead.

The first step in accepting Jesus' call is to trust Him enough to make the changes necessary to become His student, or follower. Spend some time reflecting prayerfully on Jesus' call on your life to follow Him and learn from Him.

9.4 Visiting the Sick

When our children were growing up, we scheduled "well visits" for them; but when they got sick, we called the doctor for help. If they had a common cold or a small scrape, we could help them. But when something serious came along, we did not try to help. We called our pediatrician immediately. Healthy children do not need a doctor; sick children do.

When was the last time you or your child got sick? What circumstances surrounded the sickness, and did you call the doctor? How do you feel about the chronically ill? Write your thoughts here:

_____

_____

_____

Read Matthew 9:9–11. Underline "tax collector," "sinners," and "Pharisees."

Jesus continued to recruit people to follow Him and learn from Him how to "catch" people for God. He intentionally called Matthew, a Jew who collected taxes for the Romans, to leave his collection booth and follow Him. Most Jews considered men like Matthew traitors because they not only collected money for the Roman Empire, but they also could take whatever they wanted for themselves. Jesus' choice of Matthew surprised many but signaled the nature of His mission—traitors could become followers, too.

Matthew instinctively knew how to "catch people." Matthew did not have a canned speech to give his friends about his new life with Jesus, but he knew how

to invite them to his house to meet Jesus, so he did exactly that. Jesus gladly joined Matthew's friends when the religious leaders showed up to check things out.

The Pharisees were religious professionals who knew the Law of Moses better than anyone and set themselves up as defenders of the faith. They had heard of Jesus and followed Him into the traitor's house filled with his buddies who, according to the religious laws, were "sinners."

Read Matthew 9:12–13. Underline Jesus' last statement in verse 13. Rewrite His answer to the religious leaders in your own words. You may want to look up Hosea 6:6 to read in context the verse Jesus quoted to them.

Jesus agreed with the Pharisees that those among Him were "sick" according to the Law, but then He told them that healthy people do not need a doctor. He also quoted from the prophet Hosea that God preferred "mercy" toward the sick over religious activity, or "sacrifice." Jesus' words imply that all are "sick" or "sinners" and need a doctor.

Jesus then explained His purpose for coming. His mission was to call sinners to follow Him. He did not come to serve those who considered themselves healthy or righteous. They did not need help. He came to serve those whom others considered "sinners" and "sick." Matthew and his friends serve as examples of what Jesus came to do.

Which of the two groups do you most associate with: the religious leaders or Matthew and his friends? What do Jesus' words to the religious leaders mean to you?

Christos—God's Transforming Touch

What things do you like to do that could serve as a way of exposing your friends to who Jesus is?

9.5 Putting Your Skill to the Test

I learned to fish from my grandfather. He took my two cousins and me to a nearby lake and showed us how to catch fish. He showed us everything from how to tie hooks and put minnows on a crappie rig, to how to lay and check a trot line. After he showed us how to do something, he would go back to his own poles and lines. He expected us to fish on our own. Yes, he would answer questions or get us out of a bind; otherwise, he expected us to fish. He had his own catches to make.

Go back to the skill you thought of earlier. Write about the first time someone asked you to demonstrate your newly learned skill on your own. How did it make you feel to do it on your own? How did the first time go?

Read Luke 9:1–2. If you were to diagram these verses, what three things did Jesus do toward the Twelve key followers? List them here:

_____

_____

Jesus did not call the first disciples to sit and take notes from Him as He lectured. He trained them how to "catch people" by example and teaching. He then sent them to try out their new skills. Jesus called the Twelve together. He gave them the "power and authority" to do what He called them to do and then "sent them out" to tell others about His Kingdom and to demonstrate its presence by healing the sick.

Read Luke 9:3–6. Underline verse 6 to mark the success of Jesus' apprentices.

Like my grandfather who gave instructions to my cousins and me before he sent us out to fish on our own, Jesus gave the Twelve specific instructions about what to take and how to have a successful experience. (See Matthew 10 for a fuller list of instructions.) Verse 6 says that they went as Jesus sent them and did what He told them to do—tell others about His kingdom and demonstrate His presence.

Our question to consider for this chapter is "Does Jesus call every Christian?" The answer is an unequivocal "yes!" Jesus calls all of us, and when we have said yes, we are all sent. Jesus' call on your life is not just about your career or job. Jesus calls you like He called His first followers: to no longer trust your old way of life but to learn from Him how to live in His Kingdom with Him as your King.

How have you sensed Jesus' call to follow Him in your life? Have you trusted Him as your Rescuer and Leader, and have you begun to learn how to live like Him? Have you moved beyond keeping religious rules and having correct beliefs to trying out the things Jesus has taught you as you love and serve others like Him? Yes, Jesus' call involves salvation, but it also includes the way in which you live.

For further study:
- **Luke 5:27–32**
- **Mark 2:13–17**

10—Trusting Jesus to Meet Needs: The Wedding Feast at Cana

History is spotte with the miracles of Jesus. These miracles, or signs, provide evidence that Jesus is who He says, the *Christos*, the Son of God. In our world thatverifies beliefs primarily through scientific thinking, many have questioned the authentic nature of Jesus' miracles. Some suggest His followers added these to history after His death as evidence He was the Messiah. Others suggest the ancient people had no way to explain random events or experiences so they attributed them to a miracle-worker like Jesus. However, God has always revealed Himself to people by breaking into history.

Jesus never performed a miracle to gain fame. He turned down that temptation in the wilderness (Matt. 4:5–7). Jesus intervened in His creation to demonstrate that His message held true—the Kingdom of Heaven was at hand in Him. These signs pointed to His true nature as the Son of God and helped people trust Him.

In this chapter, we will observe Jesus changing water to wine to meet the social need of a family friend. This was His first miracle recorded by His storytellers. While He resisted His mother's request on the basis of timing, He answered her request and in doing so revealed His "glory" (v. 11).

The Memory Verse for this chapter is Philippians 4:19. This verse promises that Jesus will meet all of our needs. Grow familiar with it as God's promise to those who trust Him.

Our question to consider for this chapter is "Is there anything God cannot do?" Yes, this is a loaded question. Wrestle with it, observe the episode in history from John, and then we will talk at the end of the chapter.

Christos—God's Transforming Touch

10.1 Jesus at the Wedding

My oldest daughter's wedding was our first. I remember how crazy my wife got over the details. She wrote list after list and double and triple checked each one to make sure everything would be in place at the wedding and the reception when all the guests arrived. Her hard work and attention to detail paid off. Everything went as planned at both the ceremony and the reception. Everyone had a place to sit and enough to eat, and my daughter made the most beautiful bride ever—in my humble opinion.

As a pastor, I have taken part in weddings that did not go so well. Someone forgot to order something or a natural event turned everything inside out. Those who plan such things feel more nervous about what happens than those who come as invited guests.

Have you ever planned or attended a wedding? How did it go? What was the most obvious slip-up? How did you feel as either the planner or guest when it happened? Write some of your thoughts here:

_____

_____

_____

_____

Read John 2:1–2. Underline the event, place, and people in the verses. Also, list some questions about the verses that you would like to answer. Use a commentary or Bible handbook to help you find the answers.

The episode began with John writing "on the third day" Jesus and His disciples attended a wedding in Cana of Galilee. This "third day" follows John's counting that began in chapter 1, verse 29. Verse 43 of chapter 1 tells us that Jesus decided to go to Galilee. Jesus headed north for the wedding, and on the way He called Philip and Nathanael to follow Him as His apprentices.

John tells us Jesus' mother, His newly called followers, and Jesus all attended the wedding. Most likely Jesus was the one invited, and He invited His disciples to join Him. This may have helped cause the need that would soon surface.

Read John 2:3. Underline the need Jesus' mother asked Him to meet.

Weddings held as much significance in a family's life in Jesus' day as they do now. To have a shortage of anything served to the guests was the host's worst nightmare. Jesus' mother, Mary, clearly empathized with the host's dilemma—possibly brought on by her Son's additional guests—and turned to Jesus for help. She already trusted in Him as the *Christos* and simply asked Him to demonstrate who He was by helping a friend in need. Her motivation was not for Jesus to perform in front of everyone but to meet a social need so that something as small as running out of refreshments for the guests would not ruin the marriage celebration.

Put yourself in Mary's place. How would you feel toward a friend who did not have enough for guests at his or her wedding? Knowing what she knew about her Son, would you have asked Jesus to meet the need? Pray a prayer of thanksgiving for God meeting our needs no matter how small they may seem to others.

10.2 Jesus' Intervention

"Timing is everything," the saying goes. In golf, for example, the timing of your swing makes the difference between a slice into the trees or a drive down the middle of the fairway. In cooking, timing is critical when adding ingredients and when you remove the cake or roast from the oven. In a relationship, well-timed words can break a heart or mend it. Timing matters in sports, relationships, medicine, and business. When you do something is as important as how well you do it. We all know offering air conditioners to folks in Minnesota during a January snowstorm is not good timing in the sale of air cooling units.

In what areas of your life have you observed in which the timing of something you did made the difference? Do you have any examples? Describe the situation here:

_____

_____

_____

_____

Read John 2:4–5. Underline Jesus' response to His mother and circle the word "time" in verse 4. What did Mary then say to Jesus and how did it strike you?

Jesus wondered why His mother would ask Him to get involved in something like refreshments at a wedding. It was not that He thought of the problem as beneath Him. He was, after all, the Suffering Servant-Messiah. The real issue was that of timing. Jesus said, "My time has not yet come" (v. 4). The word for "time" in this verse can be translated "hour" (NASB). Jesus had a sense of timing for when things should happen in His ministry and when He should demonstrate who He was to those around Him. He felt this was not the time or place to reveal Himself to those around Him. On the other hand, as He drew closer to the cross—the purpose of His coming—He knew His hour, or appointed moment, had come.

Take time to do a word search in the Gospel of John for the words related to time (for example, hour, time, or day). Observe how Jesus was aware of the spiritual meaning of time. Some passages include: John 7:30; 8:20; 13:1.

Jesus' mother did not pay attention to Jesus' hesitancy nor did she understand what He meant. She turned to the servants without acknowledging Jesus' words and told them to do what Jesus said to do. She felt the timing of her friend's need was more important than Jesus' sense of whether or not His "hour" had come. This was not a disregard for who Jesus was but evidence of her trust in who He was and what He could do to meet an obvious need.

What events in your life would you consider God-orchestrated timing for you? When have you sensed a certain thing had to happen at a certain time for it to be effective? Write some of your thoughts in the space below. Pray for God to reveal to you His timing for your life and how you can respond in order to be most effective for Him.

_____

_____

_____

_____

_____

10.3 Turning the Water into Wine

Jesus often used everyday objects and events to demonstrate who He was and what His Kingdom looked like. A surface reading of the stories about Him show Him in people's homes, walking down dusty roads, pointing out vineyards, talking with children, and eating bread and drinking water like everyone else. Jesus was part of the world He came to rescue from darkness. He used objects like water jars and lamps, which people used every day, to tell His story and show others how to live in His Kingdom. He could have made stars fall or lakes dry out or overflow, but He wanted people to know His Kingdom could be realized in day-to-day living.

What other ordinary things about Jesus' life do we tend to overlook as we observe Him from our perspective? What difference does it make that Jesus took part in normal life as He revealed Himself as the *Christos*?

_____

_____

Read John 2:6. Underline "water jars" and "ceremonial washing" to mark those items that you may need to explore further to get a picture of their meaning in the setting in this story.

John wrote that "six stone water jars, the kind used by the Jews for ceremonial washing," stood near Jesus when His mother gave instructions to the servants. John noted that these jars of various sizes each held "twenty to thirty gallons" of water. Archeological finds from that period show that they were made of clay and used to store bread and money. The "ceremonial washing" took place before meals and as a part of purification ceremonies.

Read John 2:7–8. Describe in your own words what Jesus instructed the servants to do.

_____

_____

The jars were empty, and Jesus instructed the servants of the household to fill them to the top. Jesus then told them to take some of the water they had poured into the jars to the "master of the banquet," or the servant in charge of the wedding feast. The servants complied.

We will find in the next section that, sometime between filling the jars with water and the servants dipping some out to take to the banquet master, the water turned to wine. This is significant because Jesus did not draw any attention to Himself nor the change of substance. He did nothing like a magic act in Las Vegas to impress an audience. He never said a word or made a motion. He simply spoke instructions, and somewhere in the middle of those acts the miracle occurred. The Creator need only to speak, and change happens.

What does this reality reveal about Jesus' identity and what was most important to Him when He performed a miracle such as this? How does an act like this help you trust Jesus as the *Christos*? Put yourself in the sandals of the servants. They knew they had filled the jars with water, but they were taking wine to the head servant.

10.4 First Impressions Count

Anyone who has interviewed for a job or introduced themselves to a new group of people knows that you should "put your best foot forward" in those situations. You may have also heard, "You can only make a first impression once, so you better make a good one." Offering your best impression first is good advice to let others know your best qualities and win their favor. The same is true with food and entertaining. You do not offer last night's leftovers to first-time guests in your home. You serve your best for those you hope to impress or honor as your guest.

Do you agree or disagree with the values just stated? How have you lived by them in your behavior toward others? What are some reasons not to put your trust in these axioms? List these in the space below.

_____

_____

_____

_____

Read John 2:9–10. Underline the comment the master of the banquet made to the bridegroom.

The master of the wedding banquet had no clue what had happened. He knew he had run out of wine, and he may have even sent someone to buy more. But not until he tasted the wine did he know his problem was solved. It was more than solved. The drink was the best he had tasted. Without his knowledge or involvement, Jesus met his greatest need at the time.

The master of the banquet went to the bridegroom, who also panicked about having no more drinks to serve, and commented on the quality of the wine (v. 10). The wise banquet master knew you put your best foot (or wine) forward, and then you offer the cheaper stuff after everyone has lost their taste for quality. But what he tasted was the best, not the cheapest. He was impressed but unaware of what had happened.

Jesus' miracle met a need of one who did not ask or trust Him to meet the need. God does that in our lives more times than we know. Part of our gratefulness to Him is acknowledging this happens without our participation in things.

Jesus also produced the best for what was needed. The Creator offered only the finest of His creation to those in need. Although the need was not like that of hunger or healing, Jesus honored the request of His mother and presented the best. We can also learn that God may sometimes "save the best for last." In the Kingdom of Heaven, the best will come when all else has run out. Heaven follows death, and the last will become the first.

What other insights might you have about Jesus and His Kingdom after observing this part of the episode? How does it build hope into your faith? What circumstances are you in now that may look as bad as the situation in the story? How does this miracle of Jesus help you? Our Memory Verse, Philippians 4:19, is a promise that parallels this event in Jesus' ministry.

10.5 Seeing Jesus' Glory

I appreciate the well-marked streets in my city. While my navigational skills seem lacking, I cannot blame the city manager for unmarked streets or poorly lit intersections. Of course, our town has the benefit of being relatively young and having a lot of land for road development. Go to an urban center or foreign megacity and you could spend hours looking for an intersection, building, or apartment number. Signs point to where you want to go. Well-marked paths help the traveler get to his or her destination.

Read John 2:11. Circle the words "signs" and "glory." Underline how the disciples responded to Jesus after this event.

John tells us this was the first "miraculous sign" of Jesus. John the storyteller moves from the witness of John the Baptist to Jesus' own witness through His signs that He is the Son of God. John recorded signs and dialogues of Jesus so the reader would trust that He is "the Christ, the Son of God" (John 20:31). These signs, or miracles, point to who Jesus is and the way in which a seeking traveler can find his or her way to trust Him.

The Bible also says that through this act Jesus "revealed His glory" (John 2:11). "Glory" is a biblical word to describe the presence of God and the honor ascribed to Him. In the Old Agreement of God, glory signified God was present and at work (Ex. 24:15–17). It was also used as a word of worship to honor the greatness of God (Ps. 104:31). John used the word "glory" to express Jesus' divine nature. He wrote that he and others had "seen his glory, the glory of the One and Only, who came from the Father, full of grace and truth" (John 1:14). In John 2:11 John taught that by turning the water into wine Jesus revealed His divine nature.

John, who was at the event, wrote that Jesus' apprentices "put their faith in him" (John 2:11). They had already left their livelihoods to trust Him to provide for them as they learned from Him. Now, they saw with their own eyes that He would provide. If He would provide drinks at a wedding, surely He could feed and clothe them.

Our question to consider for this chapter is "Is there anything God cannot do?" In life, no. He can turn water into wine and restore a tortured soul to health. In the hearts of people, yes. God by His own will cannot make someone love Him. That is the bane of free will granted by love.

You have observed Jesus' first public sign that He is the *Christos*. Prayerfully ask God to reveal to you Jesus' "glory" and build your trust in Him. Thank God for meeting needs in your life without you even asking or seeing Him meet them.

For further study:
- **John 7:1–9, 30–32**
- **John 8:12–20**

11—Helping Others Find Christ: Jesus and Nicodemus

I sat with Andy in a booth at a Mexican food restaurant. We had met to talk about his desire to trust Jesus. I knew Andy through a member of our church who had worked with him and who had patiently answered his questions about what it meant to trust Jesus. My dinner meeting was the culmination of those conversations. In the middle of our chips and hot sauce, he abruptly asked, "What do I do to shed my old skin and follow Jesus?" I explained how Jesus called us to trust Him. With our heads bowed, Andy confessed his trust in Jesus. At the end of the meal I knew I had a new brother in Christ.

Jesus hand-picked some to be His disciples, and others came to Jesus out of a genuine desire to join Him on mission but did not know what to do. We can learn from these encounters how to enter an eternal relationship with Jesus.

Nicodemus was a religious leader who came to Jesus by night and confessed Jesus had surely come from God. Jesus' description of how one entered a relationship with Him surprised the religious man; and it surprises many people today.

The Memory Verse for this chapter is John 3:16. This verse is possibly the best known Bible verse among God's people. It gives Jesus' explanation for why He came and how we can enter into an eternal relationship with Him.

Our question to consider for this chapter is "Can someone be born again and not know it?" Just as love involves a decision and the will to follow that decision, so the metaphor of being born again also includes both a decision and a will to respond to God's love in Christ.

11.1 Jesus and Nicodemus

If you were to describe yourself as a religious person, how would you rate yourself? On a scale of "I go to church for weddings and funerals" to "I go every Sunday and sometimes once during the week," where would you place yourself? Write your description here:

_____

_____

Read John 3:1. Underline the nouns in the opening sentence of the episode.

We know of Nicodemus only from John's story of Jesus. John tells us he was a Pharisee. These were some of the most revered leaders among the Jewish people. They were experts in the Law of Moses and committed to keeping them to the letter. They dressed according to religious custom. Jesus confronted them many times in His ministry (see Matthew 23:13, 15, 23). Nicodemus also belonged to "the Jewish ruling council," or Sanhedrin. This group of 71 religious leaders guided the religious culture of Israel at the time.

Read John 3:2–3. Write Nicodemus' confession in your own words in the space below. Underline the words "born again" in Jesus' reply to him.

_____

_____

_____

_____

Nicodemus came at night to talk to Jesus. He may have feared what the other religious leaders would think of him; or maybe this was the best time for him to talk alone with Jesus. He confessed that Jesus surely had come from God because no one could do the "miraculous signs" He did "if God were not with him" (v. 2). This was as far as his trust in Jesus had come, but he would soon go much farther down the journey of faith.

Jesus said that to truly enter the Kingdom He inaugurated, Nicodemus must be "born again," or "born from above" (v. 3). Jesus sensed the seeker's genuine desire to follow Him, and He described what must happen as being like that of new birth. Religion and religious activity were not enough—those were things people do. To take part in Jesus' Messiah movement, a birth into a new life had to occur. Jesus did not bring a new religion. Jesus brought a new existence that one could only experience through the mystery of rebirth.

Put yourself in Nicodemus' sandals. How is your confession of Jesus similar to his? For example, does the fact that Jesus performs miracles allow you to confess He is more than a man? How is your confession different from his? What first impressions did you have of Jesus' teaching about a new birth to enter His Kingdom? Ask God to open your heart to the conversation that follows between Jesus and Nicodemus.

_____

_____

_____

11.2 Two Births

"You can't teach an old dog new tricks," the saying goes; and the older I get the more I understand the truth of that proverb. I travel to Spanish-speaking countries sometimes. Every time I get ready to go, I resolve to learn the language. After many trips, I still can only greet, ask a few necessary questions, and say "goodbye." It seems much easier to get a translator than to learn a new language. My laziness to learn the language exposes my lack of care for those I serve.

What do you need or want to learn, but you use the excuse of age or busyness to keep you from learning? For what other reasons do we stop learning new things as we get older?

_____

_____

Read John 3:4. How did Nicodemus respond to Jesus?

_____

_____

Nicodemus took Jesus literally. His entire religious life was built upon the exact interpretation and keeping of the Law, so he wanted to know from Jesus how an adult could literally re-enter his mother's womb and start all over. He asked a logical question, but it exposed his lack of sensitivity to the things of the Spirit. You can be religious but miss the heart of the matter.

Read John 3:5–8. Highlight "kingdom of God" and underline the word "Spirit" every time it occurs.

Jesus patiently explained to His guest what He meant by the metaphor "born again." Jesus taught that one entered His Kingdom through a spiritual birth brought about by the Spirit. His was a spiritual Kingdom, not an earthly one. Nicodemus was a member of the earthly, physical kingdom of Israel that looked for a Messiah

to re-establish it to its rightful place. He was physically born into that kingdom. Jesus, on the other hand, brought a Kingdom that required its people to be born again spiritually in order to belong (v. 5).

Jesus explained that there are two births: a physical birth and a spiritual birth (v. 6). He used the word "flesh" to represent physical birth and "Spirit" and "wind" for spiritual birth (vv. 7–8). Jesus wanted Nicodemus to know that it was the work of the Spirit that brought about the kind of birth He described. Jesus compared the second birth to the wind, which we can hear but do not know where it comes from. It is a mystery, but we can know of its movement and presence.

Prayerfully ask Jesus the same question Nicodemus did. Read Jesus' response to him several times and ask God to make clear to you Jesus' lesson to Nicodemus about spiritual birth. Thank God for His patience as you ask questions like Nicodemus.

Christos—God's Transforming Touch

11.3 Jesus' Teachings

My wife teaches algebra and precalculus to high school juniors and seniors. She tells the students that math problems are like puzzles and that they should get excited about the work she gives them. She loves math. Through years of learning and teaching, she can see the solutions the students cannot until she shows them. They need tutoring and patient direction to see the world she sees. Many times they look at her and say, "I don't get it." She then returns to the problem and works it again for them. Her world of math seems foreign to them at first, but after a year (or two) of training, many leave understanding that world in new ways.

What courses did you take in high school that seemed foreign to you at first but that you understood after the teacher patiently explained things to you? Who was your favorite teacher and why? Write your reasons here:

_____

_____

_____

_____

Read John 3:9–10. Underline what Jesus called Nicodemus in verse 10.

After Jesus' explanation about spiritual birth (vv. 7–8), Nicodemus asked, like a confused math student, "How can this be?" (v. 9) He was not trained in Jesus' spiritual Kingdom. He was unclear about what Jesus meant. Jesus wondered aloud how "Israel's teacher" did not know of such things. He knew of the Law and how to be religious, but he knew nothing of what Jesus said.

Read John 3:11-15. Underline the phrases "earthly things" and "heavenly things" in verse 12. Circle the title "Son of Man" in verse 13. Read Numbers 21:4–9 for the background story of Jesus' reference to the actions of Moses in verse 14.

Jesus felt concerned that He had already told Nicodemus what He and His followers had seen, but Nicodemus had not accepted their testimony (v. 11). Jesus said He had talked about "earthly things" and Nicodemus had not trusted Him. Why should He expect Nicodemus to grasp spiritual matters? (v. 12) Jesus then revealed that only He, the "Son of Man," had come from heaven and had the authority to speak about such things (v. 13). No earthly religious leader had that kind of authority.

Jesus then drew on a story from the Old Agreement of God with Israel to help Nicodemus understand who He was. Moses followed God's instructions and lifted up a bronze serpent among the people to heal the deadly snake bites brought by God's judgment. Those who looked at the serpent were healed (Num. 21:9). Jesus said in the same way and for the same reason He, the Son of Man, "must be lifted up" (referring to the cross) and those trusting Him would have "eternal life" (v. 15).

Jesus continued in this passage to help Nicodemus trust Him. What did you learn about Jesus from what He told Nicodemus? How has this helped you trust Him as the Son of Man, who came down from heaven and who gives eternal life by dying on the cross?

_____

_____

_____

11.4 Jesus' Elevator Speech

An "elevator speech" is an answer to the question "What do you do?" This brief description of who you are and what you do in the time it takes to ride an elevator between floors lets people know your business. You craft an "elevator speech" carefully with a limited number of words, and it becomes so familiar you say it without thinking. My "elevator speech" for Legacy Church is "We help people trust Jesus, and we help them become like Jesus as we worship God, reach out in love, connect in community, grow in faith, and serve others. We want to be a crowd of witnesses to Christ-changed lives where everyone has a story of what God has done in his or her life, and we love telling and hearing those stories." Hopefully the description sparks interest from the person who asked the question, and we can talk about some part of what I have said. If the elevator door opens and the person must leave, at least he or she has heard the essence of who we are and what we do as a church.

Do you have an "elevator speech" for your church, business, or life? Can you describe your relationship with Jesus in a short period of time if someone asked you about it? Write what you may say to someone here:

_____

_____

_____

Read John 3:16. Highlight the entire verse in your Bible. This is our Memory Verse for this chapter. Write the verse in your own words here:

_____

_____

_____

This verse is an "elevator speech" for who Jesus is and what He has done for us. Jesus told Nicodemus of the nature of God and why Jesus did what He did. God is love. That love for a rebellious world motivated God to give His "one and only Son" for it, so that whoever trusts Him with his or her life will not experience eternal destruction but eternal life.

The word usually translated "believed" in the Bible is better translated "trusts." We believe in truth, ideas, and concepts. We trust people. You can believe in God but not trust Him with your life and decisions. While belief makes up part of our relationship with Jesus, the core issue lies in whether you trust Him enough to stake your life on His death, burial, and Resurrection and that His way of life is better than the one you can create.

Read John 3:17–18. Underline the words "to condemn" and "to save" in verse 17. Circle the word "not" in that same verse. In verse 18, what does Jesus say about the one who does not trust Him?

_____

_____

_____

The word translated "condemn" can also be translated "judged" (NASB) and means "to separate" or "to approve." Jesus said He did not come into the world to be its judge—that would come later (see Revelations 20:11–15). Jesus came into His creation in order to "save" or rescue the world, not to judge it (v. 17). Those who trust Him as their Rescuer are not "condemned," but those who do not trust Jesus as their Rescuer are judged already (v. 18).

Learn this core verse of faith (John 3:16). Thank God for sending His Son to rescue you and ask Him to grow your trust in Jesus as you seek to live like Him.

11.5 The Bottom Line

Our question to consider for this chapter is "Can someone be born again and not know it?" Write some of your initial thoughts here:

_____

_____

That question is like asking, "Can someone be in love and not know it?" Or "Can someone be rescued from a flood and not know it?" While babies are born without knowledge, the day comes when each child realizes he or she is a person. Every person, too, comes to a place in life and realizes who he or she is as a spiritual person and who God is to him or her. Just as love involves a decision and the will to follow that decision, so the metaphor of being born again also includes both a decision and a will to respond to God's love in Christ Jesus.

Read John 3:19–21. Highlight the first phrase of verse 19. Underline key words such as "light," "darkness," and "truth" wherever they appear. Summarize Jesus' conclusion to Nicodemus in your own words.

_____

_____

Jesus gave the religious leader His "verdict," or bottom line. Jesus, the "true light" (John 1:9), came into the world; but those He came to rescue loved their way of life (darkness) more than Him because the light of His

life exposed the darkness in their lives (John 3:20). Jesus taught that those who live by His truth are not afraid of the exposing light of His presence because they have acted through God and not through their sin-filled decisions (v. 21).

John did not tell us in this passage whether Nicodemus trusted Jesus and followed Him that night. Read John 19:38–39. Underline the names of the two men who came to Pilate and asked for Jesus' body after He was crucified, and then buried Jesus.

Nicodemus did step into the light and put his trust in Jesus. He risked his position as a religious leader along with Joseph of Arimathea to care for the body of Jesus. His actions indicated he was "born again" and walked in the light of truth as a follower of the *Christos*.

You have observed Jesus' conversation with a religious leader of Israel. Jesus patiently answered his questions and gave him clear, simple answers. Put yourself in Nicodemus' place. Make Jesus' words to Nicodemus His words to you as well. The conversation is over. What will you do? You saw what Nicodemus ultimately decided. Now what about you? .

For further study:
- **Matthew 23:13–39**
- **Numbers 21:4–9**
- **1 John 3:16–20**

12—Helping Others Find Christ: The Woman at the Well

Belief about God is not the only thing that separates people. Social, racial, and gender issues erect walls between individuals and people groups. Although grass-roots movements and government efforts seek to tear down those walls, they still remain. Jesus, the *Christos*, came to create unity among diverse groups by offering His Kingdom ways to everyone. Jesus stepped across every social, religious, racial, and gender barrier when He asked a Samaritan woman for a drink of water. He did this not only to demonstrate what His Kingdom would look like but also to rescue the woman from her life of sin and to bring salvation to her village.

After Jesus met with Nicodemus, a fully-vested religious leader, John carefully wrote of a midday encounter with a woman of another faith. Do not miss the contrast between the two dialogues. John, the follower of Jesus, wants you to see how Jesus is the *Christos* for all people.

The Memory Verse for this chapter is John 7:38. Jesus promised that if you trust Him, "streams of living water will flow from within" you. He will not only quench your spiritual thirst, but He will be a constant source of spiritual water so you will never thirst again.

Our question to consider for this chapter is "Is there anyone who cannot be saved?" Write your initial answers in the space below. Observe Jesus in this episode of His-story to answer this often-asked question.

_____

_____

_____

12.1 Stepping Across Boundaries

When I was growing up, we did not go through certain parts of town. The people who lived in those differed from me in race and social status. No one ever said, "Don't go through there because those people are different." But over the years I picked up the message and always stayed on the wider, more lighted streets around those neighborhoods. As I matured as a follower of Jesus, I realized I had developed a prejudice against a group of people simply because of where they lived and the color of their skin.

Did you have those "parts of town" when you were growing up? Do they still exist? For what reasons did you drive around rather than through those neighborhoods? Do you still hold those same prejudices?

_____

_____

Read John 4:4–6. Underline the details of the setting for this episode in Jesus' ministry.

Jesus had been in Judea and decided to go back north to Galilee. To do that He would need to travel through Samaria, the central region of Palestine. Most Jews went out of their way to go around Samaria in order to not associate with those they considered half-breeds and idolaters because of the Jews' intermarriages with non-Jews and worship of foreign gods. But Jesus led His apprentices through the Samaritan towns. He stopped at Sychar and sat by what was known as Jacob's well.

Read John 4:7–9. Underline the person Jesus asked for a drink of water. Highlight the last statement in verse 9.

A Samaritan woman came at noon (the "sixth hour") to draw water from the well where Jesus sat. Most women came in the cooler morning hours. The fact she came at noon, alone, suggests she was not part of the accepted women in town. Jesus asked her for a drink, and the woman immediately pointed out that He broke both social and racial taboos by speaking to her. Jewish men did not speak to Samaritan women. John lets us in on this prejudice by commenting, "For Jews do not associate with Samaritans" (v. 9).

Jesus modeled for His followers a Kingdom without boundaries. He stepped on religious (unfaithful Jews), racial (intermarriages between races), and social (speaking to an outcast woman) prejudices when He led His apprentices north through Samaria and asked a woman for a drink of water.

Take a moment and record the religious, racial, and social prejudices in your life. Be honest. We have all been taught prejudices. Ask God to open your heart and show you how they separate you from others.

_____

_____

_____

_____

12.2 Seeing Beyond the Obvious

We have an English Language Program at Legacy Church as part of our mission to help people trust Jesus. People from 52 different countries have come to learn English at our church facilities. One of the most difficult aspects of learning English as a second language is to learn idioms. How does a foreign student know what "a little bird told me" means without some help? Or how do you explain that something will cost you "an arm and a leg" without an interpreter? Advanced students can learn these sayings unique to English only after they have learned the basics of the language. Every language has idioms unique to its culture. You must eventually learn them if you truly want to understand the meaning of a native language.

What are some of your favorite English idioms? Which ones seem most peculiar to you? Have you ever had to explain an English idiom to someone? How did it go? Write your thoughts here:

_____

_____

_____

Read John 4:10–12. This is Jesus' answer to the woman's question in verse 9. Underline the words "living water" in both verses 10 and 11. Write the woman's response to Jesus in your own words.

_____

_____

_____

Jesus answered the woman's prejudiced comment (v. 9) with a spiritual expression that would lead to her trust in Him. However, like a foreign person learning an idiom, she did not understand His response. She answered Jesus in literal language, which showed she missed His point by not knowing what He meant by "gift of God" and "living water" (v. 10). She challenged the Jewish intruder regarding why He thought He could

offer water better than that of Jacob's well, which had provided water for centuries and served a patriarch of their religion (v. 12). Like Nicodemus, who did not know what Jesus meant by "born again," this woman at first did not know Jesus' meaning.

Read John 4:13–15. How did Jesus explain the difference between the "water" they talked about? (vv. 13–14) Underline the woman's response in verse 15.

Like a patient second-language teacher, Jesus explained the meaning of His spiritual words. The "water" He spoke of was not physical water. He offered her a relationship with Him that would quench her deepest thirst—spiritual dryness. Jesus hit a nerve, and she said she wanted that kind of water. Her answer, though, showed that she still thought in physical terms.

Put yourself in the woman's place. How would you respond if Jesus showed up in a public place while you were on an errand and asked you for a cup a coffee? Suppose you responded like the woman. He then responded to you by saying, "If you knew who I was, you would have asked Me for a cup of coffee, and I would have given you a bottomless cup of it." Ask God to reveal to you who Jesus is through this part of the encounter.

12.3 The Woman at the Well

Different aspects of religious life divide people. Some groups still hold to the dietary laws of the Old Agreement of God. Others believe they are free from any influence of those ways of living. Most Seventh-day

Adventists live out many of those dietary guidelines while some Baptists have no problem eating whatever they see in a buffet line. While the intent is not to separate themselves from others, the result of claiming one way of life as closest to how God intended causes those who think otherwise to feel left out. As you know, belief about what to eat is not the only thing that separates groups of Christ-followers. The list can fill this page.

What have you been taught about the best way to honor God by your diet? What other aspects of your faith differ from that of your friends? What impact has your different beliefs had on your friendships?

_____

_____

_____

_____

Read John 4:16–18. Write in the space below why you think Jesus turned from talking about living water and told the woman to go get her husband.

_____

_____

Jesus saw that the woman did not understand His picture of living water, so He shifted to something she did know about—men. Jesus told her to go get her husband and invite him to meet Him. She said she had no husband. Jesus may have known this by the time of day she came to the well or by her reputation beyond her hometown. On the other hand, Jesus' divinity allowed Him to know things about people you and I cannot know until told. Jesus told her she already had five husbands, so her answer to His request was "quite true" (v. 18).

Read John 4:19–20. Underline the woman's confession of who Jesus was. Circle where she claimed the Samaritans worshiped and where the Jews believed to be the holy place.

The woman changed the subject as soon as Jesus spoke of her personal life. Religion is easier to talk about than our personal sin. She confessed Jesus was "a prophet," and then she stated the basic religious beliefs that separated the Samaritans and Jews. She pointed to Mount Gerizim where the Samaritans believed Abraham offered Isaac as a sacrifice to God and where Abraham and Jacob set up altars (Gen. 12:7; 33:20). She then said "you Jews" worship in Jerusalem where Solomon built the Temple (1 Kings 5–6). If Jesus were a prophet, He could settle the age-old argument of who was right.

Jesus turned the conversation to the woman's personal life in order to expose her need for the living water He offered her. She deflected His efforts by trying to start a debate about religion. Ask God to open your heart to the Spirit's inquiries into your personal life that needs the living water of the *Christos*.

12.4 Worshiping in Spirit and Truth

Some faiths describe worship as going through a liturgy or service of worship. You must perform certain actions and say specific words or you have not worshiped. Other traditions tend to equate worship with certain styles of music and a time of proclamation, which together form a worship experience. Still others describe worship as personal, intimate moments alone with God filled with ecstasy. The ways to worship God vary as much as the beliefs about God. Worship at its core is your response to God for who He is and what He has done for you. That response in whatever form, whether alone or in a group, is your worship.

How would you describe your understanding of worship? Write your thoughts here:

_____

_____

Read John 4:21–22 for Jesus' words to the Samaritan woman. Underline the word "Father." Circle the last statement in verse 22.

Jesus refused to enter the old debate of religious correctness. He came to introduce the Kingdom of God, not settle old scores. When that "time" came, people would not worship God, the Father, on either a holy mountain or a specific city (v. 21). Jesus set aside manmade distinctions between beliefs about God and promised that the hour would come when those visible expressions of religion would no longer signal one's rightness before God. Jesus made it clear that rescue would come from the Jews rather than the Samaritans. He did not say this to show Himself superior to the woman but to declare the truth of God's Word (v. 22).

Read John 4:23–24. Underline the words "true worshipers" and "spirit and truth." Highlight verse 24.

Jesus said the time of religious division had ended, and the time had now come when the true worshipers of God would worship "in spirit and truth," the essence of worship. Jesus came to restore authentic worship of God founded upon spiritual truth rather than religious tradition. Those who worshiped God "in spirit and truth" were the kind of worshipers God sought (v. 23). Jesus said "God is spirit" and those who worship Him must do so in the ways of the spirit and truth.

Jesus offered the Samaritan woman a new way to relate to God. She thought worship meant correct belief and going to the right worship place. In His presence and Kingdom, the old religious distinctions and places no longer mattered in worship. He came to offer a personal relationship with those He rescued. This relationship is built upon sharing one's spirit with another and always telling the truth. Jesus revealed the true nature of worship: a personal, spiritual relationship based on the truth about every aspect of your life before God, who is Spirit and Truth. Jesus replaced religious doctrine with a personal relationship "in spirit and truth" with God.

Take some time to meditate on Jesus' teaching in verses 23 and 24. He taught the essence of worship for the true worshipers of God. How can you apply His teaching to your worship? In what ways can His teaching change your beliefs and practices of worship?

_____

_____

_____

_____

12.5 Spreading the Word

I sat in a restaurant in Santa Fe, New Mexico, with some coworkers when I looked up and saw someone I thought I recognized. I said to the guys with me, "I think that's Gene Hackman." We all looked to the table in the corner. "Yep, that's him," one guy said. "I don't know," said another. We talked awhile about whether the man was the actor in movies we had seen such as *Superman: The Movie* and *Hoosiers*. We continued to eat and talk about his movies and exited the restaurant right by his table. He never looked our way, but we knew it was him. I was glad my wife did not come with us. She would have invited him to sit with us and share dessert.

Have you seen someone you thought you recognized, but you were not sure until you got closer or met him or her? Write your experience here:

_____

_____

_____

Read John 4:25–26. Circle "Messiah" and "Christ" in verse 25 and underline Jesus' response in verse 26.

When Jesus explained authentic worship to the Samaritan woman, she said the Messiah, or *Christos*, would explain everything when He came. She may have understood some of what Jesus told her, but either she hid her misunderstanding or changed the topic again. Jesus said, "I who speak to you am he" (v. 26). Jesus was the Messiah, and she had to decide if she would confess who He was or continue the debate about religion.

Read John 4:28–30 and 39–41. What did the woman do and what were the results of her witness?

Jesus' apprentices returned just as He told the woman who He was. While they talked, she ran back into town and told people she may have met the *Christos* because He had told her "everything I ever did" (v. 29). This they had to see; so they went out to see Jesus. There Jesus taught them, and many of the Samaritans trusted Jesus as the Messiah "because of the woman's testimony" (v. 39). One witness to an encounter with Jesus led many to trust Jesus as the Christ.

To be a follower of Jesus means to follow Him across religious, social, racial, and gender barriers to help others trust Him through our witness to what He has done in our lives.

Confess your trust in Jesus, who is the Christ, and ask God to give you the same abandon as the woman to freely speak to others about Him.

For further thought:
- **Genesis 33:18–19; 48:21–22**
- **Romans 1:16–17; 11:1–21**

13—Experiencing Jesus' Power: Jesus Calms the Storm

One biblical truth about Jesus Christ's identity is that He is the Creator of all things. (See John 1:1–3 and Colossians 1:16–17 for examples of this.) He created everything seen and unseen, and the Bible confesses that He holds all things together. Since this is so, it follows that when "the Word became flesh and made his dwelling among us" (John 1:14) as Jesus of Nazareth, He would have control over the things that He created. When we follow Jesus through the pages of His-story, we see how He changed the course of natural events and restored people in order to demonstrate that He was the Creator. These "signs," as John called them, pointed to Jesus as Creator and *Christos*.

Jesus' power and authority over creation gives hope to those who trust Him when they experience disease and disorder in their lives. In the story of today's episode from His-story, Jesus' power over the storm gave His followers hope and confidence that He was the Christ. We can have that same hope when life's storms swell up around us.

The Memory Verses for this chapter are Philippians 4:6–7. Storms will come, and the encouragement of God's Word is to always face them with prayer and thanksgiving. Our prayerful conversation with God through the storm will make all the difference.

Our question to consider for this chapter is "Does God cause or allow the storms of life?" People have pondered this question for centuries. If God is in control and the Creator, how can killer storms happen and innocent people die? We will talk about this more at the end of this chapter.

13.1 The Whirlwind on the Lake

My friend Scott owned a sailboat. It was his hobby, and he spent many weekends repairing and restoring the 30-foot boat. One Saturday he invited my wife and me to sail with his wife and him on Lake Ray Hubbard, a reservoir east of Dallas. The skies were clear when we left the dock and began to make our way across the lake. But when we anchored for lunch we noticed a bank of clouds moving toward us from out of the west. Scott said we needed to head back to the docks because the clouds looked "a little darker than he liked them to be." About halfway across the lake, a wind hit us. It seemed much cooler than the air around us, and it was blowing in our faces. Scott told us to help him lower the sails, and he started the motor. We arrived at the docks drenched in rain and wide-eyed after a wild ride on the lake. I wondered if my experience was anything like what Jesus and the disciples experienced one day on the Sea of Galilee.

Have you have gotten caught in a storm? What were the conditions? Who were you with? Have you returned to that place since the experience? Write your answers here:

_____

_____

_____

Read Mark 4:35–36. What is the setting for this episode? What had happened before Jesus decided to go to the other side of the lake? Was Jesus alone in the boat? Was their boat the only one crossing the lake?

_____

_____

_____

Jesus had taught all day on the shore of the lake (v. 1). The crowds were so large that He had to stand in a boat out from the shore so everyone could hear and see Him. At the end of the day, He told His apprentices to go to the other side of the lake (v. 35). Mark tells us that other boats also crossed the lake (v. 36).

Read Mark 4:37. Circle the adjective that describes the wind and underline what happened in the boat.

You can literally translate the storyteller's description of the wind by "a great whirlwind." The wind blew so hard that waves began to come over the sides of the boat, causing it to become dangerously close to sinking. The low-sided fishing boat became vulnerable to the waves stirred up by the gale-force winds.

One way to apply the stories of His-story is to allow the physical aspects of each story to represent an event or aspect of our lives. This is sometimes called allegorical interpretation. For example, the physical storm in this story can represent the storms of unexpected danger we experience in our lives. The storm can stand for disease, divorce, or loss of a job in the story. Without overuse, this kind of interpretation can give us pictures of how Jesus is present in our lives.

Using this kind of interpretation, what storms currently rage in your life? How do they make you feel? Write some of your feelings here:

_____

_____

_____

_____

13.2 Trusting in Jesus' Power

My parents grew up in the panhandle of Texas. The region is notorious for windstorms and tornadoes that race through the area. I have found myself on a tractor, in a car, and in a restaurant when these West Texas windstorms blew by. I spent some of my summers growing up with my relatives there. When the town's storm siren would go off, people would drop what they were doing and head to the nearest shelter. But not my aunt and uncle. My aunt did not like the confines of most tornado shelters below ground. So when the storm alarm went off, she and my uncle would jump into the family pickup truck and drive to the edge of town to look for the funnel or weather front and wait it out there or drive in the opposite direction. I am not sure if I got my excitement for a storm from these experiences or not; but to this day when a storm approaches I go to where I can watch the clouds and lightning roll in and stay outside until I no longer feel safe.

How do you respond to storms? Does the abrupt change excite or frighten you? Recall an experience when you were with others as a storm hit. What details surrounded that event? Write your memories here:

_____

_____

_____

Read Mark 4:38. Underline the phrase that describes what Jesus did during the storm and also what the disciples said to Him.

Jesus slept as the storm stirred up the waves that threatened to sink the boat. He may have felt so tired from teaching all day that He was unaware of the wind and the waves. On the other hand, He felt so confident His "hour" had not come that He knew He and the boat would not go under. His confidence in the Father's call on His life gave Him peace in the storm. He could sleep while everyone else feared for their lives.

Jesus' newly called students woke Him and wondered if He cared that they were about to drown. They did not yet trust Jesus for everything in their lives nor did they share the confidence and trust that they were part of God's plan to rescue people through Jesus. They focused their attention more on their safety than on the mission they shared with Jesus. Their attitude reflected that Jesus' presence with them in the boat was not enough.

"Don't You care?" is what many people pray to God in the middle of life's storms. We turn to God to save us

Christos—God's Transforming Touch

from the situation rather than trusting that God's presence alone will get us through the circumstances. Have you ever prayed this prayer? You are not wrong in doing so because Jesus invites us to ask whatever is on our hearts (Matt. 21:22). Ask God to show you ways to trust Him when it looks as if your life's boat is about to sink.

13.3 Responding to Authority

My wife is a public schoolteacher. When her students get too rowdy, she says, "Class, be quiet." The students comply with her commands most of the time. Why? She has the authority to make such a request as a teacher, and she has been given the power to discipline those who insist on continuing to disrupt the lesson. Without such authority and power, chaos would reign in the classroom. In the same way, a judge can say, "Order in the court," and law-abiding citizens comply with his or her command. A judge has the authority to put those in jail who refuse. When those with authority speak, those under their authority respond—in most cases.

Can you think of other examples in which someone in authority can insist that those under his or her care do what they are told? When have you seen this work as it should? When have you been part of an incident when someone refused to comply with the one in authority?

_____

_____

_____

_____

Read Mark 4:39. Underline what Jesus said after He woke up and circle the actions of the wind and waves.

Jesus stood up from His sleep. "rebuked" the wind, and told the sea to calm. The wind died down, and the sea grew calm as the waves, driven by the wind, settled into a smooth surface. Jesus spoke, and the elements of nature obeyed.

We saw in the previous chapter that Jesus is the Creator of all things. As Creator and Sustainer of all things, when Jesus speaks, creation obeys. "And God said" is the way created things came into being (Gen. 1). "Jesus spoke" is the way created things responded to the One who created them. Jesus had the authority and power to command that which He created to do as He said. And that is exactly what happened. The wind stopped, and the sea settled down.

Jesus demonstrated His authority over the elements of wind and sea when He stood up in the boat and commanded them to "be quiet." What does this event do to help you trust Jesus as the _Christos_? What questions do you have about the event? Ask God to show you the authority He has placed in His Son's hands.

13.4 Having Confidence in Jesus

I took my youngest daughter on her first roller coaster ride at Six Flags® Over Texas near our home. I assured her the entire time we stood in line waiting our turn that everything would be all right. I explained the safety features of the ride and how no one had ever gotten injured on it. "It will be fun," I said. "Daddy would never take you to do something that would hurt you." I gave her more assurances and an opportunity to bail out, but she stayed in line and rode the ride. As we slowed to a halt at the end of the ride, she smiled and said, "Let's go again." "See," I answered, "that was fun just like Daddy said it would be."

Describe a time in which you introduced your child or friend to a new experience and all he or she had to go by was what you said about it. His or her only confidence was trusting in you. Write your experience here:

_____

_____

_____

_____

Read Mark 4:40. Circle the question marks to identify Jesus' response to the disciples' prayer.

Jesus' responded to His disciples after He calmed the storm with questions that were not intended to find out information. These were questions more like "What were you thinking?" from a mother to a child who just poured orange juice into a cereal bowl. Or "Didn't I tell you to trust me?" from a father to his son or daughter after an amusement park ride. Jesus questioned His followers like a father asks his sons, "Why are you afraid? Haven't I taught you to trust Me yet?" Jesus was not scolding them as much as encouraging them to trust Him. Did they really think the boat would sink with Jesus in it? Although they had asked a selfish question, Jesus wanted them to know that His presence alone was enough even in the stormy seas.

Matthew, one of Jesus' storytellers who heard the story firsthand from those in the boat, used "you of little faith" for the title Jesus gave His followers. Jesus used this nickname for them other times when they did not trust Him as they should. (See Matthew 6:30; 14:31; 16:8; 17:20 for more examples.) He wanted them to know what their trust in Him could accomplish.

Our Memory Verses for this chapter are Philippians 4:6–7. The writer of God's Word invites us not to be anxious about anything but to pray about anything and everything with thanksgiving. That constant conversation with God will bring a peace that will guard our hearts and minds from fear.

Prayerfully listen to Jesus' questions for the situations you face. Describe to God your circumstances as you see them. How do you answer His questions "Why are you so afraid? Do you still have no faith?" (v. 40) Ask God to teach you not to feel anxious but to trust Him in every situation.

_____

_____

_____

_____

13.5 Walking Through the Valley

One of the most difficult things I do as a pastor is walk with people through tough times. Long journeys with cancer seem the hardest for me. I have seen some healed and restored to a life of hope and health. But I have also walked with people from the diagnosis of the disease to their last breaths. With those who trust Jesus through their battles, I learn to trust Him more through their unwavering faith. "If this is what God wants for me, I will accept it and live as long as He wills. I want to be the poster child for God's grace," a friend told me once before he died. And he was. We who live after our friends have gone on to wonder why God allowed their deaths and sustains our lives. Yet, we see time and time again in His-story that God uses both the evil and the good in life to reveal Himself and His purposes.

Describe a tough experience with a friend in which you learned much about God through the time of suffering and uncertainty.

_____

_____

_____

_____

Read Mark 4:41. Underline the word that described the disciples and circle the word "obey."

Mark tells us Jesus' apprentices "were terrified" after Jesus halted the wind and waves. That one word in the NIV actually translates three words in the original language. Literally, the Bible says "they were afraid with a great fear." The word for fear can also mean "respect" and is the same word in the criminal's words to the other man crucified with Jesus when he asked, "Don't you fear God?" (Luke 23:40) The disciples were filled with both fear of and respect for Jesus because of what He had just done. The wind and waves obeyed His words! They began to see more and more the nature of whom they followed. Their trust in Jesus grew each day and with every event where He confirmed who He was.

Our question to consider for this chapter was "Does God cause or allow the storms of life?" Many believe this age-old question has yet to be answered satisfactorily. The problem is that if God is truly in control of all things and is a loving God, why does He allow life's storms to hurt and kill people? As with any question outside our human comprehension, the answer rests on faith. From a biblical worldview—seeing things as Jesus and His-story reveals them—things happen because God either allows or ordains them to happen for His greater purposes. This can only be accepted through trust in His Son and His Word. This is not a blind trust or a fatalistic look at life, but a trust that God is greater and more intentional in what He allows or ordains than what we can reason. The prophet Isaiah reminds us God says, "As the heavens are higher than the earth, so are my ways higher than your ways and my thoughts than your thoughts" (Isa. 55:9).

Jesus' closest followers learned to trust Him more after their leader calmed the storm that threatened to sink their boat. They had seen Him heal others and cast out demons. They had heard Him teach about the Kingdom He brought. Every lesson and demonstration strengthened their faith in Him as the *Christos*.

What events have you experienced where Jesus has shown who He was? What teaching of His has deepened your trust in Him and the way of life He offers you? Write in the space below your confession of how your trust in Jesus grew through one of these experiences.

_____

_____

_____

_____

For further study:
- **Matthew 8:23–27**
- **Luke 8:22–25**

14—Making a Difference: Sermon on the Mount

Jesus taught people how to live in His Kingdom in which He is King and we are His people. Every effective leader paints a picture of what the future looks like. Jesus did this in the speech we call the Sermon on the Mount (Matt. 5–7). In this message to His followers, on the side of a hill, Jesus described what life looked like with Him as Leader and King in people's lives. He answered many questions about His attitude toward the Law of Moses, which served as the foundation of God's Old Agreement with Israel. He introduced radical ways to treat others in which God's love rather than our ego motivates our actions. This sermon laid the groundwork for His ministry and for our lives as His followers.

In this chapter of His-story we will read two sections of Jesus' teachings to His first followers. One describes who we are and the impact of our actions as Christ-followers (Matt. 5:13–16). The other challenges us at our deepest levels of self-protection and pride (Matt. 5:43–48). Jesus tells us to love our enemies. By doing so we gain the reputation of being children of God. Jesus teaches us to do this as we watch what He did Himself. We trust Jesus' teaching because we see how He lived those teachings in His life.

The Memory Verse for this chapter is Matthew 5:16. The purpose of our good deeds is to help people trust Jesus. We give God credit for anything we do that is judged good so that others can praise our God.

Our question to consider for this chapter is "How many lives does one person affect?" The "six degrees of separation" theory popularized the idea that everyone is just six people removed from everyone else. If this mathematical quirk holds true, then the potential impact of each life is unlimited.

14.1 Being Salt

Spices are key ingredients in food. Sushi without wasabi tastes bland, just as chips in a Mexican restaurant require salsa to complete the native taste. Rice needs soy sauce, and most pizza is not pizza without a base of marinara sauce. Spices give food their particular tastes and identify them with the culture of origin. Salt is a universal spice. From soy sauce to wedding cakes, salt is in the recipe. Without it the food would taste flat. Salt is essential for food to taste good to the human tongue.

What is your favorite food? What spice makes it taste good to you? How much salt does the recipe call for? Record some of your thoughts here:

_____

_____

_____

When Jesus sat on the side of a hill early in His training of the twelve disciples, He taught them how people in His Kingdom would live. He gave them pictures of Kingdom life and explained what a life with Him as King would look like. Jesus began this message to His disciples by describing the character of a Christ-follower (Matt. 5:3–12). He then turned to tell how His apprentices would live (Matt. 5:13–48). Character always shows itself in behavior. Jesus made this connection when He gave His followers two pictures of what their lives would look like if they developed His character in their lives.

Read Matthew 5:13. Circle the item Jesus called His disciples and underline what it is good for if it is no longer effective.

Jesus used the metaphor of salt to describe the lives of His followers. Salt has been used for currency, trade, a health remedy, cooking, cleaning, and gardening. Salt is still used to preserve meats and fish. As I runner, I know the importance of keeping a proper balance of salt and electrolytes on long runs. We know now that the body requires a proper balance of salt for good health. When Jesus called His apprentices "the salt of the earth," He meant that their lives were an essential spice in life.

In what ways can you translate this metaphor into the worth of your life in the Kingdom of God? For example, "My life in Christ can preserve my friend during her illness." Or "I can be like salt when I sprinkle a taste of God's Word in my conversations with others." Write some of your ideas here:

_____

_____

_____

Jesus also talked more about salt that loses its "saltiness" than He did about the uses of salt. In Jesus' day, salt would be thrown on roadways or walking paths when it no longer provided taste to food. He implied when His followers no longer live out their purpose of being spiritual salt to others, He would no longer find them useful. This simply means that when we stop living our lives as the spice of God's love, we no longer live in the way Jesus intended His followers to live.

Go get a pinch or spoonful of salt from the pantry in your house or from a salt shaker. Examine it, taste it, and ask God to show you insights to what Jesus taught His disciples that day.

14.2 Being Light

When I write at home, I usually light a candle by my computer. The soft light calms me, and the flickering flame adds movement to an otherwise lifeless setting. Electric bulbs light the room, and my computer screen provides the images needed to produce my writing. I often wonder how people like Abraham Lincoln and Harriet Beecher Stowe wrote by candlelight or kerosene lamp. Life in Jesus' day was illumined with light produced by burning oil and flax in lamps of clay. If Matthew wrote these sayings of Jesus at night he wrote by lamplight. Light in any form is essential to life in the dark.

What forms of light do you find most familiar? Candle, television screen, fireplace, study light, flashlight, or sunlight through windows? Describe the usefulness of one of these here:

_____

_____

_____

_____

Read Matthew 5:14–16. Underline the metaphor Jesus used in verse 14 for His followers and underline verse 16 as His application of the image.

Jesus told His followers that they were "the light of the world." As with the metaphor of salt, this picture of their lives provided insight into how they would affect others as they went about helping people trust Jesus. Jesus emphasized one characteristic of light: you cannot hide it in the dark! A disciple would not live a hidden life. Just like a city on a hill cannot be hidden at night, so a lamp in a dark room is of no use if someone hides the light from others. Those who trust Jesus must know the light of His presence will shine in the darkness of this world through their lives. Jesus tells us we are light bearers of the *Christos*.

Jesus told His followers to let this Christ light shine. Just as the flame produces the light of a candle, so our "good deeds" produce the light of our lives. Jesus said we must do this so those who saw our light-giving actions would "praise," or honor, our Father in heaven (v. 16).

The implications of Jesus' picture of our lives are that we do carry the light of His presence and that it shines whenever we are in the dark. Jesus teaches us to let this light shine in the form of "good deeds" so others can know the God we worship. Just as light points the way on a dark night, the light from our Christ-centered service to others points the way for people to worship God.

Light a candle if you have one. As you watch the flame and see the light it gives off, ask God to show you ways in which your life is like the light. Ask Him to show you how to share that light with others today so they may know God as you know Him.

14.3 Desiring Revenge

If someone hurts you, what do you want to do to that person? If someone hurts a member of your family, what does your instinct tell you to do? Retaliation and revenge make up part of our human nature to protect ourselves and those we love and value. It is natural to desire and even execute a plan to hurt someone in the same way that person hurt you. A short survey of world events tells us this practice is not only common but expected among world powers as well as people.

What experiences have caused you to desire revenge or retaliation? What did that person do to you? Or what actions have you seen by others that tell you people by nature want justice through retaliatory acts to those who hurt them? Write some of your honest thoughts here:

_____

_____

_____

_____

_____

Jesus said He did not come to destroy the Law of Moses but to fulfill, or complete, it (Matt. 5:17). To demonstrate what He meant, He reframed six familiar laws that guided people's lives. He started with the phrase, "you have heard that it was said" followed by "but I tell you." (See Matt. 5:21–22, 27–28, 31–32, 33–34, 38–39, 43–44.) Jesus moved past the behavior of keeping the Law to focus on the motive behind the behavior. Jesus "fulfilled" the purpose of the Law by showing us the heart of the Law. Once again, His emphasis was on how we treated people rather than if we kept the Law.

Read Matthew 5:43. Underline the law Jesus told the people they had heard. Look up Leviticus 19:18 for the law in its original setting.

Jesus quoted the law to love one's neighbor, but He added a common extension of the law: "hate your

enemy." God never gave the last part as a law for His people to follow. Yet, human nature and interpretation of a law such as "eye for eye" and "tooth for tooth" (Lev. 24:17–22) led to the accepted practice of destroying one's enemy because the person had hurt you or someone you loved. Revenge rather than reconciliation became the way of life among God's people.

The law of God to "love your neighbor" makes sense for a society to exist. It also seems rational to "hate your enemy," for the person seeks to destroy what you have worked so hard to build—especially if you feel convinced God guided you to create and sustain what you have. Peace with those on your side and revenge on those who attack your side are natural and even lawful practices among people. Every society accepts some level of what Jesus said was the way things were.

Take some time to prayerfully consider your attitudes toward your "neighbor" and your "enemy." Be honest and ask God to reveal the true sentiments of your heart. Ask God to prepare your heart to hear what Jesus is about to teach you about your enemies.

14.4 Praying for Our Enemies

Did you allow God to reveal your true feelings toward your enemy as you ended our last session? If you are like me, I do not want to admit the thoughts I have toward another person when I believe he or she has offended me. I claim to be a follower of Jesus, but I find myself responding to people as any other human would. I want justice—"an eye for an eye." I want the other person to hurt like I do. Jesus called us to change how we live because the Kingdom of God is at hand. We must repent from our natural instincts and even from the accepted ways of dealing with others in order to live like Him. Life under His leadership is different from the life I would live on my own. How I treat my enemies marks a clear difference between the two.

Read Matthew 5:44-45. Circle the phrase "but I tell you" and underline the first three words of Jesus' instructions. Write Jesus' reasons for doing this in your own words in the space below.

_____

_____

_____

_____

Jesus spoke with authority when He said, "But I tell you" (v. 44). Jesus fulfilled the Law in the Old Agree-

ment of God by extending God's love beyond our neighbors to our enemies. Jesus went even further and told His followers to "pray for those who persecute you." The Jewish men present would immediately think of the Roman oppressors who harassed them and tortured their families and friends. This was no easy Sunday school lesson. Why did He ask them to pray for those who hurt them? Prayer helps us see the people we regard as enemies in the way God sees them. In God's presence we find we are more like our enemies than we want to admit—we hold the same prejudice and feelings of superiority as they do. Only God's leadership can show us how to step outside our prejudices and hurts to serve them with His love.

Jesus taught His followers that they would gain the reputation of being "sons of your Father in heaven" if they did this (v. 45). Only children of God who were born again would act this way toward enemies. People who observed their actions could give God alone credit for such attitudes. The evidence that God sees everyone alike is that God causes rain (valuable in a desert area) to fall indiscriminately on the "righteous," those who keep His laws, and the "unrighteous," those who do not. Rain has no favorites nor can it fall only on those who think they deserve it. Rain, like God's love, falls on those we judge to deserve it and those we judge to not.

Keep the person who is your enemy in mind as you ask Jesus to show you how to love that person and how to pray for that person. Confess your own prejudices. Ask God to reveal to you how His love has forgiven you from your hurts toward others. Seek to know His mercy and love. Ask that your enemy may become a follower of Jesus like you.

Christos—God's Transforming Touch

14.5 Accepting Those Who are Different

My wife and I belong to four different groups that meet each week. We like doing life with them. We have learned the enjoyment of getting to know each of the families and of sharing the joys and hurts of life together. Most of us are alike. We are about the same age, live similar lifestyles, and attend the same church. It is easy to love those who are like us. We feel happy to share our home with them once or twice a week. The challenge comes when we seek to invite those who are not like us into the group. It seems much harder to ask a neighbor, coworker, or even someone we do not like much but that needs the care of the group, than to ask someone like us who is not having problems at the time. Jesus asked if we keep hanging together as we do now, how are we different from any other social group?

Do you belong to a group of Christ-followers? If so, how has it felt difficult to include others in the group? Have you tried to join a group but found yourself unwelcome? Describe some of these experiences here:

_____

_____

_____

_____

Read Matthew 5:46–47. Circle the question marks to identify Jesus' questions. Summarize the point of these questions in the space below.

_____

_____

Jesus taught that His Kingdom was not defined by "insiders" and "outsiders." If what He brought meant only loving those like you or who agree with you, He introduced nothing but another social group. He pointed out that if we love people like us and welcome only our "brothers"—people in our tribe, denomination, or part of town—we are no different from "tax collectors" and "pagans"—people the righteous considered to have no clue about the things of God.

Read Matthew 5:48. Underline the word "perfect." Check a Bible commentary for different interpretations of this word.

Jesus attacked the tribalism created by religious, social, and racial prejudices by telling His apprentices they must not to be like others but instead be "perfect" like their "heavenly Father." The word "perfect" can also be translated "mature" (1 Cor. 2:6). Our Heavenly Father's love crosses all boundaries and accepts all who trust His Son into the Kingdom of Heaven. This is "perfect" or "mature" love. Jesus insisted that His followers love enemies and friends alike just as God loved them. In this way, they were "mature" in how they loved.

End this teaching time with the *Christos* by asking God to help you love others in the same way He has loved you. Pray that the love He has placed in your heart will go beyond the safe and natural boundaries of those like you. Ask God to give you the courage to love those who have hurt you in the same way that God loves you. Pray that you can perfect God's love in your life by acting toward others as God would.

For further study:
*   **Matthew 5:17–48**
*   **Luke 6:27–36**

15—Extinguishing Worry: Sermon on the Mount

Worry is part of life. We worry because we cannot see what lies around the corner. Most of us want to be in control. When we are not, we worry about what will happen. Too often we worry about what we will lose—job, house, health, or wealth. Worry is related to trust. I do not worry about whether my wife will be unfaithful because I trust her. The same is true of her trust in me. I do not worry whether my daughters will intentionally commit a felony because I trust their character. When I trust Jesus and what He teaches me, I find that I worry less than when I try to live the way I want.

Jesus continued to teach what life looks like in the Kingdom in which He is King. After reframing the rules of the Old Agreement of God toward others, Jesus turned to show His followers how to live in a relationship with Him. He reaffirmed acts of worship like giving to the poor (Matt. 6:1–4), prayer (vv. 5–15), and fasting (vv. 16–18). He then explained how His followers could live worry-free lives if they would value His Kingdom and trust Him (vv. 25–34). In this section of His message, Jesus revealed the secret to a worry-free life.

The Memory Verse for this chapter is Matthew 6:25. These words of Jesus are not as much a command as they are a lesson in perspective. If Jesus' Kingdom is at hand and He is King, then life with Him becomes "more important than food, and the body more important than clothes."

Our question to consider for this chapter is "Is it ever right to worry?" When does worry aid the follower of Jesus? We will return to the question after observing Jesus' words to us.

Christos—God's Transforming Touch

15.1 Storing Up Treasures

I have a retirement account. You may have a savings account or a strongbox with valuables. A child may have a piggy bank. If my retirement account or your valuables become what we treasure, that is what we will have in the back of our mind all the time. Our hearts jump when we think we have lost them. We wonder if we have enough or if that security blanket is safe. When I get a monthly report that the cash value of my 403(b) account has dropped five percent or so, I worry if it will go back up. I almost always ask the not-so-subtle question, "Will this be enough for when I retire?" "What if . . .?" becomes the prayer of my heart.

What emotions do you feel about those things you value or store away for security in another time? How do you feel when you must use a reserve or savings fund? If you have neither of these, what do you think of those who worry about such things? Write your thoughts here:

_____

_____

Read Matthew 6:19–21. Underline the phrases "treasures on earth" and "treasures in heaven." Highlight verse 21 and then write the principle Jesus taught from His example in your own words in the space below.

_____

_____

_____

_____

Jesus warned His followers not to "store up for yourselves treasures on earth" (v. 19). He described the process of going through the work of creating a place to put them, securing them there and, protecting them. To "store up" or "lay up" something takes time and effort. Jesus told His Kingdom people not to spend their time doing that. Why? All that effort will seem pointless if natural processes or people take the stuff they worked so hard to keep. In the end all their work would seem worthless. On the other hand, if they work to put away "treasures in heaven," eternal things, their efforts would not be in vain. Eternal things like relationships, love, and a lifestyle of worshipping God are not affected by the effects of decay and people of this world.

Jesus revealed a secret of life to us in verse 21. The Creator explained how He created us—our hearts follow what we treasure, not the other way around. If I want a bike as a boy, my heart will lock on to that treasure. I will begin to long and look for ways to get it. Pick any thing at any age and, according to Jesus, that is how it works. If so, to change your heart you must change what you treasure. Jesus offers the treasures of His Kingdom so that your heart will long for those things rather than things of this earth. The choice is yours.

What do you treasure? In the space below, answer this question: "What does my heart long for?" Does your heart long for things that will either decay (like a house) or that can be stolen (like money), or does it long for the things Jesus offers to you as your King? Prayerfully ask God to reveal your heart's desires to you. Ask God to show you how to change what you treasure to lead your heart to Him.

_____

_____

_____

15.2 Seeing and Serving

Do you wear glasses or contacts? Have you had LASIK eye surgery? Or do you have 20/20 vision? Do you have a "corrective lenses" requirement on your driver's license? Or are you a Navy fighter pilot with perfect vision? Many of us need help to see clearly. I cannot drive legally without glasses or contacts. Without them I cannot see far enough ahead to respond to changing road or traffic conditions. When my eyes are not "good" according to the department of transportation in my state, I am a hazard to other drivers and myself.

How would you describe your ability to see? What aids do you need to read this question? What happens when you remove your seeing aids?

_____

_____

_____

Read Matthew 6:22–23. Underline the phrase "the lamp of the body." Describe how Jesus used that metaphor for what He taught. What was Jesus' conclusion to this picture?

_____

_____

Jesus used a "good eye" as a metaphor for seeing things well. In other words, if your eyes are good, your body can move forward with ease. If your eyes are bad, or even blind, you will live in darkness and danger. Jesus taught that if we see things the way He describes them—that it is better to store up treasures in heaven than on earth—our lives will be filled with light to see things as He intended us to see them. If we see reality

otherwise, we will live like a blind person on a busy street without a guide dog.

Read Matthew 6:24. Underline the first and last sentences of the verse. What first impressions do you have about the choices at the end of this verse?

_____

_____

Jesus turned from the metaphor of seeing to that of a slave and master to further His point about storing up treasures here on earth. In doing so He revealed another secret of how He made us—we are incapable of serving two masters. We think we can be loyal to the things of this world (exemplified best by money) and still worship God. Jesus says differently. Our hearts are loyal to only one leader at a time. We cannot serve both God and money, the latter representing the things of

this earth. Jesus set up God and money as rival gods in our lives. For this reason the NIV translation capitalized "Money." Jesus gave money god-like status just like the idols among Israel in history under the Old Agreement of God that seduced His people's loyalty away from God. Money and the things it can buy draw our hearts to those things and away from the God who rescued us.

How do you apply to your life now Jesus' teachings about the "eyes" and our ability to worship only one God? Loyalty can be measured in time and money. Where do you spend most of those? Do you trust what Jesus says about your ability to serve God and the things of this earth at the same time?

_____

_____

_____

15.3 Not Worrying

It seems easy to say that life is more important than food and clothes when your pantry is full and you have to give away clothes to make room in your closet for more. So how realistic was Jesus when He told His apprentices not to worry about those things? Would that hold true if you did not have those things? Write some of your answers to these questions in the space below.

_____

_____

Read Matthew 6:25–27. Underline Jesus' direct instruction to His followers. Circle the object He used to illustrate His point.

Up to this point in His message, Jesus has taught us how to live worry-free lives. He said if we treasure things in heaven (v. 19) and keep our eyes on such things (vv. 22–23), we will not only live like He wants us to in His Kingdom, but we will find ourselves not worrying about material things. Our hearts, attention, and loyalty will all focus on God. This is why verse 25 starts with the word "therefore." Jesus basically said, "Based on what I just told you, don't worry" (v. 25).

Jesus reiterated His point to not worry by asking about the things people all over the world worry about: food and clothes. He asked, "Is not life more important than food, and the body more important than clothes?" (v. 25) Jesus illustrated His instructions not to worry by pointing His followers' attention to other creatures, the birds. He told them to observe the birds that neither plant nor harvest but have enough food to survive. Jesus reminded them that God values people more than the birds (v. 26).

Jesus then asked, "Who of you by worrying can add a single hour to his life?" (v. 27) Jesus wanted us to understand that worry adds nothing to our lives. It actually robs us of time with God and others.

Take time to memorize verse 25. This is Jesus' core lesson about worry. Then, meditate on phrases such as "Do not worry about your life" or "Are you not much more valuable than they?" or "Who of you by worrying can add a single hour to his life?" Accept Jesus' presence and pray as though you are speaking to Him in the room. Ask God to help you trust Him enough not to worry about the basics of life. Ask God to show you why you worry about such things.

15.4 Trusting God to Provide

For people who have the money for clothes, fashion more than need determines what they buy. In America, we identify ourselves by the clothes we wear. Some adopt the adage, "Clothes make the man (or woman)," and we shop accordingly. We are taught to value whether we are "in fashion." Most of us would go out and buy formal clothes to wear to a white tie event rather than say we cannot afford them or simply wear a less stylish ensemble. We can read about the "best dressed" and "worst dressed" people in the country, and we can find fashion magazines on every grocery store rack. Jesus challenged our loyalty to fashion when He told us not to worry about those things.

How attached are you to the current fashions? Would you consider yourself on top of the trends or lagging behind? Can you go to church not dressed like most of the people and feel OK? Write your thoughts here:

_____

_____

Read Matthew 6:28–32. Circle the object Jesus used to illustrate His point in these verses. Underline what Jesus called His listeners in verse 30. What instruction does Jesus give in these verses? (See verse 31.)

Jesus told His Kingdom people not to worry about what they wore (v. 28). Like the birds, He pointed to flowers in a field—possibly near where they sat to hear Him—and reminded His listeners that these plants do not work to gather materials or spin yarn to make them beautiful. He reminded His listeners that even Solomon's Temple, Israel's first Temple, in all its beauty

(1 Kings 6:19–22, for example) was nothing compared to the tapestry of their beauty (v. 29). Jesus then challenged their trust in God by asking if God cared for the perennial flowers that died every year, would He not clothe those who carried the image of God? (v. 30) He addressed them as "you of little faith," the nickname He used for them when He calmed the storm (Matt. 8:26).

Jesus returned to His instructions in verse 25 when He told them not to worry about what they ate or wore in verse 31. If they did, they would be like pagans—those who trust many gods or none at all—who chase after such things (v. 32). Nor would they trust that their "heavenly Father" knew about their need. The God-fearing Jews who heard Jesus that day would not want to be called pagans or say they did not trust the Lord for their needs. Neither would any confessing follower of Jesus. To follow Jesus is to trust Him to provide your basic needs so that you can live for Him.

The foundation for a worry-free life is to trust God to provide what you need. "Treasures on earth" would tell you that you need better things. With those values Jesus said you will worry, which adds nothing to your life.

Spend some time prayerfully separating those things you need from those things you want. Also, make a list of the things God has already provided to sustain you. Do you trust Him to continue to do that? Use the space below to record your conversation (prayer) with God.

_____

_____

_____

_____

15.5 Focusing on Jesus

Focus is the difference between winners and losers in most any field. A focused runner who follows a disciplined program will perform better than a naturally gifted runner who trains haphazardly and shows up to the starting line ill-prepared. Focused students do better than those who play video games instead of completing their homework. A person focused on his or her career finds rewards more frequently than someone who does the job and heads home as soon as the clock hits 5 p.m.

How would you describe yourself: focused or not focused? What do you focus on and what are the results? What would you like to focus on but have trouble doing so? For what reasons can you not seem to do one thing well over a period of time? Write your thoughts here:

_____

_____

_____

_____

Read Matthew 6:33–34. Underline verse 33 and the part of verse 34 that applies to your life at this time.

Jesus concluded His teaching about worry in these two verses. First, He told His followers that if they will focus on His Kingdom, His way of life, and His righteousness, they would also have things such as food and clothes. They would have no need to worry because their lives would be about trusting Jesus rather than storing up things such as food and clothes. "Put first" or "pursue first" are other ways to emphasize Jesus' words. A worry-free life came as a by-product of trusting Jesus.

Worry always focuses on tomorrow. There is enough trouble to worry about today(v. 34). Jesus said to trust Him with the unknown and the things we have no control over. The King will deal with those. Jesus instructed His followers to focus on today, seek His Kingdom first in everything, and be realistic about today's struggles. The things they worry about will fade away.

Our question to consider for this chapter is "Is it ever right to worry?" When does worry aid followers of Jesus? After observing Jesus' teachings on worry, how would you answer this question? Write your answer here:

_____

_____

_____

_____

Continue interacting with Jesus' words by writing application to His teaching. For example, you may write, "I will trust Jesus with things that cannot be known, like tomorrow, and things I cannot control, such as what people think of my clothes. I will trust Him enough to serve His Kingdom and His way of life rather than waste time and energy storing up things that can decay or get stolen." You get the idea. Confess your shortcomings and ask God to strengthen your trust in Him.

_____

_____

_____

_____

For further study:

- **Matthew 6–7**
- **Luke 12:22–24**

16—Developing Strong Faith: The Centurion

Trust is the foundation upon which all relationships are built. Without it, suspicion and doubt will prevent the openness and vulnerability required for friendship and intimacy. Trust keeps a relationship alive; loss of trust can kill what started as a lifelong love. Trust also lies at the heart of our relationship with God. We may say we believe in God, but until we trust God with our total life, we cannot have a relationship with Him. Belief and trust are not the same. I can believe you are a safe driver. Until I give you the keys to my car, however, I do not trust your driving. The same holds true in our relationship with God. To believe God exists does little to change how we live. To trust God's Son to learn from Him how to live in His Kingdom requires trust. Trust precedes change.

Someone once said that a leader is someone we trust to go to a place we would not go on our own. Jesus calls us to follow Him places we would not go on our own. He wants to be our Leader. Regardless of whether we trust Him as Leader in our lives, that is who He is for all people. Jesus' encounter with a military leader teaches us how to trust Him as our Leader.

The Memory Verse for this chapter is Hebrews 11:1. This is the hallmark description of faith in the Bible. It stands at the beginning of a list of names of people who exemplify what biblical faith is like. To know this verse is to know the essence of trusting God.

Our question to consider for this chapter is "What is faith?" "I believe . . . [an idea]" has been the modern confession of faith. The truest sense of the word means "I trust . . . [a person]." Consider which phrase begins your confession of faith, and we will return to this question later.

16.1 Arriving in Capernaum

If you ask someone who grew up in a military family where he or she is from, that person may answer, "Everywhere and nowhere. My dad served in the military." That means this person's family moved from base to base as the father was reassigned, and they never stayed anywhere long enough to put down roots or develop good friends. Some people love that about their childhood; others resent it. Military families sacrifice the stability of a home to serve their country.

How many times did you move when you were growing up? Where was your favorite place to live? Where did you have your least favorite experience? How do you feel now about the amount of moves your family made? Write some of your feelings here:

_____

_____

_____

_____

Read Luke 7:1–2. Circle the city Jesus entered and underline the phrases that describe the condition of the centurion's servant.

After Jesus taught His apprentices about how to live in His Kingdom (Luke 6:17–49), He entered the nearby city of Capernaum. This city was located on the northern side of the Sea of Galilee at the crossroads of north-south trade. Enough Jews lived there to establish a synagogue (Mark 1:21), and Jesus made the town His base of ministry in the north (Matt. 4:13). The city was important enough to the Romans' strategy of occupation to post a garrison of soldiers there. The presence of a centurion, the leader of about 100 soldiers, meant the military presence was sizeable.

As Jesus entered the town, our storyteller wrote that a centurion stationed there had a highly valued slave who was ill. This slave may have served the military leader for many years or may have proven himself trustworthy. The centurion held this servant in high honor. He did not want to lose him. We do not know the emotional condition of this military leader, but he was most likely stationed away from home; and now his most prized servant had become ill. He also may have exhausted all of his options to cure the illness and may have felt that he would lose his prized helper. All this was happening when Jesus entered the city.

Put yourself in the centurion's sandals. What did he feel? Try to sense his feelings of loss in this situation.

When have you been in a situation where someone you loved or respected was ill? Were you away from friends and family? What emotions did you feel at the time? Write some of your feelings in the space below. Thank God for His presence during that difficult situation.

_____

_____

_____

_____

16.2 Calling Upon Jesus

The essence of leadership is influence. A leader is someone who influences others to follow him or her to reach a goal or destination. Effective leaders know when and how to use their influence to achieve a personal or group-adopted goal. Anyone who learns how to effectively wield influence can lead. Those who learn best usually rise to the top of a group to lead them.

Who is the most effective leader in your life? How does he or she use influence to lead others to accomplish a goal or meet a need? Write his or her name and the goal reached here:

_____

_____

Read Luke 7:3–5. Underline what the centurion did when he heard Jesus was in his city (v. 3). Also, underline the reasons the Jewish elders gave as to why this man deserved Jesus' help (vv. 4–5).

When the centurion "heard of Jesus," he used his influence to meet a personal need. Jesus' reputation in the area had grown to the point that this military leader stationed to protect the empire's interests knew of Him. A network of informers and the curious kept Jesus on the radar of those sent to put down any rebellions against the empire. Jesus had also made the town His home base so who He claimed to be and what He taught was common knowledge. When Jesus came into town, this military leader called upon the Jewish elders with whom he had worked to go to Jesus and ask Him to heal his servant (v. 3).

The unwritten reality in these verses is trust. The military leader trusted Jesus for who He was by sending the elders to Him, and the religious leaders did not hesitate to ask Jesus to help their patron. We cannot know whether the religious elders trusted Jesus like the centu-

rion, but they did trust the one who had helped them enough to fulfill his wishes. They went as emissaries to Jesus and relayed the leader's request because they trusted him.

The elders came to Jesus and explained how this military leader of the occupation forces deserved His help. The servant of the empire had not abused his influence and power but had used both to serve the people and to help build the synagogue there (vv. 4–5). There are no unselfish motives in the request, however. The centurion did not want to lose good help, and the elders did not want to see someone so friendly to them lose good help either. Although their motives were self-serving, the request created an opportunity for Jesus to respond.

What do you find most striking about this passage? Is it the military leader's trust or the elders' desire to help an enemy of the state? Have you seen similar relationships in your company or community? Are self-serving motives the wrong way to come to Jesus? Write some of your responses here:

_____

_____

_____

_____

16.3 Respecting Authority

I have never served in the military, but I have known many who have. My understanding is that what makes a good military work is the discipline of carrying out the orders of a superior officer without question during the heat of battle. In a classroom, for example, students can entertain different options and ideas. On the battlefield, however, soldiers do not have the option of considering any action other than that given to them by their commanding officer. Otherwise there would be chaos and multiple casualties on the field of action. Respect for authority of those over you is a key element in a successful military unit. This is also true in a home, school, church, and society.

Did you serve in the military? If so, describe the importance of respecting authority and carrying out orders. If not, how have you seen authority used effectively in your own experiences?

_____

_____

Read Luke 7:6–8. Underline the first sentence of verse 6 and circle the words "deserve," "worthy," and "authority."

Jesus responded to the request of the Jewish elders. Why? He apparently had never met the centurion, and the elders were not necessarily sympathetic to His ministry. But Jesus went because He had an opportunity to demonstrate the Father's love to an enemy of His people. As He came close to the centurion's house, He was met by some of the leader's "friends" (v. 6). These were most likely friends of the empire and cohorts of the military base. Jesus had crossed into enemy territory.

The centurion's friends had a message for Jesus. They said the military leader felt he did not deserve for Jesus to come in his house or that he was even worthy enough to come to Jesus. All Jesus had to do was "say the word" and his servant would be healed (v. 7). The word for

"servant" here means "child" in the original language and reveals the affection the master had for this servant. Why did the centurion trust Jesus could do this?

He explained that he was an officer "under authority" who had people under his authority. If he gave orders to his troops, they responded. If he told his servants to go somewhere, they would go based on the authority he had over them. This unnamed military leader confessed he trusted that Jesus had the same authority in spiritual matters. He trusted that if Jesus told the illness to leave the servant, it would do just that because Jesus had authority over it.

The centurion confessed Jesus had authority over spiritual things like he did over his troops and servants. He also helps us understand the use of authority and how it works when properly used. If Jesus was the Messiah, the *Christos*, then He would have authority in all matters of life. Those under His authority would obey His spoken word. This military leader revealed an understanding of the Kingdom of God that we must have in order to participate in it.

Pray for God reveal to you what the centurion knew. Ask God to help you trust Jesus as the centurion did.

16.4 Amazing Faith

One Christmas we went to Disney World. On our last night, we went to what was then called MGM Studios Theme Park. We were amazed as we walked down the streets of the Osborne Family Spectacle of Lights. Five million lights draped over buildings and formed into Christmas trees flashed in sync with music while manmade snow fell from the rooftops! We had never seen anything like that. All we could do was wander slowly through the spectacle with hundreds of others and whisper "unbelievable" to each other. Of all the manmade things built to wow people, that one is among my top five.

What has amazed you? Was it manufactured or natural? What about the event or spectacle drew amazement from you? Write some of your memories here:

_____

_____

_____

_____

_____

Read Luke 7:9–10. Circle the word "amazed" and underline what Jesus said to those standing near Him.

Luke wrote that when Jesus heard the message from the centurion "he was amazed" (v. 9). Only two times in the Gospels do we hear of Jesus being "amazed." One was the faith of the centurion of the empire. The other was the unbelief of Jesus' family and friends in His hometown of Nazareth (Mark 6:6). The extreme trust of an enemy and the lack of trust by family and friends caused Jesus to marvel.

Jesus turned to those near Him and told them He had not seen faith like this in all of Israel (v. 9). He did not mean He had not seen anyone trust Him, because the disciples did just that. Until that point in His mission, Jesus had not seen anyone trust His words like the centurion did. Even though Jesus did not go any farther toward the house of the military leader, when the centurion's friends arrived there they "found the servant well" (v. 10).

Jesus exercised His authority over the illness of the slave, and healed him . He did this to demonstrate the truth of the centurion's confession—Jesus had the authority to tell those under that authority to act and they would. Jesus showed He was the *Christos* and marveled at someone who trusted Him at His word alone—most people do not understand such things.

If Jesus were to observe your trust in Him, would He marvel? Choose a word or phrase to describe your trust in Jesus as the *Christos* and whether or not you trust He can do things in your life like that of the centurion. This exercise is not to make you feel guilty but to help you fathom your faith in Jesus. Ask God to show you your trust in Him. Prayerfully observe the trust and actions of the centurion in this episode of His-story.

Christos—God's Transforming Touch

16.5 Developing Strong Faith

Our question to consider for this chapter is "What is faith?" Recall the faith of the centurion and Jesus' evaluation of it. Write your description of faith here:

_____

_____

_____

_____

Americans live in a culture that has equated belief with trust. If you ask, "Do you believe in God?" most would say, "yes." On the other hand if you ask, "Do you trust Jesus was the only Son of God and do you trust Him enough to live like He taught?" you would get far fewer affirmative answers. The problem with this is that the biblical concept of faith is essentially to trust someone and act like you trust that person. When Jesus called the disciples to follow Him, He did not ask them what they thought or believed about Him. He wanted to know if they trusted Him enough to drop what they were doing and become His apprentices. Most Americans believe in God. Fewer trust Jesus is the only Son of God.

James, the brother of Jesus, also wanted his readers to know the difference in belief and trust. He wrote to his friends, "You believe that there is one God. Good! Even the demons believe that—and shudder." His point was that what you do gives evidence of your trust in Jesus, not just what you believe about Him (Jas. 2:18–20).

Read Hebrews 11:1 from several translations. When you have finished, write your interpretation of this truth.

_____

_____

I like this translation of the verse, "Faith is the confidence that what we hope for will actually happen; it gives us assurance about things we cannot see" (NLT). Trusting Jesus gives us confidence that what He says can or will happen. We can be sure of what we cannot see because those things are spiritual or yet to happen. The bottom line is that we act on that trust! All of chapter 11 of the Letter to the Hebrews focuses on that—people who trusted God enough to act even though they could not see what God promised them. (For examples of this, see Noah, v. 7; and Abraham, vv. 8–10.) Those listed in the chapter were people of faith because they trusted in God—and none of them received all that God promised them (Heb. 11:39).

This chapter has focused on developing strong faith. After observing Jesus' encounter with the centurion and reviewing some other biblical passages about faith, evaluate your trust in Jesus and ways in which you can act as if you truly trust Him. Choose an area of your life that Jesus has authority over (for example, money). What does Jesus say about that in His teachings? (Conduct a word search for "money" in the Gospels and read what Jesus said.) After having read His words, do you trust Him enough to do with your money what He said about it? There are many other examples, so find an area you have trouble trusting Jesus with and ask Him to show you how your life would look in that area if you truly trusted Him as the *Christos*, the one and only Son of God.

For further study:
- **Matthew 8:5–13**
- **James 2:18–24**

17—Dealing with Doubt: Questions from John the Baptist

It is easy to trust someone who treats you nicely, especially when things go the way you expected. Trust is tested during hard circumstances or when the one you trust does not act the way you think he or she should act. Following Jesus seems easy when life is comfortable by our standards and we are healthy and well-fed. Hard times and unexpected pain can challenge our trust that Jesus is who He says He is and even raise doubts in our minds about whether we should continue to trust Him. Many Christ-followers wonder if their questions or doubts are allowed in a relationship with Jesus.

John the Baptist trusted that Jesus was the Messiah. John helped many people to trust Jesus as the *Christos* and encouraged them to follow Jesus. When John criticized Herod Antipas' marriage to Herodias, his brother Philip's wife, the king put him in prison (Luke 3:19–20). John trusted Jesus but found himself in prison for doing what he knew was right and what Jesus would have endorsed Himself. John needed assurance that Jesus was who John trusted Him to be. He sent two of his followers to inquire of Jesus. John's question can be construed as doubt. But was it? We will observe Jesus and John's conversations and discover if one who trusts Jesus can doubt and remain His follower.

The Memory Verse for this chapter is Matthew 11:6. This verse is Jesus' promise to His followers that they will be blessed if they do not stop trusting Him. Blessings come in both difficult and easy times.

Our question to consider for this chapter is "Is doubting wrong?" Some Christians fear doubts that come into their hearts about their trust in Jesus. Others invite any and all questions about this One who rules the universe. What is your initial answer to this question?

17.1 John's Question

One of the greatest disappointments in life is to trust someone who turns on you or abandons you. I had a friend with whom I shared ministry and companionship. We led our church and went on road trips together. I imagined we were brothers who could survive any and all hardships. One day my friend called and told me that he and his wife had decided to go to another church in town and would be leaving the church we had served at together. I was crushed. We worked through it and are genuinely happy to see each other when we run into each other around town. But it damaged my ability to trust someone as a friend. I hold on to some doubt with my current friends because I wonder when they will call me to coffee one day to tell me they are leaving.

What person have you trusted who ended up disappointing you? What has that experience done to your capacity to trust others?

_____

_____

Read Matthew 11:1. What instructions did Jesus give to His followers? Locate Galilee on a map.

Jesus taught His twelve disciples how to tell others about Him. Then He sent them out to do just that (Matt. 10). After He did this, Jesus continued His mission of teaching others about His Kingdom.

Read Matthew 11:2–3. Circle where John was at this time and underline his question of Jesus. What is your first impression of John's attitude when he sent his disciples to Jesus?

John was in prison because he had condemned Herod Antipas' marriage to Herodias, the wife of Herod's brother, Philip. (See Luke 3:15–20 for the complete story.) John had led many people to trust Jesus and refused their loyalty to him when they thought he may be the messiah. John had prepared the way for Jesus' public mission and baptized Him as the *Christos*. No one else had remained as loyal and supportive of Jesus. Yet, John found himself in prison because he had spoken the truth about the Roman ruler over Israel.

John sent two of his closest supporters to ask Jesus a pointed question: "Are you the one who was to come, or should we expect someone else?" (Matt. 11:3) John may have truly doubted if Jesus was the Messiah since John, who had helped launch Jesus' public ministry, was now in prison. Or he may have asked as a simple assurance to keep the faith while imprisoned. We cannot know John's heart in this, but his question represents what we ask Jesus when things do not turn out the way we think they should.

Prayerfully sit with John in prison and ask the question he asked Jesus. Also, ask God to bless the one who disappointed you. Place that person under God's care. Thank God for the friendship you knew, and ask God to keep your heart soft toward others.

17.2 Looking for Evidence

The best remedy for doubt is evidence. If you doubt your business partner's integrity but have an external auditor prove all is OK, you have no need to wonder. If a father is concerned about his son's performance at school, he can look at his son's grades and talk to his son's teacher to find out exactly how his son is doing in school. Grades and the teacher's assessment will paint the true picture. Doubt is mostly built on a lack of information or a misperception of reality. In relationships, doubt can cause suspicion that could result in a broken heart. In our relationship with God, doubt may come because we cannot see the bigger picture or want something God has no intention of providing for us.

How have you overcome your doubt about someone? What was the situation and what convinced you your questions were not necessary?

_____

_____

_____

_____

Read Matthew 11:4–6. Underline the evidence Jesus gave John's disciples to answer John's question about who Jesus was (vv. 4–5). Write the blessing in verse 6 in your own words.

_____

_____

The question John the Baptist's disciples asked Jesus was one of uncertainty. Jesus answered with evidence to assure John and his followers that Jesus was doing exactly what He said He would do. Jesus made His mission statement clear in the synagogue at Nazareth, His hometown. (Read Luke 4:18–19, which quotes Isaiah 61:1–2 for that statement.) When John asked if Jesus was "the one who was to come," Jesus pointed him to the evidence of the blind seeing, the lame walking, and the Good News being preached to the poor—each

of these implied in His statement of His purpose as the *Christos* (v. 5). Jesus essentially said, "Look at what I am doing. I am the One who I said I am and the One who you trusted Me to be."

Jesus then said to tell John, "Blessed is the man who does not fall away on account of me" (v. 6). Jesus did not say, "Hang on, I'll get you out of that mess." Jesus encouraged His friend and follower not to stop trusting Him no matter what happened. Jesus left John in prison to fulfill his role in the Kingdom. Jesus offered John hope to hold onto, not a promise to free him from imprisonment.

Spend some time in conversation with God right now. How do you feel about Jesus not rescuing His trusted friend from prison? How do Jesus' words to John help you trust Him? Quietly review Jesus' answer and ask God to use it to strengthen your trust in Him.

Christos—God's Transforming Touch

17.3 God's Messenger

My family has made it a habit for years to dress up in our finest and go with a group of friends to the Dallas Symphony Orchestra and Chorus' Christmas Celebration at the Meyerson Symphony Center downtown. We anticipate the event for weeks, knowing we will hear the best singers and players perform our favorite Christmas music. They have handbell choirs, children's choruses, and some dramatic presentation to enhance the experience. They also have sing-along songs, which are our favorites. We do that only once a year because we are in no way symphony people. But when we get dressed up and make the trip downtown, we anticipate a wonderful experience that adds meaning to our family's Christmas celebration.

What events do you make a special effort to participate in? What do you expect from the experience? Are your expectations met? Were you ever disapppointed in an event you had anticipated? Write your memories here:

_____

_____

_____

_____

Read Matthew 11:7–10. Circle the word "prophet" in verse 9 and underline the verse Jesus quoted from the Old Agreement to identify John in His-story (v. 10).

Jesus turned to those who followed Him after John's disciples left and explained the importance of John the Baptist in His-story. Jesus asked them a series of questions to remind them of their expectations when they went out to hear John's message and to be baptized by him. Jesus observed that they did not go out to see someone who was swayed by the most recent fad or religious talk (a reed blowing in the wind), nor did they go to the desert to see well-dressed royalty. They made the trek into the wilderness to see a prophet, a spokesperson who revealed the purposes of God. Jesus explained that they found exactly that in John.

Jesus went on to explain that John was not just another prophet. He was the very one the writings of God had told about—the one who would precede the messiah. Jesus quoted the prophet Malachi who said, "I will send my messenger, who will prepare the way before me" (Mal. 3:1). God shared His game plan for sending the *Christos* through Malachi, and Jesus connected that part of the plan to John. Jesus revealed that John was the one God had promised would prepare the way for the messiah. JThis gave further evidence that the Kingdom of Heaven was at hand.

Jesus connected John to God's greater rescue story that had been told since Adam and Eve left the garden. Take some time to identify other examples in which God revealed His game plan and those plans were carried out in His-story. You may want to look back to the stories of Jesus' birth. Prayerfully thank God for revealing His plans and then fulfilling them so that we are able to see Him at work. How do these examples help you with your doubts?

17.4 Greatness Defined

Other than Jesus, who is the greatest person ever born? That is not a trick question, and the answer is in Jesus' words to the people after John the Baptist's disciples returned to him in jail.

Read Matthew 11:11. Circle the name of the one Jesus described as being greater than anyone else who had been born of a woman.

Jesus declared John to be the greatest person ever born of a woman. While that is some compliment, Jesus followed it with a qualifier. Jesus said that as great as John was among humans, he would be considered the least among those who trusted Jesus and entered the Kingdom of Heaven. Jesus' Kingdom brings an entirely different value system to people's lives, including how they are judged great.

Read Matthew 11:12–14. What did Jesus say about the Kingdom of Heaven since John came on the scene? With whom did Jesus identify John?

_____

_____

Jesus explained that since the beginning of John's ministry, the Kingdom of Heaven "has been forcefully advancing, and forceful men lay hold of it" (v. 12). These are strong words from Jesus and imply power and force. Jesus described His Kingdom as advancing powerfully, and forceful men like John as part of it. The healing of the demon-possessed and other illnesses demonstrate its power. The Jesus movement was no weak fad or trend. It was the intentional invasion of God into the lives of people.

Jesus then explained that "all the Prophets and the Law prophesied until John" that this kingdom would come,

and the *Christos* would be its King (v. 13). All the laws and prophecies, including John's message, pointed to Jesus as the Living Word of God. To make His point more clear, Jesus taught them that John was the promised prophet who would precede the coming messiah. John was Elijah (v. 14). Jesus connected the dots in His-story to explain to the people what was happening before their eyes. John was the last prophet sent by God to reveal His Son who brought with Him the Kingdom of Heaven and the forgiveness of sin. Jesus wanted His hearers to get the point, so He said, "He who has ears, let him hear" (v. 15).

Read this teaching of Jesus several times. Ask God to show you the importance of His words to build your trust in Jesus as the *Christos*. Compare Jesus' words about greatness with your own evaluation of people. How do Jesus' words affect that evaluation? Ask God to give you spiritual ears to hear what Jesus is teaching.

17.5 Childhood Memories

As children we told each other rhymes such as, "Sticks and stones may break my bones, but words will never hurt me." Or, "I'm rubber and you're glue; what you say bounces off me and sticks to you." We used these sayings to ward off the hurtful words of others. While we sounded strong at the time, the words of those who said them stuck in our hearts and heads—sometimes for a lifetime.

What sayings do you remember from your childhood while you played with others? Do you remember some of the things people said that you tried to shield by the rhymes you threw back at them? Write some of your memories here:

_____

_____

_____

_____

Read Matthew 11:16–17. Circle the word "like" to indicate the metaphor Jesus used and underline the rhyme He quoted to His hearers.

When Jesus was a boy, He played in the marketplace like other children. Later, He drew on those childhood memories when He looked for a way to describe the generation He tried to reach. He said they were like children who called out to the others "Let's dance" but would not dance to their music. Or they shouted, "Let's pretend we are in a funeral procession," but they refused to mourn with their friends. Whatever one group invited the other to do, they refused. Jesus said that the people who refused His invitations to join Him were like those children in the street.

Read Matthew 11:18–19. Circle "John" and "Son of Man" to mark the subjects Jesus described and underline what He said of them.

According to Jesus, child-like people claimed that John "has a demon" because he lived separate from the people as he sought a lifestyle of holiness (v. 18). Those same child-like people called Jesus "a glutton and a drunkard" who hung out with the wrong crowd because He lived a normal life and rubbed shoulders with all people, including those whom the childish religious ones called names (v. 19). Children call people names to make them feel bad or to keep them out of their group. Jesus helped those who followed Him understand human nature and why He and His friend John had a bad reputation with some of the religious leaders.

Jesus concluded with the words, "But wisdom is proved right by her actions." In other words, we have been called names, but what we do proves whether or not we are wise. He returned to what He told John in verses 5–6: Look around for the proof you need to trust Me.

Our question to consider for this chapter is "Is doubting wrong?" After observing John's question to Jesus, how would you answer now? Write your thoughts here:

_____

_____

Someone once said that doubt was the ants in the pants of faith. Doubt does not kill faith. Iit can actually be how our trust in Jesus grows. Doubt can draw us to examine what we believe about Jesus. In doing so we find the evidence to trust Him as the *Christos*, our Rescuer and Leader.

Review Jesus' answers to John and those who followed Him that day. Write down what Jesus said that can answer some possible doubts you may have about who Jesus is. Ask God to grow your trust in Jesus.

_____

_____

For further study:
- **Luke 7:18–35**
- **Matthew 14:1–12**

18—Helping Others: Feeding the 5,000

Jesus expects His followers to join Him in the great rescue story for all people. One way we participate in this adventure is by meeting the needs of others in the name of Jesus. How do we know we are to do this? Jesus' teachings and examples are our motivation for such acts of service. Jesus used one particular event to teach His followers that He expects us to serve others. Jesus stressed that He has given us the power and authority to meet the needs of others, no matter how big their needs or how little our resources appear to be.

The feeding of 5,000 people with five loaves and two fish is the only miracle performed by Jesus recorded in all four Gospels. The only other miracle told in all four of the spiritual biographies about Jesus is the Resurrection. Why was the feeding of the people so significant? The event was evidence Jesus was the Son of God: Of Israel's God, *Yahweh*, who fed His people in the wilder-

ness with manna (Ex. 16:31–35). The Christ-multiplied meal also affirmed Jesus' words that He was "the bread of life" (John 6:35). Jesus taught His apprentices that they, too, could do such things if they would trust Him.

The Memory Verse for this chapter is John 6:35. In this lesson to His students, Jesus stated He was "the bread of life." To trust Jesus as the *Christos* is to trust Him for your basic physical and spiritual needs. Learn this verse as a promise of His provision in your life.

Our question to consider for this chapter is "How far should we go to help others?" When should we send people away to care for themselves? How do we know if someone is just being lazy or truly needs help in the name of Jesus? Answer these questions, and we will return to offer other answers later.

18.1 Teaching the Multitudes

We call them fans or "groupies." These are the people who are loyal to a rock star, movie star, or leader, and show up wherever the one they admire appears next. I was never such a fan, but I know people who follow someone they like and buy tickets far in advance of performances. They stand in line early on the night of the concert. All you hear from them the next week is what a great experience they had. People are drawn to popular people—for whatever reason they are popular.

Would you consider yourself a fan of someone? What have you done to demonstrate your loyalty to that person? If you are not a fan, whom do you know that is an avid fan of someone? What does he or she do to show love for that person?

_____

_____

Read Luke 9:10–11. Read verses 1–9 to discover where the disciples had come from and underline the town to which Jesus led them. Find Bethsaida in a Bible atlas, dictionary, or handbook. Underline the words that describe Jesus' response to the crowds that followed.

Jesus trained His apprentices through teaching and demonstration. He then sent them out to practice what they had learned from Him (Luke 9:1–6). When they returned from their practice run as servant-leaders in Jesus' Kingdom, their Leader took them to a town across the Sea of Galilee for a time of reflection and rest. But when the crowds saw them crossing the lake in boats, they trekked around the lake to meet them on the other side. The stories of Jesus' miracles and those performed by His disciples reached the ears of the multitudes. They wanted to be near Him. Even Herod heard of the disciples' work and wondered if John the Baptist, whom he had beheaded, had been raised from the dead! (Luke 9:7–9)

When Jesus and the disciples arrived on the other side of the lake near the town of Bethsaida, the crowd was there waiting for them. How did Jesus respond? Mark tells us "he had compassion on them" (Mark 6:34). Rather than sending them away, Jesus began to teach them more about His Kingdom and to heal those who came to Him (Luke 9:11). Jesus' love for the people gave Him the energy to meet their needs. He served the needs of the people out of love when many other leaders would have said, "I'm too tired. Let's talk tomorrow."

As you read the introduction to this episode in His-story, with whom do you identify the most? Are you like the adoring crowd, the tired disciples who just came off an incredible experience of serving like Jesus, or Jesus who was driven by love to serve the people although He felt physically tired? Ask God to reveal your heart to you as you observe these people in the story. Thank God for Jesus' untiring love for you and all who come to Him.

18.2 Serving the Multitudes

Part of my training for a marathon involves spin classes. These are held indoors on stationary bikes with an instructor who calls out certain movements and resistances in order to build cardio and leg strength. I like them because the exercises are set to music, and they raise my heart rate for effective training. Often the instructor will call out a movement or resistance I do not believe I can do. My heart and lungs say, "You better slow down or we are going to stop!" But I have found more times than not if I push a little harder I can do more than I think. Do not get me wrong. There are times when I slow down because I know if I want to make it to the starting line of the marathon I had better stop! But the role of the class instructor is to get me to do more than I would do on my own, thus enhancing my ability to go farther.

What experiences have you had in which a leader or instructor has pushed you beyond what you thought were your capabilities? How did you respond? What were the results of your response?

_____

_____

Read Luke 9:12. Summarize the Twelve's suggestion to Jesus in your own words. What do you think was the motivation for their request?

_____

_____

_____

Luke does not tell us when Jesus began to serve the crowd, but he writes that "late in the afternoon" His twelve disciples suggested Jesus needed to send the people away so they could get something to eat. They reasoned that since they were away from the towns and villages in a "remote place," the people needed time to go find food elsewhere. They truly cared for the needs of the people but saw no resources with which they could meet those needs.

Read Luke 9:13. Underline Jesus' command to them and the disciple's response to Him.

Jesus said, "No, don't send them away. You feed them." Remember that Jesus had just sent them out to practice serving others as Kingdom people, and they had experienced success. Rather than sending the people away, Jesus—like a good spin class instructor—stretched them beyond what they thought they could do and told them to feed the crowd on their own. The disciples—like sweating, gasping-for-air spin class participants—had a ready excuse for why that was not possible. Their inventory of food consisted of "five loaves of bread and two fish," which John tells us came from the lunch of a little boy (John 6:8–9). Philip calculated, "Eight months' wages would not buy enough bread for each one to have a bite!" (John 6:7) Jesus knew they could feed the people, but His apprentices did not trust what their Master Teacher had told them.

When have you felt God has told you to do something with the clear assumption you could do it in His power, but you had very good excuses for not doing it? How are you like the disciples in this part of the story? What would Jesus have to do to convince you that you can do exactly what He has told you to do? Ask God to give you the trust in Jesus you need to be obedient to Him.

18.3 Breaking Bread

Each Thanksgiving our church's English Language Program hosts a Thanksgiving meal for over 300 internationals and their families. We serve the meal not only as a chance for them to experience a traditional American Thanksgiving dinner but also to tell them the story of the new settlers sharing a meal with the native Americans in order to thank God for His provision to survive another harsh New England winter. I am amazed at the amount of food it takes to feed that many people. We purchase the meat. Our church members prepare and bring the other items such as dressing, sweet potato casseroles, and breads. Our director always worries we will not have enough, but every year we have so much left over that we have to carry it to a shelter or ministry.

What is the largest number of people to whom you have ever served a meal? Did you have enough food? Did you ever worry that you might run out of food? Write your experience here:

_____

_____

_____

_____

Read Luke 9:14–16. Circle the number of men in the crowd. Underline Jesus' instructions to the disciples and what He did prior to passing out the food.

Every storyteller of this event said there were 5,000 men in the crowd. We know there was at least one little boy with a lunch, so we can assume there were also women and other children. Even without the women and children, it was a big crowd.

Jesus told the disciples to seat the people in groups of 50 for convenience in serving them. (See how Jethro told Moses to organize the Israelites in order to serve them better in Exodus 18:17–23.) I wonder if there was disgust or sadness in Jesus' voice when He gave orders to

the Twelve to seat the people. He had told them to feed the people (Luke 9:13), and He knew they could do it if they trusted Him. Jesus' tone could have communicated, "Have them sit down. I'll show you again what you can do if you would just trust Me." Like a frustrated coach whose student still did not feel capable of what the coach had taught him or her, Jesus showed His apprentices again what was possible if they would trust His words.

Jesus prayed before passing out the food, just as every Jew would do before a meal. After He gave thanks for what the Father had provided, He broke it in pieces and passed it to the disciples who then gave it to the people.

Relate again to the disciples in this passage. What do you feel or think as Jesus takes the small amount of food you said was not enough to feed the crowd and then directs you to seat them so He could do what He asked you to do? Ask God to continue to build trust in your life as He shows you needs that He trusts you can meet with what He has given you.

18.4 Expecting God's Bounty

Each year I give gifts to our church leadership team. One year I gave them all hockey sticks. One of the members is from Canada, coaches a hockey team, and leads hockey chapels in our community. I wrote a Bible reference on each stick, and then we signed each other's sticks as a tangible sign of commitment to our mission and to one another. That stick sits in the corner of my office. When I see it, I know that there are six others I can count on to lead with me and that we can trust Jesus to lead and provide for our ministry together. That hockey stick is a token of our trust in Jesus and one another to be servant-leaders on the mission God has called us to complete.

What tokens of trust do you have that are reminders you can trust Jesus or others to lead or serve with you? What is the story behind the object that makes it so meaningful to you? Write your story here:

_____

_____

Read Luke 9:17. Circle the words "satisfied" and "twelve basketfuls."

When the disciples finished handing out the food Jesus gave them and the people had eaten, the storyteller described the people as satisfied. This word was used to describe fattened cattle. It was how Jesus said those who "hunger and thirst for righteousness" would feel (Matt. 5:6). The amount of food each person ate was no snack. They had enough to satisfy themselves like at a banquet.

Our chronicler also noted that each disciple picked up a basketful of "broken pieces" of bread after everyone had eaten. Jesus gave each doubting disciple an object lesson in trust. Jesus had told them to feed the people, and they had explained it was not possible. Then they carried around basketfuls of leftovers after feeding at least 5,000 people with only five loaves and two fish! We do not know what happened to the 12 baskets of food. They may have given them away to the people as they left or kept some for the next leg of their journey. But those baskets became a tangible reminder that they could trust Jesus for the needs of thousands and that He trusted them to do more than they thought they could do in His name.

What has Jesus done to "satisfy" you and your family? Prayerfully inventory the things Jesus has made available to you to meet your needs. Fill an imaginary basket of His provisions, and thank Him for giving you more than you need. Ask Him to teach you to trust Him more so you can serve others in His name.

18.5 Helping Those in Need

Almost every church has a benevolence ministry that provides for the basic needs of those who either come by or call for help. Some churches have food pantries and/or clothes closets. Others pay for utilities, food, or car needs. Some simply point those who ask to community services that may be able to help them. We call our ministry "Helping Hands." One of the most difficult aspects of the ministry is deciding whom to help. We have found our church's name on a list of service providers in the community. We are happy to be known as a church that helps those in need, but we sometimes feel overwhelmed with the number of calls and requests coming in on a weekly basis.

Our question to consider for this chapter is "How far should we go to help others?" What are some of your experiences with helping others? After observing Jesus' feeding of the 5,000, how has your answer changed? What boundaries have you placed around your resources? What are your church's guidelines for helping those in need in your community?

Jesus met the needs of those who were hungry. He taught His apprentices that there are enough resources—and then some—to meet the needs of those around them. He demonstrated that He could provide for the people, and that His followers could also do so if they trusted Him.

Read John 6:25–35. Underline the words "bread" and "manna." How are they related, and how does Jesus use them to reveal who He is?

After Jesus fed the 5,000, He and His disciples traveled to the other side of the lake (John 6:16–17). On the other side, they were met by others who wanted a sign from Jesus to prove He was the One sent from God. They referred to the miracle of manna in the desert that Moses had given to the Israelites. Jesus corrected their thinking: God the Father, not Moses, had provided

the miracle food. Jesus then explained, "For the bread of God is he who comes down from heaven and gives life to the world" (v. 33). The people exclaimed that they wanted that bread. Then Jesus said, "I am the bread of life" (v. 35). Jesus promised the people that, if they trusted Him, they would never be hungry again. Trusting Jesus and not their religious forefathers would satisfy their deepest spiritual hunger: having a right relationship with God.

Jesus demonstrated that He was "the bread of life" by physically feeding the crowd that day. His disciples learned a lesson of trust and the power of Jesus to provide. Jesus revealed who He was through His actions and teaching. He was the Sent One, the *Christos*.

Write your confession of who Jesus is after observing what He did and what He taught about Himself. How has this episode strengthened your trust in Him? Write specific areas in your life you want to trust Him with.

_____

_____

_____

_____

For further study:
• **Matthew 14:13–21**
• **Mark 6:30–44**
• **John 6:1–15**

19—Discovering the Church's Origin: Peter's Confession

"Where do you go to church?" or "Do you go to church?" are frequently asked questions. The implication is that church is a place you go rather than a person or a group of people. When we follow Jesus through the pages of His-story, we see that He created the church, not as a place you go but as a people who represent His body on earth. Church, or *ekklesia*—we will call it after its Greek name—is a group of people bound together by the Holy Spirit who trust Jesus is the *Christos*. The church lives to become like Him in every way, and loves others so they too may trust Him. People, not property, make up the Church Jesus established as the presence of His Kingdom on earth.

Jesus built the Church on the confession of Simon, one of the Twelve He chose as His apprentices. Based on that confession, Jesus changed Simon's name to Peter, or "Rock," and said He would build this new thing

called Church upon faith like Simon's. This was the start of God moving His primary rescue mission from the people of the Old Agreement in Israel to the people of the New Agreement in Christ Jesus represented in the *ekklesia*. This historic event is essential to every follower of Jesus' understanding what it means to be the Church and to be on mission with its Founder, Jesus Christ.

The Memory Verse for this chapter is Matthew 16:18. Jesus established His Church on the faith-filled confession of Peter that He was the *Christos*. To know Jesus' words here is to know His intention and purpose for your church—those with whom you share His mission.

Our question to consider for this chapter is "What is the Church?" Take a stab at your confession about the Church. We will revisit this question later.

19.1 Offering an Opinion

Everyone has an opinion about celebrities or famous people. And most people like to read or hear about the opinions of others. That is why there are so many gossip magazines, talk shows, and entertainment news Web sites. People love to talk about people. Everyone has a thought about Britney Spears or Barack Obama. Throw in George W. Bush and Paris Hilton, and you have an instant conversation. The media makes these people famous and gives information so those who care can have fodder for their next talk over coffee or a meal. We all are experts on the lifestyles and work of others. It is our nature to compare ourselves to others and share our insights about their lives.

Who are your favorite celebrities or world figures that you like to talk about with others? What issues in their lives make them interesting or at least easy to form an opinion about? Write their names and your thoughts here in the space below.

_____

_____

_____

_____

Read Matthew 16:13. Circle the name of the place Jesus was and underline the question He asked His followers.

Jesus led His band of students to the "region of Caesarea Philippi." (Use a Bible handbook or reliable Web site to read about this unique town.) The city was north of the Sea of Galilee and is distinguished from the more important Caesarea on the coast of Samaria. The southern city was under the control of Herod the Great

who improved the port city with a theater and better harbor facilities during his rule.

The northern city of Caesarea Philippi was out of reach for Herod's armies, and so it was a freer environment for Jesus and His followers. Caesarea Philippi was known for a major spring that was part of the headwaters for the Jordan River where pagans worshiped the god Pan. Jesus did not enter the city, according to Matthew, but took His followers into the region or area nearby. He clearly wanted some time away from the crowds to train His disciples.

While alone with His apprentices, Jesus asked what they had heard concerning who He was. He did not ask to know if He was popular or not. He asked to genuinely know what the disciples had heard. The opinion of others is a starting place to learning the truth about someone. Jesus also asked the question to set up the next question He would ask them. It was time to see what they truly believed about Him.

What have you heard people say about Jesus? Ask God to give you insight into why people said what they did and ways to lead them to trust Jesus if they do not now.

19.2 Considering Jesus' Reputation

Just as everyone has an opinion about others, each of us has a reputation. How would you describe the reputation of people like Adolf Hitler or Saddam Hussein? What are the universal reputations of people like Mother Teresa, Billy Graham, or Mahatma Gandhi? Our reputation is the combined estimation of others about our character or behavior. People know us by what we do and what we say. Their united opinions of us form the basis for our reputation among those who know us or hear about us.

Pick someone in your community or church and describe his or her reputation. Is it positive or negative? Is the person is aware of his or her reputation? How is your reputation similar or dissimilar to this person?

_____

_____

_____

Read Matthew 16:14. Underline the names the disciples offered as to what they had heard about Jesus. The disciples said they had heard Jesus called "John the Baptist," "Elijah," and "Jeremiah or one of the prophets." Take a minute and write why someone would have equated Jesus' reputation with those the disciples named.

John the Baptist (See Matthew 3 for background.)

_____

_____

Elijah (See 1 Kings 17–19 for background.)

_____

_____

Jeremiah (See Jeremiah 1 for background.)

_____

_____

Each of these men was a prophet who spoke for God and pointed the people to the coming messiah. The word on the street was that Jesus was another prophet who came to give people a message from God and possibly tell about the coming messiah. No one, however, had claimed that Jesus was the Messiah.

Today's world also sees Jesus as one of many prophets. In a pluralistic society like America, Jesus' reputation is one of God's several sons in the same family as Buddha or Muhammad. If you ask someone who Jesus is, he or she may say He was a good man, a teacher, or a prophet who taught about God. While this may be Jesus' popular reputation, it is not His true identity.

What is Jesus' reputation in your family, workplace, community, or school? How is it different from who you know Him as or how the Bible reveals Him to you? Prayerfully ask God to protect your heart from popular opinion and to strengthen your trust in who Jesus really is, the *Christos*.

Christos—God's Transforming Touch

19.3 Confessing Who Jesus Is

I have a reputation in my church and community. Some have positive opinions about my ministry and me. Others are not so positive and freely share their opinions about who I am and what I have done in the community in the name of Jesus. While I pay attention to people's opinion of me and my ministry because it reflects on the One I serve, my reputation with my wife and daughters is the one that really matters. We can review what others say about a decision I made or a ministry I led, but it finally comes down to asking my wife and daughters, "What do you think or feel about that?" Yes, I have my advisors and partners in ministry with whom I consult; but what I hold most important is what those with whom I share the essence of who I am think or feel about me.

Whose opinion is most important to you? Whose opinion do you look to the most when you wonder about your reputation or how you are doing? Write their names and the roles those people play in your life here:

_____

_____

_____

Read Matthew 16:15–16. Underline Jesus' question to the disciples and Peter's immediate response. Circle the word "Christ" in verse 16.

Jesus was more interested in what His chosen apprentices said about Him than what the crowds said. This was because they would carry on His mission after He returned to heaven. He needed to assess if they knew who He was and if they had trusted what He had called them to do. Jesus asked the pointed question, "Who do you say I am?" (v. 15) No other question is more important to a follower of Jesus than this one. It is the basis for our confession of trust in who Jesus really is.

Peter, one of the first chosen ones of Jesus, stepped forward and said, "You are the Christ, the Son of the living God" (v. 16). Peter trusted Jesus for who He said He was and for what He did to demonstrate that truth. Peter did not let popular opinion sway his confession of Jesus. He agreed that Jesus was the Messiah, or *Christos*, the Son of God. Jesus was more than a prophet. He was the One the prophets said would come one day to rescue the people. This is the central confession of Christianity. Jesus is the Promised One, the Messiah, Christ, for all who confess their trust in Him.

While Matthew recorded only Peter's confession that day, each disciple had to make his own confession of who Jesus was. The same is true for you and me. Neither Peter nor anyone else can make our confession about Jesus for us. At some time, we all must answer Jesus' question to us: "Who do you say I am?" This is the question of salvation, the question for eternity.

Prayerfully put yourself with Jesus in this scene from the Gospel of Matthew. Allow Jesus to ask you the same question He asked His disciples. What is your answer? Use Peter's words if you like, but the bottom line is, "Do you trust Jesus to be who He says He is as the Son of the living God?" Write your confession here:

_____

_____

_____

_____

19.4 Creating the Church

Read Matthew 16:17. Circle the word "revealed" and underline the source of Peter's understanding.

How was Peter able to confess that Jesus was the Christ? Jesus knew Peter had not figured this out without help, because man could not humanly grasp that concept alone. Jesus used the word "revealed," which means "to unveil something that is hidden," to describe how Peter knew who He was. "My Father in heaven" was the source of this truth.

"Revealed" is the word used of the biblical concept of revelation. According to Jesus and the Bible, God makes Himself known by unveiling Himself and His purposes to people. We are incapable of doing that on our own—our perspective and spiritual capacities are too limited—so God shows Himself to those He chooses so others can know Him and His ways. (See Genesis 6:13–21 where God revealed Himself to Noah, and 2 Corinthians 3:13–18 for how Paul described those who cannot know the things of God until they are revealed to them.) God, the Father, revealed to Peter that Jesus was the Christ.

Read Matthew 16:18. Circle the words "Peter," "rock," "church," and "gates of Hades."

Based on the confession of Simon, Jesus changed His follower's name. He would no longer go by his father's given name. From now on, Simon would be known as Peter, which means "rock." Jesus said that upon Simon Peter's rock-like trust, He would build His Church, or *ekklesia*. Matthew is the only Gospel story writer who

used the word "church," but it is the primary image for the people of God in the New Agreement of God in Christ Jesus. (See Acts 2, 5:11, and 8:1 for examples of this.) The Church is the visible presence of Jesus in the world today.

Jesus made one more promise to Peter. He promised that the "gates of Hades" would not prevail against the Church. Hades (*Sheol* in Hebrew) was the place of the dead and the dwelling place of demons (Ps. 89:48). The "gates of Hades" can be understood as keeping its inhabitants in as well as keeping others out. Jesus promised that even if the demons stormed out of the gates they would not prevail against His people. The *ekklesia*, the people of God in Christ Jesus, would be victorious no matter what force came against them.

Reread these important words of Jesus in verses 17–18. Write a statement of faith about the Church of Jesus based on what you read in these two verses. Ask God to reveal to you the nature and purpose of His people.

_____

_____

_____

19.5 Defining the Church

One day my father, who had retired and was in his late 60s, called me into his study and told me he had made me executor of his will. He said it was time for me to know where he stored all the legal papers, keys to safety deposit boxes, and passwords to his accounts. He wanted me to know this so when the day came I could execute his purposes among the family members. It was a solemn moment for me because it signaled the reality of my father's passing. But it also gave me encouragement that there was a way to carry out my father's wishes after he was gone. What I said as the executor of his will would be done in the family as I represented him and his desires. He said he could count on me, and I had every intention of living up to his expectations.

Have you ever executed a will for someone? Do you have a parent who has trusted you with his or her information to get to the assets after his or her death? Write about your experience and feelings here:

_____

_____

Read Matthew 16:19–20. Underline the phrase "keys of the kingdom of heaven" and what Jesus said Peter would do with these figurative "keys."

Jesus had promised to build His Body, the *ekklesia*, on the rock-like faith of Peter and declared that the inhabitants of Hades would never overpower it. He then gave Peter the authority to release and bind whatever was needed to establish God's will on earth. Jesus came to inaugurate the Kingdom of Heaven on earth. Up until this time, He alone carried the "keys of the kingdom." Now, like my father who gave me access to the information guarding his assets, Jesus gave Peter the metaphorical "keys" in order to "bind and loose" the powers necessary to carry out the Kingdom work and to combat the forces that may come from the gates of Hades.

Jesus did what every leader does—pass on his or her authority to make decisions when he or she has departed. Jesus designated Peter as the leader who would guide the *ekklesia* after He departed. Peter would have the authority to open and close the Kingdom's resources—like Pharaoh gave Joseph during the Egyptian famine—in order to serve the Church in its infancy. Jesus would later give the same authority to the other disciples so they too could carry out His mission on earth (Matt. 18:18). Peter was not the only one with the authority to access the resources of Jesus, the Son of the Living God.

So, "What is the Church?" The Church is made up of people who confess Christ as God's Son and are being used by Him to advance God's Kingdom. Jesus shared with Peter the authority to make decisions as Jesus moved toward His death and Resurrection. All of Christ's followers share a similar authority to access heaven's powers and resources as they live on mission with Him.

What does this historical exchange between Jesus and Peter mean for you as a Christ-follower today? How does this strengthen your trust in Christ? What does it tell you about the access you have to the things of the Kingdom that you do not use every day? Ask God to show you what you can "bind and loose" in order to carry out His mission call on your life.

For further study:
- **Acts 2:37–47**
- **Ephesians 2:11–22**

20—Seeing Christ for Who He Is: The Transfiguration

One characteristic of Jesus' life is that He constantly found time to connect with the Father. He stole away to private venues to spend hours alone with the One who sent Him to complete the final rescue mission for all people. Jesus knew that His coming as the *Christos* was dependent on His constant contact with the Father. About halfway through His earthly ministry, Jesus invited His three closest followers to join Him on a mountain to pray. During that retreat from contact with others, God the Father affirmed Jesus as His Only Son. God revealed Jesus' glory and connected Him to Moses and Elijah, representatives of the Law and the Prophets. Jesus' transfiguration on the mountaintop signaled He was on the path to complete His mission and that God, the Father, was pleased with Him.

This episode in His-story is one more sign that Jesus was who He said He was and that His followers could trust Him with their lives and eternities. In this chapter we will climb with Peter, James, and John to observe this miraculous experience that affirmed Jesus' identity and purpose for coming.

The Memory Verse for this chapter is Matthew 17:5. These are God the Father's words of affirmation to Jesus. Learn His message to Jesus just as the disciples overheard it as God's message to you.

Our question to consider for this chapter is "What did Jesus look like while on earth?" Sketch with words or drawings your answer to this question. Observe Jesus from the pages of Matthew's story, and then revisit this question.

20.1 On the Mountaintop

God likes mountains. You may first ask, "How do you know that?" and then "Why is that important?" When we observe the biblical record, significant events related to God's purposes took place on mountains. The ark settled on a mountaintop (Gen. 8:4). Abraham offered Isaac as a sacrifice on a mountain (Gen. 22:2). Moses received the Law of the Old Agreement from God on a mountain (Ex. 19:1–3). God used Elijah to defeat the prophets of Baal on a mountain (1 Kings 18:19). We can find other examples, but these examples allow us to say that God used the location of mountains to move along His purposes on earth. Mountains are important places because of the events that took place there. Of course we cannot build a belief system on this observation. However, when we see one of God's chosen servant-leaders going to a mountain, we can anticipate that something significant may happen there.

What other mountaintop experiences do you recall from the biblical record? Do you agree or disagree that God uses the place of mountains to do some of His significant work? What role have mountain experiences played in your relationship with God?

_____

_____

Read Matthew 17:1. Underline the time marker in the verse and circle the names of those Jesus took with Him to the mountain.

"After six days" from Peter's confession of Jesus as the Christ, Jesus led three of His closest followers to a mountain. Luke tells us He took them there to pray (Luke 9:28). Jesus withdrew from the crowds who followed Him and took Peter, James, and John to a quiet place to talk to His Father in heaven. Jesus invited these three servant-leaders to an intimate place of prayer. His purpose was to equip them for their future roles of leadership they would hold in the Kingdom once He ascended to heaven. Prayer was a leadership habit He desired for them to develop. Like Moses, who took 73 men with him to a mountain to worship (Ex. 24:1), Jesus took three with Him to pray.

We learn two leadership lessons from Jesus by this description of His movements. First, Jesus separated Himself from the masses to commune with the One who had sent Him. He chose a mountain, away from the distractions of town, to do this. Servant-leaders on mission with God must intentionally find places away from the drone of everyday life to listen to the One who called them on mission. Second, Jesus handpicked three from the Twelve to experience His most private moments with God. Jesus chose twelve but spent more time with these three to ensure they knew Him and His mission fully. Letting them observe His prayer time was one way to equip them.

Describe a special time you spent with God away from the busyness of life. What happened and what did you sense was God's purpose for leading you there? In the quietness of this moment, observe the ways in which God has revealed Himself and His purposes to His chosen leaders.

_____

_____

_____

_____

20.2 Morphing on the Mountaintop

At the writing of this chapter, my oldest daughter is pregnant with our first grandchild. I cannot wait to be part of this child's growth. I have not met one grandparent who has said anything negative about being one. Someone said you have fun all day and get to give them back before you go home. Now that I like. While we wait for the child to be born, she is growing inside her mother's womb. She is morphing from a zygote into an infant during the nine or so months of gestation.

Paul used the word *morph* ("formed" in the NIV translation) in Galatians 4:19 to describe Christ forming in the Christ-followers whom he had helped trust Him. He used another form of the word when he wrote to the Christians in Rome that God's plan was for them "to be conformed to the likeness of his Son" (Rom. 8:29). In the first verses of chapter 12 of his Roman letter, he told his friends to experience metamorphosis by the renewing of their minds (Rom. 12:2). Change, or morphing, is part of a Christ-follower's experience with Jesus. It also describes what happened in an instant to Jesus on the mountain with Peter, James, and John.

Read Matthew 17:2–3. Underline the word "transfigured" in verse 2, and circle the names of those who appeared with Jesus in verse 3.

Matthew wasted no words in his description of what happened on the mountain. "There he was transfigured" (v. 2). The word behind our English word *transfigured* is translated from the Greek word from which we get *metamorphosis*. In front of His three closest friends, Jesus instantly changed—like a caterpillar into a butterfly—but His change involved more than natural changes. Matthew wrote Jesus transfigured and "his face shone like the sun, and his clothes became as white as the light [of the sun]." Mark described Jesus' clothes as "whiter than anyone in the world could bleach them" (Mark 9:3). Since Jesus was the "light of the world," it would follow that in full disclosure of who He is He would shine beyond what words can describe (John 8:12). Moses reflected the glory of God on the mountain. Jesus was the glory of God.

Matthew then tells us that both Moses and Elijah appeared in front of them "talking with Jesus" (v. 3). What were they talking about? Luke tells they "spoke about his departure," or death and Resurrection that would come (Luke 9:31). Why Moses and Elijah? Remember when Jesus spoke of John the Baptist? He said that up until John, "the Prophets and the Law prophesied," or told about the coming messiah (Matt. 11:13). Moses was the Law giver, and Elijah represented the prophets. Moses established the Law as the basis of the Old Agreement; Elijah did not die (2 Kings 2:11). Jesus fulfilled the requirements of the Law, and He fulfilled the prophecies about the messiah. The culmination of God's work in His-story stood together on the mountaintop as Jesus' followers watched it all.

Write in your own words the significance of the meeting of Moses, Elijah, and Jesus on the mountain where Jesus was transfigured. How does this episode in Jesus' life help you trust that He is the *Christos*?

_____

_____

_____

_____

Christos—God's Transforming Touch

20.3 Stunning the Three Disciples

Jesus' metamorphosis from what He looked normally like into the shining Person of glory stunned Peter, James, and John. Like someone who had just seen the most spectacular display of power or beauty, they were speechless—except for Peter. He always had something to say or was the first to respond to a situation. Leaders are like that. While the two others stood staring at Moses, Elijah, and the altered state of Jesus, Peter blurted out an idea to memorialize the moment.

Read Matthew 17:4. Underline what Peter wanted to build for Jesus, Moses, and Elijah.

Peter offered to build three "shelters" ("tabernacles" in the NASB) for Jesus and His guests. The word for "shelters" in this verse is the same word used to describe Jesus' incarnation in John 1:14: "made his dwelling among us." The connection there was with the Tent of Meeting in which God met with Moses while in the wilderness (Ex. 27). Jesus was the physical presence of God among us just like the Tabernacle housed the presence of God in the wilderness.

Shelter has another connection with the Old Agreement of God. God instructed the people of Israel to observe a Feast of Tabernacles (Lev. 23:33–43). Soon after the Day of Atonement, they were to "live in booths [or shelters] for seven days" in order to remind the people they lived in portable shelters after they came out of Egypt. This took place in the "seventh month," which would fall in our September/October time frame. Some commentators believe Peter offered to build the shelters for the three to commemorate the feast that was close in time to the event. Others suggest that Peter wanted to build shelters like that of the Tent of Meeting to memorialize the event.

Read Mark 9:6. Underline Mark's explanation of Peter's suggestion.

Mark added, "He did not know what to say, they were so frightened." The translators put Mark's commentary in parentheses to show it was the writer's remarks and not part of the event. Luke, the other Gospel writer who recorded this event, said Peter simply "did not know what he was saying" (Luke 9:33). Fear and uncertainty caused Peter to blurt out the suggestion to build shelters for the three.

Jesus did not respond to Peter's suggestion. Something else would happen to break into their dialogue (v. 5).

Put yourself in Peter's place. Write some of your feelings about seeing such an event. Also, based on the connection of "shelter" with the Old Agreement of God and Mark and Luke's comments, what do you believe Peter was thinking as he offered to build the shelters? Given the moment, was it a good idea?

_____

_____

_____

20.4 God's Presence in the Cloud

I was on a backpacking trek with friends once in the Pecos Wilderness, New Mexico, when we found ourselves walking above the clouds that had settled in a valley below the trail. We could see the tops of the clouds. It looked like we were in a plane above them, but our feet were on the ground. As the morning progressed, the clouds rose and others gathered with them to form a milky soup of moisture that we walked in the rest of the day. Plants and trees dripped with wetness, and our visibility became limited to about five feet in front of us. The staccato sounds of drops falling on leaves struck between our measured steps along the mountain trail. I much preferred walking above the clouds than in them. Still, there was something mysterious and unique about trudging through the mist that limited our perspective to the person and patches of forest right in front of us.

Have you ever walked above or in a cloud like we did? What memories do you have from that experience?

_____

_____

Read Matthew 17:5. Circle the words "cloud" and "voice" and underline the message from the cloud.

As if seeing a transfigured Jesus standing with Moses and Elijah was not enough, a "bright cloud enveloped them." The brightness was like the shining clothes and face of Jesus that shone as the glory of God. Remember, the presence of God was in a cloud that led Moses and Israel out of Egypt (Ex. 13:21–22). Moses would have remembered his trip into the cloud of God's presence to receive the Law of the Old Agreement (Ex. 24:16–18). The cloud of God's presence on the mountain in His-story "overshadowed" (NLT) Jesus and the others.

All three storytellers of this event, Matthew, Mark, and Luke, record that a voice came from the shining cloud. Matthew wrote that the voice said, "This is my Son, whom I love; with him I am well pleased. Listen to him!" The voice of God from the cloud of His presence affirmed His love and pleasure in His Son. God's voice also told the three apprentices of the King to "listen" to Him. This was a similar message from the voice that came from heaven at Jesus' baptism. (See Matthew 3:17 and compare that message to the one in chapter 17.)

The presence of God continued to unfold on the mountain in front of Peter, James, and John. How do the connections with the Old Agreement, Jesus' baptism, and the event itself strengthen your trust that Jesus is the *Christos*? Write your expanding confession here:

_____

_____

_____

_____

Christos—God's Transforming Touch

20.5 Showing Honor to God

We stand as we worship in song on Sunday mornings at my church. We teach that when we are in the presence of God we stand out of respect and honor. So as we sing praises to who He is and what He has done, we stand. Sometimes we all are seated by the worship leader for an announcement or interpretation of the day's theme. When we begin another song, no one is asked to stand; but as the song progresses, someone will stand up, then another, and then others. People stand as the words they sing encourage them to stand in honor and worship of God. Sometimes everyone ends up standing. Other times those standing are scattered throughout the crowd of worshipers like trees in a field of grass.

Do people stand while you worship with music at your church? Is it spontaneous, or do people stand only when directed? What are your beliefs/feelings about this practice of worship? Write some of your thoughts here:

_____

_____

Read Matthew 17:6–9. Underline what the disciples did when they heard the voice in the cloud and what Jesus said and did as a response. Also, underline what Jesus told them as they came down the mountain.

The disciples fell on their faces out of fear of God's presence (v. 6). What would you do after seeing and hearing what they saw and heard? Face to the earth is another posture of worship, and the disciples hid their faces as God's voice came from the shining cloud. Like other times, Jesus touched them and told them not to be afraid (v. 7). When they heard His voice and felt His touch, they looked up. The cloud, Moses, and Elijah had gone and only Jesus in His pretransfigured clothes remained (v. 8).

No storyteller writes that anything else was said after Jesus told His disciples not to be afraid. Sometimes worship cannot be told in words. As they came down the mountain, Jesus told the three not to "tell anyone what you have seen, until the Son of Man has been raised from the dead." Why would Jesus do this? Jesus refused the temptation of people trusting Him because of spectacular displays in the wilderness (Matt. 4:5–7). The demonstration of God's favor and His conversation with Moses and Elijah were for Him, not the masses. After Jesus had demonstrated who He is in His Resurrection from the dead, then the three could tell of this event of affirmation that Jesus was the "Son of Man," the Promised One.

You have observed an episode in His-story that affirms Jesus is the *Christos*. It followed Peter's confession and set the stage for Jesus' final trips to Jerusalem that would result in His death, burial, and Resurrection. If you were Jesus what would be the significance of such an event as you sought to carry out the mission call of the Father on your life? How does this event in Jesus' story help your trust in Him as it helped Peter, James, and John?

_____

_____

For further study:
*   **Mark 9:2–13**
*   **Luke 9:28–36**

21—Accepting God's Will: Jesus Predicts His Death

Every leader states his intentions to those he leads. Great leaders do this consistently and choose strategic moments to present their intended objectives. Jesus had accepted His mission to be the Suffering -Servant Messiah when He stepped up for John to baptize Him. From that time on, He lived out that mission; He recruited, trained, and sent others to share that mission along with Him. However, there was one thing only He could do. Only Jesus could be the final "once-for-all" sacrifice for the sins of all people. He knew that His death that rescues all people was His calling alone. So as He led others to be servant-leaders in the Kingdom He came to establish, He explained to them why He must ultimately go to Jerusalem and experience death as the Father had called Him to do.

After Jesus was changed on the mountain before Peter, James, and John, He returned to public ministry to demonstrate who He was and what His Kingdom looked like. As He went about leading and serving others, He stopped to tell His closest followers His intentions to go to Jerusalem where He would face death but would be raised in three days. This chapter is about some of those times Jesus shared His intentions with those He led.

The Memory Verse for this chapter is 1 John 2:2. This verse explains Jesus' reason for dying. In one sentence John summed up Jesus' work on the cross for all people. To know this verse is to know why Jesus died.

Our question to consider for this chapter is "Did Jesus want to die?" Did He accept death on the cross as His mission? Those are two different questions we will talk about later.

Christos—God's Transforming Touch

21.1 Understanding Jesus' Mission

Servant-leaders have a mission, a plan, an agenda. That is why they lead. They have made themselves a servant to that mission. They are compelled to lead others to do what they sense must be done or that which can help the most people. Martin Luther King Jr. announced his intentions when he said, "I have a dream." New York City knew what their leaders would do after the attacks of 9–11 when Mayor Rudy Giuliani promised them they would rebuild the city. Parents are servant-leaders when they lead by telling their children their plans to send them to college or to show them support as they become independent.

Who is a good leader who constantly tells you where he or she is leading you? How does that make you feel about the future? If you are a leader, what are some intentions you have made clear to those whom you lead? What were their reactions?

_____

_____

Read Matthew 16:21–23. Underline Jesus' message to His disciples (v. 21) and Peter's response to Him (v. 22). Underline Jesus' response to Peter (v. 23). Also read Luke 9:22.

After Peter's confession that Jesus was the *Christos*, Jesus took the opportunity not only to affirm His disciple's declaration but also to explain again what being the *Christos* meant. He was the Suffering-Servant Messiah who would die to take away the sins of the world. Every follower has an idea of how the leader should lead and who that leader should be. Peter was no exception.

So when he heard Jesus explain that Him being the Messiah meant going to Jerusalem to die, Peter was shocked. He basically said, "Over my dead body!" (v. 22) He missed the part about Jesus being raised in three days. He could not allow the One he just declared to be the messiah to suffer and die like a common criminal.

Jesus responded to Peter's heroic promise by saying, "Get behind me, Satan!" (v. 23) How was Peter like Satan? In the wilderness, Jesus had refused any shortcut to the Kingdom that was empty of suffering. For Peter to remove suffering from Jesus' mission was to miss the point of why He came as the *Christos*. Peter got the answer right as to Jesus' title, but he missed the point of Jesus' mission. Jesus corrected His anxious follower and again explained why He had come.

What images do you have for Jesus as Leader and Rescuer of all people? Where have your preconceptions of who He is differed from who He says He is? How are your feelings like those of Peter and how are they different? Write your thoughts here:

_____

_____

_____

21.2 Hearing Good News and Bad News

My older sister has had breast cancer. I remember the day she told us and that the prognosis was good. But the process of surgery and chemotherapy would not be so good. The good news of healing was buried under the reality of cancer. An added fear was that she had walked through fighting off melanoma cancer some 10 years earlier. It seemed she just could not get away from it. She called the other day to tell me she got her five-year, all-clear report from the doctor. We celebrated on the phone together. The good news had come to pass, and the bad news of cancer was no longer the topic of our discussion.

What news have you heard from a friend or loved one that was good news mixed with the bad? Which one struck you the hardest? What was the outcome of the news? Did things happen as you had hoped or as feared?

_____

_____

Read Matthew 17:22-23. Underline the setting. Underline three things Jesus told the disciples would happen to Him. Also read Luke 9:44–45.

Jesus and His closest followers had just experienced His metamorphosis on the mountain where He met Moses and Elijah (Matt. 17:1–9). When they came down from that miraculous experience, they immediately encountered a man with a demon-possessed son whom Jesus healed (vv. 14–18). When the disciples gathered back together in Galilee, Jesus felt it necessary to explain again what was going to happen as a result of His being the Suffering-Servant *Christos*.

Jesus honestly portrayed to them what would happen as He completed His mission as the "Son of Man," God's Sent One. Jesus laid out the bad news with the good news. He said He would "be betrayed into the hands of men," and that they would kill Him. However, Jesus told them that "on the third day he will be raised to life" (v. 23). Like Peter who missed Jesus' promise of His Resurrection, so the disciples heard only that Jesus would be betrayed and killed. How do we know this? Matthew tells us "the disciples were filled with grief." If they had heard the whole message, their response would have been different.

You and I live on the other side of the cross and empty grave. We know the whole story; yet we are like the disciples. We tend to pick and choose what we hear Jesus say to us. However, we hear differently than the disciples. We tend to ignore the part of Jesus' message that He must suffer and die, and we embrace the promise of the Resurrection. Both aspects of Jesus' life are significant. The disciples grieved over Jesus' coming death and missed the hope of His Resurrection. We often revel in the promise of Resurrection. However, we forget that we, too, must suffer as part of our apprenticeship with Jesus.

Christos—God's Transforming Touch

Which of the two parts of Jesus' message do you embrace most? The cross or the Resurrection? Why? Ask God to call you to hear Jesus' complete message and to understand how significant both parts are to who He is.

21.3 Turning Back

At a week-long speaking engagement in the Rocky Mountains, I led a group of hikers up a mountain trail so we could say we had made the 11-mile round trip and seen the view from the peak. Ultimately, I was not a good leader that day (and night), but along the way I did stop the group and tell them about the next section of terrain. I then said that anyone who did not feel they could go on should turn around and return to the conference center. I had climbed the trail many times and knew it became steeper and more rugged the closer we got to the peak. Stopping and explaining what the next section was like helped the hikers know what to expect and to evaluate whether they wanted to continue. No one ever turned back. Some should have. But that is another story.

Have you ever been in a situation in which the leader told you what was coming and you had a choice to continue or quit? Describe the situation and your decision here:

_____

_____

_____

Read Matthew 20:17–19. Underline the details of Jesus' prediction about His death that are different from the others He has made so far.

In this episode of Jesus' life, He was leading His band of apprentices to Jerusalem. At this time in His-story, opposition to Him had grown in proportion to His popularity. The "chief priests" and "teachers of the law" had confronted Him and even had begun to plot His demise (Matt. 12:14). Jerusalem was the center of religious life for the Jewish people, and the most powerful and influential leaders were there. For Jesus intentionally to go there was to jeopardize not only His ministry but also His life.

As He made the trip to religious headquarters and His harshest enemies, He pulled together His Twelve chosen future leaders and explained to them again what He foresaw would happen when they got there (Matt. 20:17). Jesus was not warning His followers as much as He was spelling out the completion of His mission. This time Jesus explained that the religious leaders would condemn Him to death and then hand Him over to the "Gentiles," or Roman leaders, to execute Him (v. 18–19). Jesus included one more time the fact that on the third day He would be raised to life!

Jesus did not give His closest followers an "out" to return home because of His message about the future. He did that with others who followed Him (Luke 9:57–62), but He expected the Twelve to follow Him to the end—and the new beginning. Matthew does not tell us the response of the disciples this time. Maybe their grief (Matt. 17:23) had turned to wonder. Maybe they had begun to trust Him that this was to be the way things would happen.

What have you heard several times from Jesus through the biblical record that you have begun to accept as

God's will for your life? What things did Jesus teach that you still struggle with to make part of your behavior? Prayerfully write those things here:

_____

_____

21.4 Completing the Mission

Leaders make decisions. Servant-leaders make decisions related to completing the mission with which God has entrusted them. When leaders make decisions, those who work for them or who have volunteered to serve with them react to their actions. Some followers cheer bold decisions. Others grumble. Still, others become fearful. Any decision made by a leader can disrupt the status quo of those he or she leads, and people will respond differently to that disruption.

If you are a leader, how have some of those whom you lead responded to some of your bolder decisions? If you work or volunteer for a leader, what has he or she done that caused you to question his or her decision? Write your experiences here:

_____

_____

Read Mark 10:32–35. Circle the words that described the people's and disciples' responses to Jesus announcing He was headed to Jerusalem. Underline the names of the two disciples who approached Jesus after He told them of His death.

Jesus led His group of followers to Jerusalem. He had been there previously, but the atmosphere was tenser and the possibility of resistance from the religious leaders was greater than ever before. Mark wrote that Jesus' disciples were "astonished" at His decision to lead them to Jerusalem. They must have wondered why He would risk His life like that. Why did He not withdraw like He had done before when the tensions seemed strong? Luke wrote that the disciples did not understand what Jesus had told them because "its meaning was hidden from them" (Luke 18:34).

Mark also noted that "those who followed were afraid." What did they fear? This was a large group of followers who may have chosen to follow Jesus either because He had healed or fed them, or they knew someone who had experienced one of His miracles. To lose Jesus in Jerusalem jeopardized their source of hope. They also may have simply feared for Jesus' life and did not want Him to put His life in danger.

Jesus sensed what those who followed Him felt. Once again He pulled His closest followers apart from the larger group, explained His mission, and told them why it took Him to Jerusalem. He had come to be the Suffering-Servant Christ. This meant He must suffer and die at the hands of those He came to rescue. Verses 33–34 contain the description of what would happen in Jerusalem. Verse 35 tells us James and John, who had been with Jesus and Peter on the mountain of Jesus' transfiguration, approached Jesus with a request. They had totally missed the meaning of Jesus' mission and were ready to cash in on what they believed to be beneficial to them.

Which of the people in the story do you associate with? Are you "astonished" at some of the decisions Jesus makes as He leads you, or are you more often "afraid" by the things He leads you to do? How did His decision to lead them to Jerusalem challenge their trust in Him? Take time to thank God for Jesus' resolve to complete His mission as the Messiah even though His closest followers did not support Him.

21.5 Our Atoning Sacrifice

Jesus' death on the cross was not an imposter's failed attempt to become a hero. From the perspective of those who followed Him, Jesus' choice to go to Jerusalem to face death must have seemed confusing. Later, we will stand at the foot of the cross and wonder with the disciples what went wrong. Yet if we trust Jesus, then we will trust His Word. Since He stated His intention three different times to go to Jerusalem and predicted His betrayal three different times, we should accept in trust that this was the way things were supposed to happen. Jesus never waived in His understanding that His mission was to face the cross and the Resurrection. Too often, we prefer Jesus to act the way we want Him to rather than the way He chooses to act as our Leader.

Read 1 John 2:2, the Memory Verse for this chapter. Underline what the verse says Jesus is and underline the recipients of His sacrifice.

Jesus knew why He had to die, and He tried to explain it to His disciples. Like us, they were dense in the matters of God. Not until after the events that Jesus predicted happened were the disciples able to understand His words. When John was inspired by the Holy Spirit to explain who Jesus was, he wrote, "He is the atoning sacrifice" (1 John 2:2). That trip to Jerusalem and death on the cross resulted in Jesus dying as the "atoning sacrifice" required by God to satisfy His requirements of righteousness. His death paid the debt we owed God for our sins—"not only for ours but also for the sins of the whole world." Jesus became the final sacrifice so that people could be at one with God. To trust Jesus is to accept that His death, burial, and Resurrection were God's way of making us right with Him.

Our question to consider for this chapter is "Did Jesus want to die?" Jesus intentionally walked into His death when He led His followers to Jerusalem. It may have looked like He had a death wish and wanted this to happen. There is a difference, however, between a megalomaniac and a servant-leader on mission. Jesus no more wanted to suffer and die by crucifixion than you or I would. Jesus accepted the will of His Father in heaven as His own because He trusted Him. Jesus chose to lay down His life for those He loved because that was His mission as the *Christos*.

You have observed Jesus' intentional choice to go to Jerusalem. You have read His prophecy that told His followers exactly what would happen, and you have seen their responses. End this chapter by telling God the ways in which you accept (trust) His will for Jesus' life and then by confessing whether you trust His will for your life—even if it means suffering so others may be rescued eternally. Be honest with God. Seek ways to live out your trust in Him as your "atoning sacrifice."

For further study:
- **Luke 9:21-27, 43-45**

22—Responding to God's Word: The Parable of the Sower

"Once upon a time . . ." "In a galaxy far, far away . . ." "The Kingdom of Heaven is like . . ." These are the lines to stories that make us want to know what happens next. They catch us in the middle of our own stories and draw us to another time and place to walk with someone else for a while. We want to let the person lead us to places we have never dreamed of and teach us lessons we could only learn by joining him or her on the journey. Stories tell the meaning of life and connect us together. They lead us on adventures to face danger and challenges we never would face on our own. And the one story is His-story—the story of Jesus, the story of our rescue and hope for eternity.

Jesus told stories. The biblical storytellers call some of them parables, which literally means "to cast alongside of." Jesus laid these stories alongside life to explain some Kingdom aspect. These stories help His followers know what life is like with Him as their Rescuer and Leader. The parables are Jesus' way of revealing secrets of His Kingdom that lessons with bullet points and Power-Point slides just cannot tell. The Parable of the Sower, the title of this Kingdom story, tells how people's hearts are like different types of soil that are ready or not ready to receive the good news of who Jesus is.

The Memory Verse for this chapter is Proverbs 4:23. This saying supports Jesus' story. We must guard our hearts because they are the "wellspring of life" where the seed of God's Word settles and grows. Learn this truth as a way of life and a warning of what will happen if you neglect it.

Our question to consider for this chapter is "How can a person know the condition of his or her heart?" Chew on this as you walk through the Parable of the Sower.

Christos—God's Transforming Touch

22.1 Using Parables

The *Gift of the Magi* by O. Henry is one of my favorite short stories. Its simple story line and the sacrifices of the most cherished gifts for a loved one move my heart. I also like the more obscure short stories such as *The Princess and Curdie* by George MacDonald and not-so-obscure ones like *The Chronicles of Narnia*. Each of these provides insight into human nature and the ways of God through children and characters of the imagination. I prefer these stories to commentaries, but I traffic more in the verse-by-verse explanation of words and principles than I do stories. Adulthood and responsibilities take away the adventure of story and replace them with scholarship and information. That is one reason I love returning to Jesus' parables.

What are some of your favorite short stories? What is your favorite kind of reading? Or do you spend more time watching DVDs, movies, or television? If so, what stories do you like in them? Write your answers here:

_____

_____

Read Mark 4:1–2. Circle the ways in which Jesus taught the people that gathered to hear Him.

A part of His-story is that Jesus told stories while teaching. Jesus taught many ways. One way He taught was by extended lessons as in the Sermon on the Mount (Matt. 5–7). Another way was by demonstration, as when He calmed the storm (Matt. 8:23–27). Jesus taught so people would trust Him and, like a loving parent who uses many methods to train up a child, Jesus used teaching methods common to His day.

Jesus became a popular teacher among the people. Crowds followed Him as He taught about the Kingdom He came to establish. In these verses, Mark tells us that Jesus taught using parables. Jesus used these short stories taken from everyday settings to teach some aspect of the Kingdom of God. They were simple, easy to remember, and usually had a single lesson that those who heard them could take away and discuss long into the night.

Why do you think Jesus spoke in stories? Why did He speak in parables from everyday life rather than using more imaginative stories? You may want to take some extra time to read the parables recorded in Matthew 13 and Luke 15 for representative parables of Jesus.

22.2 Differing Soils

In America and other developed countries, we farm with machinery that covers acres of land in a day. Whether it involves planting, weeding, or harvesting, mass production with massive farm equipment produces what is needed to feed millions. Those of us who live in cities and towns have less and less to do with the growing and preparing of our food. That is why we have grocery stores and fast-food restaurants. While some people decide to grow their own vegetables or fruit, a plot of land overseen by an individual to feed a family or two is not so much a part of the American landscape any more. So to try and understand anything about farming in an ancient, agrarian society will be a leap for us all.

Do you grow anything to eat for you or your family? If so, have you ever shared your harvest with others? If you do not grow your own food, would you like to try?

Read Mark 4:3–8. Read the story at least twice, and then write in the space below what you believe to be the main point. When you have finished, go back and circle the four surfaces the seed fell upon and underline what happened when the seed fell on each.

_____

_____

_____

Jesus told the crowd, "Listen!" (v. 3) The crowd had become noisy, and Jesus wanted them to hear what He was about to say. The details of Jesus' story came from the everyday life of His hearers. They all had prepared a small plot of earth, bought seed, thrown it onto the tilled ground, and worked and prayed for the seed to take root and grow something they could eat or sell in the market. There was no genius to the content of the story. There were no secrets hidden between the lines Jesus spoke. The meaning of the story was simple and straightforward so that anyone standing on the side of the lake that day could understand it.

Check the heading before this story in your translation of the Bible. Most translations call this the Parable of the Sower. After reading it a couple of times and paying attention to the details, what would you say the story is more about: the farmer or the surfaces the seed fell upon? There is no right answer. This is an exercise in letting the passage offer its meaning rather than you simply accepting the translation editors' decisions. What is the focal point of the passage? The farmer casting seed or the ground it fell on or the results after it fell? Did Jesus tell the story to illustrate how He as a farmer spread the seed of the Kingdom? Or did He tell it to help the people see how their hearts were like

the different surfaces? Or was it a promise that the Kingdom He brought would have varied results when He introduced it and that some of those results would multiply "thirty, sixty, or even a hundred times"?

Ask God to put you in the crowd who heard Jesus' story and to show you its meaning for you.

22.3 Teaching the Mysteries of the Kingdom

I teach as an adjunct professor at a theological institution. A couple of times a year the school offers a conference with a noted scholar to talk on a topic beneficial to theological education. One year I went with the student minister on our staff to hear a well-known British philosophy of religion professor talk on the existence of God in a postmodern world. He was typically British in his dress and accent, but his reasoning and language were foreign to my biblical studies mind. After his first presentation to the group, I turned to the student minister and asked, "What did he say?" We both laughed and were thankful for the question and answer time that followed. I had not spent much time in the world of philosophy, but I learned much that day. I felt thankful that minds like this professor's were on the front line of thought to explain God's existence to an unbelieving world.

Whom have you heard speak before but did not get his or her message the first time? Did you have an opportunity to talk to the speaker in a different setting and ask questions in order to understand more fully?

_____

_____

Christos—God's Transforming Touch

Read Mark 4:9–12. Underline Jesus' final words of the story in verse 9. Circle the word "parable" where it appears in the verses. Write in your own words why Jesus said He spoke in parables. Note the prophet He quoted in verse 12.

_____

_____

_____

_____

Jesus ended this story with His familiar phrase: "He who has ears to hear, let him hear" (v. 9 and later in verse 23). It meant something like, "If you were listening, I just said something important. Pay attention." He wanted His hearers to grasp the importance of what He had just told them.

When the disciples got alone with their teacher, they asked about the important of the story (v. 10). Jesus told them that He had given them "the secret of the kingdom of God" (v. 11). He meant He had taught them lessons like the Sermon on the Mount, and had demonstrated the power of His presence through healing others and performing miracles. These stories revealed more secrets to what He was doing on earth. But for those who were simply curious or listened to trap or distract Him, the stories would be "parables," stories that seemed to have no meaning to their lives. Jesus said this lack of understanding fulfilled Isaiah's prophecy. Some people would see but not understand, or hear but not comprehend. Otherwise they would "turn and be forgiven" (v. 12).

Responding to God's Word means having an open and willing heart to first accept who Jesus is and then desire to learn from Him to be like Him. While Jesus' words seem to eliminate some people from knowing Him, He actually provided deeper insights into His Kingdom to those who trusted Him and wanted to learn from Him. In which of the groups of listeners do you belong?

22.4 Examining the Heart

As a teacher and a pastor, I have found that most learning happens after the presentation rather than during it. I look forward to talking with students after class who desire to know more about what I just taught. Their interest and energy enthuses me to continue my ministry of teaching and preaching for those who want to know about the things of God. Of course there are always those who want to argue or make their point about a passage or lesson, but that is part of the process of learning, too. Any good teacher allows it—up to a certain point.

Describe a time you learned more about something after a speaker's presentation when you had time to process with him or her. What made that time meaningful and the topic clearer for you?

_____

_____

_____

_____

Read Mark 4:13–20. Create two columns on a separate sheet of paper. Write the different kinds of ground in the original parable in one column (for example, the path, rocky places, and thorns). Then write out Jesus' explanation for each kind of ground in these verses.

Jesus' teaching is more like an English literature teacher explaining Homer's *Iliad* than a storyteller at a public library. But for students these times are necessary to know the full meaning of a lesson. Jesus took the time to explain to His apprentices the details of the story He had just told the crowd.

Although verse 13 may sound like a negative statement, Jesus was simply saying that this was an easy parable to understand. If they had trouble understanding this one, just wait until He told them more. Therefore, He launched into Parables 101 and explained how each part of the story represented an aspect of how people accepted Him and His message about the Kingdom of God. The farmer, Jesus, sowed the seed of the message or Word. That message fell on different hearts of people—some hard, and some fertile to receive it. The seed of the message can only grow in proportion to the readiness of the soil, or heart. Jesus knew that not everyone would accept His Word. However, like a grateful farmer who harvested the seed that grew 30, 60, or 100 times its number, Jesus embraced those who trusted and followed Him. Like the farmer, Jesus went about His work of telling others and trusting God to prepare the hearts of those who heard Him.

This parable is also easy to apply to our own heart condition. Go back to your list of the kinds of soils and what happened to the seed that fell in each type. Which one is most like you in your acceptance of Jesus' message of who He is and what He wants you to do with your life? Ask God to help you be like the disciples and ask Jesus about the parts you do not understand or about which you want to know more.

22.5 Casting Seed into Hearts

Jesus' parable of the farmer casting seed on different soils is my model for preaching. My job as a preacher/teacher is to cast God's Word faithfully into the hearts of people. Like the farmer, I trust God as to where the seed falls and whether each person will accept it. My job is to teach people the message of Jesus. His job is to prepare their hearts to receive it. This takes pressure off me to produce the harvest. As with seed that finds good soil and produces a harvest without the farmer, so anyone who preaches or teaches in the Kingdom leaves the ultimate work of growth up to God. Grades in a grade book or the number of responses at an invitation do not tell the condition of a person's heart before God. Every faithful sower of God's Word must trust the "Lord of the harvest" for the results of his or her labor.

Do you teach a Sunday school class or another group of people? How do you know when one of your students "gets it"? Which teacher, preacher, or writer has taught you the most about the things of God? What makes it so easy to learn from that person? How can you teach or write like him or her? Write your thoughts here:

_____

_____

_____

_____

Our question to consider for this chapter is "How can a person know the condition of his or her heart?" Another question to consider is "How can a farmer know the condition of his field?" After reading Jesus' story and explanation of the parable, how would you answer these questions? Write your answers here:

_____

_____

_____

_____

_____

Jesus told this parable not so people would have a lesson in farming, but so they would become aware of their spiritual condition. This lesson is important for Jesus' disciples so they will not get discouraged when they see people refusing the message of the Kingdom. Or when they see people start following Jesus enthusiastically but quit due to hard times or things of the world seducing them away from Christ. There will be those who, like the disciples, have fertile hearts. These people will enter the Kingdom, live for the King, and produce fruit for their entire lives.

The story has also been preserved so people who read or hear it will stop and examine their own hearts about their receptiveness to Jesus' message. While some may hear it as a meaningless story by a simple man, others will see themselves in the story and "turn and be forgiven" (v. 12).

This story of the different soils also reminds us to "guard" our hearts for they are "the wellspring of life" (Prov. 4:23). Like a farmer who tills and weeds the ground so seed can grow into a crop, we must guard our hearts so they will stay fertile for the things of God.

Given Jesus' description of the soils in His parable, in what ways can you guard your heart? Write your thoughts here:

_____

_____

_____

Once again, ask God to apply the message of this parable to your life with Him today. The story and its application are timeless, and Jesus' Spirit can reveal to you what is true for you today in your relationship with Him. Listen prayerfully so you may hear Jesus' message for you.

For further study:
- **Matthew 13:1–23**
- **Luke 8:1–15**
- **Luke 15**

23—Searching for Significance: Greatest in the Kingdom

We live in a culture that equates greatness to bigness. We hold those who have large companies, churches, or ministries as great. We are taught early on that those with higher grades and more accomplishments are greater than those with less. Those with more votes or market share are greater than those with lesser shares. Yes, great means big and notable. But does that same meaning translate into the Kingdom of Heaven Jesus introduced when He came? How does the definition of greatness in our world translate into Jesus' world? Or can it? On the other hand, did Jesus talk about being great at all? If so, how does His description fit into the world in which we find ourselves?

One day while Jesus was walking with His disciples, He overheard them talking about who was the greatest among them. Peter, James, and John had just come down from the mountain where Jesus had been joined by Moses and Elijah, and His appearance had changed before their very eyes. Maybe they were the greatest? Or maybe those who could not heal the man's demon-possessed boy surely would never be called great among the Twelve due to their ineptness in spiritual matters? This conversation led Jesus to describe what it means to be great in His Kingdom, and His answer may surprise and confuse you. But then again, most things where Jesus is King are different from the kingdom of this world in which we live.

The Memory Verse for this chapter is Mark 9:35. Jesus reversed the categories of greatness when He spoke.

Our question to consider for this chapter is "Is it wrong to want to be recognized?" Is there such a thing as godly ambition? Observe Jesus' lesson to His disciples as they struggled with this concept.

23.1 Ranking Among the Disciples

In the world of running, everyone knows exactly where they rank compared to the rest of the field. Chip timing and finishing times posted on the Internet by age group and overall finishers leave no doubt where one ranks in a particular race. I like knowing where I finish when I run. I usually fall in the middle of my age group and just under twice the time it takes the winner to finish a marathon. At age 54, I am OK with that; but I always want to improve. Get me in a group of runners, and we will almost always discuss the number of races we have run and the usual finishing time of our runs. Before long we all know who has the fastest times and who is ranked first among us. We then move on to the next topic, but the pecking order is set for the rest of the conversation.

What do you do in which you know your ranking order? Maybe it is measured by title, salary, production, grades, or number of international trips. Write what you would rank first in among a group of peers. How does this rank connect to your identity and confidence?

_____

_____

_____

_____

Read Mark 9:33–34. Underline the location of the conversation and Jesus' question to the group in verse 33. Circle the last word in verse 34, which was the topic of the disciples' discussion.

Jesus made His way to His adopted hometown of Capernaum after His transfiguration experience on the mountain. Along the way, He overheard His apprentices arguing about something. Rather than confronting them on the road, Jesus waited until He got into the house. When everyone was inside and settled, He basically asked, "So what were you guys arguing about out there?" (v. 33) The word translated "argue" can also be interpreted "dialogue" or "debate." Groups cannot go long without some dispute arising among them. But this argument particularly interested Jesus; He asked them point-blank about the topic of their debate.

Mark wrote that none of the disciples would tell Jesus what the discussion was about because "they had argued about who was the greatest" (v. 34). Like children embarrassed after getting caught talking about something they knew their parents disapproved of, Jesus' apprentices looked down at their dusty feet and hoped no one else would speak when He addressed them. They knew they had argued—raised their voices—about something Jesus may not approve of, but why?

Read Matthew 5:3 and 11:29. If you were Jesus' student and you heard His teaching, how would an argument about who is the greatest in the group be out of place? The disciples also may have felt embarrassed because they were talking about who would be the greatest in Jesus' Kingdom, while He had talked about suffering and being killed. They looked beyond His suffering to their new positions of greatness. How do you relate to the disciples? Have you ever had a similar discussion with others?

_____

_____

_____

_____

23.2 Being First in the Kingdom

Jesus introduced an upside-down Kingdom. If you start with how you and I value significance, Jesus' teachings seem not only odd but backward. He valued the poor and the outcast, and refused to hold any title or position. He shied away from public applause, and He had a bad reputation among the religious leaders of His day. His value system is so different from our natural and learned values that people today have trouble accepting His ways as valid—true, but not practical. Jesus' lesson to His students is one of those ideas that if accepted literally would turn our world upside down.

Read Mark 9:35. Circle the words "first," "last," and "servant." Write what you think these values would look like in your family or church if you took them at face value and tried to live this way.

_____

_____

_____

Jesus sat down and called the Twelve chosen students to listen. We may expect Him to scold the group for arguing about such an ego-centered topic like who was the greatest among them. Rather than scolding, Jesus redefined greatness for them. Kingdom leadership is different from earthly leadership.

The word for "first" is the word from which we get our prefix *proto*. It means "first in line or series." We can interpret it to mean great as the first one in rank or as the first one in line, or leader. We all understand that concept. What we do not understand are the words Jesus connected to being first. He said those who want

to be great in His group "must be the very last, and the servant of all." We get our theological word *eschaton*, meaning "the end time," from the word "last," and we get our word *deacon* from the word "servant." Those concepts were as foreign to being great to the Twelve as they are to us today. What did Jesus intend by this strange connection of ideas?

To lead or be great in the Kingdom where Jesus is King, we must be like the King and share His values. Follow Jesus to the cross, and you will find He was the servant-leader of the Kingdom movement. Yet when evaluated by the world's leaders and their values, He clearly was ranked "last" and as a "servant." But Jesus' significance did not come from His ranking in opinion polls or titles held. He came to "glorify" the One who sent Him (John 17:1). He found His significance and was evaluated as "great" by His audience of One.

Read also Mark 10:41–45 for another time Jesus pulled His disciples aside and taught them the values of Kingdom leadership.

Apply Jesus' teaching to your life today. Sit with His disciples and hear His teaching on greatness for the first time. Ask God to show you where you have adopted the world's value system and to help you live like Jesus.

23.3 Welcoming Little Children

I love watching the volunteers greet children in our church's child care area on Sunday mornings. Their eyes light up as they raise the tone of their voices and open their arms to receive each child. They are so happy to see the children and anticipate their learning time with the children each week. It is just as interesting to watch the children's response to the workers. Some fly into the waiting arms of a volunteer. Others cling to Mom or Dad and must be coaxed to let go and trust the one to whom they have led the child. Either way, the children are welcomed into the room of a caring, prepared volunteer who is ready to help these children trust Jesus.

Whom do you know who is great at greeting children? What seems to be the key to children trusting that person so freely while they may have suspicions of others? Write some of your thoughts here:

_____

_____

_____

_____

Read Mark 9:36–37. Circle the lesson object of Jesus' lesson in verse 36. Write in your own words what Jesus wanted His disciples to learn from Him in verse 37.

_____

_____

Jesus loved object lessons. Parables are verbal object lessons, but Jesus often used a person or something from life to make a point. After He sat down and challenged the disciple's on their argument about who was the greatest among them, He called a child to Himself and stood the child in front of the Twelve. The child must have felt intimidated by the all-adult audience staring at him. Then Jesus took the child in His arms and made His point.

Jesus said that "whoever welcomes one of these little children" in His name, welcomes not only Jesus but also "the one who sent" Him (v. 37). Jesus wanted people to welcome Him like they do children: with open arms and trust, just as they are. He did not want them to welcome Him like they would someone whom the group had decided was great or who had declared himself great among them. To welcome a child is to embrace, accept, and appreciate the child for who he or she is, not for his or her accomplishments or wealth. Jesus did not want earthly categories to create barriers among His people. He wanted them to freely accept one another for who they were and who He saw them to be. Jesus did not want them to judge the greatness of each person. Jesus also added that to welcome Him was to welcome His Father who sent Him.

Become one of the disciples as Jesus stood the child before you, embraced the child, and offered His lesson to you. How do you apply Jesus' simple object lesson to your relationship with Him today?

_____

_____

_____

_____

23.4 Being Like a Child

I recently found some notes I had kept from when my girls were children. My oldest wrote to me one day (I will spell the words correctly for you.), "A teddy bear is a good thing. I like them. They are fun. Why are they fun? They just are." Not genius, but simple and true from the mind of a seven-year-old. I also had recorded the thoughts of my youngest who was four at the time. She had coughed, and I had said, "Bless you." She responded, "That's not a bless you. That was a cough." She knew the difference between a cough and a sneeze, and she was not going to let Dad get by with mixing blessings. One thing about children is that they see the world simply and honestly tell you what is on their minds. Adults, sadly enough, learn to be more cunning in order to protect themselves or to gain advantage over others by putting people in their places.

What about children draws you to them? Or do find children more annoying the older you get? Do you have any examples from your own children that remind you of their simple reasoning and open hearts? Record some of your memories here:

_____

_____

_____

_____

_____

_____

Read Mark 10:13–16. Circle the main characters in this episode of His-story. Underline Jesus' primary teaching in this passage.

One day some children ran up to Jesus to touch Him, but the disciples pushed them back (v. 13). Surely, they thought, someone as important as the Messiah had no time for children. That was their mistake. Mark wrote that Jesus became angry with His students and ordered them to let the children come to Him. Why? Jesus said, "the kingdom of God belongs to such as these" (v. 14).

Jesus then made clear the truth of the moment to everyone listening: "Anyone who will not receive the kingdom of God like a little child will never enter it" (v. 15). He then took the children in His arms and blessed them by placing His hands on them (v. 16). What did Jesus mean when He said that unless we receive the Kingdom of God "like a little child" we will not enter in? What was Jesus referring to when He said to be "like a little child"?

_____

_____

_____

_____

_____

There are many possibilities to apply Jesus' words, but the simplest is that children wanted to be with Jesus. They wanted nothing from Him but His attention and embrace. They had yet to learn the art of negotiation to have things their way, like the rich young man Jesus encountered in the next episode in Mark's story of Jesus (Mark 10:17–22). Children trust without assurances. They find their significance in those they trust rather than what they think of themselves or what their friends tell them. Until we come to Jesus in that way, Jesus said we will never enter the Kingdom He brings to us.

Take some time to meditate on the trust and thoughts of a child. Apply those to Jesus' object lesson with the disciples. How can we become like children in our trust of Jesus as the *Christos?*

_____

_____

_____

23.5 Seeking Success or Significance

Someone once mused that we, as adults, spend our early years seeking success and our later years seeking significance. Somewhere along the way some of us figure out that someone will always be more successful than we are by world standards. We often figure out that what others say about us is not who we are or want to be. On the other hand, some people fight through life hoping to gain enough notice and wealth to be recognized as important or feel they are significant in some way. One of the mysteries of who Jesus, the Christ, was is His lack of desire in any way for human accolades. He found His significance in who He was as God, the Father's Only Son, who was sent on a rescue mission to give His life so others may live. His Kingdom was not of this world, and His ways were nothing like ours when it came to influencing others or living His life. Greatness was service; significance came from living out God's mission call on His life.

Do you agree or disagree with the opening observation in this lesson? If you agree, where are you between seeking success and significance? If you don't agree, how would you describe generally what adults seek in different stages of their lives? What is it about Jesus' attitude about these things that baffle or inspire you?

Our Table Talk Question is "Is it wrong to want to be recognized?" Given your review of Jesus' teachings in this passage, write some of your thoughts here.

_____

_____

_____

We all long to be recognized for who we are. That need starts when we are children and grows proportionally with the attention our parents, guardians, and peers give us—or don't give us. Wanting to be recognized is not the issue. We all have that need. How or in what ways we find that recognition is the rub. Jesus pointed to children as examples of those who "get" Him and His Kingdom. Children are content with being who those who love them tell them they are before someone tells them otherwise. As we grow up, we begin to find ways and categories that define us. It is in pursuit of those things that lead us away from who we are as Jesus sees us.

Jesus came to say, "Trust me. How I see you is significant enough. You don't need to pursue what others classify as success objects or push others down so you will stand out. My love and acceptance is enough. Trust Me. I made you and I know this about you."

Spend some time reading the message above. Prayerfully ask God to show you how He sees you and ask for help to trust Him like a child trusts a loving parent.

For further study:
Matthew 18:1-4
Luke 9:46-50
Luke 22:24-30

24—Deciding to Forgive: The Parable of the Unmerciful Servant

The story of God is about forgiveness. From when Adam and Eve sought to be as wise as God to Jesus' Resurrection to this present day, God has been patiently working to make it possible for all people to accept His forgiveness so they can have the relationship He created them to have with Him. Jesus, the *Christos*, is the culminating act of God to make His forgiveness accessible to everyone. The problem is that we do not function naturally in a world with forgiveness. We understand revenge, justice, and getting our due; but forgiveness—unless experienced—is foreign to our nature and thus our actions. Jesus came to forgive. His motive for this divine act was love—love born out of compassion for those He created, even though they had turned away from Him and even killed Him.

Prior to His rescuing work on the cross, Jesus taught His followers what forgiveness in His Kingdom looked like. He instructed them how to forgive someone who offended them (Matt. 18:15–17). After one lesson, Peter stepped forward and asked for all of us, "How many times shall I forgive my brother when he sins against me?" (Matt. 18:21) That is the question Jesus answers in this chapter.

The Memory Verse for this chapter is 1 John 1:9. This is God's promise. When we agree with Him that we have sinned and that we have crossed the boundaries He has set up for us, He will remain faithful and true to His character. He will forgive us—just as He said.

Our question to consider for this chapter is "Is forgiving and forgetting the same?" The English poet Alexander Pope said, "To err is human. To forgive divine." But what about forgetting the error? We will return to this question later.

24.1 Forgiving Others

Where I live, drivers do not read a speed limit sign as the maximum speed at which you can drive. They read the sign as the minimum speed. On most streets if you drive the posted speed, you will not only get passed but also get honked at for getting in someone's way! The same is true on interstates around our state. Most speed limit signs on the open road are 70 miles per hour. If there is no highway patrolman clocking drivers with radar, many drivers will pass far exceeding that limit. The word on the street is that if you stay within 10 miles per hour over the limit, you will not get stopped. That means no ticket, no fine, and no increase in your insurance rates. So the goal becomes to push the limit of the law rather than to drive within the boundaries it has put there for you.

If a speed limit sign reads "40," how fast do you drive? Be honest. What circumstances "allow" you to go over the speed? What do you think of others who speed by you without getting a ticket for it?

_____

_____

Read Matthew 18:21. Underline Peter's question to Jesus. Why do you think/feel he asked that?

_____

_____

Jesus invested His days equipping His apprentices to live and lead in His Kingdom. The Kingdom way of life was different from anything they had previously known, so He patiently taught them new ways of living that challenged their human nature and old ways of life. One lesson Jesus taught His followers was how to forgive someone who offended them (Matt. 18:15–17). Offending others is inevitable. Our choices and words hurt feelings and cross the boundaries of others. In order to live like Jesus, His followers must learn to forgive like Him. Jesus' forgiveness is more divine than human.

As soon as Jesus ended His lesson on forgiveness, Peter came up to Him to find out the limits of what He told them to do (v. 21). Like a driver who tests the speed he can go without getting a ticket, Peter questioned the limit to this new "speed of life." Forgiveness of someone who continually offends you must have some limit to it! Peter chose the perfect number seven as the maximum number of times to forgive someone. That was God's number—from the seven days of creation. Surely that is all Jesus could expect of His followers.

To get the full effect of Jesus' teaching on forgiveness, ask God to bring to mind someone who has or is currently offending you. The person may have seriously offended you or just irritated you. Either way, ask God to place that person and his or her offense on your heart. Ask God to teach you to forgive like Jesus.

24.2 Repaying Debt

We owe a mortgage on our house and have some credit card debt. We have paid off one car and still owe some on another. Next to our house payment, reducing the amount of college loans for our daughter's college expenses challenges our monthly budget. We tithe to our church, give to other mission causes, save for retirement, and have a small emergency fund. We are like many Americans who live with debt and work to free ourselves from its bondage, so that we can live on a cash-only basis and invest more in Kingdom causes. We got ourselves into the debt. It is our responsibility to get out of it. But it sure would be nice if those we owe would just say, "We no longer hold you to your debt. It's forgiven. Keep what we loaned you, and you don't have to give us any more of your money."

Debt can be a huge problem in our lives. It is a bondage that keeps us from living freely for Christ. What is your debt situation? What would you do if you asked all of those you owe to forgive your debt, and they did? What would you do with the money you spent each month paying off debt? Write your thoughts here:

_____

_____

Read Matthew 18:22–23. Underline the number of times Jesus told Peter to forgive someone who offended him (v. 22). Underline the phrase "the kingdom of heaven is like," and circle the story's main character.

Jesus answered Peter's question about forgiving others with a hyperbole, an exaggeration not intended to be taken literally. Jesus multiplied Peter's hypothetical number seven to the extreme number of 70 x 7, or 490 times! Peter wanted a limit to forgiveness for others. Jesus said by His answer there was no limit.

Peter must have had a look of confusion on his face, so Jesus continued with a story, a story about forgiveness. Jesus began with the phrase, "The kingdom of heaven is like . . ." Take some time to find these Kingdom stories from Jesus by using a concordance or an online search engine. They begin with this or a similar phrase. Each one describes an aspect of Kingdom life that Jesus calls His followers to live out. This one is about "a king who wanted to settle accounts with his servants" (v. 23).

Read the Kingdom story, Matthew 18:23–34, all at once. Read the story as a whole and let Jesus' message challenge your attitude about forgiving others.

Too often, we miss the simplicity of Jesus' stories because we dissect them to better understand each part. But in doing this, we miss the power of the whole story. Jesus' parables and stories are whole within themselves. Before we pick them apart as if they were a frog in seventh-grade biology, we must hear them as Jesus first told them.

Listen to the story by reading it two or three times. Ask someone to read it to you. Of course, do not forget Jesus told the story in response to Peter's question about forgiveness. Ask God to show you the meaning of the story for your life.

24.3 Pushing the Limits

Let us go back to the speed limit discussion from earlier. Say you drove like many others and acted like the speed limit sign was really a minimum speed sign. You push the limits above the posted speed. Then when you look in your rearview mirror, you see a black and white police car with the lights flashing. As you pull over to make room for the car to pass, it follows you to the side of the road. You try to remember how fast you were going. Both cars stop. The officer approaches you and informs you that you were going 12 miles over the posted limit. What are your next words to him?

What do you do when you get pulled over for speeding or another traffic violation? Do you try to explain your situation and ask for forgiveness? Or do you ask if the officer's radar is working well? Write a conversation and its outcome here:

_____

_____

_____

_____

_____

Read Matthew 18:24–31. Circle the two main characters in the story. Underline what each did for the one who owed him money.

Jesus used a common practice in His day as the setting for His story. Although slaves were owned by their masters, they were allowed to carry on their own lives as long as they did what their owner wanted them to do. As property of the owner, however, slaves were subject to the owner's will and could be bought and sold as the owner pleased. While foreign to our lives today, this was a common situation in Jesus' day. Those who heard Jesus' story understood every aspect of it. Jesus was not condoning slavery in this story. He used its familiarity among His hearers to illustrate His message to His followers about forgiveness.

The story is about forgiveness and the ability of two men to show forgiveness. Jesus told of a king who granted forgiveness, and a slave who received forgiveness but would not forgive those who owed him. The king forgave

an unbelievable amount of debt instead of imprisoning his servant because he "took pity" on his pleading servant (v. 27). The twist of the story is that the forgiven slave left the mercy of his master and went straight to a fellow slave who owed him practically nothing and demanded he pay up even though that slave begged for mercy (vv. 29–30). When the other slaves saw this and learned what the king had done, they went to tell the king (v. 31).

What is it about the forgiven slave's action that sits so wrongly with you? What makes the slave's refusal to forgive his peer so inappropriate? Write your feelings here:

_____

_____

_____

_____

24.4 Showing Compassion

Forgiveness is the child of mercy and compassion. You forgive because someone has loved you enough to forgive you. Until that moment, you naturally seek justice or revenge to gain what you have lost. Forgiveness is not natural. It is a learned behavior from the leadership and love of Jesus. We taught our children to forgive because we were taught to forgive. Our parents learned the practice from their parents, and so on. But the source of this practice is the mercy and compassion found in the heart of God. This is why Jesus taught it as a core value in the Kingdom of Heaven on earth. To have the heart of God is to forgive others—even when they do not deserve it.

Can you recall the first time you were forgiven? What were the circumstances? Why did it make such an impact on your life? On the other hand, have there been instances when you have withheld forgiveness or not received forgiveness when you sought it? How did those experiences make you feel?

_____

_____

_____

_____

Read Matthew 18:32–34. Underline verse 33. It is the heart of the story's conclusion.

When the king heard of the injustice committed by his forgiven slave, he called him in and reminded his slave what he had done for him (v. 32). He then asked the rhetorical question (a question with an obvious, expected answer), "Shouldn't you have had mercy on your fellow servant just as I had on you?" (v. 33) "Of course" is the expected answer. Forgiveness is about more than getting you off the hook. Forgiveness frees you to forgive others; the king expected as much from his servant.

Because of the servant's selfish misuse of the his mercy, the king dispensed justice instead. He turned the servant over to jailers who were allowed to torture him until he paid (v. 34). Again, this act recorded in the story does not condone the act of torture. It is how a secular king would deliver justice in that day. In a world with a king, there was no "due process," only the will of the king.

What is right about the king's actions? What message did the king send to the rest of his servants through his actions? What is foreign to your experience and reasonability in this story? What is the overall lesson Jesus wanted His followers to learn from this story?

_____

_____

_____

24.5 Receiving Mercy

Jesus was serious about His followers forgiving others as He forgave them. Jesus' forgiveness would cost Him His life. His sacrificial death was not only His mission; it also signaled how God could forgive all people who trusted that sacrifice. Jesus' death was a demonstration of God's love and mercy. Those forgiven by that sacrificial act should pass it on to those who sin—cross boundaries—against them. Jesus concluded His Kingdom story with the king's act of justice. He then drove the point home with Peter, who asked the question, and those with him.

Read Matthew 18:35. Underline the condition for which God the Father would treat Jesus' followers like the king did his unforgiving servant.

Jesus words seem harsh to those who do not know Him. However, this promise of justice instead of mercy is consistent with the character of God. The other side of God's mercy is His wrath that flows from His justice. Jesus said that if His followers did not forgive "[their] brother from [their] heart," His followers were like the unforgiving servant who had not truly grasped what God had done for them. God would then have no choice but to extend to them justice rather than mercy. Jesus' teaching here is consistent with how He taught His followers to pray, "Forgive us our debts, as we also have forgiven our debtors" (Matt. 6:12).

Our Memory Verse connects to Jesus' teaching here on forgiveness. Read 1 John 1:9. Circle the first word in the verse and then underline the words related to God.

John, who followed Jesus, told his readers to confess their sins. This means to agree with God that their behavior is sinful and separates them from an eternal relationship with Him. If they would do this, he wrote, God would be faithful to His Word. God promised that if they trusted Jesus as Rescuer and Leader, He would forgive them from all of their unrighteousness. So where is the justice in Jesus' warning in Matthew 18? John said God would be just. God is just in His forgiveness because His demands for righteousness were satisfied in Jesus' death. Rather than dispensing wrath, God offers mercy.

Our question to consider for this chapter is "Is forgiving and forgetting the same?" After reading Jesus' story and the Memory Verse, how would you answer this?

_____

_____

While our minds cannot forget the pain or injustice others inflict on us, we must act as if we have forgotten those hurts. Why? Because this is how God acts toward us. We deserve God's justice, but we receive God's forgiveness through our trust in Jesus as our Rescuer and Leader. God is faithful and just to act toward us as we confess our sin and seek His forgiveness. We are to treat others in the same way.

Forgiveness is easy to receive but difficult to give. As you end this chapter, affirm God's forgiveness in your life as you confess your sin and need for Him. Thank Him for the unmerited favor He has shown you. Prayerfully ask God to give you His love so you can forgive those whom He has already forgiven in Jesus, the *Christos*. Pray as Jesus taught you to pray, "Forgive us our debts, as we also have forgiven our debtors" (Matt. 6:12).

For further study:
- **Luke 17:3–4**
- **James 2:12–13**
- **Matthew 6:9–15**

25—Loving Your Neighbor: The Parable of the Good Samaritan

As Jesus moved toward the cross, He continued to tell stories that taught people how to live in His Kingdom. These were stories with a purpose. Jesus told them in such a way that no one would miss the point. He wanted everyone who heard them to make a decision about Him. One of Jesus' most popular Kingdom stories is what we call the Good Samaritan (Luke 10:25–35). When we learn about the hero of the story, we scratch our heads at what motivated an outsider to care for someone who easily could have walked past him for prejudiced reasons if he were lying on the ground.

The story invades our own religious and ethnic prejudices. It challenges us to cross the barriers we have built around ourselves when it comes to serving the needs of others. It also forces us to examine why we care for others. Do we do it because we are all members of the human race and survival of the species depends on it?

Or do we do it to gain points for God, as the religious leader implied? Do we care for those with needs because that is what our King and God would do? Are we not supposed to act like Him who rescued us and adopted us into His family? Become familiar with this timeless story. It could change how you live your life.

The Memory Verse for this chapter is Luke 10:27. This verse describes our relationship with God in its simplest form. In Luke's story of Jesus, the religious leader quotes the core confession of the Old Agreement of God. Matthew (22:37–40) and Mark (12:29–31) record it as a response to the question concerning the greatest rule given by God.

Our question to consider for this chapter is "Should Christians always be kind?" Is it always wise to stop and help someone on a dark street or busy highway?

25.1 Testing Jesus

I have a friend who believes differently from me about eternal life and how you get there. Our conversations revolve around the differences between a belief in reincarnation versus Resurrection, and Jesus as the only way to God versus the many ways to God people have acknowledged around the world. Our friendship keeps our discussions safe, but we do not lack emotion or conviction as we seek to understand each other and why neither of us will budge from our positions. Our common beliefs are that there is a loving God who cares for His creation, and as God's image bearers we are to treat others as God would. We struggle with eternal life.

Do you have a friend with a different view of eternal life and how to obtain it? What are the points of disagreement and agreement in your conversations? Write some of them here:

_____

_____

_____

Read Luke 10:25–26. Underline the question asked by the "expert in the law" and Jesus' return question. Circle the word "test" in verse 25.

By this time in the story of Jesus, the religious leaders had sought to discredit Jesus' teaching and popularity. He had become too much of a threat to the religious status quo among the Jewish faithful, and the leaders wanted Him stopped. Not all religious leaders were opposed to Jesus, as we saw with Nicodemus in John 3. However, in this episode, an "expert in the law" wanted to trap Jesus with a question about eternal life. If Jesus

answered with something other than what the religious experts would say, the people would have to make a choice. Tradition and tenure were on the side of the Jewish scholars.

In the evangelistic stories about Jesus, we read of scribes who sought to kill Jesus. Jesus had little patience with them. (See Matthew 23 in which they are called "teachers of the law.") Some translations call a scribe an "expert in the law" or "lawyer." These were the professional religious leaders who spent a lifetime learning the laws of God, interpreting them, and explaining them to the people who trusted their leadership. The people respected them as the best source of knowing and interpreting the rules and ways of God.

One day, one of these experts in the Law came to Jesus in order to "test," or "trap," Him (Luke 10:25). The lawyer had no other motive for testing Jesus than discrediting Him in front of His followers and the people. He asked Jesus what he had to do (the operative word) to obtain eternal life. The lawyer clearly saw eternal life as something you obtained for yourself by keeping the rules of God.

Jesus accepted the question at face value and answered the lawyer with a question (v. 26). If the lawyer wanted to talk in terms of the Law, Jesus would gladly start there. Jesus always started with people where they were. He knew the scribe's motives, but invited His adversary to answer a question with the hope the lawyer may come to trust Him as the Messiah.

Whom do you respect as a religious authority in your life? Have Jesus' teachings challenged what you have heard from that person or from your religious tradition? How have you dealt with those conflicting concepts?

_____

_____

_____

_____

25.2 Getting Attention

Growing up with the last name Wilkes, I always found myself near the back on the last row in elementary school classes. At graduations, I sat with the other students whose last names began with letters near the end of the alphabet. In my alphabet-ordered life, starting at what seemed to me the back of the line, getting recognized became a priority. One way I did that was to try and answer questions asked by the teacher. That seemed a way to get attention that did not involve being sent to the principal or having a note sent home to Mom and Dad. I became rather competitive with my grades and felt really pleased when a teacher or professor acknowledged a correct answer or noted a remark. I have come to realize that kind of recognition was outside my identity in Christ; accolades by teachers was never really about who I truly was. If it were not for my encounter with Jesus, I would have made a great scribe.

Did you use right answers to get recognition in school, or did that not matter to you? What other ways did you seek to be recognized in front of your peers? Write some of your experiences here:

_____

_____

Read Luke 10:27–28. Look up the references in the record of the Old Agreement in order to read the context of the original statements by God (Deut. 6:5). Underline Jesus' two responses to the expert's answer.

Rather than proving Himself to His challenger by answering his question, Jesus asked the scribe to answer his own question. Jesus would let the "expert" play his hand first. The lawyer quoted the most famous of God's guidelines for his people: "Love the LORD your God with your heart . . . soul . . . strength . . . and mind" (Deut. 6:5). He even added, "Love your neighbor as yourself" (Lev. 19:18). The expert on the law answered with what he had been taught and studied his whole life. His answer agreed with Jesus' summation of the Law when a different scribe asked Him to state the greatest of the commandments (Mark 12:29–31). The lawyer got it right. What would the Teacher say?

Jesus responded by saying the lawyer had answered his own question correctly. The data fit the inquiry, but did the expert get more than a right answer? Jesus told him that if he would do those very things he would "live."

Christos—God's Transforming Touch

The only problem is that no one is capable of keeping those two requirements of God their entire lives. They are God's purpose for our lives, but we are incapable of doing those things on our own. If the man wanted to know what he must do to get eternal life, Jesus said that the lawyer knew the answer to that question. If he could do that, he would obtain eternal life.

The scribe's answer to Jesus' question is our Memory Verse for this chapter. Do you know it? If not, take time to make it part of your knowledge about your relationship with God. If you already know it, meditate on what it says. Allow God's Spirit to examine your life and reveal where you need His help in loving Him with that part of your life.

25.3 Dealing with Experts

Right answers are not enough to get you recognized in school. You must present yourself as inquisitive and insightful. When I was pursuing my Ph.D. studies, I enjoyed the discussions in my seminars. A student would present a paper for the first hour, and the next hour was spent challenging and inquiring about the content of the paper. Most discussions were truly about learning the subject matter and benefiting from the one who had become the subject matter expert in the group. Some in the group, however, wanted the other seminar members to know their intelligence at the expense of the presenter. These graduate students would become aggressive in their inquisition and relentless in pointing out the failure of the one who had prepared the paper. You soon knew who was there to learn and who was there to establish him or herself as the lead dog in the group. Those were the peers you feared on the day of your presentation. These people would have made better scribes than me.

In what setting have you found yourself in which someone in the group wanted to make sure he or she was superior to others? It could have been in an organizational or academic setting. It could have been among friends in a dinner club or small group. How did he or she go about letting others know his or her knowledge?

_____

_____

Read Luke 10:29–30. Underline the scribe's question in verse 29. What is the setting of the story Jesus told in verses 30–36?

_____

The expert in the Law could not let Jesus go. He had come there to trap Him, and he would not leave until he had done so. Now that Jesus had validated him by releasing him to live as he had answered, the scribe refused Jesus' acceptance. Like a Ph.D. candidate who wanted to point out the inadequacies of a peer at a seminar table, he pushed for another answer. He asked, "Who is my neighbor?" In a world of ethnic and social prejudice, Jesus could cause more of a stir with His answer here than with the previous question. The scribe must have felt proud of himself. This was going to be good.

Jesus again refused to enter the combative argument the trained lawyer posed. Instead, Jesus told another story that painted a picture of life in His Kingdom. The lawyer wanted to debate. Jesus wanted him to understand what He had come to do. So He told a simple story filled with danger, kindness, risk, and fear. The lawyer would not let go until he had proven himself right. Jesus would not let go because He loved the man He would die to rescue.

Read, at least twice, the entire story Jesus told to answer that question. Familiarize yourself enough with the details to tell a child or friend Jesus' story sometime in the next 24 hours.

25.4 Having Compassion

I seldom stop to help someone with a flat tire on the freeway. I guess I have heard too many stories of people getting hit by speeding cars while trying to help that harden my heart. I tend to think someone else will help or they have already used a cell phone to call for help—as if they had someone to call or a cell phone to use like me. Sometimes I will help push someone out of an intersection into a gas station. I have also rolled down my window to ask someone stopped in the street with a raised car hood if I could call someone to help. When I pull up on a wreck that I have witnessed or where no help has arrived, I do stop and offer assistance. But I wonder what I would do if I came upon someone of a different race lying in the street bloodied and clearly in pain in a different part of town than mine. Surely I would stop then.

What about you? What are your habits about stopping to help others in need? What scares you about helping? How do you feel when you go past someone in need or when you stop to help? Write about your experiences.

_____
_____
_____

Read Luke 10:30–35 again. Circle the characters in the story and underline what happened to them or what they did in response to the situation. Underline Jesus' question to the scribe at the end of the story.

Jesus told a story about a too common experience among those who risked traveling between Jerusalem and Jericho. The road was notoriously dangerous. Gangs of bandits or robbers would leap from the jagged terrain, surround a traveler, and rob him of all his belongings. Jesus added that this particular time the bandits not only robbed the man but "beat him and went away, leaving him half dead" (v. 30).

The irony of the story is that both of the religious leaders, the priest and the Levite, crossed over to the other side of the rode and did not help the man (vv. 31–32). They had good reasons. If they were on their way to serve their turn in the Temple of Jerusalem and they touched the man, they would become ceremonially unclean and could not do the work of serving God and His people.

A Samaritan, a man of the same race and religion as the woman at the well we met in John 4, was the one who stopped to help. Jesus said the unlikely helper had "pity" on the wounded man (v. 33). He then cared for the man and made provision for his recovery (vv. 34–35). If the Samaritan was religious, it did not get in the way of helping others. Maybe his faith gave him the courage to do what he did.

Christos—God's Transforming Touch

Enter the story by meditating on each character. How are you like or unlike them? Include the wounded man in your imagination. Ask God's Spirit to reveal the true nature of your heart.

25.5 Showing God's Love

When I was growing up, my neighbor was the one who physically lived in the house next to mine. Going to a neighbor's house literally meant going next door. Now, the proximity of "my neighbor" and "next door" are nanoseconds away. I have neighbors in Cuba, China, and Canada via the Internet. I see my neighbors where I serve as more than the two couples that live on either side of us. Those who are members of the family of Legacy Church are more like neighbors than those who live on the same block of houses as me. This nearness of distance is a reality, but it can create a problem when it comes to community. If I spend all my time building relationships with those in my social and technological networks, never walking next door to invite my neighbors over for dinner, then the dark side of a virtual community has replaced authentic community.

Who are your neighbors? Where is "next door" for you? Are you most involved in the physical community in which you live, or in other networks of relationships?

Read Luke 10:36–37. Circle the word "neighbor" in verse 36. Underline the response of both the scribe and Jesus in verse 37.

Once again Jesus let the expert in the law answer his own question. The "neighbor" in the story and

in our lives is the one who has "mercy" on those in need. Neighbors in Jesus' Kingdom show God's love in tangible ways to people in need. Jesus brought a Kingdom with no boundaries. No ethnic, social, or religious barrier built by people could stop His love for them. His followers are to live the same way.

Jesus judged the scribe correct in his answer. If the scribe still wanted to do something to inherit eternal life, he could "go and do likewise" (v. 37). To tell a Jewish religious expert to go do what a Samaritan did was a hard pill to swallow. It would be like telling a prominent white preacher in deep southeast Texas during the civil rights movement to go and do what a poor black man did to help a bleeding white man on the side of the road. The implications of Jesus' teaching were enormous. Yet, He warned us we would have to change how we live because the Kingdom of Heaven was at hand.

In what ways you can "go and do likewise" to someone in need? In the global village in which we find ourselves, that may mean going to a foreign country or serving in your own neighborhood. Jesus taught that wherever someone was in need, His Kingdom people were to act like the Samaritan who stopped to help the bleeding Jew. Prayerfully write out some actions you can take to meet the needs of those in your global neighborhood.

_____

_____

For further study:
- **Mark 12:28–34**
- **Romans 7:7–12**

26—Learning to Pray: The Lord's Prayer

Prayer is to our relationship with God what conversation is between spouses—without it you can live in the same house for years but never know the heart of the other. The two are committed to caring for the basic needs of each other; but there is no intimacy, no friendship. They have nothing but habits learned over years of living around each other. People assume longevity equals love. But if people ever stayed in this couple's house for more than a few hours, they would soon realize that while the two like and respect each other, they no longer love each other. The outward signs of a marriage are there, but the reality of love is gone. Too many followers of Jesus who have been exposed to religion for a long time may feel like the couple described in this paragraph. They have been around the teachings and person of Jesus for a lifetime, but they either do not know how to talk to Him anymore or they have simply filled the space with other things. So like a familiar spouse or friend, they never take the time to enter into conversations of meaning and intimacy.

In this chapter Jesus taught His apprentices how to pray. You may have memorized this prayer from your childhood, or you may have heard it only from others. As Jesus introduced Kingdom life to His students, this is how He taught them to pray.

The Memory Verses for this chapter are Matthew 6:9–13. Jesus taught this as how His disciples should pray. Memorize this prayer to have in your heart and mind the basics of a conversation with God.

Our question to consider for this chapter is "Does God always answer prayer?" Let us spend time with how Jesus taught us to pray and use His lesson as the starting point of this question.

26.1 Learning the Basics

My wife and I taught our two girls the English alphabet by singing the 26 letters to the tune of "Twinkle Twinkle Little Star." We also wrote and recited them. They eventually learned to say and write them so they could assemble them into words, sentences, paragraphs, and stories. The foundation of literacy is to know the alphabet. We were fortunate to have parents who taught us to read and write, and we know this is a skill essential to our daughters' doing well. Too many in the world are not literate. Those of us who know these things have an obligation to teach others.

How did you learn or teach your children the English alphabet? Have you tried to learn a language foreign to you? How did you go about doing it? Write some of your experiences here:

_____

_____

_____

_____

Read Matthew 6:5 through the first line of verse 9. Circle the words "when" (v. 5) and "how" (v. 9). Describe the context of Jesus' teaching here:

_____

_____

_____

_____

When Jesus introduced how the Kingdom life looked, He took time to explain the basics. He first made sure no one fell into the trap of doing good things to call attention to oneself (Matt. 6:1). He then set three basic acts of religion—giving alms, prayer, and fasting—in the context of serving God and others (vv. 2–18).

Pause and read Matthew 6:1–18 to get the full effect of this part of His Kingdom message.

Jesus' primary message was that we are to do these things only in service to God and others, not to gain recognition from others for our apparent spirituality. Appearances matter only among those who are keeping score to see who is the most religious.

Luke records this basic prayer of Jesus as a response to one of His disciple's request to teach them how to pray just as John taught His disciples to pray (Luke 11:1). Luke noted this came after Jesus had been "praying in a certain place." His followers finally made the connection between Jesus' extended times of prayer and His powerful life. They wanted to learn to pray like Him.

Traditionally, this prayer is known as the "Lord's Prayer," accenting that Jesus is the source of its content. Roman Catholics know it as "Our Father" from the first two words of the prayer. However, it is really the disciples' prayer; for Jesus taught them to pray it so they would have the foundation of a conversation with God.

If you already know this prayer, take time to quietly repeat it. Pause after each phrase to hear again the words that Jesus taught you. Also allow God's Spirit to test your heart in relation to giving to the poor, talking to Him, and fasting as part of your spiritual habits. You may know the words and perform the acts, but do they aid your friendship with God? Why?

26.2 Addressing Our Father

I want to be a good father to my daughters. We continue to have good relationships as they are now young adults and starting their own careers and families. Their father remains a positive part of their lives. I am fortunate to have a loving father. Whenever I hear the name "father," I have positive memories and feelings toward him. Some people are not so fortunate. Their biological father may have left or abused them, and a stepfather never was who they had hoped or prayed for. All of this is to say that when Jesus teaches us to call God "Our Father," not everyone starts in the same place in their attitudes toward Him.

What was your relationship with your father growing up? How would you describe your relationship with him now? If you are a father, how are you doing in your relationship with your children? Write some of your thoughts here:

_____

_____

_____

_____

Read Matthew 6:9–10. Circle the word "Father" and write the phrases related to God in your own words.

_____

_____

_____

_____

Jesus' model prayer for His disciples addressed God as "our Father in heaven" (v. 9). Jesus intended this prayer to be said together with other followers due to the emphasis at the beginning being "our Father," not "my Father." While your individual relationship with God is important, this prayer is said with all first person plural pronouns: our, us, and we. This is not a private prayer. This prayer is for all followers of Jesus to share together.

Jesus called God His "Father." (See Matthew 16:17 and John 5:17–23 for examples of this.) Jesus taught His disciples to address God in the same way. This term of endearment also teaches that the Christian God is not aloof and uninterested in people. God can be intimately involved, like a father in the life of a child, if we allow Him to do so. Yet Jesus taught us to respect the holiness of God by acknowledging His name was holy or "hallowed" and set apart. God is our Father, but He is to be respected as the God He is.

Jesus then taught us to ask our Father in heaven for some things. Children do that with their fathers. These are requests related to the purposes of God, not our personal needs. The first request is that we pray the Father's "kingdom come." This was Jesus' purpose in coming: to introduce the new-creation Kingdom on earth. Our prayer should match His purpose. The second request is that we pray God's "will be done on earth as it is in heaven." This means we pray that God's purposes, as they exist in His presence, happen here on earth—and we are the agents of those purposes.

Take time with this part of Jesus' lesson on how to pray. Meditate on what it means to call God Father, to acknowledge His holiness, and to pray that His will be done on earth now just as the way it is in heaven.

Christos—God's Transforming Touch

26.3 Asking for Our Needs

Children expect their parents to provide food for them. Caring parents gladly give food to their children to sustain them. One of the great tragedies on our planet is when a parent cannot feed a hungry child. Parents who are able to feed their children teach them to thank God so the children can acknowledge the source of their nourishment and to be grateful for it. If God is "our Father," then it follows we should feel free to ask Him for an essential item for our lives: food.

How were you taught to ask and be grateful for food in your family? Do you remember asking for food, or did it always seem to be there when you needed it? Did you say a prayer before your meal to thank God for it? Do you still do that? Write some of your answers here:

_____

_____

_____

_____

_____

Read Matthew 6:11. Underline the words "daily bread." What is the significance of receiving the Word daily?

After Jesus taught His apprentices to trust God as their Heavenly Father and to ask that His purposes be realized on earth as they are in His presence, He then taught them to ask for their basic need of food. Prayer involves asking; our Father expects His children to ask. Jesus, however, taught us to request only a daily portion of food. This is like God the Father who taught the people of Israel to pick up only a day's worth of manna in the wilderness (Ex. 16). Truly trusting God is to ask for only what is needed for today rather than asking for a full pantry of items to choose from when we want.

Later in this same message, Jesus told His followers to make it a habit of asking, seeking, and knocking. In these actions they would receive and find, and God would open doors for them. He concluded that if we who are evil know how to respond to our children when they ask, how much more would our "Father in heaven give good gifts to those who ask him!" (Matt. 7:7–11)

Too often, what happens is that our list of needs turns into a list of wants. We wonder why God does not give us those. In the ABC's of prayer, Jesus taught us first to ask for our basic needs on a daily basis. If we would express our trust in God this way, we would have no reason to worry.

Read Matthew 6:25–33 for Jesus' reasons for trusting God with our basic needs rather than worrying or pursuing them ourselves.

Jesus taught us to trust our Father in heaven by asking Him for our daily portion of food. How does this part of the prayer apply to your life? Do you take for granted the amount of food you have? Have you moved on to other requests, or do you pause each day to ask and thank God as the source of your basic needs?

26.4 Asking for Forgiveness

Jesus taught His disciples to ask God, our Father, about spiritual matters. We often forget the importance of this part of the elementary prayer Jesus taught us. Both forgiveness and protection from spiritual temptations are part of Jesus' model prayer.

Read Matthew 6:12. Underline the word "forgive" and circle the word "as."

Jesus taught His students to ask God the Father for forgiveness. Why? We have lived as if we were gods, and we have crossed the boundaries He has constructed for our lives. As with food, God lovingly supplies forgiveness. However, our asking acknowledges God as the source and fosters our gratefulness. Jesus added that we are to ask our Father to "forgive us our debts" in the same way that "we also have forgiven our debtors" (v. 12). Our acceptance of God's grace is demonstrated in how we forgive others. Do you remember the story we read earlier in which Jesus told of an unforgiving servant whose master forgave his debt, yet he refused to forgive a fellow servant? (Matt. 18:23–35) This part of the disciples' prayer carries with it the same message. To accept God's forgiveness is to grant the same forgiveness to others.

Read Matthew 6:13. Underline the two requests Jesus teaches us to pray in these verses.

Jesus taught us to ask our Father to lead us away from temptation and to deliver us from the devil (v. 13). Why would God add these requests to our alphabet of prayer if He does not tempt us? (Jas. 1:13) One reason we need our Father to "lead us not into temptation" is because we are so poor at overcoming temptation when we encounter it. A loving parent leads his or her child away from the temptation to drink poisonous liquid or play in the street because the child has no knowledge or experience to avoid such dangers. The child needs the parent's protection and guidance. We are all like children, no matter our age, when it comes to avoiding temptation.

The next request acknowledges both the existence of the evil one and our need for the Father to rescue us from Satan's plans to destroy us. We find ourselves weak before the methods of Satan (Eph. 6:11). In this prayer, we admit our weakness. We ask our Father in heaven to deliver us from the influences of the one bent on our destruction. This is not a prayer of fear but an acknowledgement of our Father's power over evil and His constant protection over us.

If God measured His forgiveness toward you in the same way you have forgiven others, what would it look like in your life? Is there someone whom you need to forgive as God has forgiven you? Do you seek God's help in times of temptation and acknowledge the reality of the evil one and God's power over him? Write your personal prayer built upon the disciples' prayer.

_____

_____

_____

26.5 Accepting the Conditions

Jesus ended His model prayer for His followers with one last word of explanation. It may seem odd that He repeated a condition of forgiveness, but the warning is necessary to help us understand that our requests are not about us but about serving others. Only one request in the prayer is about physical things, and it is limited by daily amounts. All the other requests deal with the spiritual realm and our relationship with God as His children. Prayer is more about entering the presence of God and seeking His purposes than it is about us asking for more stuff.

Read Matthew 6:14–15. Circle the word "if" in both verses and underline God's promised responses to those conditions.

The longer version of verse 13 did not show up in manuscripts of the story of Jesus until later. The earlier versions of the text do not include it, and later translators note this by putting that part of the verse in a footnote or in the margin. Check a commentary to read more about this particular verse and the different versions that are available.

Jesus repeated His warning that if we forgive others, God will forgive us; if we refuse forgiveness, God will withhold His forgiveness from us. This is not a matter of salvation but of whether or not we accept the fact that God's forgiveness is not ours alone. This frees us to forgive others in order to introduce them to life in Christ's Kingdom. How can God forgive us when if we turn around like the ungrateful servant and refuse to forgive those He sent His Son to die for? How we treat others when they offend us is evidence of whether we have truly grasped what God has done for us through Jesus, the *Christos*.

We have likened this prayer of Jesus to the ABC's of a language. From this basic prayer can come prayers that deepen our relationship with God. Every aspect of this prayer is a window into the nature of God.

Memorize and meditate on this prayer as a primer on how to converse with God. As it becomes familiar to you, pause at different phrases and meditate on that portion of the prayer. Other times, allow your prayer to expand one of the topics. For example, when you pray may "your kingdom come . . . on earth as it is in heaven," ask God to show you how to introduce Kingdom ways in all you do that day. When you pray for "daily bread," ask God to show you how little you really need and how you can share your excess with those in need. Allow this core practice of following Jesus to grow as you grow in your relationship with the *Christos*.

For further study:
- **Luke 11:1–4**
- **Exodus 16:1–8, 13–26**

27—Growing God's Kingdom: The Parables of the Mustard Seed and Yeast

Every movement that has made a difference in human history began with a small group of believers who lived out their passion for a cause. Their numbers grew until others began to notice them. Some eventually changed governments and the way of life for those around them. Women can vote in America now because Susan B. Anthony and others created a movement to allow women to vote around the time of the Civil War. It was not until 1920 with the adoption of the 19th Amendment to the U.S. Constitution that women received the right to vote. What started as a conviction that women, just as men, had a right to vote grew into a movement that made it possible for the first woman to run for president in 2008.

Jesus came to bring God's will "on earth as it is in heaven" (Matt. 6:10). His coming established a beachhead for the Kingdom of God on earth. It appeared to be a small movement among peasants and outcasts. We know it grew to capture the hearts of billions and was the single most important influence on Western civilization. What looked like a carpenter trying to become a messiah with a ragtag band of followers turned out to be the Son of God marching through history to change the hearts of people.

The Memory Verses for this chapter are Matthew 13:31–32. These verses record Jesus' description of how His Kingdom would grow. To know this is to grasp how the Jesus movement grows around you.

Our question to consider for this chapter is "How does the Kingdom of God grow?" We live in a world of project plans with goals and objectives. Jesus knew of no such thing. He knew of agriculture and how things grow. Let us observe two Kingdom parables Jesus told.

Christos—God's Transforming Touch

27.1 Using Similes

A simile is a part of speech that compares two unlike things in order to help the hearer or reader understand better. For example, "She sings like a bird" or "He cooks like a chef" give you comparisons of a person's skill. "She was pretty as a picture" or "He slept like a log" create mental pictures to help you grasp the speaker's meaning. Good communicators use similes to make their message more vivid and to help their hearers walk away with pictures to hang the message upon.

What common similes have you used or heard? Write those most familiar to you in the space below. Or pick an object or idea and write a simile for it. For example, "My son eats like a _____," or "I felt like a _____ in the last meeting as I made a presentation."

_____

_____

_____

Read Luke 13:18. Underline the phrase "the kingdom of God" and circle the word "compare."

Jesus illustrated what He had come to do. He did this by healing on the Sabbath, a feat that caused both believers and skeptics to question how they viewed the Law (Luke 13:10–17). He taught lessons in which He compared what He was doing with common things in people's lives. These comparisons, or Kingdom stories, helped people understand more fully something that was new that they could not see naturally.

Jesus asked a rhetorical question when He taught those around Him, "What is the kingdom of God like? What shall I compare it to?" The "kingdom of God" is the same as the "kingdom of heaven" in Matthew's story of Jesus. While all four storytellers used the broader concept of the Kingdom of God, Matthew used the narrower term for his fellow Jews. The concepts are synonymous, and Jesus used them interchangeably. The Kingdom of God is wherever Jesus rules as King in the hearts of people. Jesus used stories and comparisons to cast a vision about what His rule would look like in the lives of people.

We get our English prefix *homo*, meaning "the same," from the original word meaning "to compare." Words like *homogeneous* and *homogenous* use this prefix. Jesus was about to use a word picture to paint how His Kingdom would affect the lives of those who trusted Him to be the Ruler and Rescuer of their lives.

Jesus used comparisons from everyday life to describe what the Kingdom, or rule of the Christ, would look like. Use a concordance or search engine and explore the many references to the Kingdom of God/heaven in the stories of Jesus. Record some of the references here:

_____

_____

_____

27.2 Comparing God's Kingdom to a Seed

Go to your pantry where you keep the herbs and spices. OK, go to a nearby grocery store and find the aisle with herbs and spices. Look for the bottle or container labeled *mustard seed*. Buy the product. Then open the bottle and pour the seeds in the palm of your hand.

They look relatively small compared to the pumpkin seeds sitting near them in the store. If you take one of the seeds outside and drop it on the ground, say next to a full-grown oak tree, you can see the contrast in size. But that small seed can produce a tree-sized plant. If you have access to the Internet, search for an image of a fully developed mustard seed plant, and you will see what that small seed will become.

What other seeds do you know that look small compared to the size of the full-grown plant? What are some other things that begin small but grow to be large? Write your ideas here:

_____
_____
_____

Read Luke 13:19. Underline the man's results from planting the seed.

Jesus used an analogy to describe how His Kingdom would grow. He may have done this because some may have wondered about the size of His group and the influence of His movement. As things heated up in Jerusalem related to Jesus' popularity, some followers may have wondered what would come of the Messiah's efforts. The application of this picture is immediate and clear. The contrast is of the seed's smallness and the largeness of the plant it produces.

According to Matthew, Jesus explained, "Though it is the smallest of all your seeds, yet when it grows, it is the largest of garden plants and becomes a tree" (Matt. 13:32). Jesus used the object lesson of a common seed to teach that this "smallest of all your seeds" would

become as large as a tree. A mustard seed plant can grow up to eight feet and look like any other tree. Jesus wanted His followers—then and now—to know that while the Kingdom of God looked small compared to a kingdom like the Roman Empire, the seed of its message will grow beyond what is apparent at the beginning. His-story has proven Him right.

What applications can you make of Jesus' parable? What does it tell you about His Kingdom, your faith, His influence, your efforts in His name, and your church? Size is not the only application. What about the seed dying to produce the tree? Meditate on Jesus' words and write some of your thoughts here:

_____
_____
_____
_____

27.3 Comparing God's Kingdom to Yeast

I love going to my parents' home for Thanksgiving or Christmas. In addition to spending time with family I do not see much during the year, I love the home-cooked meals. I fear that when that generation of cooks passes away we will all be dependent upon mass-produced foods. I know my family will depend on cafeterias and food stores when we are left to cook for ourselves. Homemade bread and pies are my favorite holiday food items. Mother begins the day before the meal by mixing, kneading, and letting the dough rise. As a child I never understood how if you set a pan of dough on a counter and covered it with a kitchen towel, somehow it would rise past the top of the pan and then bake into the best tasting bread. My dad, who was a chemist, tried to explain it once, but I was too young to care. I just wanted a slice of hot bread.

Do you bake homemade bread? If so, what is your secret for making good bread? If not, who is the best cook you know? Have you ever seen the yeast he or she puts in bread to make it rise?

_____

_____

_____

Read Luke 13:20–21. Underline the word "yeast" in verse 21. What did the woman do with the yeast? Check the footnotes or margin in your translation for an explanation of "large amount" in verse 21.

Jesus presented a second comparison to how His Kingdom would grow. A seed that produced a tree is obvious to many due to its outward appearance. Yeast's

effect on flour is less conspicuous but still changes the nature of the dough. Both produce growth and change. Jesus taught that the Kingdom of God He brought would grow and produce change in the hearts of people.

Yeast is smaller than a mustard seed. It is a fungus that causes fermentation with the flour, which produces carbon dioxide and ethanol that is trapped in bubbles and makes the dough expand. (That is all I remember from my chemist father.) The point is that this seemingly small ingredient changes the entire nature of the flour to create a tasty, life-giving food when baked. A footnote in my Bible equates the amount of flour the woman worked her yeast into to about 22 liters! That was just the flour. Imagine how big the bread would have been if she had not separated it into smaller pieces after it rose. The amount of the flour may give a hint to the potential size of Jesus' Kingdom.

Meditate on this simile like you did the mustard seed. Ask God to show you its meaning so it will build your trust in Jesus and your confidence in His Kingdom's growth in your life and the lives of others. Write some of your thoughts here:

_____

_____

_____

27.4 Comparing Analogies of Yeast

Jesus used the analogy of yeast that causes bread to rise in a positive way to explain how His Kingdom would grow. But Jesus and other biblical writers did not always use this object in a positive way. One way to understand the full meaning of a word or concept in the Bible is to study it in other contexts. Let us see how yeast is used throughout the biblical record. We can then compare its use to how Jesus used it in His Kingdom parable. This principle of interpretation can be described as comparing Scripture with Scripture to understand the Bible.

Read Exodus 12:14–20. Circle the word "yeast" everywhere it appears and write your summary of God's instructions in the space below. What is the historical context for these verses?

_____

_____

The removal of yeast from the home was part of the Feast of Unleavened Bread, which was part of the Passover event when God delivered Israel from slavery in Egypt. Yeast in this context is a metaphor for sin and was to be removed as a sign of preparing the peoples' hearts for their rescue by God from their enemies. In this context yeast had a negative connotation.

Read Luke 12:1. Underline the word "yeast" as well the last word in the verse, "hypocrisy."

Jesus used the analogy of yeast with His apprentices as a metaphor for the hypocrisy of the religious leaders prior to His use of it in a parable. He warned that the hypocrisy of the religious leaders among His followers would be like the infiltration of yeast in a lump of dough. Once it was "kneaded" into the group, it would be hard to guard against.

Read 1 Corinthians 5:6–7. Circle the word "yeast" everywhere it appears. What did Paul equate it with in this context?

_____

_____

_____

In this passage, Paul used yeast as a metaphor for an unrepentant person in the church. He insisted they remove the sinful person like yeast from their home. He may have had in mind the Old Agreement command to clean yeast from a home as a sign of God's deliverance of His people.

Yeast is used in the Bible both positively and negatively. Jesus' use of it in the parable of the yeast is the only positive context for the image. All others use it to represent something we need to remove from our lives.

Take some time to apply to your life today each of the passages of Scripture in which yeast is used. Ask God to make it a word picture that teaches you about His character and how He wants you to live. Write here or in a journal some of the applications to your life.

_____

_____

_____

_____

27.5 Assessing Technology

I am currently typing this sentence in a room in which I am the only living thing. My office has shelves filled with books, lamps that give light, and a vent that blows conditioned air. I sit in a steel and plastic chair with cloth covering and type on plastic keys that send electrical impulses that appear on a screen, which I can print on paper. However, I am the only living thing in the room. Sometimes I light a candle or turn on some tunes, but nothing is alive but me. My point? Jesus' classroom for His Kingdom was in the living creation from which He drew images and comparisons to teach His students how to live as Kingdom people. I fear that I miss something by sitting in my technologically top-heavy office rather than being in Jesus' creation.

Our question to consider for this chapter is "How does the Kingdom of God grow?" Summarize Jesus' teachings on this topic in the space below. Begin with His introductory phrase: "The kingdom of God is like . . ."

_____

_____

_____

_____

Jesus' Kingdom is more like a seed that grows into a plant than a strategic plan. It infiltrates people's lives like yeast that spreads through a lump of dough rather than like a program of evangelism. Business technology has too often replaced the ways of creation in how we see the church growing and influencing our world. When we try to impose technology on natural processes, we may be able to produce more things faster, but we can also fabricate something that was not intended in nature. Jesus chose things that grew naturally to describe His Kingdom, rather than comparing it to how Rome built its government or how the Phoenicians built ships.

Yes, organization and manufacturing have met the world's needs in many ways. However, those same techniques may not be as effective in creating environments in which the Kingdom of God can grow.

This truth remains a mystery. If we are to take Jesus' words at face value in its original context, we must let them teach us rather than us trying to fit them into our technological habits. Technology is not bad. It is snowing outside as I write. I much prefer this manufactured environment than the one outside right now. But to be a follower of Jesus we must not overlook the pictures He chose to reveal to us how His Kingdom works.

Take some time to observe how you explain or plan for growth in your church. How is it like Jesus' parable and how is it like the tools of business you have brought to it? In what ways have those tools helped you? In what ways have they possibly distracted you from Jesus' teaching about these matters? Write some of your thoughts here:

_____

_____

_____

_____

_____

_____

For further study:
- **Matthew 13:31–35**
- **Mark 4:30–33**

28—Giving God Everything: Jesus and the Rich Young Ruler

Are possessions bad? Is wealth a blessing from God to those who deserve it? Is it really harder for rich people to enter Jesus' Kingdom than the poor? We could go on with questions that arise out of the episode of Jesus and the rich young ruler. Yet, a careful look at the conversation between Jesus and the young man followed by Jesus' words to His disciples teach a clear message of what keeps so many from entering God's Kingdom.

Three of four writers who wrote of Jesus record this episode. We learn from Matthew that the one who approached Jesus was young (Matt. 19:20). Luke tells us he was a ruler (Luke 18:18), and all three confirm the man was wealthy (Mark 10:22). This rich young ruler represented those who were both successful and pious in Jesus' day. The assumption was that someone like the young man was surely "in" with God. Some still hold that assumption today, but Jesus' words are as challenging now as they were then. As with the young man who came to Jesus wanting to know how to have eternal life, the choice remains with us. Will we choose our wealth and success or will we choose Jesus for how we enter the Kingdom of God?

The Memory Verse for this chapter is Matthew 6:33. This verse is from Jesus' inaugural message about His Kingdom. He told His first followers to make His Kingdom their priority and all the objects of life would follow—not the other way around. Jesus' words to the rich young ruler are consistent with these.

Our question to consider for this chapter is "Does God ask us to give everything away?" Many have interpreted Jesus' command to the young man as intended for all of His followers.

Christos—God's Transforming Touch

28.1 Asking the Ultimate Question

"How do I get to heaven?" is not so much the question people ask me these days. They seem more interested in how they can make life better now than what life will be like later. As a pastor, I spend more time talking with people about their jobs, families, and the meaning of life than I do about life after earth. But sometimes someone will bring up the topic. When I ask the person what he or she thinks, 9 times out of 10 answers go something like, "I am trying to do the best I can; and if I don't do anything really bad, I know I'm going to heaven." Most people in my small world who have not been introduced to Jesus still hold on to the idea that they can do something to obtain eternal life with God.

First, where do you stand on the subject? What are your personal views about how to obtain eternal life? If you have had a similar conversation with someone, how did he or she answer? Write your thoughts here:

_____

_____

_____

Read Matthew 19:16–26. Read the entire story once or twice without stopping. Read it like you would an episode in a novel. Observe both sides of the story to see what is going on. You will recognize events we have studied before. Return to verse 16 and circle who approached Jesus and how he addressed Jesus. Underline his question to Jesus.

This episode in Jesus' life begins rather mildly. "A man" comes up to Jesus with a question. Mark wrote that the man "ran up to him and fell on his knees before him"

(Mark 10:17). Luke tells us he was a "ruler," which was a general term for those in the ruling class of the day. He addressed Jesus as "Teacher," which was also a general term that gives us no hint to his motives in asking. However, his question betrayed his motives.

The man wanted to know, "What good thing must I do to get eternal life?" He approached Jesus humbly and asked what the one "good thing" was he could perform in order to gain eternal life for himself. We will discover as we move through the story that he had gained wealth and kept all the rules of the faith through his own efforts. Having things was part of his way of life. He wanted to know from this popular teacher what he had to do to "get eternal life" for himself. If he could have that, his life would be complete from his perspective.

What part does doing the "good thing" play in your relationship with God? How much do you depend on doing what you believe God wants you to do to feel confident you will have eternal life? Be honest. Ask God to reveal your true feelings. Come to God as the man came to Jesus. Then listen to the words He gives you.

_____

_____

_____

28.2 Understanding the Answer

My father and I worked on the family cars when I was growing up. I loved spending Saturday mornings changing spark plugs, changing the oil, or taking care of something more major like adjusting the timing. We shared the work of keeping the family station wagon and his work car running smoothly. One of my disappointments with progress is that I can no longer work on my car. Environmental laws and computerized components complicate what used to be simple tasks. Now, I pay someone else to do the work I once could do myself. When I do take my cars to the local garage, or "maintenance center," I find myself asking an old school question and getting a mechanic's answer. The answer makes me realize that I should not have even asked the question. I just need to pay the bill and leave.

Have some things in your life changed to the point that what you once knew about them is so outdated you feel silly even asking questions now? How has your knowledge or understanding changed as it relates to something you have done for a long time and how have you kept up? Write some of your thoughts here:

_____

_____

_____

Read Matthew 19:17–19. Underline Jesus' question to the man and what He told the man to do to "enter life." Look up the Old Agreement references to the commandments Jesus recited to the man to see their original context.

Jesus turned the man's question back on him just like the maintenance center manager turns my questions back on me. The question should be about the One who is good, not the thing that is good. Jesus redirected the man's question away from his efforts that would make him "good" to the only One who is good—God (v. 17). Jesus then answered by refocusing the man's attention from "having eternal life" to "entering life."

The man wanted to work a deal like he would in the marketplace, something he was very good at. Jesus wanted the man to enter a new way of life with Him. Jesus affirmed God's commandments as the way to life. So if the man wanted to enter life by his own efforts, Jesus offered the path he should follow to do so.

The man arrogantly asked which ones to obey (v. 18) like an experienced climber asks which 14-thousand-foot peak in Colorado you want him to climb next. He was ready to make the deal. Jesus obliged and gave him a list of laws from the core commandments God gave Israel, the Ten Commandments (Ex. 20), and what Jesus would call the second greatest commandment (Lev. 19:18). "Keep these and you will enter the life you ask about," Jesus said. This part of the conversation is similar to the one we observed between Jesus and the expert in the law which led Jesus to tell the story of the Good Samaritan. (Luke 10:25–28).

Put yourself in the place of the young man. Ask God to help you know the young man's heart and Jesus' answers to him as well as how those same answers apply to you.

28.3 Understanding the Place of Money

I live in a relatively wealthy suburb. Type *median household income Plano, Texas*, in an Internet search engine and you will find the median household income is above the national level by quite a bit. (See what your city's household income is compared to the national level.) Given my city's level of income, people in our town most likely have more things than others in the country because they have more income with which to purchase things. The question for the Christ-follower is not necessarily "Is all this stuff bad?" but "How am I investing what God has loaned me to help build His Kingdom?" But even the answer to that last question assumes I get to keep my stuff. Jesus' command to the rich young ruler was to sell everything, give all the proceeds to the poor, and follow Him. Why do you think Jesus told him to do that? Is that Jesus' command to all of us—no matter our household median income?

Write what you found from your Internet search and your answers to the questions above.

_____

_____

_____

Read Matthew 19:20–22. Underline the man's next question to Jesus (v. 20). Underline the three things Jesus told the man to do if he really wanted to be "perfect" (v. 21). In verse 22, circle the word "sad" and underline why he felt that way.

After Jesus listed the commands the man must keep to enter life with Him, he said, "All these I have kept" (v. 20). Mark and Luke wrote that he said he had done those things "since I was a boy" (Mark 10:20; Luke 18:21). He wanted to know what he still lacked for eternal life. Mark tells us that Jesus "looked at him and loved him" (Mark 10:21). The command that follows is born of that love, not to scold or trip up the man. Jesus always gave everyone a chance to trust Him.

Jesus told him to do three things to be "perfect," or "complete." (See Matthew 5:48 for another use of the

term.) The young man was to go, sell all of his possessions, and give the money to the poor. He was then to come back and follow Jesus (v. 21). By doing these things, Jesus said the man would be complete in his effort to do the "good thing" and to have "treasure in heaven." (See Matthew 6:19–21 for more about treasures in heaven.) Jesus knew the man's wealth had become his treasure, and his ability to gain it had become his way of life. Jesus wanted the man to dethrone the god of wealth by using money for the one thing it was not intended for. Jesus wanted the young man to give it all away.

Matthew observed that when the young ruler heard Jesus' final offer, "he went away sad" (v. 22). The young man grieved his situation because his wealth had become his god. He did not know how to live or die without what he thought was his.

Jesus' words to the rich man are not for all. However, they are for anyone who trusts that his or her wealth can buy the way into eternal life or who cannot follow Jesus only. What do Jesus' words mean to you? Meditate on His words to the rich man and ask Him to show you how they apply to your wealth and values.

28.4 Understanding a Hyperbole

Jesus' teaching to His students on wealth and entering His Kingdom rocked their world. If we take what He said plainly without over-interpreting it, the same bombshell will land in our world. Yes, Jesus spoke in metaphors and similes. But His message to His followers about wealth and entering His Kingdom are not grammatical tactics. Jesus made it perfectly clear that the path to wealth and the way to eternal life are separate roads. To travel one path in order to enter the other is difficult and almost impossible.

Write your first responses to Jesus' words as the rich man walked away and Jesus turned to His disciples.

_____

_____

Read Matthew 19:23–24. Answer the following questions: Did Jesus say a rich man could not enter the Kingdom of Heaven? (v. 23) What did Jesus mean by His use of the hyperbole about the camel and the eye of a needle? Write your answers here:

_____

_____

_____

_____

After the rich young ruler left grieved over the thought of selling all of his possessions and following Jesus, Jesus stated the obvious: "It is hard for a rich man to enter the kingdom of heaven" (v. 23). Jesus could have pointed to the man as he walked away with his head down and said, "Look, see how hard it is for a guy with all that wealth to follow Me." I translate Jesus' observation to say, "I'm telling you, a rich man enters the Kingdom of Heaven with difficulty" (v. 23). Jesus wanted His followers to know that wealth and success were not essentially good things in relation to the things of God. They can be greater hindrances than helps, according to Jesus.

Pause here and list ways in which your wealth has hindered you from following Jesus completely. For example, the more you have the more time you must spend caring for it all.

_____

_____

_____

Jesus followed up His observation of the man with an exaggerated picture to make His point. "It is easier for a camel to go through the eye of a needle than for a rich man to enter the kingdom of God" (v. 24). In light of the man's initial question to Jesus, He made sure everyone knew wealth and success cannot get a person into heaven. The impossible act of a camel going through a needle's eye was easier than trying to buy your way in or be religious enough to get into His Kingdom.

Jesus pushes the edges of our sensitivities about wealth and success with His truth-telling. We may attempt to say we are not wealthy and successful and that Jesus' words do not apply to us. However, just the fact that you own this book, can read it, and search for things on the Internet places you among the wealthy of this world. Do not compare yourself to the neighbors on your street or those on the other side of your town. Jesus' Kingdom is global, and His values and teachings apply to every culture and people. Ask God to help you see your wealth from a global perspective and to show you how His observation of the rich young man and wealth applies to you—no matter how disturbing it may seem.

28.5 Entering the Kingdom of God

Jesus' Kingdom neither holds the same values nor functions the same way as this world. Jesus told us to "repent," or "change your heart and how you live," because "the kingdom of heaven is near" (Matt. 4:17). To trust Jesus as the ruling King is to enter His Kingdom with the intentions of adopting His values and way of life. You cannot say you trust Jesus and not seek Him and His Kingdom first. The beauty of the story of Jesus is that those who followed Him struggled with the same issues we wrestle with today.

Read Matthew 19:25–26. Underline the disciple's response to Jesus and His answer to their question.

The disciples understood Jesus' comparison of a camel and the eye of a needle, and they were "astonished" (v. 25). This word means to "strike a blow," or "knocked out." It is the same word used to describe the crowd's response to Jesus' teaching at the end of the Sermon on the Mount (Matt. 7:28). What Jesus said was like a blow to the stomach. How could it be that a rich man cannot get into the Kingdom? The disciples, like us, wanted to know, "So, if rich people who represent your blessings can't get in, how can we who are not so successful or wealthy get in?" The Jews wondered at Jesus' teaching. If it was easier for a huge animal to go through a tiny hole at the end of a needle, how could those who bore the pleasure of God in the form of wealth and health not enter Jesus' Kingdom?

The value systems of our fallen world—even our religious world—equate well-being with God's favor. The rich young ruler was the poster child for that worldview. Surely, bad things happen because people are bad, and good things happen because people are good. But Jesus' Kingdom does not work that way. As we have seen, He made it clear that wealth and success cannot buy your way into eternal life. If that is true, who can be saved?

When Jesus saw His follower's astonishment, He said, "Humanly speaking, it is impossible. But with God everything is possible" (v. 26, NLT). In other words, "You're right. Given how people think it works, it is impossible. But God has another way, and if you trust that way, everything is possible—including entering the Kingdom of God without wealth and success." Jesus introduced a different way to enter His Kingdom than that of the religious and material world.

For further study:
- **Mark 10:17–31**
- **Luke 18:18–27**

29—Responding to God's Invitation: The Parable of the Wedding Banquet

The rich young ruler's interaction with Jesus challenged our perception of who is eligible to enter the Kingdom of Heaven. Jesus told a story the week before His death that confronted that perception at a deeper level. After Jesus entered Jerusalem and was praised by the people (Matt. 21:1–11), He entered the Temple courts and threw out the money changers (vv. 12–13). Later He told two stories. One was about two sons: one who obeyed his father and the other who did not (vv. 28–32). The other was about a landowner who sent his son to take back his vineyard from rebellious tenants; instead the tenants ended up killing the son (vv. 33–44). Matthew wrote after the second story, "When the chief priests and the Pharisees heard Jesus' parables, they knew he was talking about them" (v. 45). Needless to say, the religious authorities were not happy with Jesus' implication that they were the unrighteous and wrongdoers in these stories.

It was in this atmosphere of conflict that Jesus told the story of the invitation of a king to a wedding banquet (Matt. 22:1–14). At this time in His-story, Jesus refused to back down from those who sought to discredit Him and to draw the people He came to rescue away from Him. This story, like the two before it, appears judgmental. Yet, Jesus sought to ensure that no one missed His call to all people to join Him at the wedding feast in His Kingdom.

The Memory Verse for this chapter is Matthew 22:9. This verse describes for whom the Kingdom feast had been prepared. Learn it as a reminder that "anyone you find" is an eligible guest at the table of salvation.

Our question to consider for this chapter is "Who can be a part of God's Kingdom?" While the answer is easy, those at the banquet table may not be able to accept it.

Christos—God's Transforming Touch

29.1 Preparing a Banquet

The reception dinner for my oldest daughter's wedding was held at the Texas Sports Hall of Fame facilities in Waco, Texas. The guys loved it. If they got bored with the table conversation, they could wander through exhibits that included people like Tom Landry, Carl Lewis, and Mary Lou Retton. It was not your usual wedding dinner location, but it was reasonably priced, and the groom liked the idea. We sent out an invitation list that fit the size of the facility and the food we ordered. We had two fears: either too many would show up and we would run out of food, or too few would come and we would eat Italian pasta and salad dishes for a year. We had fun putting on a dinner to celebrate our daughter and her husband. We were honored by those who accepted our invitation and celebrated with us.

Name some places where you have attended a wedding dinner. What was unique about each place? Did you know the hosts? How did they feel at the dinner? Write some of your memories here:

_____

_____

_____

_____

Read Matthew 22:1–2. Circle the words "parables" and "like." Underline the phrase in verse 2 that sets up the simile of the Kingdom.

Jesus told another "parable," or story, about His Kingdom. In these stories, He taught the values and practices of those who trusted Him as their Lord and lived His way of life. As our model of servant leader-ship, He used these stories to cast His vision: what His mission would look like when He completed it. A compilation of these vision stories paint a picture for us to see what His Kingdom looked like as He saw it.

The setting of this story is "a king who prepared a wedding banquet for his son" (v. 2). The king was the only one who spoke or acted in the story, thus making him the central figure. Jesus told this and other stories directed at the religious leaders in Jerusalem. He wanted them and those they led to know exactly what His intentions were and whom He came to rescue. This context helps us grasp the meaning of the parable.

Read Matthew 22:1–14. As with the other parables, read it through once or twice in one sitting. Try to "hear" the story. Put yourself in the noisy Temple courts filled with faithful followers of God who were there for the Passover festival. Try to hear Jesus' voice over the crowds and feel the tension in the air as the religious leaders in their official garb stand next to you, mumbling as they hear the story unfold. Watch for the eyes of the people as Jesus tells the different parts of the story. Find whom you associate with the most in the story.

29.2 Inviting Guests

What if you planned a party and invited guests, but no one came? That would hurt. On the other hand, when my daughters were growing up the standard among their friends was to rent a local pizza parlor or game house and invite 10 or 12 to join in the food and festivities. Sometimes I wished not everyone had come when I had to pay the bill for the event.

What were some events you planned when everyone showed up? How did that make you feel? Have you ever planned an event and sent out invitations, but no one came? What did you do then? Write some of your experiences here:

_____

_____

_____

Read Matthew 22:3–4. Underline the response of the invited guests in verse 3, and circle the last two words describing the event in verse 4.

The context of this story suggests Jesus had history in mind as He told it. He was in Jerusalem at Passover, and the religious leaders challenged Him openly. They knew He was telling stories with them in mind (Matt. 21:45). This story of the invited guests refusing to accept the king's invitation is similar to the religious leaders' current refusal to accept Jesus as the *Christos*. It was comparable to the rejection of the prophets and the messages God gave them to tell of His coming. Jesus summarized the history of God's relationship with His people and their rejection of His Sent One to them.

Every Kingdom parable has a singular message, but the details help make it clear. In this story, the king equates to God who hosted a banquet for His Son, Jesus. His "servants," God's prophets, went to let those who were invited in the Old Agreement through Abraham, Isaac, and Jacob to come celebrate His Son. However, they refused (v. 3). The king sent out more servants or messengers to let them know everything was prepared for a typical wedding banquet, but none responded (v. 4). God sent out prophets including John the Baptist

to say the celebration was ready. The invited religious leaders refused to accept His invitation.

How would you feel if you were the king and your guests refused your invitation? Since this is a metaphor of God inviting His people to accept His invitation to celebrate His Son, how do you think God feels about people's rejection of His invitation to trust Jesus is His Son? Write some of your thoughts here:

_____

_____

_____

29.3 Joining God

Most of us do not intentionally reject God's invitation to join Him in what He is doing in His-story to rescue

all people to Himself. When reminded that our lives count most when we serve God's purposes, we agree and momentarily look for ways to participate in God's work around us. However, most days we get lost in work, family activities, hobbies, and entertainment. We miss hearing God's promptings and seeing His work around us. We want our lives to count for things spiritual and eternal, but we get so caught up in physical and temporal things that we miss the other. We miss so much while doing so little.

Evaluate your life currently. Would you say you are aware of God's guidance in your life and make adjustments to serve Him? Do you spend more time on things immediate and wonder how God could ever use you in His plans? Write your evaluation here:

_____

_____

Read Matthew 22:5–7. Underline the responses of the people to the king's invitation (vv. 5–6) and also the king's response to their actions (v. 7).

The first group ignored the king's invitation and went on with their lives as farmers and businessmen (v. 5). There is nothing inherently wrong with their choices. People are supposed to make a living and care for their families. The problem occurs when making a living gets in the way of finding life. These invitees gave up a chance to feast with the king by choosing to work their chosen jobs and eat at their own tables.

Another group was invited to the banquet, but they seized the king's servants and killed them (v. 6). Why guests would do this is a mystery except that it runs

consistent with history when God's prophets were captured and killed. (For examples, see Nehemiah 9:26, Jeremiah 2:30, and Jesus' own words in Matthew 23:29. The servants represented the king whom the guests had decided to no longer honor.

In reacting to the last group's horrific response to a dinner invitation, the king exercised his power and authority and had their town destroyed (v. 7). Their acts of murder signaled a deeper issue of rebellion; the king would not tolerate such sedition. Some commentators believe Jesus was foretelling the destruction of the Temple in A.D. 70. The king's actions are similar to the landowner's actions toward his tenants in Matthew 21:40–41.

The invitees' responses to a king's request seem odd. How has your work or outright rebellion kept you from saying yes to God's invitation to join Him in things spiritual and eternal? Ask God to show you these things in your life, and how you and I are like those in the story who said "no" to the king.

29.4 Being Part of God's Kingdom

One characteristic of Jesus' Kingdom is that it is not always made up of those we expect to be there. Jesus continually challenges our ideas of who is "inside" and who is "outside" God's acceptance. History includes God's sovereign choice of Israel to bring His rescue mission to all people. Jesus is the Promised One sent by the Father to fulfill every requirement of righteousness that God commanded of Israel. Through Jesus' sacrificial death, burial, and Resurrection, all people have access to God's rescuing love. As we will see in the biblical story called The Acts of the Apostles, God led Peter and Paul to fulfill Jesus' "Great Commission" (Matt. 28:19–20) and to carry the message of Jesus beyond the boundaries of the Jewish nation to all people groups. Jesus' story of the king commanding his servants to invite "anyone you find" parallels God's call through the *Christos*.

When you look at those you know who are clearly captured by God's love, does it surprise you that they are part of God's family? What is unique about their lives that tell you God has done a special work in their hearts? What about your own story? Write some of your observations here:

_____

_____

_____

_____

Read Matthew 22:8–10. Summarize what the king did in this part of Jesus' story. Underline verse 9, the Memory Verse for this lesson.

The king made a surprise move in response to his invited guests' refusal to attend the banquet. He sent his servants into the streets to invite anyone they found (vv. 8–9). All the people were his subjects. Those he had invited were too busy or rebellious to accept the king's invitation to his son's wedding banquet. The king widened his invitation to include all people, not just his invited guests.

The servants obeyed the king and went out into the streets and gathered "both good and bad" and filled the banquet hall to capacity with guests (v. 10). Now that the invited guests had said no to the king's invitation, the banquet was opened to any and all who would attend. The servants recruited people from the streets, not just the respected places.

This part of the story reflects Jesus' invitation for all to join Him in His Kingdom. The religious leaders rejected Him as the Messiah, so He turned to tax collectors, prostitutes, and Samaritans to fill the empty spots at His Kingdom banquet. The "good and bad" replaced the "invited" guests at the banquet. Jesus' story reflected what was happening before the very eyes of those who heard it.

Jesus' story told of how His Kingdom was open for all people, both "good and bad." Who are some "good" people you expect at the wedding banquet of the King? Who are some people others could label "bad" who clearly have said yes to the King's invitation? Write their names and your feelings toward them here:

_____

_____

_____

29.5 Wearing the Right Clothes

I like the current relaxed attitude toward formal wear in churches. When I began as a pastor in the late 1980s, suits were required of all church leadership and expected of members. When someone came into the sanctuary in casual clothes, he or she stood out among the well-dressed assembly. Now, the opposite is true. When a person or family comes to our church dressed in anything other than casual attire, people notice. We know they are first-time guests and offer to help them feel at home, although we all can see they are over-dressed for the occasion.

Have you ever visited another church or went to at an event and instantly realized you did not get the memo on how to dress? Describe the event and your feelings.

_____

_____

_____

Read Matthew 22:11–13. Underline how the king addressed the guest and what set this guest apart from the others. Compare Jesus' description of what the king did with the man to Jesus' words in Matthew 13:42, 50; 24:51; 25:30. What does this image depict in Jesus' stories?

_____

_____

_____

One guest accepted the king's open invitation but showed up improperly dressed for a wedding banquet. The king condemned him and had him cast out into the darkness of the evening to spend with those who refused the first invitation. "Wedding clothes" in this story can represent something similar to how the Apostle Paul described our new life in Christ. He wrote that trusting Jesus and following Him through baptism is "like putting on new clothes" (Gal. 3:27, NLT). The man in the story came to the banquet but had not dressed in a way to honor the king. By not making the effort to dress appropriately, the man indicated he did not respect what it meant to say yes to the king's invitation. Therefore, the king judged him accordingly. Saying yes to the King's invitation means accepting the responsibility of making adjustments in life to show you are headed to the banquet.

Read Matthew 22:14. Circle the words "invited" and "chosen."

Jesus ended His story in a surprise. He explained that everyone is invited (called) but few are chosen (elected). These words of Jesus have caused great discussions in churches and seminaries over the centuries. (Examine a reliable commentary to learn some of the several inter-pretations of this verse.) For our purposes, Jesus' words are clear in the context in which He spoke them: many were invited to the banquet but those who actually sat down to the meal were few in comparison. Compare this with the history of God's invitation to all people to trust Him. The number who actually "clothe" them-selves in His way of life is much fewer in number than those invited. The same will hold true for eternity.

Read the story through again without stopping. Prayer-fully ask God's Spirit to guide your heart to the parts of the story that apply to your life today. Record some of the things He reveals to you in the space below.

_____

_____

_____

For further study:
- **Luke 14:16–24**
- **Galatians 3:26-29**

30—Pursuing Those Far from God: The Parable of Lost Things

We have what is called an Amber Alert system in America that is designed to notify all law enforcement, transportation, and news agencies in order to find an abducted or missing child. This system was put in place after a tragic abduction and murder of a nine-year-old girl named Amber who lived in Arlington, Texas. Now a nationwide organization is in place to help find and recover missing children. One child's death provided a way that others would not have to suffer the same end.

Jesus taught that His mission was "to seek and to save what was lost" (Luke 19:10). He was God the Father's one-person alert system to find those who were spiritually lost. Since Jesus' mission was to the lost, you would expect His stories and actions to reflect that mission. His actions toward Nicodemus (John 3), the Samaritan woman (John 4), and Zacchaeus (Luke 19) show how He sought out the lost and rescued them. Jesus' parables recorded in Luke's story of Jesus (chapter 15) tell of His love for the lost. Like Matthew 13, Luke 15 is a collection of Jesus' parables that explain why He came and whom He sought to reach. Jesus told of a lost sheep (vv. 3–7), a lost coin (vv. 8–10), and a lost son (vv. 11–32) in this chapter. Each story ends with a celebration of the found object. We will look primarily at the story of the lost son, his waiting father, and his jealous brother, and hear Jesus' heart as He pursued those far from God.

The Memory Verse for this chapter is Luke 19:10. This verse is in the context of Jesus' blessing of Zacchaeus. It is a form of Jesus' mission statement as God's Servant-Leader. He came "to seek and to save what was lost."

Our question to consider for this chapter is "How far can a Christian sink into sin?" Read the story of the lost son.

30.1 Welcoming Sinners

Several years ago I had the opportunity to have one of my books translated into Chinese. I had gone to mainland China twice, so I was excited about having the message of servant-leadership after the model and teaching of Jesus in the language of those who served the church there. A Chinese friend had translated the book, and we had taught it together there. The only problem was that the publisher asked that I pay for the first printing. I did not have the money at the time for such a project. I went to my father and asked if he would provide half the money for the first printing, and I would provide the other half. My mother and father had gone to China, too, and knew the potential of training so many followers of Jesus to lead like Jesus. They graciously gave me the money, and the book is in print today.

When have you gone to your parents to ask for money? What were the circumstances, and how did they respond? Record your memories here:

_____

_____

_____

Read Luke 15:1–2. What prompted Jesus to tell the stories of lost things? Read Luke 15:11–32 in one sitting. Circle the story's three main characters. What would you title this parable? Write your answers here:

_____

_____

_____

_____

_____

The three "lost" stories about a sheep, a coin, and a son were prompted by the religious leaders' dismay that Jesus "welcomes sinners and eats with them" (v. 2). They reasoned that if He was the *Christos*, then Jesus surely would not break their rules about becoming ceremonially unclean by touching and being with "sinners." Jesus disregarded the religious barriers the "Pharisees and the teachers of the law" had created to separate the righteous and the unrighteous. Jesus had a reputation among the religious insiders for preferring the outcasts over themselves. Jesus told these stories to help them see why He as the true *Christos* had come.

Read Luke 15:11–12. Underline the father's reaction to the younger son's request.

The third of Jesus' stories in response to the religious leaders' criticism of Him begins with a son's request for his portion of his father's estate (v. 12). This was not completely uncommon in Jesus' day, and the son's request would not have raised any eyebrows. The father, who had already allotted what part of his estate would be bequeathed to each son, gave the younger son his portion without comment or question.

This story is not an allegory—a story in which each of the details directly represents something else. The actions of the characters are the focus of this story, not the characters themselves. Be careful not to equate the father to God and the son to you or the older brother to a fellow church member. Jesus told the story to help the religious leaders see why He "welcomes sinners and eats with them."

30.2 Squandering Money

My first year in college was a disaster for me financially. Although my parents had shown me how to manage money, the temptations to live beyond my means at the university almost broke us both. Someone was always saying, "Let's go to a movie" or asking, "Anyone want to go get something to eat?" Friends seemed to always be doing something that cost money. Soon my allowance for food and necessities was gone. I overdrew my account so many times the bank knew me by my first name when I called to make arrangements to put more money in my account. It was not pretty. I am grateful for my parent's patience while I learned to live within the money I had to spend.

When in your life did you find yourself living beyond your paycheck or resources? Was it a time of rebellion or just good times? Did you ever "hit rock bottom," as the cliché goes? Describe your situation(s) here:

_____

_____

_____

Read Luke 15:13–16. Describe in your own words the progression of the son's demise in the "distant country."

_____

_____

_____

Like any young person with wealth and no rules to guide him or her, the young man in Jesus' story traveled to a "distant country" and began to live it up (v. 13). As anyone who has lived that way before learns, no amount of money lasts forever. The son spent all of his father's estate. To top that off, a famine hit the country where he partied (v. 14). His hunger drove him to hire himself out to a pig farmer. He became so hungry he would have eaten the pigs' food if someone had given it to him (vv. 15–16). Picture this: a son of a very wealthy man taking care of religiously unclean animals in a foreign country. Every advantage he had back home had been squandered in his desire to live a life of his own.

Wealth and undisciplined freedom are a curse without maturity. The son's actions were probably not evil, just typical of a young man who had too much money and no discipline. This is why we in America see so many young film, rock, and sports stars struggling with life when they seemed to have the life everyone wants. If freedom from controls and unlimited wealth are life's highest goals, then what we see in celebrity gossip magazines, television shows, and Web sites will sadly continue.

To what extent are unlimited freedom and wealth a part of your life? How can those be advantages and how can they be hindrances to a life as a follower of Jesus? Ask God to give you a loving heart rather than a judgmental one for those who find themselves in the son's situation.

30.3 Yearning for Home

Between my freshman and sophomore years of college, I sold books door-to-door for about four weeks. A friend had recruited me to join his sales team. As soon as the semester ended we headed off to Nashville, Tennessee, for sales school. After a week of memorizing sales talks, we drove to Terra Haute, Indiana, rented a room, and started knocking on doors. One of my worst emotional fears is rejection by anyone. No amount of training and encouragement from my sales team leader could buffer me from the no's I received daily. It was not long before I called my father, who was a manager at a refinery back home, and asked him if I could get a job with him for the rest of the summer. Living at home and going to work with my dad every day had to be better than knocking on doors nine hours a day. The reality of how good I had it back home soon replaced the thrill of adventure and the promise of living on my own.

Have you ever given up what you thought was a great plan and gone back home when things did not work out the way you planned? What were the circumstances and what made you drop your plans and go home? Write some of your experience here:

_____

_____

_____

_____

_____

Read Luke 15:17–19. Underline the first phrase in verse 17. Circle the word "sinned" in verse 18 and the phrase "no longer worthy" in verse 19.

The first phrase in verse 17 can be literally translated, "having come unto himself." One day the son woke up, "came to his senses," and realized the farmhands back home on his father's farm had it better than he did. He rehearsed in his head and heart his true feelings. He would tell his father he had "sinned against" him, and that by his actions he was "no longer worthy" to be his son. He would feel happy to get treated like one of his

father's hands if his father would allow him to return home. The son's confession in the story is similar to the confession those far from God must make in order to return to Him.

Read Luke 15:20–21. Underline the first phrase in verse 20 and the verbs that describe the father's actions when he saw his son returning.

Repentance without action is only guilt. The son in the story stopped planning his trip home and started that way. The surprise in the story is the father's reaction to the son's return. He clearly looked for him regularly because "while he was still a long way off" the father ran to meet his son (v. 20). Rather than scolding or advising, the father had "compassion" for his son. This is the same word for the Samaritan's compassion for the man on the road (Luke 10:33) and the compassion Jesus had for the multitudes who were like sheep without a shepherd (Matt. 9:36). The father ran to embrace his lost son who had returned home.

Meditate on both the father's and son's feelings as they embraced. Ask God to show you the son's repentant heart and the father's compassionate heart.

30.4 Welcoming a Loved One Home

We have a family in our church whose son served in Iraq during the war. The first time he was coming home from the war, they invited people over to a house filled with food and friends to celebrate their son's safe return. Signs stood in the yard, and everyone waited in anticipation for him and his father to come home from the airport. Shouts, hugs, and tears flowed from everyone as they greeted the beloved son who had returned home from war. During the festivities, the family paused to say thanks to God for their son's safe return and for the families of those who had lost a son or daughter in the battles. Few experiences match the emotions and anticipation of a loved one coming home.

Have you ever been part of a reunion like this one? Describe the experience and your emotions here:

_____

_____

_____

_____

_____

_____

Read Luke 15:22–24. Underline in verse 24 the reason the father wanted to have the banquet and circle the word "celebrate" where it occurs in the verse.

The father ignored the confession of his repentant son. He immediately put a robe on him, put a ring on his finger to signify his status as a son, and put new sandals on his traveled feet. He then instructed his servants to prepare a feast to celebrate his son's return (vv. 22–23). What was the reason for his joy? He said, "This son of mine was dead and is alive again; he was lost and is found" (v. 24). His words are reminiscent of the line in the 19th century hymn "Amazing Grace:" "I once was lost, but now am found." The son who was lost came home; the father wanted to celebrate.

Without asking what the son had done with his money, the father threw a party. He cared more about his flesh and blood than his estate. His extravagant expression of joy resulted in a celebration that signaled the worth of the lost son's homecoming. The theme of this story is the compassion and celebration of the father at the son's return. Celebration over finding a lost sheep and a lost coin are the themes of the previous two stories from Jesus. God rejoices when one of His lost children comes home. Jesus had come to seek the lost and rejoice when they were found.

The Memory Verse for this chapter is Luke 19:10. Jesus said this at the home of Zacchaeus, an infamous tax collector in Jericho. It was Jesus' mission statement as God's Servant-Leader who came "to seek and to save what was lost." Jesus' mission lines up with this story of a father's love for a found son. Learn this verse to remember why Jesus came as the *Christos*.

Christos—God's Transforming Touch

30.5 Life Does Not Always Seem Fair

There were two sons in Jesus' story. The father and repentant son teach us of a waiting father's love expressed in celebration. The elder son in the story reveals the heart of many who question why our Heavenly Father would be so forgiving of one who acted so irresponsible and rebellious. Surely living right and keeping the rules counted for something?

Read Luke 15:25–28. How did the older brother respond to the sounds of celebration at the house? Underline what the father did when he found out his son's feelings about the party.

As the older brother came in from the field, he heard party sounds coming from the house. He asked a servant what was going on. After learning that his bratty brother had returned and his dad had thrown him a party instead of throwing him out, the older son pouted and refused to join the fun (vv. 25–28). But the father loved the older brother just as he loved his younger son. He came out and explained to him why he did what he did.

Read Luke 15:29–32. Describe the older brother's feelings in your own words in the space below. Underline the father's answer to him (vv. 31–32).

_____

_____

_____

"It's not fair" was the older brother's response to the party. He had done his duty and his job, and Dad had never thrown a party for him. Even worse, his little brother spent his part of the family wealth, broke all the moral laws, and he still got the goods! "It's not fair." Again, the patient, loving father explained that while all he had was his older son's too, he was compelled to celebrate his lost son's return. We never hear if the big brother ever joined the party.

Remember why Jesus told the story of the lost things? (See Luke 15:1–2.) Whom do you think Jesus was thinking about when He added the response of the older brother? How was the older brother's attitude toward the father's love and celebration like those of the Pharisees and scribes who criticized Jesus?

_____

_____

_____

The story of the "Prodigal Son" is a story of a son who lost his way and a loving father who embraced the son who returned home with a repentant heart. It is a story of a jealous older brother who refused to join the celebration because his pride insisted the father was not fair in his actions. It is a story of each of us—we are the lost son and the jealous older brother when we are prideful, and we are the loving father when we act like Jesus.

Who are you in the story today? Do you need to repent and go home? Do you need to forgive and embrace a lost child? Do you need to give up your pride and celebrate the return of those who have a change of heart and come to the Father? Take some time to ask God to reveal the depths of Jesus' story and heart to you today.

For further study:
- **2 Corinthians 2:5-11**
- **Hebrews 4:14-16**

31—Understanding God's Grace: The Parable of the Vineyard Workers

Grace is an odd concept in a world of wages and rewards. We have grown up in a capitalistic economy in which we receive pay for work. Ideally, the more work we do, the more pay we get. That is how we accumulate wealth. This way of thinking has infiltrated religion as well. We sense that the more good we do, the more God will bless us; and the more bad we do, the more God will punish us. We see everything—both in the world and in the Kingdom of God—as *quid pro quo*, or one thing in return for another. But Jesus continually challenged that way of thinking and surprised both His followers and His enemies with a different economy.

This Kingdom story about a vineyard owner who hired and paid workers is sandwiched between two similar stories of Jesus. When the disciples asked how they were to get into the Kingdom after the rich young ruler walked away, Jesus said, "But many who are first will be last, and many who are last will be first" (Matt. 19:30). Jesus then told this story. After finishing it, He said, "So the last will be first, and the first will be last" (Matt. 20:16). We can conclude that the story we will soon study has something to teach about how following Jesus can change our view of "first" and "last" and how God treats all of us with His grace.

The Memory Verse for this chapter is Romans 2:11. The verse simply states, "God does not show favoritism." Read the context of the verse in Paul's Letter to the Romans. This truth supports what Jesus taught His disciples through the story of the vineyard workers.

Our question to consider for this chapter is "Is God fair?" Check out a newspaper, news Web site, or cable news show. Based on these sources, what would be your first answer?

Christos—God's Transforming Touch

31.1 Finding a Job

One summer when I was still in high school I worked in a field that grew boxwood plants for a nursery. The field was in the rice-producing lands outside Beaumont in southeast Texas. Needless to say about that part of the world, the amount of humidity in the air often matched the air's temperature. My only job was to walk down each row of eight-inch-tall plants and chop weeds away from them. This was so that other workers could come in later and dig the plants up, place them in pots, and sell them to individuals and builders. It was a lonely, miserable, meaningless job. So why did I do it? Same reason many young men take a job like that in high school: I needed the money for my car and dates.

What jobs have you worked simply because you needed the money? Was the work hard and pointless? Share your experiences here:

_____

_____

_____

_____

Read Matthew 20:1–2. Underline the familiar introduction: "the kingdom of heaven is like." Circle the main character of the story and the word "denarius."

Try to look past the chapter divisions and headings in your translation of the Bible. See how this story of Jesus follows directly after His encounter with the rich young ruler and His dialogue with His disciples about riches and entering His Kingdom. We know this is one of Jesus' vision-casting parables about His Kingdom by the introductory phrase: "the kingdom of heaven is like."

Once again, Jesus used a story from everyday life to explain a reality about His rule and His Kingdom. Remember, too, that the story is a simile in the context of the discussion about how people enter the Kingdom. It is not an allegory in which we try to match the details of the story with the things of God. Jesus told this parable to make one main point. Our job is to discover that point.

Jesus told a simple story with a setting and characters common to His hearers. A landowner wanted to hire workers for his vineyard. He went out and found some day laborers and agreed to pay them a day's wage, which is the meaning of a denarius (vv. 1–2). The action of the story has begun. We wonder where Jesus is going with this story.

Read the entire parable through once or twice. As in lessons past, have someone read or tell you the story so you can hear it like the disciples heard it. What twists in the story surprised you the most? What questions does the action of the landowner raise for you? Write some of your thoughts here:

_____

_____

_____

31.2 Hiring Workers

Do you recall the 1993 Oscar-winning film *Schindler's List*? It is the story of German businessman Oskar Schindler who saved the lives of Polish Jews during the Holocaust. Schindler did this by spending his fortune employing Jews in his factories and bribing German military officials to protect the Jewish men, women, and children on his "list." This moving portrayal of a man who gave all his money in order to save the lives of others paints a picture of God's love for us.

If you have seen the film, what scenes moved you the most? What do you think motivates a person to do such a selfless thing?

_____

_____

_____

Read Matthew 20:3-8. Underline the different times the landowner went out to hire workers. Circle the word "right" in verse 4, and underline how the owner wanted the workers to be paid in verse 8.

From early morning until an hour before sunset, the landowner went out about every three hours and hired workers to work in his vineyard. There does not appear to be any urgency to hire the number of workers he hired. His simply seemed interested in giving the men in the marketplace work. He graciously offered a second group whatever was "right" if they would go to work for him (v. 4). Another interpretation for "right" in this verse is "fair" (MSG). The owner promised a fair wage for their work. They accepted his offer (v. 5).

He did this three more times. At the end of the work day, men were still standing around in the marketplace waiting for work. The owner wanted to know why they had been there all day, and they said no one had offered them any work (vv. 6–7). They were willing to work, but had no opportunity to do so until the owner offered them a job. Finally, at the end of the day, the owner

had the workers line up to be paid, "beginning with the last ones hired and going on to the first" (v. 8).

The owner clearly had the means and the desire to give the men of his town jobs, so he continually went out and hired them. He promised the first group a day's wage and the second group "whatever is right." He simply told the last groups to go to work. The owner graciously employed those who did not have jobs.

In what ways are the landowner's actions like God's actions toward us? What would you have felt if you were one of the men invited to work? Have you ever been in this situation? Ask God to give you a heart like that of the landowner who hired those who did not have jobs although he apparently had no pressing need to employ them.

Christos—God's Transforming Touch

31.3 Paying Workers

Much of my writing is under a "work for hire agreement." That means I write for a publisher, who pays me an agreed upon amount and owes me nothing more for my work—even if a million copies are sold. The agreement usually means the publisher owns what I have written and can publish it in almost any form that best benefits the publishing company. As a writer, you go into the contract knowing this and sign it because you are happy for the opportunity to write and have your thoughts put in print.

Once I signed such an agreement for a certain amount of money. I completed the project and waited for the check to come in the mail. When the check came, I opened the letter looking for the amount I had agreed to in the contract. I looked a second time. The check was twice the amount of the agreement. Something must have been wrong. I called the publisher, and he said they had looked at my work and felt it was worth twice the contract amount; so they doubled my pay. I thanked him and God for the undeserved experience of grace.

Have you ever received more than you had agreed to work for? In what form did it come? Did others know about it? What did they say or do? Write some of your feelings here:

_____

_____

_____

_____

Read Matthew 20:9–12. Underline in verse 12 the complaint of those who worked all day.

The landowner lined his employees up in order of those who worked the least to those who had labored all day, and paid them all. Those he hired last received a day's wage, a denarius. Those who worked longer were promised "whatever is right" and also received a full day's wage (v. 9). That was definitely more than the "right" promised to them. When it came time to pay those who had worked since early morning, they expected more than the others; they received the same amount (v. 10).

Every one of the workers was surprised by the owner's payment; especially those who worked all day. How could it be fair for those who worked only one hour to receive a full day's wage and they received only the same amount? They complained the owner had made the one-hour workers equal to those who had "borne the burden of the work and the heat of the day" (v. 12).

The surprise payments by the owner created joy for those who did not deserve it and anger for those who thought they deserved more when they compared themselves to the others. Jesus made the point that it is not when we get in the Kingdom that is important. The important thing is that we are in the Kingdom. The undeserving got more than they deserved. The all-day workers got what they were promised. Everyone was "equal" in the owner's eye.

Put yourself in the place of the "one-hour" workers, the "whatever is right" workers, and the "all day" workers. How would you have felt when the owner paid you? Be honest and record your feelings here:

_____

_____

_____

31.4 Questioning the Landowner's Decision

"It's not fair," was one of our oldest daughter's favorite complaints while growing up. She felt convinced we were more lenient on her younger sister than on her. She married a "first child," too, and he has his own stories of favoritism for younger siblings. I admit we did let our youngest have a later curfew her senior year in high school than we allowed our oldest, but we tried our best to be fair to them both. If one complained about the unfairness of it all, we would simply resort to listing all the things we did for them and ask them how that was fair. That usually ended the discussion, but not the sentiment.

Did you have a brother or sister who you knew your parents treated better? How about an employer or teacher? Write some of your feelings and examples of unfairness here:

_____

_____

_____

Read Matthew 20:13–15. Circle the word "friend" in verse 13. Underline the owner's reasoning in verse 15.

The owner answered the complaints of the all-day workers by first calling the spokesperson of the group "friend." This revealed his benevolent heart and an understanding of their feelings. However, he reminded them he was not "unfair" to them because he had paid them exactly what he said he would pay them (v. 13). His desire was to pay the last hired the same as the first hired (v. 14). Here we see again how the last and the first hired to work are equal.

The owner then let those who complained know that it was his money they were grumbling about. He had a right to do with it as he pleased. How did they have the right to be envious about his generosity? (v. 15) The first hired were envious of the owner's generosity toward the last hired. The first got what they were promised, but they could not live with the fact that those who worked less received the same. The owner made it clear it was his desire to pay everyone equally. He could use his money to pay whomever he wanted.

Jesus wanted His disciples and the religious leaders to hear this part of the story. The owner's generosity was like that of His Father's grace given first to those He had chosen to "work" for Him. Those who were hired last in the "eleventh hour" received the same grace as those who served God for centuries. The first had become envious of the Father's grace toward the last.

How can you apply the owner's words to the grumbling workers to your understanding of God's love toward all people? What biases do you share with the grumbling workers? What do the owner's actions tell you about God? Write some of your thoughts here:

_____

_____

_____

31.5 Loving Everyone the Same

Growing up in church I thought Jesus' words "the last will be first, and the first will be last" was a promise that if I got at the end of the line it would be OK because somehow I would get to be first in the line. I spent a lot of time at the back of lines waiting to miraculously end up at the front. I soon discovered Jesus did not reveal a secret to getting ahead but the way in which God hands out His love. Our designations of first and last do not match how God sees things.

After Jesus finished His parable of the landowner and how he paid those he hired to work for him, Jesus said, "So the last will be first, and the first will be last" (v. 16).

Underline Matthew 20:16 in your Bible. The last will be treated equally as if they were the first.

This truth stands on both sides of this story. Jesus wanted His students to understand that God's grace, like the owner's wages, is given according to His desire and purposes, not as we value it to be given.

Our Memory Verse for this lesson is Romans 2:11. Paul wrote that God does not "show favoritism." In that context he wrote that God picks no favorites when it comes to His judgment (Rom. 2:5–10). The same is true of God's grace and love. Jesus' story in this lesson demonstrates this truth.

Our question to consider for this chapter is "Is God fair?" The answer to this question is a matter of perspective. The first hired in Jesus' story would say God is not fair. They worked all day and received the same pay as those who worked one hour. Like the older brother in the story of the lost son, some people think God is not fair because it seems those who live in sin and then at the last minute trust Him for their rescue get saved. However, if we will stop and consider God's gracious act of love toward us in His Son, then we would say God is

more than fair. We receive what He promised us when we trust Him. We, the last or least deserving, find that we will receive a full measure of God's grace.

Read through the story one more time. Then prayerfully ask God to help you understand what Jesus wants you to learn from this story for where you are in your life now. The point of the story is God's equal love for all. Ask God's Spirit to reveal this truth to you and to help you see and treat others as God sees them.

For further study:
- **Romans 3**
- **Deuteronomy 24:14–15**

32—Seeking God During Grief: Raising Lazarus

Death of a loved one is one of the deepest pains we must bear. The loss of a spouse, child, parent, grandparent, or friend covers our hearts like a wet fog, and we wonder if we can get up the next morning and continue our lives. How do you keep going without the one you loved so deeply? Grief that follows such a loss can be as debilitating as a disease. It can lead to depression and giving up on our own lives. We get through grief two ways. One way is to have another loved one at our side to love us and remind us of the reasons we still have to live. The other is to have hope—hope that death is not the end of our loved one's life nor our own. Some day we will be reunited with the person. Where does that kind of hope come from?

Since Jesus was the *Christos* who came to bring the Kingdom of God on earth, He had to deal with the one issue that plagues every human: death. He would show us He knew our fear of it and the grief that tortured those left behind. Jesus did just that when He raised His close friend Lazarus from the dead. This miracle is not only more evidence that Jesus is the Christ who brings eternal life to all who are dead in sin, but it also foreshadowed His Resurrection that would soon follow. Jesus is the hope that sees us through our grief.

The Memory Verse for this chapter is John 11:25. This verse records one of Jesus' "I am" sayings. Here He tells us He is "the resurrection and the life." If we trust Him we will have life even though we die physically. This is a key confession of our trust in Jesus as the *Christos*.

Our question to consider for this chapter is "Who can help me deal with my grief?" Think about a time when you pondered this question and what you discovered.

32.1 Arriving at a Funeral

When a loved one dies, we drop what we are doing and go to the family. We get a substitute. We change a flight. We call our boss to say we will not be in to work. Death disrupts our routine when it takes a loved one. We do whatever it takes to be near those who love the person when he or she is gone. This is why Jesus' response to the sickness and death of his close friend Lazarus seems odd at first. He waited until His friend died before He started toward the house where Lazarus' two sisters and friends grieved.

Read John 11:1–16 for the background to the events to follow. Read verses 17–20. Circle the number of days Lazarus had been buried and the names of his sisters.

By the time Jesus came to Bethany, the home of His close friends, Lazarus had been in the grave four days. The house was filled with friends who had come to grieve with Mary and Martha (vv. 17–19). Jesus had known about Lazarus' sickness days earlier but did not go then to heal His friend. Jesus told His apprentices, "This sickness will not end in death. No, it is for God's glory so that God's Son may be glorified through it" (v. 4). Later Jesus told them "Lazarus had fallen asleep;" He would go and "wake him up" so that He would be glorified through the miracle (v. 11). Jesus' followers began to use "fall asleep" to describe someone's death (1 Thess. 4:13). Jesus was not wrong in His prediction that Lazarus' sickness would not "end in death" because He knew He would "wake him up" and Lazarus would live.

As Jesus approached the house, Martha went out to meet Him while Mary stayed behind (v. 20). Jesus loved this family (v. 5), and Mary and Martha were significant players in the story of Jesus. Jesus taught us the value of being with Him above daily chores through His lesson to Martha (Luke 10:38–42). We know Mary as the one who sat at Jesus' feet in Luke 10 and the one who anointed him with expensive perfume, which Jesus said she did to prepare Him for His burial (John 11:2).

Which of the characters in this story do you relate to the most in your experiences with losing a loved one? What would you think or feel about a close friend who showed up four days after your loved one's funeral? Write some of your thoughts here:

_____

_____

32.2 Questioning Jesus

"If only . . ." is a phrase I sometimes hear when I am with someone who has lost a loved one after a long sickness. "If only the doctors had done . . ." "If only I had seen the signs earlier." "If only I had not listened when he told me he was OK." The game of "if only" drives us crazy trying to find a way to get our loved one back. However, death is permanent until Christ returns. The game of "if only" adds to our grief when we think we have discovered how we could have saved the one we love so that he or she could still be with us.

Have you ever wrestled with "if only" in the loss of someone you loved? Did it help or confuse you? Write some of your memories here:

_____

_____

Read John 11:21–24. Underline Martha's "if only" phrase in verse 21. How were Jesus and Martha talking about two different things? Write your answer here:

_____

_____

_____

Martha addressed Jesus as "Lord." She was not only His friend, but she had also come to trust Jesus as the *Christos*. This is why she told Jesus that if He had been present during her brother's sickness, Lazarus would not have died. Her "if only" was that "if only" Jesus had been there He could have healed him. Lazarus did not need to be dead now. We cannot hear the tone of her voice. It may have been one of disappointment and confusion as to why someone she knew loved them did not show up until four days after Lazarus' death. Jesus may have sensed her tone and assured her, "Your brother will rise again" (v. 23). Jesus referred to the miracle He was about to perform; Martha thought Jesus spoke of "the resurrection at the last day" (v. 24).

Sometimes we place all our trust in Jesus for the future. Like Martha, we trust Jesus is the *Christos*. We know that if He were present things would not happen the way they do. Our true trust is that He will help us "at the last day." We tend to think, "It will all be better in the end because Jesus will be there, but I sure could use His presence now!" Jesus so wanted Martha to know what was about to happen, but she could not see past her grief and disappointment in Jesus to hear His clear words that her brother would "rise again."

How are you like Martha? Do you ever say to Jesus, "If You had only been here . . "? Is your trust in Him mostly relegated to the future and eternity instead of the present? Do you trust His clear words for today? Write some of your answers here:

_____

_____

_____

_____

_____

32.3 Failing to Communicate

As I write, our country is in the primary stage of the elections leading up to the national conventions that choose the candidates for president in November. This year it is exciting to watch because the field of potential candidates is so diverse. As in any presidential race, those running make promises; the people will decide if they trust the candidates' words enough to elect them to lead. Every voter has a reason to want a certain candidate to win, and every candidate is happy to offer that reason. The moment of truth comes when the voter marks his or her ballot that says, "I want you to be president."

What is it about a local, state, or national candidate that causes you to vote for him or her? What is the deciding issue or factor that gives you the confidence to vote for that person? Write some of those important issues here:

_____

_____

_____

_____

_____

_____

_____

Christos—God's Transforming Touch

Read John 11:25–27. Underline or highlight Jesus' words to Martha that define who He is.

When Martha said she knew her brother would rise "at the last day," Jesus may have pointed to Himself and said, "Look at me. 'I am the resurrection and the life. He who believes in me will live, even though he dies; and whoever lives and believes in me will never die'" (vv. 25–26). Jesus said that resurrection was not some day but that He was the hope of resurrection. In Him exist life both now and eternally. The word for "believe" is best translated "trust." Belief in our culture tends to mean "belief in an idea or concept." The biblical meaning of this word is "to trust a person." Martha believed in a resurrection some day. Jesus wanted her to trust Him for that future day as well as for the present.

Martha's confession was like that of Peter's at Caesarea Philippi: "Yes, Lord . . . I believe that you are the Christ, the Son of God, who was to come into the world" (v. 27). Martha agreed with Jesus' revelation that He was who He said He was and that she would stake her life and eternity on Him.

Jesus' "I am" statement in verse 25 is our Memory Verse for this lesson and a core confession of our trust in Him as the *Christos*. Jesus' Resurrection is the linchpin to our trust in Him as God's Son. Without it Jesus is but another human who died heroically for others. But He revealed His uniqueness in His words to Martha. He confirmed them in His raising of Lazarus. He sealed their truth when God raised Him from the dead on the third day (John 20). Martha's confession becomes our confession when we trust Jesus at His word and observe the power of His Resurrection.

Take time to memorize Jesus' revelation of Himself as "the resurrection and the life." Is Martha's confession your confession of who Jesus is? Do you trust that He is the Son of God? If not, what things still cause doubt in your head and heart that Jesus is not who He revealed Himself to be?

_____

_____

_____

_____

32.4 Being a Humble Leader

Humility is the ability to give credit where credit is due. As a proponent of servant leadership, I believe in doing ministry in teams. Teams are more effective than individual effort in many ways. A servant-leader who leads a team is humble when he or she gives credit to the team for a job well done. Too many times a leader will accept the rewards and accolades of success without acknowledging those who did all the work to experience the success. This is a leader who has not made him or herself a servant-leader to the team. Humble leaders always acknowledge they are only as good as those with whom they serve.

Name a leader you know who willingly recognizes those who make his or her success possible. How are you like or unlike him or her? Write some of your thoughts here:

_____

_____

_____

Read John 11:41–42. Circle the name of the One Jesus gave credit to for what He was about to do.

After Martha's confession, Jesus made His way to the tomb of His friend Lazarus. On the way, Jesus cried (v. 35). He cried when He saw Mary crying with all those with her. They did not realize who Jesus was. He did not cry because He empathized with their grief. He cried because they still did not trust that He was the *Christos*; He was their hope and the power over death.

When Jesus went to the tomb, He stopped. Before He did anything, He acknowledged His Heavenly Father (v. 41). This was a common practice of Jesus. He did nothing without direction from the Father (John 10:14–18). Jesus acknowledged His Father before He fed the 5,000 (John 6:11). Jesus was humble and recognized His unique relationship with God the Father. Jesus thanked the Father for hearing His heart. (Perhaps Jesus cried tears of joy because at that moment the Father confirmed in His heart He would raise His friend from the dead.) Jesus said He knew that His

Father always heard Him, but He voiced the prayer so those who heard Him would "believe that you sent me" (John 11:42). Jesus wanted those who were about to see Lazarus come from the tomb to know that it was a work of God in Jesus, not a magic trick or anomaly of nature.

How often do you publicly give God credit for your success? Do you pray openly to ask God to help you and those with whom you work or play? Can others say they know you trust God for all that happens in your life? Whisper Jesus' prayer as your own and ask God to reveal Himself to you through it:

_____

_____

_____

32.5 Trusting Jesus

I have a friend who trusted Jesus to be "the resurrection and the life," not just for eternity but for now. One day a woman in our church died of an infection. We were at the hospital beside her and her husband when she died. We said a prayer of hope and thankfulness for her life, and then I suggested we all go to the waiting room while the nurses prepared the body of our friend. As we shuffled out of the room, my friend turned around, went back into the room, and closed the door. I turned and followed him in while the rest of the family went to the waiting room. My friend knelt by the bed and began to pray that she "wake up" and be healed so she could be the wife and mother God intended for her to be. For a moment, my faith was ignited and I sensed the possibility of her waking. I knew my friend and his absolute trust in Jesus and His Word. He continued to pray. I joined him, but after some time our friend remained unresponsive. As we rose to walk out he said, "I know God wanted to raise her. I don't know why He didn't."

Have you ever exercised that kind of trust in Jesus? What are your thoughts and feelings about my friend's actions? What have you done to demonstrate your absolute trust in Jesus and His Word? Write some of your thoughts here:

_____

_____

_____

_____

Read John 11:43–44. Underline Jesus' command to Lazarus in verse 43 and His instructions to the crowd in verse 44.

After giving witness to the Father, Jesus cried out in a loud voice, "Lazarus, come out!" (v. 43) The stone that covered the grave had been removed (v. 41). As soon as Jesus shouted His command, Lazarus came out dressed typical for someone who had been buried (v. 44). There was no mistake that he was the one they had buried. Jesus then told the crowd to unbind him from his grave clothes and release him to his family (v. 44).

The details of this event parallel Jesus' Resurrection. The stone rolled away from the tomb and the cloth covering Lazarus' face are part of Jesus' Resurrection story (John 20:1–7). Jesus clearly raised Lazarus from the dead to demonstrate His own Resurrection was possible. Remember, too, Jesus had already raised Jairus' daughter (Mark 5:22–43) and the widow's son at Nain (Luke 7:11–17). These, combined with the raisingof Jesus'

friend, pointed to Jesus as the *Christos* who is King over His creation and the very Son of God.

Of course, Jesus' Resurrection was different than these experiences. Jesus restored life to Lazarus and Jairus' daughter, but they died again. Jesus' Resurrection was different. He was raised to eternal life. And His Resurrection is the promise of Resurrection eternal life for us as well.

Our question to consider for this chapter is "Who can help me deal with my grief?" After observing this episode in the story of Jesus, we can see two direct answers to this question. Our trust that Jesus is "the resurrection and the life" gives us the hope we need to continue and the promise of seeing our loved one in Jesus. We also see that friends who walk through the valley of death with us are a gift from God to help us continue.

Thank God for sending Jesus to demonstrate His power over death and for the hope He gives us when we deal with our grief. Return to this story to see Jesus' compassionate heart for His friends and His purposeful actions to reveal who He is.

For further study:
- **Mark 5:22–43**
- **Luke 7:11–17**

33—Sacrificial Giving: Anointing at Bethany

Giving is an issue inside and outside the Christian community. Inside, members are challenged to give a portion of their money to the programs, ministries, and missions of the church. The weight of debt, salaries, and property maintenance send leaders out to raise funds to keep the organization afloat. Gifts become obligation, and giving as an act of worship falls off the joyful scale. Those inside the church need a dose of Mary of Bethany's heart for giving. Outside, skeptics of organized religion have a hard time with multimillion dollar facilities and budgets when poverty sits so near what appear to be edifices to personalities. Judas' complaint to Jesus fits their attitude.

Jesus was in Bethany during the last week of His life attending a dinner in His honor. Martha and Lazarus' sister, Mary, anointed Jesus' feet with expensive perfume and wiped His feet with her hair. Judas criticized the woman's wasteful action, which he said could have been used to help the poor. But Jesus defended Mary and proclaimed that her sacrificial action was done in preparation for His burial. Jesus blessed her gift and reminded Judas that the poor would always be present to receive his gifts.

The Memory Verse for this chapter is Proverbs 15:8. This ancient proverb reveals the reality that God prefers prayers from those who love Him over sacrifices from the wicked. Compare this proverb to Mary's gift and Judas' remark.

Our question to consider for this chapter is "Does God need anything we give Him?" God is complete in Himself, so the purely theological answer would be "no." However, gifts are tokens of affection and appreciation from the giver, and also a part of worship.

33.1 Throwing a Party

My father was able to retire early. To celebrate the event, his five children and their families hosted a dinner in Dallas. My mother and father drove six hours to get there, and my sisters came similar distances to join the celebration. We gathered in a private dining room, ate, shared stories, and heard again how God had made it possible for my parents to retire earlier than they had planned. My parents also took time to share their plans with us and invited us to join them as often as we could. It was a celebration of the passing of one stage of their lives and the beginning of another. I remember thinking how much the event had cost, but in the same nano-second I told myself it was still not enough to honor my parents who had given so much.

What dinners have you been part of that honored someone else? What was the occasion, and what part did you have in it? Was the expense worth the honor given? Write some of your thoughts here:

_____

_____

_____

Read John 12:1–2. Underline the places and people mentioned in the verses. Review where they were before and locate Bethany on a map.

Jesus returned to Bethany after He had raised His friend Lazarus from the dead. John, whose story of Jesus we follow here, marked the time as "six days before the Passover," the annual Jewish feast that commemorated God's deliverance of Israel out of Egypt. "Bethany was less than two miles from Jerusalem" (John 11:18), and

Jesus chose to stay with His friends during the festival season. The religious leaders had told the people in Jerusalem to alert them if they saw Jesus in the city. They wanted to arrest Him (John 11:57). This may be a reason why Jesus chose to stay outside of the city.

John set the scene by identifying the house as the one "where Lazarus lived, whom Jesus had raised from the dead" (v. 1). That was all the address the followers of Jesus needed in those days. Everyone knew where the man "Jesus had raised from the dead" lived. John also told us that the family had prepared a dinner in Jesus' honor one evening (v. 2). Mary and Martha continued to be grateful for Jesus' act of love that resurrected their brother and wanted to honor him with a meal. John noted that "Martha served," which was consistent with her personality. Remember how, in Luke 10:38–42, she let her "love language" of service distract her from sitting at the feet of Jesus? John also wanted us to know that Lazarus was healthy and "among those reclining at the table" with Jesus.

A grateful family hosted a dinner to honor Jesus, their friend and the *Christos*. Prayerfully step into the biblical setting and hear the celebration with laughter and stories of people who not long before were mourning the death of one of those sitting among them. Ask God's Spirit to let you feel the joy that surrounded Jesus when tensions were so high in the city.

33.2 Giving Gifts

The single most expensive gift I have personally given my wife was a dishwasher. Yes, a dishwasher. Her birthday is December 25, so I thought I would combine her Christmas and birthday gifts and give her something really nice. We needed a dishwasher. I shopped for, purchased, and had installed an expensive dishwasher without her knowing it until she came in from work that day. Let me just say I let her pick out the next expensive gift. We agreed that the big gifts in the future would be agreed upon before I purchased them.

What was the most expensive gift you have given to your spouse or a friend? How was it received? How did it improve your relationship? Write your experience and the reason for the gift here:

_____

_____

_____

Read John 12:3. Underline what Mary poured on Jesus' feet. Read similar accounts of this event in Matthew 26:6–13 and Mark 14:3–9.

Mary, the sister of Martha and Lazarus, is the one who sat at Jesus' feet in Luke 10. Martha served (v. 2), and once again Mary placed herself at the feet of Jesus. While Jesus and the guests reclined at the dinner given in His honor, Mary poured about a pint of expensive perfume oil on Jesus' feet. The gift was substantial. John noted its worth to show the value of Mary's gift. Normally, a small portion was poured on a person's head to honor him or her. (Psalm 23:5 gives a similar picture.) Mary poured the entire amount on Jesus' feet. This was a sign of her humility toward the One she honored. She wiped the excess oil from His feet with her hair, and the "fragrance of the perfume" filled the entire house.

Mary not only gave a costly gift to Jesus, but she also offered it in a way that honored Him, not her. Like the unnamed woman in Luke 7, Mary approached Jesus while He reclined and stood at His feet to show her appreciation and honor of Him. She worshiped at His feet and served Him by wiping His feet with her hair. Humility, not pride, was in her heart that night. While Martha's "love language" was service, Mary's was gifts.

Gifts are tangible tokens of the heart. We give them to show a person how much we appreciate or honor him or her. Gifts are part of worship and have been since God taught His people how to worship (Deut. 16:16– 17). Bringing a gift to honor God is an act of worship that costs you something. Mary's gift to Jesus was very expensive. It may have been something she cherished quite highly. She gave it all to Jesus in an act of worship.

What is the most costly gift you have given God in worship? Do not write it down, but recall what motivated you to give it and how you felt after you had given it. If you have not given a costly gift to show your

Christos—God's Transforming Touch

appreciation and worship of God, list the reasons you have not and ask God to guide your heart in this matter.

33.3 Resenting the Gift

In the middle of Mary's tender act of worship, one of the disciples blurted out that they could have sold the perfume and used the proceeds to feed many poor people. I have heard similar arguments from members of churches who wonder why we spend so much on (pick a topic) and not give more to the poor. There is a fine line between investing in things to equip and build up the church and serving the needs of people in our mission field. This has always caused tension in churches.

What are some of your thoughts on this matter? How do you balance what you spend to care foryour family with your investment in serving the needs of others? Write some of your thoughts here:

_____

_____

_____

_____

Read John 12:4–6. Underline the name of the person in these verses. Circle the words "betray" in verse 4 and "thief" in verse 6.

Mark observed that "some of those present" questioned Mary's actions. However, John singled out "Judas Iscariot, who was later to betray him," as the one who raised the objection (v. 4). Judas asked why something "worth a year's wages" could not have been sold and the money given to the poor (v. 5). Those who are self-promoting always try to make themselves look better than the truly humble. Who could disagree with such a worthy notion? Mary's act was viewed as less valuable after Judas offered this other option.

John, the writer of this story of Jesus and a disciple of Jesus, was present at this event. He was the only disciple who followed Jesus all the way to the cross (John 19:25–27). He knew all the disciples well. He had been with Jesus from the beginning of His ministry until His return to heaven. He knew Judas, and he freely stated that Judas' comment was not "because he cared about the poor but because he was a thief" (John 12:6). How did he steal? John added, "as keeper of the money bag, he used to help himself to what was put into it." Judas served as the treasurer of the group, and he freely took for himself what he wanted from the group's resources. While Judas' statement seemed noble, his character was not.

Compare Mary's actions and apparent motives with those of Judas. Mary never spoke but worshiped Jesus. Hers was a humble act of giving an expensive gift and wiping His feet with her hair. Judas did nothing but speak of what sounded like a nobler deed.

Which of the two are you most like? Be honest. Do you criticize others and offer greater ideas with no cost to yourself? Or would you more likely take something you highly value and invest it in a worshipful act to Jesus?

_____

_____

_____

_____

_____

33.4 Defending Mary

I have four sisters. I was the second child born to my family. Growing up, occasionally one of my sisters would come home from school and tell me what someone had said or done that hurt her feelings. "Go beat him up" was her request. None of the offenses were worthy of such action, so I never had to exercise my big brother authority on their classmates. Still, I know I would have taken up for my sisters if the occasion warranted it.

Are you a big brother or sister in your family? Did you ever defend a sibling because he or she asked you to? Or did you ever have a brother or sister take up for you? Write your experience here:

_____

_____

_____

Read John 12:7. Underline Jesus' response to Judas and why Jesus said Mary had "saved" the perfume.

Like a big brother protecting his sister from a bully, Jesus answered Judas immediately and told him to leave Mary alone (v. 7). The story does not indicate that Judas spoke directly to Jesus. His comment could have been offhanded and thrown out into the room for all to hear. Jesus, however, took the comment as if directed to Him. He did not tolerate the remark of Judas. He knew Judas had not only stolen from the group but also would eventually betray Him to the religious leaders. There was no place for insincere remarks that discredited genuine acts of worship in His Kingdom.

Jesus then explained why Mary had taken the actions she did. The wording of the sentence is difficult in light of what had just happened. We could interpret Jesus' words as "It was intended that she should save this perfume for the day of My burial, but she chose to use it now to worship Me." Mark recorded Jesus' words in his story of Jesus as "She poured perfume on my body beforehand to prepare for my burial" (Mark 14:8). Judas saw her actions as wasteful. Jesus saw them as prophetic and a "beautiful thing" (Mark 14:6).

Spend some time putting your self in Mary's place in the story. How would you feel if, when you gave a gift worth a year's wages to Jesus, some pious person said it could have been used for a better purpose? How would you feel at Jesus' defense of your actions? Write some of your feelings here:

_____

_____

_____

_____

33.5 Honoring Jesus

One characteristic of a Christ-follower is that he or she cares for the poor. A criticism of American Christians is that they spend more on themselves than on those in need. One way we have tried to meet such needs at our church is through a Helping Hands fund. We use those funds, which are given freely by the membership, to help people in our network of relationships with everything from utility bills to car repairs. We have also partnered with our school district to serve the needs of some in a student-age parent program and an after-school care program. These partnerships have led to opportunities to know and serve others in the name of Jesus.

What contact do you have with those in need? What does your church do to serve them? How does your family participate in the lives of others to serve them in the name of Jesus? List your responses here:

_____

_____

_____

_____

_____

Read John 12:8. Circle the words "poor" and "me."

Judas wanted to sell Mary's give and give the money to the poor. Jesus put that comment in perspective when He quoted an Old Agreement law that everyone in the room would have recognized. He reminded them, "You will always have the poor among you." They knew the rest of the word from God: "Therefore I command you to be openhanded toward your brothers and toward the poor and needy in your land" (Deut. 15:11). Caring for the poor was to be a lifestyle of service for all of God's people. If everyone had followed God's instructions, there would be no need to sell Mary's gift.

Jesus then put the situation in perspective when He said, "but you will not always have me" (v. 8). In light of His death, Mary's gift was justified. Jesus was among them only as long as it took to accomplish His mission of laying down His life as a ransom for many. The poor had been with them, and would remain with them until He returned.

Jesus was not belittling the needs of the poor by His comment. Jesus directed his response to Judas who tried to discredit Mary's gift in light of Jesus' coming death, burial, and Resurrection. Jesus talked about the poor because Judas brought up the topic. Jesus genuinely cared for them when He reminded the group of God's command "to be openhanded" to them.

If you had been in the group that saw Mary's gift, heard Judas' criticism, and heard Jesus' response, what would you have felt and concluded from the event? What lasting impression of that dinner to honor Jesus would have stuck with you? Use the Memory Verse, Proverbs 15:8, for some insight on this. Write some of your thoughts here:

_____

_____

_____

For further study:
- **Matthew 26:6–13**
- **Mark 14:3–9**

34—Practicing Authentic Worship: Triumphal Entry

Jesus told the Samaritan woman that the day would come "when the true worshipers will worship the Father in spirit and truth" (John 4:23). There would be no need for places of worship, priests, or traditions. The Father seeks those who "worship in spirit and in truth" (John 4:24). When Jesus entered Jerusalem for what turned out to be the final week of His life on earth, the people who saw Him riding on a donkey spontaneously began to worship Him. They sang a psalm, covered His path, and waved palm branches over His head. They were not in a place of worship but standing along a road. They were not dressed for worship but in everyday clothes. They did not follow the prescribed liturgy for worship but sang and shouted what was on their hearts. They authentically worshiped the Coming King.

Jesus' entry into Jerusalem recorded in Luke 19 marked the beginning of the end of Jesus' mission on earth.

That week's activities resulted in His death, burial, and Resurrection. His choice of a colt that had not been ridden and the songs and praises of the people signaled the King's humble entry into the bastion of religious authority and power. The people praised the King while the religious leaders plotted His death.

The Memory Verse for this chapter is Isaiah 29:13. This verse is Isaiah's condemnation of the people's worship in his day. The people on the road who worshiped Jesus represent authentic worship. Learn the Old Agreement verse to evaluate your own worship habits.

Our question to consider for this chapter is "How can I make sure my worship is genuine?" Become familiar with the Memory Verse and how the people worshiped Jesus when He entered Jerusalem, and then you have a place to start.

Christos—God's Transforming Touch

34.1 Dreading Opposition

Several years ago I led a meeting at our church that would define the direction we would take for years to come. As part of updating our constitution and bylaws, more than one item had become a point of contention between those who wanted to ratify the changes and those who did not. While I always seek a win-win situation in decision-making, the leadership team and I knew there were about four issues that could not be compromised; those issues were the focus of the meeting. It was scheduled for a Sunday evening, and everyone knew it would be a long, hard family meeting. My point is not the meeting, but the dread and uncertainty that led up to the actual meeting. I so wished I would get sick or that an "Act of God" would stop it from happening. None of that happened. After weeks of prayer, preparation, and communication, we entered the auditorium to address the issues.

Have you ever dreaded or wished you did not have to attend a meeting or event, but it was your job or responsibility to do so? What was the situation and how did you feel leading up to the encounter? Write some of your thoughts here:

_____

_____

_____

_____

Read Luke 19:28. Underline the place Jesus was going.

Jesus was in Jericho outside Jerusalem at the house of Zacchaeus (Luke 19:1–10). There He told the story of a returning king who judged his servants for how they managed his assets while he was away (Luke 19:11–27). This story is similar to the one recorded in Matthew 25:14–30. Jesus told this story to answer the expectations "that the kingdom of God was going to appear at once" (Luke 19:11). He told the story in graphic detail that ended in reward and punishment. Such a story would cause its hearers to decide whether the servant had done what the king desired.

Luke described Jesus as leading His followers by using the phrase, "he went on ahead" (Luke 19:28). As in Mark 10:32, Jesus led His future servant-leaders in the Kingdom toward Jerusalem. The religious leaders had already put the word out that if anyone saw Jesus, he or she must report to them so they could arrest Him (John 11:57). Jerusalem would be the location for the clash of His Kingdom of Heaven and the kingdom of religious law. Jerusalem was the city of David, which held the seats of both Israel's ancient kings and the "mercy seat of God." Jesus led His followers there as He promised He would. They must have wondered if His predictions of what would happen would come to pass there, too.

Put yourself again in the place of the disciples as they came near Jerusalem. They felt the tension in the air and knew what could happen if a spark lit the fire of disagreement between Jesus and the religious leaders. What did they feel? What would you have felt? Would you have followed Jesus into the city?

_____

_____

_____

_____

34:2 Following Instructions

Every day with Jesus brought fresh encounters with God. One day He stopped a storm on the sea. Another day He turned and told His apprentices to feed 5,000 people. Later, He sent them out two-by-two to heal, teach, and meet the needs of anyone they met. Following the *Christos* and trusting His words must have been challenging in so many ways. Excitement, confusion, and fear mingled together to make faith a living reality for those closest to Jesus. They learned to trust Him no matter what He said to do—whether or not they knew His reason.

Which instructions that Jesus gave His disciples would have challenged your trust in Him the most? Can you get a feel for how the disciples felt by this time in His-story to have the confidence to do without question whatever He asked them to do? Record some of your thoughts here:

_____

_____

_____

_____

Read Luke 19:29-32. Underline the places identified in the verses and underline Jesus' instructions to the two sent to get the animal. Read the parallel accounts in Matthew 21:1–3 and Mark 11:1–3.

As Jesus approached Jerusalem He made a peculiar request of His followers. Near the towns of Bethany, the home of Lazarus, and Bethphage, He sent two of His followers to find "a colt tied there, which no one has ever ridden" (v. 30). They were to untie it without asking permission. If asked what they were doing, they were to say, "The Lord needs it" (v. 31). Without question, the two went ahead of the group and found the colt just as Jesus had said (v. 32).

What was Jesus up to in His instructions to His disciples? Matthew, who quoted more of the Old Agreement prophecies than any other writer of the story of Jesus, reminded us that the prophet Zechariah had told Israel, "See, your king comes to you, gentle and riding on a donkey, on a colt, the foal of a donkey" (Matt. 21:5; Zech. 9:9). Jesus purposely chose to ride into Jerusalem on a colt that had not been ridden. It was a sign that announced His kingship and demonstrated the kind of king He was.

Put yourself in the place of the two unnamed disciples. By this point in His-story, would you have trusted Jesus enough to go without question to retrieve the colt? Had you seen enough to trust Him or would you still be questioning His identity?

_____

_____

_____

_____

34.3 Celebrating Jesus' Arrival

My wife was a cheerleader sponsor for four years at the senior high school where she taught. Every year the school would put on a small homecoming parade that highlighted the football team, cheerleaders, band, and homecoming court. The route was about a half mile, and it ended in the gymnasium where the pep rally was held. There were not so many people at the beginning of the parade, but by the time it got to the school, the streets were lined with people of all ages. The sounds of the band and honking horns brought people out of their houses to see what the noise was about. The parents and friends of those in the parade combined with those curious about what was happening in their neighborhood made for a large, lively crowd.

Does your local high school have a homecoming parade? How big is it? Does the school advertise it, or do people know by word of mouth? Describe the event here:

_____

_____

_____

Read Luke 19:33–36. Underline in verse 34 the disciples' response to the owners' question and what the people did in verse 36 as Jesus approached the city.

The disciples did exactly what Jesus said (v. 33). When they were asked by the owners of the donkey what they were doing, they said exactly what Jesus told them to say, "The Lord needs it" (v. 34). They then brought the colt to Jesus, put their coats on it as a sort of saddle, and lifted Jesus onto it (v. 35). Maybe they had begun to understand what Jesus was doing since they put Jesus, the King, on the donkey themselves. Kings have servants who do that sort of thing.

As Jesus continued toward the city, other people joined the disciples who walked beside Him. Someone laid a cloak on the ground for the donkey bearing the king to walk upon and soon "a very large crowd" began to lay their cloaks on the road in front of Jesus (Matt. 21:8).

Matthew and Mark added that others cut palm branches and laid them on the road (Matt. 21:8; Mark 11:8).

The closer Jesus got to the city gate, the more people gathered to see what was happening. Like a parade that starts with a few at its beginning and swells as it moves along, the number of people who gathered to honor the Coming King grew. Jesus rode toward Jerusalem as the gentle and humble king promised by the prophets, and the people responded by honoring Him as their King.

Join the crowd on the side of the road as Jesus passed. You probably heard from a friend Jesus was on His way into the city. You wore an outer cloak and stood under a palm tree such as grew everywhere. What would you do? Ask God's Spirit to show you some of the joy and anticipation felt by those who stood along the road.

34.4 Worshiping Jesus

Our confession of worship at my church is "God created me to live a life of worship in response to who He is and what He has done for me." Worship is a lifestyle that can happen wherever we are because the Holy Spirit dwells within us. Worship can be in the form of anything that is done to honor God. We can worship while we hold an infant or sing aloud as we drive. We try our best to help people see that what we do on Sunday mornings is only one of many ways that we worship God. You need no building, choir, or preacher to worship. These things may enhance and focus your experience, but worship comes from the heart in response to God's grace and goodness, no matter the setting or props.

How do you describe worship? Recount one or two experiences where you spontaneously responded to God's presence and grace outside the gathering of the church in a building.

_____
_____
_____
_____
_____

Read Luke 19:37–38. Circle the words "praise God" in verse 37. Underline the song from the Old Agreement the people sang in verse 38.

Luke tells us that as the road turned toward the Mount of Olives, "the whole crowd of disciples began joyfully to praise God in loud voices for all the miracles they had seen" (v. 37). The response of worship was joyful praise. The object of worship was God. The reason for worship was "all the miracles they had seen." The people spontaneously worshiped God in response to what Jesus had done for them through the miracles. Luke noted the crowd was made up of disciples, those who had been with Jesus when He performed His signs and miracles.

The crowd's praise included a phrase from a song they knew by memory. Psalm 118 was a song of praise to God as King and included the words the people shouted, "Blessed is he who comes in the name of the LORD" (v. 38; Ps. 118:26). They shouted and sang other sentences of praise: "Peace in heaven and glory in the highest!" Matthew and Mark recorded that the people shouted, "Hosanna," which means "save" and called Jesus "the Son of David" (Matt. 21:9; Mark 11:9). The people worshiped Jesus as the Coming King and Messiah whom they longed to know.

Read the three accounts of the people's response in Matthew 21:9, Mark 11:9-10, and Luke 19:37-38. See how Jesus helped them see and worship who He truly is by finding and riding a donkey. How does this event help your trust in Jesus as the *Christos*?

34.5 Praising Jesus as King

While the people praised Jesus as the Coming King, the religious leaders approached Jesus as an intruder. While the people called upon Jesus to "save," the religious leaders insisted Jesus shut down the parade of praise. While the people laid down their cloaks and palm branches to honor the King, the religious leaders mocked Him by calling Him "Teacher." The contrast of praise and resistance was stark that spring afternoon outside Jerusalem.

Christos—God's Transforming Touch

What other differences do you see when you read the the religious leaders' response to Jesus' ride to Jerusalem?

_____

_____

_____

_____

Read Luke 19:39–40. Underline Jesus' response to the Pharisees' insistence that He make the people be quiet.

The religious leaders did not like the people's worship-filled response to Jesus. For many reasons they did not want the Jesus movement to grow. One reason was because such outbursts of worship did not fit into the prescribed methods they had supported. Our Memory Verse for this chapter is Isaiah 29:13. This passage is God's condemnation through His prophet of the people's worship in Isaiah's day. God described their worship this way: "They honor me with their lips, but their hearts are far from me. And their worship of me is nothing but man-made rules learned by rote" (NLT). The religious habits of the Pharisees who told Jesus to stop the praise and worship parade fit that description.

Our question to consider for this chapter is "How can I make sure my worship is genuine?" One way to answer this is to compare your worship habits to the worship of the people who praised Jesus and to the worship described by the prophet Isaiah.

Luke is the only writer who recorded this confrontation. John mentioned that the religious leaders threw up their hands and said something like, "There's nothing we can do. Look, everyone has gone after Him" (John 12:19). Jesus answered their insistence that He make the people be quiet by saying, "if they keep quiet, the stones will cry out" (v. 40). Jesus, the Creator, rode into Jerusalem not only to rescue the people but also to restore His creation (Rom. 8:19–22) and eventually bring "new heavens and a new earth" (Isa. 65:17; Rev. 21:1). Jesus knew that if His creatures stopped praising Him, His creation would pick up the chorus!

Jesus did not just come to save us so we can go to heaven some day. He called us to change how we live, for the Kingdom of Heaven is at hand. His ride to Jerusalem signaled He was nearing the place and time that the Kingdom and King would rule.

End your time with this episode in the story of Jesus by writing your own praise to Jesus. Let this time be a time of evaluation by God's Spirit and a time of celebration of Jesus. If you like, physically sing or lay down a coat on the floor to honor the present *Christos*. Let your praise be authentic and spontaneous.

_____

_____

_____

_____

_____

_____

For further study:
- **Matthew 21:1–11**
- **John 12:12–19**

35—Overcoming Hypocrisy: Jesus and the Pharisees

The number one complaint about Christians I hear from those who are far from God remains, "They are a bunch of hypocrites." Pick a topic, and those I talk to seem to think our actions do not match our words. For example, they ask why some Christians support a costly war and claim to love everyone. Or why the divorce rate among Christians is the same as for everyone else. I have heard many questions as evidence that those far from God have little confidence in those who say they know God. Why? Because those who wear the title Christian seem so unchristian to them.

Jesus did not show anger often. However, He was red-faced angry when He confronted the religious leaders in His final week on earth about their hypocrisy. Their leadership not only put a burden on the people by weighing them down with religion, but they also led the people away from seeing Jesus as the *Christos*. Let us be

honest. The religious leaders would not have called Jesus was not nice in the Sermon of Woes in Matthew 23. Yet His love for the people and His frustration with the obstinate religious leaders produced a scathing report of their leadership and a lesson to all who may say one thing and do another in the name of God.

The Memory Verse for this chapter is 1 Peter 2:1. Peter admonished his readers to rid themselves of "hypocrisy" since they had been "purified . . . by obeying the truth so that you have sincere love for your brothers, love one another deeply, from the heart" (1 Pet. 1:22). This verse warns against the sin of religious hypocrisy.

Our question to consider for this chapter is "What is an authentic person?" Jesus' message to the religious leaders helps answer this question. Observe Jesus' confrontation with the leaders and then return to answer the question.

35.1 Exposing Temple Worship

An integer is a whole number that is not a fraction. The word comes from the Latin word which means whole. Integrity comes from the same word and refers to being whole, complete, or sound. A whole number is an integer. It is not divided. A person of integrity is a person who has an undivided, or sound, character. He or she is the same person in public as in private and can be trusted to be honest no matter the situation or question. This person is not divided between his or her words and actions. This person is whole.

Who do you know whom you can describe as a person of integrity? Write the person's name and list examples as to why you would describe him or her that way.

_____

_____

_____

_____

Read Matthew 23 in its entirety. Note each time the word "woe" is used.

This is a pivotal episode in Jesus' last week before His death, burial, and Resurrection. In it He confronts the hypocrisy of the religious leaders who sought to kill Him and who led the people away from Him. We will not cover all of His complaints; but in order to understand the ones we do study, we need to know the full context of His message.

Reread Matthew 23:1–4. Underline whom Jesus addressed and whom He spoke about. Underline verse 3 as the heart of His message.

After Jesus entered Jerusalem (Matt. 21:1–11), He went to the Temple. There, He became incensed over the abuses of the money changes who converted public currency into Temple money in order to worship there (vv. 12-13). He threw the money changers out. He healed people in the Temple and began an ongoing debate with the religious leaders who sought to discredit Him before the people. Matthew 22 records a parable and several debates with the leaders who came up to Him in the Temple. It is in the middle of these confrontations and debates that Jesus turned "to the crowds and to his disciples" (Matt. 23:1).

Jesus did not seek to abolish the leadership God had established for His people. Jesus affirmed that they "sit in Moses' seat" of authority (v. 2) and that the people "must obey them and do everything they tell you" (v. 3). The problem Jesus had with them was that they were not men of integrity. They said one thing but acted in another way. Jesus would have none of it. He said they "tie up heavy loads and put them on men's shoulders, but they themselves are not willing to lift a finger to move them" (v. 4). They loved to tell people what to do—especially what God said to do—but they did not love or serve the people by showing them how to live as God taught.

"Practice what you preach" is a cliché in some circles. It comes from Jesus' judgment in this passage. How do you apply this truth to your life? Would you consider yourself a person of integrity? Ask God to reveal where you are "whole" and where you are "divided."

35.2 Deciding Whether to Tithe

My wife and I tithe. We have since we got married over 30-plus years ago. We have tried to model this spiritual habit for our children and their families without making it a matter of their standing with God. We also ask the leaders of our church if they tithe. Not all of them do, and we seek to encourage them to exhibit their trust in God by giving a portion of their wealth as an act of worship to invest in people and projects that yield eternal value.

How do you view tithing? Do you have friends you talk to about the practice? What is your church's teaching on the practice? Write some of your insights here:

_____

_____

_____

_____

Read Matthew 23:23–24. Circle what Jesus called the religious leaders and underline "the more important matters" the leaders neglected (v. 23). Underline the second title Jesus called the leaders and write in your own words what He meant by the images in verse 24.

_____

_____

_____

Jesus said "woe" to the religious leaders. This term can also be interpreted "what sorrow awaits you" (NLT). These verses represent the fourth "woe" Jesus gave to the leaders. In this indictment, He called them hypocrites, or play actors, because they set aside a tenth of the spices they used on their food to show their devotion to the Old Agreement laws (Lev. 27:30; Deut. 14:22–23). They tithed the tiny pieces of "mint, dill and cummin" but did not practice the more important parts of the Law such as "justice, mercy and faithfulness" (Matt. 23:23). (Also read Micah 6:8, which mentions the important matters of the Law.) It was easier to count out spices at a meal than to show real people godlike justice, mercy, and faithfulness. Jesus said they "should have practiced the latter, without neglecting the former" (v. 23). Tithing matters, but treating people with a heart like God matters more.

Jesus called the leaders "blind guides" (v. 24). This was an oxymoron such as, a "wise fool" or a "pretty ugly" person. They were like blind men leading a tour of the city when it came to the things of God. Leviticus 11:4 and 23 did not allow God's people to eat camel or gnat-like insects as food. These leaders strained their water for gnats but sat down to a meal of camel! How could anyone follow their example?

It is easy to accept Jesus' criticism of the religious leaders' inconsistencies and say, "how terrible of them."

Christos—God's Transforming Touch

What about us? What practices are in line with the "law" of religion but prevents people from trusting Jesus? Take some time to allow God's Spirit to examine your heart as you hear Jesus' words in a new way.

35.3 Having a Clean Heart

Dressing up and going to church while paying workers unfairly during the week are signs of a divided life. If I tell people I follow Jesus yet gain my profits on the backs of workers who live in sub-standard housing and have little to eat, I have made a mockery of my faith. To look like I trust Jesus on the outside while living for myself on the inside is idolatry and gives those far from God another reason not to trust Jesus.

What have you witnessed or done yourself that is similar to the examples listed above? Why is it so easy to look religious, yet live so irreligiously? Write some of your observations here:

_____

_____

_____

Read Matthew 23:25–26. Circle the words "outside" and "inside." Summarize Jesus' complaint to the religious leaders in your own words.

_____

_____

_____

In this "woe" and the "woe" that follows Jesus identifies the heart of hypocrisy. Our English word *hypocrisy* comes from the Greek theater and means "to play act." Greek actors wore different masks to play different characters in the play. Hypocrisy is wearing a mask to play a part different from who you really are. The outside mask covers the true identity of the one acting.

Jesus decried the religious leaders' practice of super holiness when they kept their cups ceremonially clean on the outside but left the inside filthy. Like tithing dinner spices, these experts of the Law looked holy beyond the religious traditions. However, Jesus pointed out that the inside of their clean cups were "full of greed and self-indulgence" (v. 25). He was telling them to clean the inside of their hearts and the outside would be clean, too (v. 26).

Jesus had already taught in answer to the question of eating food with unwashed hands that "the things that come out of the mouth come from the heart, and these make a man 'unclean'" (Matt. 15:18). (Read Matthew 15:1–20 for the full story.) Our hearts are the issue, not our religious practices. Jesus did not come to reform religion. He came to change our hearts.

According to Jesus, how did the teachers of the Law and the Pharisees "play act" or wear masks,? What are some contemporary practices of religion that make it easy to wear a mask of piety while having a heart dedicated to "greed and self-indulgence"? Ask God's Spirit to examine your heart in these matters and to lead you to repentance and change.

35.4 Exposing the Religious Leaders

As a pastor I have served many families during the death of a loved one. Families have different priorities when it comes to caring for a loved one after he or she dies. Some embalm and put the body in an airtight casket, encased in a sealed crypt with a big headstone. Some cremate the body, while others cannot afford much more than a cardboard casket placed in a shared grave. At the graveside, some family members leave after the last prayer while others stay until the graveyard workers have lowered the casket and covered it with the pall-bearers' flowers and some dirt. We all cover the fact that the body of the person we love will eventually decay and, as God said, "dust you are and to dust you will return" (Gen. 3:19).

What are your feelings and thoughts about how you want your family to care for your body when you die? What is your attitude toward your body in light of your relationship with God in Christ Jesus? Write some of your thoughts here:

_____

_____

_____

_____

Read Matthew 23:27–28. Underline the object to which Jesus compared the religious leaders (v. 27). Underline what Jesus said was "inside" the leaders (v. 28).

Jesus continued His indictment of the religious leaders for their outward appearance not matching their inward motives by comparing them to "whitewashed tombs." Once a year near the time of the Passover Festival, the graves were painted with a white chalk so that the pious—especially the priests—would not become ceremonially unclean for the festival (Num. 19:16). Although the graves looked clean and freshly painted

on the outside, rotting and decay still lay on the inside. This reality was the basis of Jesus' metaphor for His judgment of the leaders (v. 27).

Jesus applied His image to the religious leaders by the fact that they appeared on the outside as "righteous," or clean by following the religious Law. But on the "inside," they were like the dead bodies in the graves. They were "full of hypocrisy and wickedness" (v. 28). The word for "wickedness" actually means "without law." While they looked like they kept the law by their clean outward appearance, they actually did not keep the intent of the law by their inward motives, which Jesus had mentioned previously (v. 25).

Jesus continued His rant against the leaders of religion by exposing their hypocrisy of looking like righteous Law keepers when they lived lawless lives. We may think of this as hideous or the worst kind of sin among religious leaders. In fact, we see examples every year of a publicly known religious leader who is exposed for private sins. But before we point our fingers at them, Jesus' words apply first to us. Anyone can look religious, but no one can hide a wicked heart forever. Jesus would not tolerate a divided life of righteous appearance and private lawlessness.

Listen to Jesus' words again and sit in the presence of God's Spirit. Allow Him to expose the things you allow in your private life but cover up in your public life so others will see you as "righteous." Do not pray for others. Pray for yourself. Pray that you will never be what Jesus called a "whitewashed tomb."

35.5 Warning Jesus' Followers

Peter was Jesus' closest follower. After Jesus' death, burial, and Resurrection, he became the leader of the Jesus movement. When he was in prison in Rome toward the end of his life, he wrote to those who trusted that Jesus was the *Christos* to help them be like Jesus. You would expect that some of Jesus' teaching would show up in his letter. The Memory Verse for this chapter is 1 Peter 2:1. Peter told his readers to rid themselves "of all malice and all deceit," and "hypocrisy" since they had been "purified . . . by obeying the truth so that you have sincere love for your brothers, love one another deeply, from the heart" (1 Pet. 2:1; 1:22). Peter was present when Jesus fired off seven rounds of "woes" at the religious leaders. When he wrote the Christians in Asia Minor, he remembered Jesus' words. He instructed those who claimed to be Jesus' apprentices to make sure they were people of integrity and to remove all "deceit" and "hypocrisy" from their lifestyles. Peter passed on a Kingdom value that should govern every heart that has been given to the King for His service.

Our question to consider for this chapter is "What is an authentic person?" We know from Jesus' confrontation with the religious leaders what an authentic person is not. If we could use one word as a synonym for authentic from Jesus' teaching it may be "whole," or "one." Jesus did not like the fact that the religious leaders looked one way on the outside while living another way on the inside. He hated their divided lives and insisted they be whole, or leaders of integrity.

Jesus taught His followers an important Kingdom value in His heated indictment of the religious leaders. While the message was initially for them, His closest follower Peter reminded all of Jesus' apprentices to rid their lives of all hypocrisy. No play acting allowed. No masks welcome. Honesty and integrity are the highest values among God's people.

The easiest response to Jesus' words is, "Not me. That's _____ (fill in the blank with a name)." But we all live with some appearances, and we all can justify them in some way. Ask Jesus to make you a person of integrity. Be obedient to follow what He puts in your heart to do in order to make that happen.

For further study:
- **Matthew 22:15–46**
- **Matthew 23:1–36**

36—Preparing for the Apocalypse: Signs of the End Times

In the early 1970s Hal Lindsey's *The Late, Great Planet Earth* swept across America and brought the message of the end of the earth to life for many. In the mid-1990s it was Tim LaHaye and Jerry Jenkins' *Left Behind* series that captured the imagination of people around the world as they, too, made the cryptic message of the Revelation of John a reality for modern minds and hearts. The popularity of these books and the innumerable articles, books, Web sites, and radio talk shows that followed demonstrate that in a world of chaos, terror, and war, everyone wants to know how history will end.

Jesus' disciples wanted to know the same thing. Since Jesus was the *Christos* and had come to set up His Kingdom, surely He would know the timetable to the end. He could explain it to those whom He called as servant-leaders in His Kingdom. His-story as recorded in the Scriptures had a clear and purposeful beginning.

The disciples wanted to know if it had the same kind of ending. Jesus taught His disciples the signs of the end times, but He cautioned them not to guess an exact time for it to happen. He instructed them instead to be ready at all times for His return. Jesus' words were filled with mystery and warning for His followers. One message is clear in Jesus' words about the end: Keep watch and be ready because any day could be the day of the King's return.

The Memory Verse for this chapter is Matthew 24:42. This verse sums up Jesus' message about the end times and His return. Make it the source of your hope that His-story will end as He has written it.

Our question to consider for this chapter is "When do you expect Christ to return?" Walk through Jesus' teaching on this topic.

Christos—God's Transforming Touch

36.1 Expecting the End

Every story has an ending. Sometimes when reading a book, I am tempted to turn to the last chapter to see what happens. Usually the ending resolves conflict between the main character and a nemesis or ties the loose ends of subplots and minor conflicts together into a nice package. Some endings are predictable, while others come as a surprise. Some endings I hope for, others I regret. When the end comes, the story is complete. The end of the story most often answers the questions raised in the story or explains the paths the storyline took after it began.

How does your favorite story end? Do you like it because it was what you hoped for, or was it something unexpected? When in the story did you anticipate the end? Did you ever look ahead to see what would happen? Write some of your thoughts here:

_____

_____

_____

Read Matthew 24:3. Circle the word "this" and underline the phrases "sign of your coming" and "the end of the age."

Jesus left the Temple courts and led His disciples to the Mount of Olives. On the way, He told them that not one stone in the Temple would be left on the other (v. 2). When He finally sat down with His disciples, they wanted to know when "this" (the destruction of the Temple) would happen and what would be the "sign" of His coming as King with "the end of the age" they were in (v. 3). What followed is Jesus' description of the end

of His-story. We get our theological word *eschatology*, the study of end times, from the Greek word for "the end," *eschaton*.

Read Matthew 24:4–8. Circle the phrase "watch out" in verse 4 and underline verse 8.

Jesus answered their questions in a straightforward manner. He spoke of concrete events and situations, but He never said when they would happen. He first told them to "watch out," which is the theme of His answer to them (v. 4). He warned them that others would come and claim to be the *Christos*. These others would deceive many into believing them (v. 5). We know from the history that followed that there were those who claimed to be messiahs and tried to throw off the Roman rule only to fail in the end.

Jesus then told His students that "wars and rumors of wars" and "famines and earthquakes" would happen, but "the end is still to come" and these events would be only "the beginning of birth pains" for the end (vv. 6–8). These were some of the "signs" of "the end of the age" before Jesus' coming as the King.

Jesus pointed out hints to the end of history for His disciples. As a follower of Jesus, what current events can you say Jesus may have had in mind as "signs" of His coming? List some examples here:

_____

_____

_____

_____

_____

_____

36.2 Enduring to the End

Often things get worse before they get better toward the end of a story. The hero is wounded or a lover is betrayed. A villain appears to gain the upper hand or disease looks like it will destroy the strong. The one we thought would survive to the end is written out of the storyline, and we are left trusting lesser characters to finish the plot. Someone believes a lie and acts as if it were true, or high school sweethearts end their marriage of 25 years. A good story is built off of a real story—like the one Jesus lived and foretold to His disciples.

Go back to your favorite story. What happened just before it ended that made you wonder how it would end or whether the main character(s) would survive? What other twists happened that made you curious about the end? Write some of your memories here:

_____

_____

_____

Read Matthew 24:9–14. Make a list of things Jesus said would happen before "the end will come." Underline that phrase in verse 14.

Jesus continued to list what would happen that would signal "the end." He warned as He had before that His followers would "be persecuted and put to death" (v. 9; Matt. 5:11–12; 10:17–20) and that this would be the sentiment of "all nations" before it was all over. We can read in the Acts of the Apostles about both persecution and death of Jesus' disciples (Acts 5:17–18; 7:54–60). We can also read about Christian martyrs in today's newspapers.

Betrayal, false prophets, and deception will be hallmarks of the day (vv. 10–11; 2 Pet. 2:1–3). Wickedness will increase and disciples' love for Jesus "will grow cold" (v. 12; Rev. 2:4). But there will be signs of hope, too. Jesus foretold that "he who stands firm to the end will be saved" at the end, and that in the middle of all this the message of His Kingdom will be told throughout the entire world as a witness to all people (vv. 13–14). When all of this is taking place Jesus said, "the end will come." Jesus promised an end to history, and He provided evidence as to when the ending would come.

Some have tried to attach specific times to the conditions Jesus outlined for His disciples. Some have pointed to the perceived increased number of wars, famines, and earthquakes today as evidence of nearing the end. Others have made an effort to tell the story of Jesus to every nation through satellite networks or missionary experiences so that when "all nations" have heard, the end will come. Still others have pointed to increased wickedness, violence, and persecution of Christians around the world as sure signs that Jesus' coming is at hand.

What things do you personally point to as signs that Jesus' words to His disciples are relevant to our world today? What hope or fear does His promise of endurance give you? What do you feel about the Good News of His Kingdom being preached to everyone? Record your answers here:

_____

_____

_____

_____

_____

Christos—God's Transforming Touch

36.3 Expecting the End of the Age

One event in a story usually marks its end. Lovers embrace and promise their love forever. Long lost friends are reunited to celebrate finding one another again. A sick one is healed, an enemy defeated, someone becomes pregnant, or father and son are reconciled over lifelong differences. Wars end or new adventures begin. A story can end in many ways. To write an ending, the author must let the reader know without a doubt that the final event or conversation ends the story he or she is trying to tell. All the plot lines converge in the event, and there is no question this story has reached its climax. Jesus described the final event that would end history. When His disciples saw this happen on the pages of history, they could be certain it was the end.

What were the final event(s) in your favorite story that let you know the story had ended? Did the good guys win? Was love restored? What happened? Answer here:

_____

_____

_____

Read Matthew 24:30–31. Underline the phrase "the Son of Man" that occurs twice in verse 30. What will the Son of Man send His angels to do? (v. 31)

_____

_____

Up to this point, Jesus had given a list of signs that signaled the end of the age and His coming was near. In verse 30, Matthew records "the sign" that will let Jesus' students of eschatology know this was the end. The Son of Man will appear in the air, "coming on the clouds of

the sky, with power and great glory." Everyone will see Him coming, and they "will mourn." Why mourn? Jesus' coming will bring not only His eternal presence but also His judgment over a fallen creation and sinful creatures. Those who do not know the King or have not expected His return will mourn that they had not prepared.

Jesus continued to spell out the clear sign of His coming in the end. He told His disciples that He would send His angels or messengers to "gather his elect" from all over creation. His coming would be an ingathering of those He has chosen as His own. "Elect" means "to be chosen" and is a title in the written letters of the New Agreement given to Christ-followers (Titus 1:1; 1 Pet. 1:1). At His return, Jesus will gather to be with Him those chosen by Him through their trust in Him.

This final sign of the end of the age and of Jesus' coming is affirmed in Paul's earliest description of Jesus' coming (1 Thess. 4:16–18). Jesus will return in the sky for all to see, at the sound of a trumpet and the presence of attending angels, for the purpose of gathering His people to Himself. Both Jesus and Paul's words confirm this as the sign of the end. While some may wonder if the end is near; no one will question when it happens.

How does this teaching of Jesus strengthen your trust in Him as the *Christos*? When He comes, do you trust you are one of "the elect" because you have trusted Him as your Rescuer and Leader? If He came today, would you mourn with those who saw the Son of Man in the sky but did not know Him? Ask God to give you the confidence to wait expectantly for Jesus' return.

36.4 Looking for the End of the Age

Predicting the end of time has become a rather large industry. Books and articles, television and radio shows, and multimedia Web sites abound with information that promises to point you to the proximity in your lifetime of the *Christos*' return. Just type *end times* in an Internet search engine and you will find links to sites that list today's headlines, world events, and leaders, along with explanations of biblical passages that supposedly fulfill Jesus' predictions of the end. You can buy DVDs, books, and pamphlets, and go on "end time" tours to help you know when the end will come.

What have you read or depended upon to help you know when Jesus will come? If you do not read about the topic, how would you describe your attitude and faith about His coming? Record your convictions here:

_____

_____

Read Matthew 24:36–41. Underline verse 36. Circle the word "as" in verse 37.

After Jesus told His disciples how history would end, He warned them not to try and guess when it would end. Jesus taught them not to worry about tomorrow but to seek first His Kingdom. Then all the other things, including His return, would follow (Matt. 6:25–34). Jesus revealed a secret of when He would return—only God, the Father, knew the exact time in His-story when the Son of Man would come and the age would end (v. 36). Some manuscripts add that "not even the Son" knows that time. What Jesus provided were evidences the end was near and what the end would look like when it occurred.

What are we to assume it will look like when Jesus does come? Jesus said it would be just like "in the days of Noah" (v. 37). (Read Genesis 7–9 for the details about Noah's story.) God had revealed His plan to Noah, who carried out that plan. But the people who were around during those days went about life as usual (vv. 38–39). Jesus said it will be this way when He comes. Two people will be doing daily chores and "one will be taken and the other left" (vv. 40–41). Jesus' point was that people would be going about life as usual when the Son of Man comes. Like Noah and his family, only those who trusted the Word of God would expect Jesus' return. Yet, the particular time would come as a surprise to all.

How does this portion of Jesus' answer to His disciples' questions about the end help you formulate your understanding of His return? Which points are clear and which are unclear? Who will you go to for help to

Christos—God's Transforming Touch

understand more fully these teachings of Jesus? Record your responses below:

_____

_____

_____

_____

36.5 Staying Alert

One day I came home after a day's work and realized we had been robbed. We had no alarm system then. The thieves had broken the sliding glass door that opened into the back yard, unlatched it, and then helped themselves to our new stereo system. That seemed to be their target because nothing else was missing. The police said the perpetrators had not been there long before I had come home. I wished I had come home earlier that day. After the police left, Kim and I worried that if someone broke in once, someone else could do it again. We eventually bought a home with an alarm system, but that experience has kept us a little nervous about what goes on at our home when we are not there.

Have you ever had someone break into your home? What were the circumstances? How did you feel at the time? How have you prevented it from happening again?

_____

_____

Read Matthew 24:42–44. Underline the phrases "keep watch" in verse 42 and "be ready" in verse 44. Although no one knows the day or time of His coming, Jesus said to stay alert and be prepared, for He will come (v. 42). Like a homeowner who knew the hour in the night a thief was planning to rob, we are to keep watch so we will be ready for His coming (v. 43). (Read also 1 Thess. 5:2, 4 for this illustration.) Jesus said He would come "at an hour when you do not expect him" (v. 44). In order to be ready when He unexpectedly shows up, be ready as if each day were the day of His coming.

Jesus assured His disciples that if they watched for His certain return they could see signs that His return was near. If they stayed prepared for His coming, they could live lives of hope and joy that history had an ending and they would share it with the King.

Our question to consider for this chapter is "When do you expect Christ to return?" Review the passages chosen from Matthew 24 along with the parallel passages in the "For further study" list below. Formulate your own confession of the end times. Consult other Christians and Christian writings to build upon your confession. Always make sure you give the Bible priority over other writings about the end of history. Record your confession here:

_____

_____

_____

_____

For further study:
- Mark 13:1–37
- Luke 21:5–36

37—Observing the Lord's Supper: Jesus' Last Hours with His Disciples

The Lord's Supper, Communion, and the Eucharist are names the Christian Church has given Jesus' last Passover meal with His closest followers. Jesus' last meal with His followers was a picture of the fulfillment of the Passover meal God gave Israel to remember their exodus from Egypt. It also pointed forward to when Jesus would die as the Passover Lamb for the sins of all people.

Jesus intentionally shared a traditional Passover meal with His followers in order to complete His mission as the *Christos*. Judas had gone to the religious leaders to work a deal to turn Jesus over to them (Luke 22:3–6). Jesus knew this and sent Peter and John to prepare the meal for Him to share with the Twelve one last time (Luke 22:7–13). In that intimate setting, Jesus provided a visual of His sacrifice on the cross the next day.

The celebration of the Lord's Supper is something the church has practiced since early in its history. While Christians have some disareement about the meaning of the supper, it is an important practice for the church today. Some churches take the elements of the supper every time they gather. Others schedule it four or five times a year. Taking the meal is one way we identify ourselves as members of the Body of Christ.

The Memory Verse for this chapter is Matthew 26:28. Jesus explained that the cup in His final meal represented His blood that would be shed on the cross and that was the sign of a New Agreement.

Our question to consider for this chapter is "Why did Jesus institute the Lord's Supper?" Observe this episode in Luke's story of Jesus in order to develop your own answer.

Christos—God's Transforming Touch

37.1 Celebrating with Family

We mostly celebrate birthdays, anniversaries, and holidays around meals. Families sharing a meal seems to add meaning to whatever we celebrate that day. The presence of those closest to us, along with meals spiced by conversation and stories, gives family and friends a chance to know one another at a deeper level. Food and time spent in a relaxed setting with those we trust let us be ourselves and share thoughts and feelings we would not share in any other setting.

What is your most recent memory of a meaning-filled meal with friends or family? What was the occasion? Who was there? What one thing did you hear that you would not have heard at a business dinner? Write about your memories here:

_____

_____

_____

Read Luke 22:1–16. Circle all the words connected to the Passover. Underline the word "suffer" in verse 15 and the phrase "kingdom of God" in verse 16.

Jesus knew His mission would soon be complete on the cross. Tensions had heightened throughout the week leading up to Passover, and Judas had agreed to betray Jesus to the religious authorities. All the signs pointed that the time of His suffering was at hand. Jesus had come to Jerusalem during he Feast of Unleavened Bread, or Passover (Ex. 23:15; Deut. 16:16). It was one of the three annual feasts God gave to Israel in the Old Agreement, which served as a reminder of God's great deliverance of Israel from bondage in Egypt.

Luke records that on "the day of Unleavened Bread," the day leaven was to be removed from the home, Jesus sent Peter and John to prepare the traditional meal for His followers (Luke 22:7–8; Ex. 12). After getting everything together, Jesus sat down with His disciples "when the hour" of the meal had come (v. 14). We have no record to show that Jesus had done this with His disciples before. The Passover meal was designed to be taken in the home with family. We can assume each of the disciples and Jesus observed the meal with their families in the years prior to this night. Given the circumstances and significance of what was happening, Jesus asked the Twelve to share the meal with Him as His family.

When they were seated around the festival meal, Jesus told them He wanted to share this Passover with them before He suffered for them (v. 15). Jesus wanted them to see that He was the fulfillment of this ancient meal that pointed to God's ultimate deliverance in His Son. Jesus told His followers He would not eat this meal again "until it finds fulfillment in the kingdom of God" (v. 16). Jesus promised He would not celebrate this feast again until He returned to rule eternally in His Kingdom. The ancient meal pointed to the future promise of His return.

What significant connections do you see between the prescribed Passover meal in the Old Agreement and Jesus' completion of it on the cross? How do you relate to the possible feelings of the disciples as they shared the meal for the first time with Jesus?

_____

_____

_____

_____

37.2 Sharing the Cup

One part I like about wedding traditions in America is the rehearsal dinner. At that dinner the bridal party takes turns making toasts to the bride and groom. These are words in the form of blessings or promises of support for the soon-to-be spouses. I like it when a friend from childhood chokes up talking about his friend's fiancée because he has come to love her as much as he did his friend. Or I love it when a bridesmaid cannot make it through her speech because tears of affection prevent her from speaking any more about the bride whom she knows is choosing to make her husband her new best friend. These words of blessings tell the stories of friendship and love that give everyone present a deeper appreciation for the wedding event the next day.

What words of blessing have you spoken that over-whelmed you? Where were you? How did you know the person? Have you stayed connected to him or her since the event? Write some of your memories here:

_____

_____

_____

Read Luke 22:17–18. Circle the word "cup" in verse 17 and underline "the kingdom of God" in verse 18.

After Jesus told His followers how badly He wanted to share this memorial meal with them, He took a "cup" from the meal, blessed it, and told His students to share it among themselves (v. 17). He then told them that He would not eat this meal again "until the kingdom of God comes." He would "not drink again of the fruit of the vine" until the coming of that same Kingdom (v. 18). This was the last meal, the last Passover, Jesus would take until He returned to fully establish His Kingdom.

Jesus took "a cup" from the table to tell them this was His last meal. He took "the cup" from the Passover meal as part of His pictorial parable to explain His death. "A cup" goes with Jesus' desire to "eat" with the disciples, just as "the cup" goes with His explanation of His mission as the final Passover Lamb.

Reread verses 15–18. Summarize what Jesus tried to tell the Twelve about the significance of the meal they were about to eat together. What applications can you make of His words for your life today? Thank God for Jesus' promise of a completed mission and future return.

_____

_____

_____

Christos—God's Transforming Touch

37.3 Sharing the Bread

When I was growing up, I always wondered why the little squares of bread we took in the Lord's Supper tasted so flat and the juice that accompanied it so lukewarm and sour. I just accepted on faith that religious food tasted bad to emphasize the spiritual nature of it all. That was until I took part in my first Seder meal. A Messianic Jewish rabbi (a Jew who trusts Jesus is the *Christos*) hosted a modern Passover meal for our church. He showed us the elements of the ancient meal and how he believed they pointed to Jesus as the Messiah. The tastes mixed the sweet charoset and parsley dipped in salt water. The bread was matzo bread, unleavened flat bread that was more like a cracker than a slice of bread from a loaf. The rabbi explained that removing yeast from the house and bread was part of cleansing one's life of sin before killing and eating the sacrificial lamb. I finally made the connection between the bland, prefabricated, small squares of bread in the Lord's Supper and unleavened bread of the Passover meal.

Have you ever attended a Seder meal? If so, what parts of the meal stood out to you? What tastes lingered? What parts connected to your church's current practice of the Lord's Supper? Write some of your thoughts here:

_____

_____

_____

_____

Read Luke 22:19. Underline the verbs in verse 19 and compare the last phrase, "Do this in remembrance of me," in several translations. Choose the translation that best interprets the phrase for you. Also read 1 Corinthians 11:23–24.

Jesus took the unleavened bread of the Passover meal, gave thanks for it in prayer, broke it into smaller pieces, and gave it to His disciples. Jesus then connected Himself to the unleavened bread of the Passover meal by saying, "This is my body given for you." Jesus associated His body, which would be given as the final Passover sacrifice the next day, with the bread Israel had taken for centuries as part of the meal that commemorated God's great deliverance of His people from Egypt. Jesus was God's Great Deliverer who would rescue not only the people of the Old Agreement, but also all people from bondage through His death.

Jesus then told them as they took the bread to eat it to remember what He had done for them. Paul described Jesus as doing the same things (1 Cor. 11:23–24). Every time the followers of Jesus tasted the unleavened bread, they were to remember that He gave His body for them on the cross. This was His mission. This was His act of love. They were to remember that always.

What are your earliest memories of taking the elements of the Lord's Supper, or Communion? When did the connection between the bread of the Passover meal and Jesus' body become clear to you? What meaning does it hold for you now? Write your thoughts, feelings, and memories here:

_____

_____

_____

_____

37.4 Pointing to the New Covenant

Whenever Kim and I attend the wedding of one of our friend's children, we hold hands and renew our vows to each other by whispering the vows repeated by the bride and groom. This is a way of letting one another know what we promised to each other 30-plus years ago still means what it meant then. We give each other our rings again like children sneaking notes to one another during a church service. We accept the pastor's prayer of blessing as our own. Rather than simply observing the wedding ceremony, we participate in a way to share the meaning of the moment with those who enter the marriage covenant for the first time.

Have you ever renewed your vows? If you have remarried, what was the meaning of the vows as you shared them? Did the pastor or priest describe your marriage as a covenant? Write some of your thoughts here:

_____

_____

_____

_____

Read Luke 22:20. Circle the words "new covenant."

Luke writes that "in the same way" Jesus "took the cup" after supper. After they finished the prescribed meal of the Old Agreement, Jesus took a cup of blessing from the table and gave it to His followers. He said, "This cup is the new covenant in my blood, which is poured out for you." Through Jesus' death, burial, and Resurrection, God made a new covenant, testament, or agreement with people. In the Old Agreement, an annual sacrifice provided the forgiveness of sins and made the people "right" or "righteous" before Holy God. This was done on the Day of Atonement. (Read Leviticus 16 for background on the Day of Atonement.)

Jesus said His death would be the final sacrifice that would satisfy God's requirements for righteousness once for all by equating His blood to the drink of the Passover meal. His death would be the basis for God's New Agreement with people and the way they could be made "right" before Holy God. The Passover of the Old Agreement was fulfilled when Jesus shed His blood on the cross. He was the final sacrifice and the New Agreement between God and His people. He wanted those He had trained to be servant-leaders in His Kingdom not to miss what was happening before them.

Place yourself among the disciples at the table with Jesus. The bread and cup are familiar to you, but Jesus' words are fresh and somewhat confusing. Prayerfully ask the questions they may have had as Jesus gave them the bread and wine. Ask what they may have connected and what they may have missed as Jesus made the analogy between His body and blood with the bread and cup.

37.5 Exposing the Traitor

The name *Judas* means "traitor" to this day. A traitor like Benedict Arnold stains the pages of America's history, but none compares to the betrayal of Jesus by one of His chosen followers. Jesus knew of Judas' cowardly act of selling Him out for 30 pieces of silver, and He acknowledged Judas' actions to the other 11 followers. Jesus, however, did not call his name or even address him harshly as Jesus had some of the religious leaders. Judas' decision to turn Jesus over set the course to the cross and allowed Jesus to complete His mission as the Suffering Servant *Christos*. It ended with Judas taking his own life (Matt. 27:5).

What do you know about Judas? Look up his name in a Bible dictionary or encyclopedia to read more about him. Take notes from your research in the space below.

_____

_____

_____

_____

_____

_____

Read Luke 22:21–22. Underline what Jesus said about Himself and what was to happen to the one who would betray Him.

Sometime in the evening—Luke wrote it happened immediately after Jesus gave His disciples the bread and cup—Jesus announced that one of the group at the table would betray Him (v. 21). We know Judas had already made the deal with the religious authorities to hand Jesus over to them when the time was right (Luke 22:3–6). Jesus let His followers know that He knew what this betrayer had done. Jesus did not expose Judas by giving His name, but basically said, "You know who you are." I have always wondered how Judas responded when Jesus said that. What was the look on his face? Did his heart almost jump out of his chest? Did he wonder how Jesus knew what he had done, just like a teenager wonders how his or her parents found out that the place he or she had asked permission to go the night before was a lie to cover up the real destination?

Jesus drew a line of distinction between His willful choice to go to the cross and Judas' choice to turn Jesus over to the religious leaders. Jesus said He, the Son of Man, would go His way according to what had been "decreed," or "appointed," to happen. Jesus would fulfill the mission call of the Father for His life. His path was certain. God would use the evil choice of Judas to accomplish His purpose for His Son. God redeemed betrayal into the way redemption came to all people. However, Jesus said "woe" to the one who would betray Him (v. 22). We know from Matthew's account of Jesus' story that Judas' life did end with a "woe."

Our question to consider for this chapter is "Why did Jesus institute the Lord's Supper?" Now that you have observed the setting of Jesus' last meal with His followers, how would you answer this question?

_____

_____

_____

_____

Jesus provided a tangible, visual parable of His sacrificial death for all people by identifying Himself with bread and wine in the Passover meal. It is a memorial to His death and a promise of His final deliverance when the King returns.

For further study:
- **Mark 14:22–25**
- **1 Corinthians 11:23–26**

38—Practicing Humility: Jesus Washes the Disciples' Feet

Humility is hard to define, but we know it when we see it. The Bible described Moses as "more humble than anyone else on the face of the earth" (Num. 12:3). The context of that description was when Miriam and Aaron thought they could lead as well as Moses. When God judged the two, Moses intervened and prayed that God would not destroy them. God altered His sentence (Num. 12:13–14). Humility is trusting God enough to take up for those who are trying to get your job.

John was the only evangelistic writer to include the episode of Jesus washing His disciples' feet on His last night with them (John 13:4–17). After Jesus said one of the disciples would betray Him, they argued again "as to which of them was considered to be greatest" (Luke 22:24). This was an interesting twist of dialogue that went from questioning who among them would betray Jesus to who would be the greatest (vv. 23–24).

Jesus had told them He was the fulfillment of the Passover promise who would die for them, and they were talking about their status in the group. The disciples were far from practicing humility. Not one of them would wash the others' feet as a courtesy to prepare them for the meal. But Jesus modeled not only humble servant-leadership for them, but His mission as the Suffering Servant-Messiah for those who trusted Him.

The Memory Verse for this chapter is John 13:15. Jesus told His disciples He had given them an example to follow among themselves.

Our question to consider for this chapter is "Do humble people know they are humble?" Humility is what humility does. We choose our actions based on who we believe ourselves to be. Let us follow Jesus from the table to His disciples' feet to how He describes it for us.

Christos—God's Transforming Touch

38.1 Having Confidence as God's Servant

Humble people are confident people. They do not have an unrealistic confidence like a Superman I-can-do-anything, but rather a quiet certainty that they know who they are and what they can do. They go about their assignment with poise and purpose. Humility is a source of confidence because it is a realistic picture of who we are before God and alongside others. Humble people know their strengths and status, not as measuring sticks to defeat others or stroke their own egos, but as resources to know what they can offer and from where their strength comes.

Write the name and characteristics of someone you consider a humble person. What are some things he or she does or does not do that signal humiliy to you? Would you also describe this person as confident?

_____

_____

_____

Read John 13:3. Underline the three things Jesus "knew" as He got up from the table to serve His disciples by washing their feet.

John tells us Jesus was confident of three things. He knew "the Father had put all things under his power, and that he had come from God and was returning to God" (v. 3). Each phrase reveals an aspect of Jesus' humble confidence that got Him up from His place as the King to wash the feet of His pupils. To "put all things under his power" is a reference to Jesus' authority over all creation and spiritual realities. (Read Ephesians 1:20–23 for more on His authority.) Jesus knew He

was the Creator, the Second Person of the Trinity, and that God had "placed all things under his feet" (Eph. 1:22; Ps. 8:6.) Jesus also was confident that He had come from God. His miraculous birth was evidence that He was uniquely God's Son. God, the Father, was His source of life. John also tells us Jesus knew He was returning to His Father. Jesus had no doubts that after He suffered and died He would return to His Father in heaven where He would dwell eternally (John 20:17).

Jesus' God-given authority, the certainty of where He had come from, and the assurance of where He was going combined to create in Him an humble confidence. It prevented Him from entering the argument about who is the greatest and propelled Him to show His love for those He called to join Him (John 13:1).

Followers of Jesus can have the same humble confidence as Jesus. How? Paul wrote to the Christ-followers in Ephesus that "in Christ Jesus" they had been raised to sit in the heavens with Him to show the "richness of his grace" (Eph. 2:6–7). All true Christ-followers trust that they came from God; that God prepares for them a mission-driven, vision-drawn life; and that they will return to God when their mission is complete. When you have confidence in who you are and who you belong to, you can have a humble heart. That confidence allows you to serve rather than compete with others.

38.2 Serving Humble Leaders

For a little over two years I worked for a multimillionaire's private foundation that funded Christian camps and camp programs. He had a heart for telling others the story of Jesus. He invested millions of dollars in creating environments where children, teenagers, and adults could experience the rescuing love of Jesus. He did not act or dress like someone with a lot of money. Often when he was at a camp working on some project, people would mistake him for a camp staffer who could help them locate Mr. Piper. He would then smile and say that he was Mr. Piper. Working for Mr. Piper taught me that it is better to invest money for the Kingdom than to look like you have it.

Whom do you know who could insist people treat him or her as someone important but acts and looks like everyone else? What are some things you know about the person that points to his or her humility? Write your description here:

_____

_____

_____

_____

Read John 13:4–5. Underline what Jesus did after John's description of His source of confidence.

Jesus got up from the Passover meal after revealing to His followers that He was the fulfillment of the ancient promise of deliverance, and laid aside His outer robe. Dressed only in His tunic, He looked like a common household servant. Jesus wrapped a sheet-like towel around His waist (v. 4). He then put water into a basin used to wash guests' feet and began to wash and dry the feet of His students who reclined at the table (v. 5). Humility is leaving your position of leadership, taking up the towel of service, and meeting the needs of others.

Jesus modeled humble service to others as He left His place of leadership, dressed like a household servant, and did the work of a common slave to meet the need of pride and misunderstanding among His followers. His descent from the Passover Lamb to a common slave reflected His riches-to-rags descent from heaven to take on the form of God's Suffering Servant *Christos*. (Read Philippians 2:5–11 for details of His descent.) Next to the cross, Jesus demonstrated no greater act of humility for those who trust Him as their Leader and Rescuer.

Do not miss the connection between verse 3 and verses 4–5. Humble acts of service come from having a confidence of whose you are, who you are, and your commitment to the mission call of God on your life. Servant-leaders like Jesus can leave their positions of leadership to serve the most menial need of those they lead when their service to the mission and love for those they lead outweigh their need to be in leadership.

Pause and reflect on Jesus' intentional acts of service to His followers. What situations do you face that may call for similar acts of humble service to others?

_____

_____

_____

38.3 Understanding Jesus' Role as Servant

Leaders lead. Servants serve. In the leadership language of the world, neither one does the other's work. We expect our leaders to stay out front, look good in public, and represent the cause. We do what we can to keep them doing those things. In the early stages of the start up, we expect the leader to do anything to get the movement or business going. But after some successes, the leader can recruit or hire others to do the things he or she did in the trenches. Is not the point of getting to leadership to get as far away as possible from the dirty work? Do we not pursue the corner office for the perks and compensation packages? Leaders deserve those things, right? They are supposed to have proved themselves as the hardest workers and deserve the luxuries that surround them. A CEO would never be seen mowing the office building's grounds or cleaning one of its toilets. Janitors do those things.

What are some common expectations of leaders in your organizations, church, or school? How would you feel, for example, if your school principal served in the cafeteria line one day or the CEO of your company was cleaning a toilet when you went in to wash your hands before lunch? Write some of your thoughts here:

_____

_____

_____

Read John 13:6–11. Verses 6–9 record Jesus' dialogue with Peter. Summarize it in the space below. Verses 10–11 are Jesus' words to the whole group. Record His message to them in your own words.

_____

_____

_____

_____

When Jesus came to Peter after washing the feet of other disciples, the lead disciple wanted to know if Jesus

planned on washing his feet (v. 6). Jesus said that He did but that Peter would not understand what He was doing until later (v. 7). Peter said no such thing would happen. Jesus replied that unless He washed Peter's feet Peter would "have no part" with Him (v. 8). In typical Peter style, the wary disciple said, "give me a bath, then!" (v. 9, my own translation).

Peter resisted the humble servant leadership of Jesus. Why? He may have felt that what Jesus was doing should have been his job to do and that he had failed to do it. Like a child with a guilty conscience, he wanted to make up his misdeed to his Teacher. He also may have felt washing feet was not what the Messiah was supposed to do. He had already refused Jesus' description of His suffering in Caesarea Philippi (Matt. 16:21–22). Surely the *Christos* would not do the work of a slave. Whatever his reasons, Peter refused his Leader's service.

Jesus answered Peter's initial question by explaining that what He was doing looked strange now but would make sense later—either when He explained it after washing their feet or after He was crucified, buried, and raised on the third day. When Peter said Jesus would never wash his feet, Jesus replied that unless Peter allowed Jesus to serve him, Peter would not be part of the Kingdom ruled by the Suffering Servant *Christos*. Jesus refused Peter's perception of the *Christos* and told the disciple to accept Him as a suffering servant. Otherwise, Peter had missed everything Jesus had tried to teach him. Like James and John who naively agreed to suffer with Jesus, Peter unwittingly said he was all in.

Put yourself in Peter's place. What feelings and questions do you have about your leader washing everyone's feet? Have you ever had someone wash your feet?

_____

_____

_____

38.4 Learning to Serve

When my daughters were growing up, we expected them to help with chores around the house. We did not say, "Go empty the dishwasher," without first showing them how to do it and where to place the dishes in their proper places in the cabinets. We helped them several times but eventually expected them to empty the dishwasher, put the dishes in their places, and fill it up again with dirty dishes. Leadership is sometimes like parenting. You must show people what you want, coach them how to do it, and then release them to do it alone.

What have you have taught others that involved showing, coaching, and releasing them to do the task on their own? Who has taught you well in this way?

_____

_____

_____

_____

Read John 13:12–15. Underline the words "Teacher" and "Lord" in verse 13. Circle the word "example" in verse 15.

Jesus finished the dirty task of washing His followers' feet, put His cloak back on, and reclined again at the table with them (v. 12). The King returned to His rightful place among His chosen leaders. Jesus explained that they trusted Him as their "Teacher" and "Lord," and they were correct in doing so because that was what He was to them (v. 13). Point made. Jesus then continued. If He who was their Teacher and Master would lower Himself to such a menial task as doing the work of a slave, they should do the same for one another (v. 14). Jesus, the One to whom they had made themselves apprentices, said He had established an "example" of what they should do for one another as He had done for them (v. 15). The word "example" is the same word in James 5:10 that means "an illustration or example." Jesus' humble act of service was an example of how they were to serve one another.

Some followers of Jesus have taken Jesus' words as instruction to literally wash each other's feet. When they share the Lord's Supper, they set aside a time to wash the feet of those who are fellow Christians. Most interpreters agree that Jesus did not mean the literal act of washing dirty feet. His actions were an example of service we should show each other. His example was the entire picture of leaving His place of leadership to meet a need among those He led. Greatness was in the form of a servant. The Leader acted like a slave.

How have you interpreted Jesus' teaching to His disciples? What are some ways you can "wash the feet" of those you lead? Make a date to do what God puts on your heart before you leave this study session.

_____

_____

38.5 Following Orders

Teams fall apart when the players do not follow the coach's instructions. When I coached t-ball for my daughter and her friends, it drove me crazy that the first graders would not follow my instructions on where to throw the ball or where to stand. Add in the instructions from the parents in the stands, and it was more often chaos than a game. We got better over the season, but we were never great. I can only imagine what a professional coach goes through when multimillion dollar players decide to play their own game.

What experiences in your life are similar to mine? Have you ever coached or led a team? Did the players follow your leadership or not? What were some of the results of those situations?

_____

_____

_____

Read John 13:16–17. Circle the word "blessed."

Jesus reminded His squabbling followers that He established an example for them to follow. They also were not to think a "servant is greater than his master, nor is a messenger greater than the one who sent him" (v. 16). He referred to them as servants and messengers. Their role was to do what their Master told them to do. Humble service was a hallmark of those who followed the Suffering Servant *Christos*.

Jesus told His students that a blessing exists for those who serve like Jesus. Joy comes from serving others in His name and living out the call to be a servant and messenger in the Kingdom of God. Jesus not only insisted His players play according to His rules, He promised they would be glad they did. This is how things work in the Kingdom of the Suffering Servant.

Jesus has provided a clear and challenging example of how we are to humbly serve in His name. Spend some time in prayer asking God to reveal to you ways in which you can take up the towel of service in His name to meet the needs of others. Commit to do those things in a given period of time.

For further study:
- **John 13:1–30**
- **Mark 10:35–45**

39—Seeking the Counselor: The Holy Spirit

Abandonment is humanity's greatest fear and its deepest hurt. From birth we want and need others to care for us. If somewhere in our stories a loved one or friend abandons us, the hurt can wound us emotionally so we will struggle to trust anyone else again. Divorce, death, or willful decisions take people from us; we must deal with the feelings of rejection, abandonment, and fear. Without someone to fill our need for love, we are left to live fearful, lonely lives.

After Jesus washed His disciples' feet, exposed Judas' treacherous plot, and predicted Peter's denial, His disciples were afraid. To them it looked as if the Kingdom of God was crumbling before their eyes. They had signed on with the *Christos*, whom they trusted would rescue Israel and restore it to its status among the nations as God's chosen tribes. The previous week of His-story had brought conflict and imminent danger to the Kingdom movement. Jesus could read the fear in their eyes, and like a loving parent He comforted them. He promised He was "going to prepare a place" for them and that He would return to take them there (John 14:2–3). He would leave but not abandon them. Jesus promised "another Counselor" who would be their advocate, and would teach and guide them in His absence (v. 16).

The Memory Verse for this chapter is John 14:26. Jesus promised that His Holy Spirit would teach and remind His followers everything He had said to them. They were not to worry because He would be present with them. We share that same promise.

Our question to consider for this chapter is "How does the Holy Spirit help me?" Jesus was careful to spell out the answer to this question to His apprentices.

39.1 Sending the Counselor

When our girls were younger and my wife and I had to travel together, we would ask one of their grandparents either to come to the house and stay or have the girls stay at their place until we returned. We are fortunate to have loving, supportive parents on both sides of our family. The girls loved staying with their grandparents. When we called from wherever we were, the girls were content and cared for. Yes, we all missed each other, but for the time being the separation was fine because the grandparents were the next best thing to the parents—and sometimes the girls said they were better!

Who do you trust to leave your child(ren) with when you have to travel or go to work? What is it about those you leave your children with that allows you to leave them when you must? Write some of your feelings here:

———————————————————————

———————————————————————

Read John 14:16–18. Underline the names Jesus gave the Holy Spirit in verses 16–17. Underline Jesus' promise in verse 18.

Jesus continued to encourage His followers in the face of His death by telling them He would ask His Father to send "another Counselor" (v. 16). The word "counselor" comes from the Greek word that literally meant "to call alongside" and was used for a legal assistant or advocate who pleads the case of another person (1 John 2:1).

One of the titles for the *Christos* was "Wonderful Counselor" (Isa. 9:6). As the *Christos*, Jesus was the promised Counselor of God's presence. Notice Jesus said that

His Father would send "another Counselor" (v. 16). "The world," or those who did not trust Jesus to be the *Christos*, would not be able to receive, see, or know Him. Jesus' followers, on the other hand, would be able to know the "Spirit of truth . . . for he lives with you and will be in you" (v. 17).

Jesus said that He would not leave His followers "as orphans" and that He would come to them as promised (v. 18). Jesus would not abandon His followers after His death. He would be raised from the dead, ascend to heaven, and send "another Counselor" to be with His followers as they continued His mission.

Begin to formulate your understanding of the Holy Spirit in your life by recording what Jesus taught about His Spirit in the space below. Add to this listing after each of Jesus' five teachings on the Holy Spirit.

———————————————————————

———————————————————————

———————————————————————

———————————————————————

39.2 Teaching After Jesus

My college Greek professor, Dr. Cutter, was one of my favorite teachers. There were not that many Greek majors, so we got to know one another very well. He patiently taught the other students and me how to read, translate, and interpret both classical and New Testament Greek. Though he joked with us, he would get very serious when it came to getting our translations right or understanding a nuance of grammar or context. Once during my senior year, he was called out of town for a week. He asked me to teach his classes. Most of the time I administered tests, but I did get to teach some, too. I must admit I was proud to stand in my teacher's place and teach others what he had spent three years imparting to me. When he returned, he approved of my work; I have never lost my love for teaching since.

Did you have a teacher who not only taught you but gave you responsibilities beyond that of other students? Describe some of your experience here:

_____

_____

_____

Read John 14:25–27. Underline in verse 26 another name for Counselor and what He will do. Describe in your own words what Jesus meant by the peace He gives in verse 27.

_____

_____

_____

_____

Jesus reminded His students that He had taught them while He was present with them. And He would not leave them without a teacher (vv. 25–26). His Father would "send in my name," the Counselor, "the Holy Spirit." Jesus spoke of the Trinity when He taught about the Father, Himself, and the Holy Spirit. The Spirit would "teach . . . all things" and bring to mind all that Jesus had taught His students (v. 26). Jesus taught the ways of the Kingdom; those would not be lost in His physical absence. His Holy Spirit would come and teach "all things" about the Kingdom and remind His students of all He had taught them.

Jesus said He would leave His peace with them (v. 27). Peace is not just the absence of conflict. Jesus faced conflict and even created it. The peace Jesus gave would not be "as the world gives." Armies, revolutionaries, and terrorists believe their violence will ultimately bring the peace they envision. But peace to Jesus was the rest that comes from knowing whose you are and why you were born. The peace Jesus gave His followers was a clear mission for their lives. It was the certainty that His Kingdom rule would come no matter what. Based on this reality, Jesus reiterated for them not to let their hearts be troubled or to be afraid (v. 1.)

Add to your understanding of the Person of the Holy Spirit in the space below. What parts of Jesus' teaching about God's Spirit apply to your life and faith today?

_____

_____

Christos—God's Transforming Touch

39.3 Being a Witness

We who trust Jesus to be the *Christos* serve as witnesses to who He is and what He does in our lives. Like witnesses in a courtroom who give their version of a story from their vantage point, we have the privilege of telling others what we see and know to be true from the perspective of our relationship with Jesus. We who are citizens of the King gladly tell "our side of the story" to those who ask about what we have experienced. But we are not alone in our take on events and circumstances. Jesus taught us that the Holy Spirit helps us see things from God's perspective. It is not our opinion or understanding alone that makes a difference to others. The Holy Spirit reveals the things of God through His Word to us so we can be truth-filled witnesses for Him.

Have you ever been a witness in a courtroom? Under what circumstances? How was your witness received? What was the outcome of the trial?

_____

_____

_____

Read John 15:26–27. Circle the word "testify" in both verses. Write in the space below the two whom Jesus said will testify about Him.

_____

_____

This is the third of five descriptions of the Holy Spirit by Jesus in John's story of Jesus (John 14:15–17; 14:26; 15:26; 16:4–11; 16:12–15). Each one reveals a different aspect of the person of the Holy Spirit. In John 15:26, Jesus said He would send the Spirit from the Father to them. Earlier He said He would ask the Father and the Father would send the Spirit (John 14:26). This statement is not a contradiction but demonstrates the unity of Father, Son, and Spirit.

Jesus said the Spirit of truth would "testify about me" (John 15:26). We get our English word *martyr* from this Greek word that can also be translated "witness." To testify is consistent with the Holy Spirit's work as the Advocate. Jesus testified about Himself as the *Christos*, about His departure and the Spirit's coming. The Holy Spirit would witness to who Jesus is and help people trust God's Word.

But the Spirit would not be the lone witness to who Jesus is. His disciples would also "testify" because they had been with Him "from the beginning" (John 15:27). The disciples had the advantage of being with Jesus from the time He called them to join Him on the messianic mission. When it came time to replace Judas as one of the Twelve, those who were eligible were those who had been with Jesus since "beginning from John's baptism to the time when Jesus was taken up from us. For one of these must become a witness with us of his resurrection" (Acts 1:22).

Jesus said people would know Him through the combined witness of the Holy Spirit and His followers. As a follower of Jesus, what does this teach you about your role in witnessing to others about who Jesus is?

_____

_____

_____

_____

_____

39.4 Leaving the Disciples

I will never forget the day my wife and I left our oldest daughter standing at the door of her college dorm. We had come the day before with all of her furniture and supplies, arriving at the dorm at 6:30 a.m. to move her in. We finished a little after noon, and it was time to make the three-hour drive back home so I could preach the next morning. After we prayed for her, hugged her, and made each other let go of the other's hand, my wife and I turned toward our car to leave. I will never forget looking back over my shoulder and waving one last time to my grownup baby girl. We would leave her many more times, but the first time was the hardest. We hurt as we left her at the door, but we knew it was for her good. We had to let go so she could become the young woman God envisioned her to become.

Describe a time when you left a loved one because you knew it was best for them. What was the circumstance? What were your reasons? Write your experience here:

_____

_____

_____

Read John 16:7–11. Underline the phrase "for your good" and the reasons Jesus said it was best for Him to go away.

The context of this fourth teaching of Jesus about the Holy Spirit is persecution (John 16:1–4). Jesus explained that while they feared what others may do to them in His absence, the Holy Spirit would take His place and guide them through the trials. Jesus said it was "for your good" that He went away. If He stayed and did not complete His mission, the Counselor could not come to empower and guide them (v. 7).

Jesus then added to what the Holy Spirit would do when He came. Jesus taught that the Holy Spirit was the Counselor, or Advocate, on the disciple's behalf (John 14:26). Yet, for those who did not trust Jesus to be the *Christos*, the Counselor would not defend them but prosecute them. The Counselor for God would "convict the world of guilt in regard to sin and righteousness and judgment" (v. 8). The Holy Spirit would go before Christ's witnesses to "convict the world" about their relationship with God. Their sin is they refused to trust Jesus was the *Christos* (v. 9). The Holy Spirit showed that Jesus' return to the Father meant He brought righteousness through His death, burial, and Resurrection. The Counselor of God would witness that "the prince of this world," Satan, has been judged and condemned by the work of Jesus (v. 11).

The Holy Spirit will advocate and empower the followers of Jesus. That same Holy Spirit will convict those who do not trust Jesus about who He truly is. How does this part of the Holy Spirit's advocacy apply to your life? Write some of your thoughts here:

_____

_____

_____

39.5 Listening to the Holy Spirit

There are some things you just do not tell your children until they are ready. For example, at the time of this writing our youngest is about to graduate from college.

She has a job already lined up to begin three months after she graduates. She has begun to realize that the "college season" is about to end, and she will be responsible for 100 percent of what she needs to live. Now it is time to talk straight about debt, spending, housing, and the joy and burden of living on your own. We can add weight to our caution about safety, saving, and being careful about how she invests her time, talent, and treasures. When she was six these sorts of conversations would have frightened her, and she would have no point of reference or recourse to respond to what we told her. Some children have had to deal with those things at a young age. We are fortunate that our daughter did not have to wrestle with the hard stuff until she was prepared to do so.

What conversations have you held off with your children because they were not ready to hear the stark truth of a situation? When do you plan to discuss such topics? Or if you have already had those dialogues, how did they go? Write some of your experiences here:

_____

_____

_____

Read John 16:12–14. Describe in your own words what Jesus adds to our understanding of the role and work of the Holy Spirit in the disciples' lives.

_____

_____

_____

Like a wise parent, Jesus told His followers that He had more to tell them but it was "more than you can now bear" (v. 12). He may have had in mind His suffering

or the horrors they would face in their own deaths as martyrs for Him. Whatever kept Jesus from sharing with His disciples, He said when the "Spirit of truth" comes He would lead them "into all truth" (v. 13).

Jesus insisted He never spoke unless the Father first prompted Him (John 5:19, 30). In the same way, Jesus said the Holy Spirit "will not speak on his own; he will speak only what he hears" (John 16:13). The Holy Spirit would not misspeak the words of the Father or the Son. He would also "bring glory" to the Son by affirming what He said and did (vv. 14–15). After Jesus' Ascension (Acts 1:9), the Holy Spirit came just as Jesus promised (Acts 2:1–4). And as they say, "The rest is history."

Complete your catalog of what Jesus taught about the promised Holy Spirit and write your own understanding of Him from what you have learned. Share it with one person in the next week to see what it "sounds" like. Spend time in prayer to hear what Jesus said the Holy Spirit would do for us.

_____

_____

_____

For further study:
* **John 14:1–31**
* **John 15:18–27**

40—Staying Connected to Christ: The Vine and the Branches

"Now that I am a Christian, how do I know what I am supposed to do?" is a question I often hear from people who have recently trusted Jesus to be their Rescuer and Leader. What would you tell them? Christ-followers who have known Jesus for years wonder the same thing—especially when their lives have not changed and they see little evidence that Jesus is as important as they say. Jesus expects us to change. Jesus expects His Kingdom people to show evidence that they have been with Him and learned a new way of life from Him.

Jesus intently taught His apprentices in the last hours He had with them. John 14–17 are some of the most intimate words Jesus shared with His followers. He promised another Advocate, the Holy Spirit, would come when He left. He prayed for Himself and His disciples before He was arrested (John 17). Jesus also explained how they must stay connected to Him in order to be like Him. Jesus gave them a simple analogy of the relationship between a branch and a vine as the picture of how they should relate to Him so they could do what He called them to do. Jesus' teaching to His first disciples is for us today as we seek to be with Him in order to be like Him.

The Memory Verse for this chapter is John 15:5. Jesus gives us the secret to how our lives intertwine in Him and how He makes a difference in our lives. This is a key concept in becoming like Jesus in our everyday lives.

Our question to consider for this chapter is "Can you know someone else is a Christian?" Jesus taught elsewhere that you will know a person by his or her "fruit," or actions. While you cannot know a person's heart, you can see what he or she produces by his or her actions. See what kind of fruit Jesus expects from His followers.

40.1 Giving One Last Analogy

When I ran my first marathon, a friend came alongside me at about mile 10. He had run many more marathons than me, and we had trained together. It was good to see a familiar face while I ran on that February morning. As we ran he told stories of his runs, asked how I was doing, and generally kept my mind off the pain that was building in my legs with each step on the pavement. As long as I stayed with him and listened to him, my body and mind moved along as it was trained to do. I felt OK. When I broke stride with him and quit listening to him, my mind and body began to convince me this was the craziest thing I had ever done and that I needed to stop that minute and go home. When I was "with" my friend, I did well. When I ran "on my own," I almost quit. I finished the run and have finished several marathons since. But that day, I learned the importance of staying with someone in order to learn from and be encouraged by him or her.

What have you done that you soon realized if someone else was not there to help or encourage you, you would have never done it? Write your experience here:

_____

_____

_____

Read John 15. Read the chapter in its entirety to gain the context of Jesus' important teaching here. Return to verse 1 and underline who Jesus said He was and who the Father was in His analogy.

Six times in John's story Jesus used the phrase "I am" to identify Himself. "I am" is the name God gave Moses when His servant asked what he should tell the Egyptians about who had sent him (Ex. 3:14). Jesus was God in flesh. In John 6:35, Jesus said, "I am the bread of life." In John 8:12, He said, "I am the light of the world." In John 10:11, He said, "I am the good shepherd." In John 11:25, He said, "I am the resurrection and the life;" and in John 14:6, He said, "I am the way and the truth and the life." Here in John 15:1, Jesus said, "I am the true vine," but He also added a second figure. He said, "My Father is the gardener."

On the last night with His disciples, Jesus gave one last analogy of who He was as the *Christos*. He said He was like a vine and His Father was like the gardener or "vinedresser" (NASB). The vine was a familiar image for Israel (See Psalm 80:8–19 and Ezekiel 19:10–14 for examples of this). But in each of these Old Agreement images of Israel as a vine, the picture was one of failure and judgment. Jesus said He was the "true vine," the vine to replace the failed one.

Jesus described Himself as a vine and His Father as the one who cared for it. He then applied the analogy to His followers. What are the first images that come to your mind when you read Jesus' words? Write some of your thoughts here:

_____

_____

_____

40.2 Pruning Branches

We have a couple of crepe myrtle plants in our back yard. They provide superb landscape presence, and their blooms are beautiful in season. They also grow fast and tall. A crepe myrtle plant can look like a tree in a year or so. Every other year, I trim the branches down to look like I planted five-foot sticks in the ground. The first time I pruned it, Kim thought I had killed the thing. But within two or three weeks small, green sprigs began to sprout from the "sticks." By the end of the growing season, it was beginning to look like a full budding plant again. The plant actually looks better and is healthier during the years I prune the limbs than when I do not.

Do you care for any plants? Do you prune the plants or do you just let them all grow as they will? What do you know about pruning? Write your thoughts here:

_____

_____

_____

_____

_____

Read John 1:2–4. Underline what Jesus said the Father does to the branches (v. 2). Underline the recurring word, "remain," in verse 4.

The purpose of a vine is to produce fruit; the purpose of the vinedresser is to care for the vine so it can produce the most fruit. Jesus said the Father did what any good vinedresser would do with branches that bear no fruit—He cut them off. Those branches that gave fruit, He "prunes" or literally "cleanses," to make it "even more fruitful" (v. 2). God desires for us to produce fruit with our lives. Jesus said that God will cut off those who do not produce fruit, but He will prune those whose lives give Kingdom fruit.

Jesus told His disciples that they were already "clean," or "pruned," because of the message He had given them (v. 3). They were healthy to produce fruit with their lives because they had been with Him, and He had taught them how to live for Him. The secret to staying healthy or clean is to "remain" in Him (v. 4). Remain can also be translated "abide" (NASB). Like a vine and branch, our relationship with Jesus is reciprocal. If we remain in Him, He will remain in us. Jesus also stated the obvious truth that a branch cannot bear fruit alone. Without a support system of branches and roots, the nutrients needed to produce fruit can never get to the branch. In the same way, Jesus said, we cannot bear fruit unless we have a vine-branch relationship with Him.

Apply this part of Jesus' analogy to your own life. Which of the images relate to where you are in your relationship with Jesus? Ask God to show you the health of your relationship with Him.

_____

_____

_____

40.3 Cleaning Up the Plant

Part of spring cleaning in my yard every year involves picking up dead branches that have fallen from the trees throughout the winter. Wind and ice cause some to fall to the ground, creating a project for me as the days grew warmer. Those on the ground are dead, useless to a tree trying to rise out of its winter sleep to produce again its fruit of seeds and leaves. The limbs on the tree look dead, too. There are no leaves or evidence of growth, but their connection to the tree ensures hope they will soon have leaves again. Those on the ground that I pick up and put in the alley for the city truck to take to the landfill have no chance of producing growth. All they are good for is organic compost or landfill trash.

What are some of your chores during the spring to clean up from the winter? Do you enjoy doing these, or would you prefer someone else tend to these sorts of things? Express your feelings here:

_____

_____

_____

Read John 15:5–6. Circle the word "branch" (or "branches") in both verses. How did Jesus compare the branch that "remains" in Him and the one that does not? Write your answer here:

_____

_____

_____

_____

Jesus moved the analogy to His disciples and Himself. He is still the vine, the source of support and life for the branches which the Father tends; but here He identifies the branches. We are those branches. Between the life of the vine and the care of the Father, we serve like a fruit-producing branch. And if we stay in a vital, vine-branch relationship with Christ, He promised we will "bear much fruit" (v. 5). Jesus shot straight with His disciples: "Apart from me you can do nothing." Meditate on those clear words for a while. No matter how much we want to do or even the large amount of good things we do, without our continual relationship with Jesus we can do nothing for Him or His cause.

This analogy is a core image of our relationship with Jesus every day. We cannot expect to produce any fruit in our lives by deciding to "remain in Him" one day and going about our busyness of life the next. We either abide with Him or we will become like those branches I pick up at the end of winter and put out in the alley for the city truck to haul away (v. 6). Self-sufficiency is not a hallmark of a Christian. We are 100 percent dependent on our Vine to produce any kind of fruit in our lives. And when we do so, we can confess with Paul, "I can do everything through him who gives me strength" (Phil. 4:13).

John 15:5 is the Memory Verse for this lesson. Begin to learn it now. Take the time to identify some practical ways you can "remain" in Him. Spiritual practices like Bible study, prayer, and fasting may start your list.

What can you do to ensure you are in constant contact with your Source of life and fruitfulness?

_____

_____

_____

40.4 Producing Fruit

Jesus lived and taught in an agrarian society. More people live in urban and suburban environments than when Jesus chose His analogies of Kingdom life. My girls still think of fruit as being in the produce section of the grocery store. Few of us plant, care for, and keep plants so we can eat their fruit. Jesus used the image of fruit several ways. He used it as evidence of whether or not someone was a false prophet (Matt. 7:15–20). He used it as a way to tell what kind of a person someone was (Luke 6:43–44). And He cursed a fig tree on His way to Jerusalem as a parable of what would happen to those who did not produce fruit for Him (Matt. 21:19). Fruit is the output of one's life; the kind of fruit grown tells much about the person and the nutrients he or she depends on to produce it.

Use a concordance or online Bible search engine to find the many ways fruit is used in Jesus' story. Record some of them here:

_____

_____

_____

Read John 15:7–8. Circle the word "if" at the beginning of verse 7 and the promise that follows. Underline what will give the Father glory in verse 8.

One way we remain in Christ is through prayer. Jesus told His students that if they abided in Him, to "ask whatever you wish, and it will be given you" (v. 7). The promise is built on the condition that they "remain" in Him and His Word in them. The former is a prerequisite for the latter. The word for "wish" does not mean to wish, as in "make a wish." It can mean "to will or purpose." Jesus is not a genie or Santa Claus that gives us what we wish for. As we abide with Him, we learn His heart. Soon our requests are desires in line with His. He gives us those so we can bear fruit for Him, not to be healthy, wealthy, and wise. (See a principle similar to this in Psalm 37:4.)

The evidence that we are apprentices to Jesus is in our actions—what we produce with the investments of our time, talents, and treasures. This fruit of our life is what brings "glory," or "honor," to God. Jesus has said that we are to do our good deeds so others may see them and "praise your Father in heaven" (Matt. 5:16). Our actions point either to ourselves or to God.

But what is the "fruit" we are to produce? Some say the fruit is the result of our evangelistic efforts and are the people we lead to Christ. Others point to the "fruit of the Spirit" Paul talks about in Galatians 5 (vv. 22–23). Still others say our fruit that glorifies the Father is our good deeds which reflect the Kingdom and King to whom we belong (Matt. 5:16; Jas. 2:14–17). I suggest it is all of the above. When we abide constantly in Christ, others will come to know Him. His character will show in our lives, and we will live like Kingdom people.

Does the fruit of your life honor God? Review the verses above and ask the Holy Spirit to reveal this to you.

40.5 Obeying Jesus

One way I know that my children love me is that they do what I tell them to do. This is because if they follow my instructions it means they respect me and value who I am and what I tell them as their father. To obey what I say is another way of saying, "I love you, Daddy." On the other hand, disobedience can indicate a lapse of respect or, over an extended period of time, evidence they no longer love or respect me enough to follow my leadership. To obey someone is to demonstrate one's love for him or her. Not to obey means something else is going on.

Respond to the concept that obedience is to love someone. Do you agree or disagree? In what other relationships might this statement hold true?

_____

_____

_____

Read John 15:9–11. Underline the form of the words "love" and "obey" in verses 9–10. Circle the word "joy" in verse 11.

Jesus reminded His students that He had loved them just as the Father had loved Him. Jesus had an abiding, vital relationship with the One who sent Him. It was this Father-Son love relationship that was the source of His strength and courage. He offered that same kind of relationship to His followers (v. 9). Jesus then described what that love looked like. Just as He obeyed His Father's commands to show His love to Him, so His disciples should love Him by obeying His instructions to them (v. 10). The prophet Samuel said, "To obey is better than sacrifice," and Paul observed that Jesus was "obedient to death [His Father's will]—even death on a cross" (1 Sam. 15:22; Phil. 2:8). Jesus highlighted obedience over feelings and obeying as the clearest evidence of love between Him and His followers.

Why would He tell them this? He wanted the joy He knew through obedience to be part of their relationship with Him so they may then have "complete" joy (v. 11). Love is lived out in obedience to the One who laid down His life for us and called us to the adventure of being His Kingdom agents in the world. This love produces a joy of life that only Jesus and those who follow Him can ever know. If we abide in that love each day, Jesus promised our lives will be filled with joy and purpose.

Can you say you have the kind of joy Jesus promised to His disciples in your life? How is it the same? How is it different? Spend more time meditating on how obedience and love fit together in a relationship—especially your relationship with God. If you like to draw or are an artist, draw an image of what Jesus has said in this passage. Show it to someone you trust and explain to them which of Jesus' teachings it represents.

For further study:
- **Galatians 5:16–26**
- **James 2:14–26**

41—Examining Your Heart: Jesus' Betrayal and Arrest

Your attitude toward Judas may be, "There's no way I'd ever do a thing like that! Turn Jesus over to His enemies for a measly 30 pieces of silver? What a jerk." Judas did perform a wicked act toward the One who came to rescue him. But when we observe Jesus' reaction to what he did, we see how He calmly accepted His disciple's actions. Once again, the ways of the King and the Kingdom seem counter-intuitive to our natural sensitivities. In the end Judas' choices made it possible for Jesus, the *Christos*, to complete His mission as the Suffering Servant-Messiah.

On the night Jesus shared the Passover meal with His followers and washed their feet, His traitor left to get those who would arrest Him. Jesus and the other disciples went into the night to the Garden of Gethsemane where Jesus submitted to the will of His Father and the way of the cross (Matt. 26:26–44). This is the setting

of Jesus' arrest and the whirlwind events that led to His crucifixion. Judas was the catalyst God used to orchestrate the plan for Jesus' capture and arrest. And while it is a dark moment in the story of Jesus, God redeemed even this scene to bring salvation to all people.

The Memory Verse for this chapter is 1 Corinthians 10:12. Paul warned his readers to be careful not to fall, even though they believed they were standing firm. This parallels the Proverb: "Pride goes before destruction, a haughty spirit before a fall" (Prov. 16:18). Biblical wisdom warns that we all are susceptible to a fall.

Our question to consider for this chapter is "Does Judas represent all of us in some way?" The seed of what he did is in all of us. Observe his act of sedition and discover the places in which you may be turning Jesus over to those with whom you have made alliances.

41.1 Handing Jesus Over to the Authorities

In this and the following episodes in the story of Jesus I have little that I can relate to from my life. No personal anecdote or historical reference I can think of will measure up to the depth of emotional, physical, and spiritual pain Jesus experienced during the hours of His betrayal, trial, crucifixion, and death. I have had people resist my ideas and even orchestrate my departure from ministry, but I have no reference for the depth of betrayal Jesus knew when Judas came in the night to hand Him over to the authorities.

As hard as Judas' act was to accept, Peter, who was Jesus' closest friend and swore to never leave His side, turned on Him as well. Jesus had to know a pain of rejection few have experienced. These next chapters cover the dark and chaotic events that will appear to defeat God's plan. As we stand at the empty tomb, we will see that what looked like the end was really only the beginning to the Kingdom Jesus came to establish among us.

As we move into this part of His-story, if you are familiar with these events, ask God to make them fresh to you. Ask the Holy Spirit to reveal those things that apply to you directly as one for whom Jesus suffered.

Read Matthew 26:1–47 for the setting of this chapter. Return to verse 47 and underline all the people Matthew listed.

The story writers tell us that as Jesus finished praying in the garden, Judas, one of the Twelve, arrived with a crowd of people to take Jesus to the religious leaders for trial. Matthew wrote that the crowd was "armed with swords and clubs," more the weapons of a mob than a trained army. The writers of the story of Jesus also let us know that the group had been gathered and sent by "the chief priests and the elders of the people" (v. 47). These were the religious leaders who had been in conflict with Jesus since He began His public ministry and who had been plotting His arrest for some time.

The religious leaders had assembled a mob of people to capture Jesus after Judas had agreed to lead them to his leader. Blind allegiance allowed the mob to do whatever they said to do. Trumped up charges given by corrupt leaders led the crowd to follow Jesus' betrayer into the garden to capture Him. Clearly the religious leaders had painted Jesus as a dangerous rebel, or there would have been no need for a "crowd" carrying weapons. We begin to see the absurdity of their charges through the actions of their followers. They wanted Jesus removed from public life and would do whatever needed to try and stop Him.

What mobs have you seen on the news or read about that clearly were brought together by leaders to make a scene or to capture someone? Have you ever been part of a group that was driven more by emotional frenzy than by clear reason and purpose? Write some of your ideas about how such a mob forms and how people could so easily become part of it here:

_____

_____

_____

_____

_____

_____

41.2 Turning Jesus Over to the Crowd

On a trip to Albania, I quickly realized that men greeted one another with a kiss. Instead of a handshake or a hug, these men gladly kissed one another on each cheek and heartedly embraced. You could tell there was nothing but friendship and a warm welcome intended by their actions. After a week of serving with some of them, when it was time to leave, I found myself accepting their customary greeting and goodbye. I began to grasp how such actions showed friendship in a way a handshake would not. I felt honored that they saw me as one to whom they could freely show their friendship. I did not, however, bring the practice home with me. I still shake hands, even with my best friends.

Have you been in a culture where kissing was part of the common practice of greeting someone? Did you ever experience such a greeting? How did it make you feel? What did the practice teach you about the culture and people who practiced it? Write your experience here:

_____

_____

_____

Read Matthew 26:48–50. Circle how Judas addressed Jesus and how Jesus addressed Judas.

Judas had prearranged with the mob that the One he greeted with a kiss was the One they were to seize (v. 48). This would be similar to someone saying, "The one I shake hands with, take him." A kiss was common among men of that day. It seems odd to us now due to our different customs. There is nothing special about Judas' kiss other than the sinister motive behind

it. Judas went directly to Jesus and addressed Him as "Rabbi," which meant "Teacher" (v. 49). Judas had called Jesus by the same title earlier when Jesus had told Judas he would betray Him (v. 25). Judas is the only disciple who addressed Jesus as "Rabbi" in Matthew's story of Jesus. Judas then kissed Jesus.

Judas called Jesus "Rabbi;" Jesus called Judas "friend." (v. 50). This word for friend was what you called a partner or comrade, not a close friend. It would be similar to a formal greeting like, "My good friend, it is good to see you again." Judas used the formal title of Rabbi. Jesus used the formal title for friend.

Jesus said, "Do what you came for" (v. 50). In the margins or footnotes of some translations the editors suggest another interpretation of Jesus' words: "Why have you come?" The difference is based on a tech-

Christos—God's Transforming Touch

nical reading of the short phrase in Greek. Jesus clearly knew what Judas had come to do. If the question is the correct reading, then Jesus was either asking a rhetorical question or getting Judas to confess openly what he had done, which Judas did tell. The members of the mob stepped up and seized Jesus.

A common greeting of the day between a teacher and his student became a signal of treachery and betrayal for all time. Put yourself in the scene. Watch it unfold as Jesus' story writers tell it. Feel the night air. Smell the burning torches and lanterns (John 18:3). Hear the noise of the mob. Watch Jesus.

41.3 Using a Sword

Soldiers defend their comrades in arms. Loved ones come to the side of the other when they feel threatened. Parents instinctively protect their children. Friends take up for friends in a fight. You can test the depth of your relationship with someone by how they respond in a situation where you are in danger or attacked. Acquaintances step back in conflict. Friends step up. Danger is the crucible of one's love and care for another. You know you have a true friend when he steps into the same situation as you and risks his safety for you.

Have you ever had someone step up to defend you or risk his or her life for you? Have you ever done that for someone else? What was the situation? How did it affect you or the one you defended? Write some of your thoughts here:

_____

_____

Read Matthew 26:51–52. Underline Jesus' teaching in verse 52 during these quick actions by His disciple.

As soon as one in the crowd grabbed Jesus, one of those with Him drew his sword and cut off the ear of "the servant of the high priest" (v. 51). John tells us Jesus' "companion" was Peter and the servant's name was "Malchus" (John 18:10). What was Peter doing with a sword? Fishermen are not usually too adept at wielding swords. One of Jesus' disciples armed with a sword seems atypical of His teachings. However, just before Jesus went to the garden to pray, He had told those in the room with Him, "but now if you have a purse, take it, and also a bag; and if you don't have a sword, sell your cloak and buy one." The disciples said they had two swords among them (Luke 22:36–38). Previously, He had told His students to take nothing with them as He sent them out to tell others about Him (Luke 9:3–6). Things had changed since that time. Jesus had warned His disciples before they left the upper room to prepare for the perilous days ahead. Peter was the first to follow his Leader's orders.

Jesus responded sharply to Peter. He told him to put the sword away, and then said, "For all who draw the sword will die by the sword" (v. 52). Jesus was not teaching passivity for all who follow Him. But He clearly warned that those who choose to solve problems with force will be subject to the same consequences of force in their own lives. "Our struggle is not against flesh and blood," Paul wrote (Eph. 6:12). The battles of the Kingdom of God are fought in the spiritual realm. To draw the sword may be to fight in the wrong battle. That was clearly the case in the garden with Jesus. Why? Jesus explained next.

Stay in the scene as you meditate on this passage. Be Peter. Be Malchus. Listen to the mob as a disciple of Jesus. Hear Jesus' words. What would they mean to you then? Now? Watch Jesus heal the ear of His enemy. What lesson do you learn from that act by your Leader?

_____
_____
_____

41.4 Defining True Power

True power is to have it and refrain from using it. Anyone in power can launch an attack or send armies into battle. Scarce are those who have unlimited power but do not use it. As the saying goes, power corrupts, and absolute power corrupts absolutely. In Jesus' day, Herod the Great, Pilate, and the chief priests all possessed and used power to hold and expand their positions. Power is the way of the world to defend ourselves, defeat others, or acquire what we want or argue is rightfully ours. Refusing to use power or resources when we feel threatened or challenged in order to allow a higher purpose to find its way into the lives of others is a sign that we may be closer than we think to becoming like Jesus.

What are some of your thoughts on the use of power? What do agree with in the paragraph above? What do you disagree with in the paragraph above? Write some of your thoughts and feelings here:

_____
_____
_____
_____

Read Matthew 26:53–54. Summarize Jesus' continued response to Peter in the space below.

_____
_____

Jesus said that if He wanted to start a fight, He could do so. Swords and clubs were child's toys compared to what He could bring down on the mob if He wanted. He asked the rhetorical question that if He asked His Father, could He not command "more than twelve legions of angels" in a moment (v. 53). A legion was about 6,000 soldiers. You do the math. Jesus' point was, if they wanted a fight, He could bring one on. This sword for sword action was like boys pushing each other on a playground compared to what He had access to if He wanted to use it. But Jesus would save the legion of army angels for later. He had another job to do. He would soon demonstrate a different kind of power—the power found in Him as King and among those who were His people.

If Jesus had asked His Father to send in the angelic cavalry to save the day, His mission as the Suffering Servant *Christos* would not be completed. A bigger plan was at work. Jesus asked, "How then would the Scriptures be fulfilled that say it must happen in this way?" (v. 54) John added that Jesus said, "Shall I not drink the cup the Father has given Me?" in reference to His prayer of submission to suffer in the garden (John 18:11). Isaiah's prophecy of the *Christos* told of His suffering through which He would "bear their iniquities" (Isa. 53:11). Jesus came to suffer and die for the sins of the world, not to wield earthly power like a sword. Only a cross would fulfill the Scriptures that told the story of a suffering *Christos*.

Christos—God's Transforming Touch

Continue to listen to Jesus. His life was threatened, and He had access to unlimited power to end the threat. Yet He chose to refuse the use of that power, be arrested, and begin the journey to the cross. What do His actions and words reveal to you?

41.5 Arresting Jesus

Jesus wanted all those present at His arrest to know that it was not of their doing. Instead, it was part of a greater story line of which they were simply players. His-story was coming to its climax, and Jesus seized the moment to tell His disciples and captors that even their acts at night in the garden was God's doing, not theirs.

Read Matthew 26:55–56. Circle the word "rebellion." Underline "the writings of the prophets."

Jesus turned to the larger crowd and asked if they really thought He led the kind of rebellion that required clubs and swords to capture Him (v. 55). When had they ever seen Him call men to arms or incite a rebellion against the Romans? Although other so-called messiahs had done that, they had no evidence of such actions by Him. Jesus reminded them again that their actions had nothing to do with reality, only the wishes of the ones who sent them. Jesus stated that if He was such a threat to them, they could have arrested Him any day when He openly taught in the Temple courts. "What's up with that?" He challenged them.

What was happening before their eyes took place so "that the writings of the prophets might be fulfilled" (v. 56). Luke tells us that in the upper room before the group followed Jesus to the garden to pray, He reminded them of Isaiah's words: "and he was numbered with the transgressors." Isaiah's prophecy must be fulfilled in Him (Luke 22:37; Isa. 53:12). The Suffering Servant *Christos* would be identified as a common criminal—someone who broke the law, was arrested, sentenced, and executed. Jesus revealed the Father's purposes in the dark events of the night. What happened there had been set in motion centuries before this motley band of mercenaries followed a traitor through the night to arrest Jesus. His-story was being written right before their eyes.

"Then all the disciples deserted him and fled" (v. 56). Jesus was alone in the night. One had betrayed Him. All the others had deserted Him. Only the hired hands of His enemies remained near Him to lead Him to His death. Few scenes in history, film, or literature show such tragedy or sadness as this. All Jesus had done for His friends did not count for more than a miscalculated swing with a sword and desertion into the night. Jesus was left alone to complete the mission the Father sent Him to complete.

Meditate on the Memory Verse, 1 Corinthians 10:12, and our question to consider for this chapter, "Does Judas represent all of us in some way?" Reflect on the events in this episode of the story of Jesus, the *Christos*. Ask the Holy Spirit to reveal the motives of your heart no matter what they expose.

For further study:
- **Luke 22:47–53; 23:1–5**
- **John 18:19–24, 28–40**

42—Seeing Christ's Love: The Crucifixion

Christianity cannot exist without the crucifixion of Jesus. Without His trial, suffering, and death, Jesus would not have completed the Father's mission. He would not be the *Christos*. The story of Jesus includes the apparent failure of an earthly kingdom through His death at the hands of those He came to rescue. Only through His Resurrection could He establish the Kingdom of Heaven. Jesus' death on the cross was an intentional act of love that Jesus told His followers about long before it happened. His death is the fulfillment of the Passover promise and Day of Atonement.

The mob seized Jesus in the garden and handed Him over to the religious leaders who had sent them. The ruling body conducted a prearranged "trial" in the middle of the night (Matt. 26:57–68). Early in the morning these religious leaders decided Jesus must die. They took Jesus to Pilate, the Roman governor, to complete their wishes (Matt. 27:1–2). Pilate initially refused their request. In the end keeping peace and his job were more important to Pilate than trusting Jesus for whom he knew Jesus to be.

The Memory Verse for this chapter is John 15:13. Jesus told His disciples that there was no greater demonstration of love than for someone "to lay down his life for his friends." He then demonstrated that love when He died on the cross for them and for us.

Our question to consider for this chapter is "Could Jesus have chosen not to die?" The answer is "yes" and "no." As fully God and fully human, Jesus had every option not to die. However, the Son came to do the will of the Father so the Scriptures could be fulfilled. To show the ultimate act of God's love for all people, He had to die.

42.1 Humiliating Jesus

Fear is sometimes as great a motivator as truth. Fear mostly grows out of self-protection. Truth, on the other hand, frees us to risk everything. People who have gained or been given power are often more concerned with keeping that power than knowing the truth. Why? Truth can disrupt their status quo, which they have worked hard to create and then keep. Fear of losing what they have gained can be like a fog on the coast of Maine in March. The fear keeps them from seeing the rocky shore of truth they are about to crash into. We want to keep what we have worked so hard to gain. Anything or anyone who threatens our status becomes a threat to us. Fear motivates us to protect ourselves from the threat of others. Truth frees us to serve them.

When have you feared someone because he or she threatened to take your job or injure your status? When has knowing the truth about a person or a situation motivated you to change your mind and risk your position in order to make the truth known?

_____

_____

_____

_____

Read John 19:1–15. Underline Pilate's responses to the religious leaders. Highlight Jesus' words to Pilate in verse 11.

Jesus' "trial" before Pilate began in John's story of Jesus in chapter 18:28–40. The religious leaders brought Jesus to the Roman governor. They wanted Jesus killed but they had "no right to execute anyone" (v. 31). To placate the mob that would not go away, Pilate had Jesus flogged and ridiculed by his soldiers. They mocked Jesus by putting a crown of thorns and robe on Him. The bored soldiers enjoyed mocking those they were sent to control.

When Jesus was brought out to the crowd in His battered and humiliated state, Pilate tried again to hand Jesus back to those who brought Him (John 19:4–5). When the leaders called for crucifixion, Pilate retorted that he still saw no reason to execute this man (v. 6). The leaders of the people said their laws had cause for His death: "he claimed to be the Son of God" (v. 7). John wrote that when Pilate heard this "he was even more afraid" (v. 8). This accusation sent Pilate back into the palace to question Jesus further. When Pilate tried to force Jesus to talk by explaining that he had the power to crucify Him, Jesus replied, "You would have no power over me if it were not given to you from above" (v. 11).

Pilate returned with Jesus before the crowd, and the dance of power continued. The Jews subtly reminded Pilate he was there to protect the interests of Caesar. If he let Jesus go, Pilate would not be doing his job (vv. 12–14). The leaders went so far as to claim Caesar as their king, a lie and sacrilege to their faith (v. 15).

Put yourself in Pilate's place. How would you have responded to the crowd if you were in his position with his mission to keep the peace for the empire? Be honest.

_____

_____

_____

_____

42.2 Enduring the Cross

The cross of Jesus' day was a tool of execution. We have turned it into a piece of jewelry. The cross was an instrument of death designed by the empire to keep its subjects in line. Some wear it like a good luck charm. The wooden cross was stained with blood and pieces of flesh. We polish it, engrave it, and imprint it on stationery as a sign of our faith. When we look at the cross that Jesus died upon, we cannot help but see the depth of His love. Only the love of One who did not deserve to hang there but allowed Himself to suffer such a painful death could be the motive behind what He did.

Do you wear a cross as a piece of jewelry? Do you have images of the cross in your home? What do these mean to you and what do you hope they say to others? Write your answers here:

_____

_____

_____

Read John 19:16–22. Underline the characters and places mentioned in the passage. Underline the message Pilate had nailed above Jesus on the cross.

After being badgered by the religious leaders, Pilate "handed him over to them to be crucified" (v. 16). The Roman soldiers assigned to crucifixion duty went about the prescribed process to execute those put under their charge. Jesus carried a part of the wooden cross upon which He would be crucified to where the biblical writers knew as "the place of the Skull" (v. 17). There He was nailed to the wooden death machine with a man sentenced to death on either side of Him (v. 18). To the people walking by, Jesus was just another criminal the Romans disposed of that day.

Pilate wanted to make a point. He ordered a sign in three languages, Aramaic, Latin, and Greek, to be hung above Jesus. The sign read, "JESUS OF NAZARETH, THE KING OF THE JEWS" (vv. 19–20). As representative of the empire, Pilate wanted to make sure that anyone seeking to be king would know his fate would be the same. The religious leaders did not like the governor's message and asked that he change it. They feared what would happen to them when people realized that they had to come up with something Jesus did not claim for Himself in order to have Him executed (v. 21). The irony is that the "notice" was true, though few believed it that day. Pilate would have no more of their petty wishes and ordered the sign to remain (v. 22).

Compare John's description of Jesus' execution by the Romans with the other biblical writers' accounts. What does John tell us that the other writers do not? What is his unique message in telling what he did about Jesus on the cross? Put yourself in the place of the different characters in this part of the story and consider what each one saw from his or her perspective that afternoon.

42.3 Standing at the Foot of the Cross

At this point in Jesus' execution, it may appear all was going according to the plans of the religious leaders and the Roman soldiers. The leaders got what they wanted; the soldiers got to divide up the clothes of the one they killed as part of their work. Those who stood at the foot of the cross must have seen that Jesus had lost control

Christos—God's Transforming Touch

of His mission to establish the Kingdom of God. The chaos of the last 12 hours must have made them wonder if their trust was in vain. However, upon reflection and inspiration by the Holy Spirit, John lets us know that the soldiers' gambling for Jesus' undergarment was part of God's plan for the *Christos*. Jesus' instructions to His mother and disciple were not sentimental words but signs of His leadership even at the end.

Read John 19:23–24. Underline the Old Agreement passage John quoted in verse 24.

We learn there were at least four soldiers who executed Jesus by the fact that they divided His clothes "into four shares, one for each of them" (v. 23). Jesus' undergarment had some value since it was seamless, so His executioners decided to cast lots to gamble to see which of the four got it. John tells his readers that this act was also part of God's plan to rescue all people through Jesus. He remembered Psalm 22:18: "They divide my garments among them and cast lots for my clothing." The Roman soldiers were not in control that dark day. God was.

Read John 19:25–27. Underline Jesus' instructions from the cross to His mother and disciple.

Only John tells us of Jesus' instructions about His mother from the cross. John was the only disciple who had come to the cross with Jesus' mother and two other women disciples (v. 25). The others had deserted Him in the garden and had not returned to Him. Peter had denied Him and was nowhere to be found. John recorded Jesus' instructions for him to care for His mother. John took Mary, the mother of Jesus, into his home (v. 27). John is "the disciple whom he loved" and he identified himself in his story of Jesus this way (John 13:23; 19:26; 20:2; 21:7, 20). This is not a title of pride but one of humility that told others of Jesus' great love for him. He was honored to be chosen to care for Jesus' mother after Jesus returned to heaven.

John provided two more insights into the death of Jesus that demonstrated God's purposes and plan in it. What do these two facts about Jesus' death do to help you trust Him as the *Christos*? Stand at the foot of the cross. Watch the soldiers. Hear Jesus' words to those He loved. Prayerfully feel what they may have felt. Ask God to use those feelings to strengthen your trust in Jesus.

42.4 Recognizing It is Finished

When I wrapped up writing my dissertation and turned it in to my supervising professor, I walked away from his office and said, "It's finished!" When I conclude writing this study of the story of Jesus, I will say, "It's finished!"

Then I will reflect on what I have written before I soon begin my next project. When I cross the finish line of my next marathon, I will shout, "I'm finished!" I will have completed my training, diet, and preparation to complete the run, and I will joyfully announce the work is done and the celebration can begin. Part of my motivation for beginning something is to confidently say "I have completed what I started." Few things feel better. I know I will never finish my ministry to my wife, family, or church, or my apprenticeship to Jesus in this life. But when the day comes to leave this life for the next, I hope to say humbly, "It's finished. Let's get started on eternity."

What have you done that when you said, "It's finished!" it meant more than just words? How do you feel after you have completed something very difficult? Describe some of your experiences here:

_____

_____

_____

Read John 19:28–30. Highlight Jesus' final words on the cross (v. 30).

John moved quickly to Jesus' death by simply writing, "Later" (v. 28). John wrote Jesus sensed that "all was now completed." This is the same word for "finished," which Jesus used as He died (v. 30). Jesus knew He had completed His mission as the Suffering Servant *Christos*. He then "gave up his spirit" and died (v. 30).

Knowing what was about to happen, Jesus asked for something to drink. Matthew 27:34 and Mark 15:23 tell us Jesus refused a drink while on the cross. This may be because He did not want to be under the influence of anything but God's leadership during His suffering. Here Jesus took it possibly because His mouth was dry and He needed it to speak. This is another unique description of events by John who was near Jesus when He died.

"It is finished" were Jesus' final words on the cross (v. 30). Only John recorded these words. The other evangelistic writers said Jesus "cried out again in a loud voice" (Matt. 27:50; Mark 15:34). John heard what He said. Jesus announced that He had accomplished what the Father had sent Him to do. His death was not an accident or a failed attempt to be a king. It was, from beginning to end, the reason He came to earth. His announcement was one of victory and accomplishment, not resignation to circumstances or defeat by those more powerful than Him.

After announcing His victory, Jesus "bowed his head and gave up his spirit" (v. 30). The battle was won. The mission was complete. The Son had fulfilled the wishes of His Father. The final sacrifice of the New Agreement fulfilled all the sacrifices of the Old Agreement. Jesus truly was "the Lamb of God, who takes away the sin of the world" (John 1:29).

Record some of the reasons you have observed in His-story as to why Jesus' death on the cross was the completion of His mission from the Father.

_____

_____

_____

_____

_____

Christos—God's Transforming Touch

42.5 Evidence of His Kingship

After Jesus' announced His completed mission and died, the plan of God continued. Every detail of the events after His death pointed to Jesus as the *Christos*.

Read John 19:31–37. Underline the details that explain what happened after Jesus' death. Underline in verses 36–37 the reason John gave for these things happening.

The cruelty of crucifixion cannot be imagined by our civilized minds. To ensure death by suffocation the Roman soldiers were ordered to break the legs of the criminals. This would prevent the criminals from pushing themselves up to take a breath as they hung on the cross. The soldiers did this to the others crucified (v. 32). When they came to Jesus, the soldiers saw He was dead. But to ensure He was dead, one of them thrust a spear into His side, and blood and water gushed out (vv. 33–34).

John wrote into his story of Jesus that he saw this himself and was writing to give witness to its truth. He said he did this "so that you also may believe," or trust Jesus as he did (v. 35). Upon reflection and inspiration of the Holy Spirit whom Jesus promised, John pointed to two Old Agreement passages that were fulfilled by what he saw (vv. 36–37; see Ps. 34:20; Zech. 12:10). Every act down to the last wishes of those who orchestrated His death was part of God's eternal plan for the *Christos*.

Read and become familiar with the Memory Verse for this chapter (John 15:13). Jesus' own words to His closest friends told of His willing death for them.

Remember these words of Jesus as you reflect on His purposeful death for you. His motivation was not duty alone but His deep love for those He came to rescue.

Take some time to write a prayer of gratitude to Jesus for His suffering and death for you. Put in your own words your worship and love for Him as you meditate on His mission that was completed on the cross for you.

_____

_____

_____

_____

_____

_____

_____

_____

_____

For further study:
- **Matthew 27:27–66**
- **Luke 23:26–56**

43—Accepting Christ's Love: The Crucifixion

We have a ministry in our church called From the Dust. This group of nonprofessional musicians travels to prisons several weekends a year to present the story of Jesus to the inmates. They play rock-n-roll oldies and blues. They also pause throughout the concert to tell how but for the grace of God they would be in the same place as the inmates. Every time they come back with stories about the number of inmates who trusted Jesus for the first time.

Luke tells that as Jesus gave up His life on the cross, one of the condemned criminals executed with Him realized who Jesus was. Jesus told the man he would join Him in Paradise that day (Luke 23:39–43). Luke also recorded the tearing of the veil in the Temple upon Jesus' death and the centurion's confession that He was a "righteous man" (Luke 23:44–49). He also told who risked claiming Jesus' body and the burial process that

led to His disciples finding the empty tomb on the third day (Luke 23:50–56). These incidents from Luke's story of Jesus affirm His love for all people and how His love was extended to the least deserved and least expected.

The Memory Verse for this chapter is John 1:12. John opened his story of Jesus with the truth that "to all who received him, to those who believed in his name, he gave the right to become children of God." The events in this episode of His-story confirm John's message to all of us.

Our question to consider for this chapter is "Is it ever too late to believe in Jesus?" Does God rescue those inmates in prison in the same way He rescues everyone else? Does God accept even a "death-bed confession" as valid for rescue by Jesus?

43.1 Taunting Jesus

Jesus claimed to be the Messiah. It would follow, then, that those who saw Him as a messiah like all the others would mock Him as He apparently hung helplessly on the cross. We know the religious leaders and passersby took turns taunting Him to display His messianic powers by coming down off the cross (Matt. 27:39–43). Jesus neither answered nor acknowledged them.

Enter into the story as a person passing by the crucifixion of Jesus that Friday. After asking around who the criminals were and why they were being executed, what feelings would you have toward all three of them? What if you had asked your religious leader that question, and he told you the one in the middle claimed to be the Messiah? You knew Him as the carpenter from Nazareth. What would you say?

_____

_____

_____

Read Luke 23:39–43. Underline the second criminal's comments (vv. 40–42) and Jesus' reply to him (v. 43).

Jesus was crucified between two other men (Luke 23:32). As the religious leaders heaped insults on Him, one of the criminals joined in the chorus. He took up the chant that if Jesus was the *Christos*, why did He not save Himself? (v. 39) They all had missed the kind of King and Kingdom Jesus offered them. The other man dying with Jesus challenged his cohort in crime and confessed that they were getting what they deserved. However, he knew that Jesus had done nothing wrong (vv. 40–41). He then turned and asked Jesus to

remember him when He came into His Kingdom (v. 42). This man may have been near Jesus as He was tried and led to the cross. He may have heard Jesus as He asked the Father to forgive those who crucified Him. Something Jesus did or said combined to cause this man to trust Jesus for who He is.

Jesus sensed the criminal's trust and heard the man's defense of Jesus' innocence. Jesus answered his request by saying, "today you will be with me in paradise" (v. 43). Jesus did not promise to accept the man in His return to set up His Kingdom on earth, but He would embrace the man in heaven that very day.

We know from the fuller story of Jesus that the man's trust in Jesus was not as full as one of His chosen twelve disciples. We also know from the biblical stories and letters that follow Jesus' story that there is more to trusting Jesus than a simple confession at one's death. Before we get hung up on whether or not this man was a "Christian," think back to Jesus' own story about the owner who hired workers throughout the day and paid those who worked one hour the same as those who worked all day (Matt. 20:1–16).

What are your initial feelings about Jesus' words to the criminal on the cross? How does Jesus' response build your trust in Him? What questions does it raise for you? Spend time in thankful prayer for Jesus' heart for those who least expect it and those who least deserve it—people like us.

_____

_____

_____

_____

43.2 Watching Jesus Die

One of the several mysteries of Jesus' death was the darkness that "came over the whole land" for three hours (v. 44). Since Jesus was the Son of God, "the light of the world" (John 8:12), what did it mean when this darkness covered the land? We know that Moses approached a "thick darkness where God was" after receiving the Ten Commandments from God (Ex. 20:18–21). So, God can dwell in darkness. But John wrote in his first letter that "God is light; in him there is no darkness at all" (1 John 1:5). If there was darkness at Jesus' death, does that mean God was not present?

What initial conclusions do you have about the meaning of the darkness that fell at Jesus' death? Write your answers here:

_____

_____

_____

Read Luke 23:44–46. Underline the three things Luke recorded at Jesus' death in these verses.

Matthew, Mark, and Luke recorded that darkness came over the land from noon until three in the afternoon (v. 44; Matt. 27:45; Mark 15:33). Luke tells us this was because "the sun stopped shining" (v. 45). The others agreed it happened, but gave no cause. Some interpret this event to mean God withdrew His presence as Jesus bore the sins of the world upon the cross. This interpretation is based on Jesus' cry from the cross: "My God, my God, why have you forsaken me?" (Matt. 27:46) Jesus was truly forsaken as He died for the world's sins. The second event Luke recorded was that the curtain

separating the Most Holy Place from the Holy Place tore from top to bottom (v. 45; Ex. 26:31–33). The Holy of Holies (NASB) was the place the high priest entered on the Day of Atonement to sprinkle the blood of the sacrificial goat on the "mercy seat" of God to atone for the sins of the people (Lev. 16:15–19). No first-century Jew would miss the meaning of this act of God when Jesus shed His blood and died as a sacrifice.

Luke then wrote that Jesus called out to His Father and "breathed his last" (v. 46). All four writers of the story of Jesus recorded Jesus' death (Matt. 27:50; Mark 15:37; John 19:30). They vary on what He said as He died, but Jesus died. He did not faint; He died. This is essential to the truth of the Resurrection that will follow and core to the story's message. (Read 1 Corinthians 15:3–5 to see the importance.) Jesus' death was part of God's plan to rescue all people through the "once for all" sacrifice of His Son for their sins (Heb. 7:27). Take time to read the cross references and background

Christos—God's Transforming Touch

verses mentioned to expand your understanding of Jesus' death. Use a commentary or a study Bible to discover the meaning of this even in the Bible. Stand in the dark at the foot of the cross with John and Jesus' mother, Mary. Thank Jesus for suffering and dying for your sins.

43.3 Trusting Jesus

The last two people to trust Jesus before His burial were a criminal and a centurion. These are unlikely candidates for Jesus' love. Yet, their trust in Him serve as examples for all who wonder if Jesus would love them as they are. Many people resist going to church or joining Christians in a small group because they feel unworthy to be part of a group whose membersseem to have it all together. We who follow Jesus know better. We can point to these two men's trust in Jesus as examples that all people matter to God. Anyone at any time can place their trust in Him.

Who in your network of friends and family may consider themselves unworthy of God's love? For what reason(s)? Have you considered pointing out the trust of the criminal and centurion as people like us who were undeserving, yet worthy of God's love through Jesus?

_____

_____

Read Luke 23:47–49. Underline the three people or groups Luke noted as they reacted to Jesus' death. What do each of these groups represent for us today?

_____

_____

_____

When the darkness settled over the land, Jesus cried out to His Father and died. Luke recorded how a soldier and two groups of people reacted to Jesus' death. The centurion, who was possibly in command of the death brigade that afternoon, had observed Jesus from Pilate's palace to His death. He "praised God and said, 'Surely this was a righteous man'" (v. 47). Matthew and Mark recorded his confession as, "Surely he was the Son of God!" (Matt. 27:54; Mark 15:39)

Luke then tells us when the crowd who had gathered to watch the spectacle saw what had happened, they "beat their breasts and went away" (v. 48). Their reaction was similar to the man in Jesus' story who beat his chest in repentance. Their reaction also mirrored Isaiah's instructions to the people to repent by beating their chests (Read Luke 18:13 and Isaiah 32:11–13 for these background stories). Repentance and regret may have been their reaction after seeing and hearing such events.

"Those who knew him," Luke wrote, simply "stood at a distance, watching these things" (v. 49). In stunned silence, those who had followed Jesus to the cross watched Him die alone in the darkness. The centurion praised God. The people beat their chests. Jesus' followers stood quietly, watching and listening as the final minutes of Jesus' life on earth unfolded.

Which of the groups do you associate with as you stand and watch Jesus die? Do you praise God like the centurion? Do you beat your chest in repentance like the people? Or do you stand in silence before the sacrificed *Christos*? Write your thoughts here:

_____

_____

43.4 Burying Jesus

We all have things we say we believe in. However, most of us are never tested to see if we will stake our lives on these beliefs. For example, I believe that if I jump out of a plane with a properly packed parachute and have received proper training, I will float safely to the ground. But I have never tried that nor been in an emergency situation in which I was forced to test my belief. I have also said I trust my friends, but I have not yet had to risk my life or reputation for them. So I can say I am their friend and that I would do anything for them. But until I do, they and I will never know the extent of my friendship for them.

Have you faced a situation in which what you have thought or believed was tested by forcing you to act? What was it? If you have not, what can you imagine that would cause you to risk something for the sake of someone or something you trusted to be true? Write your thoughts here:

_____

_____

_____

_____

Read Luke 23:50–54. Circle the man's name, the group he belonged to, and the place he was from. Underline what he did that risked his well-being.

After Jesus died someone had to care for His body and bury Him. A surprise person came out of the shadows to do this. All four writers of the story of Jesus tell of a man named Joseph from Arimathea who went to Pilate and asked for the body of Jesus (vv. 50–52). The unique thing about this man was that he was a secret follower of Jesus. He was also a member of the Council, or Sanhedrin, the group of religious leaders who orchestrated Jesus' death. Luke tells us he "had not consented to their decision and action" to have Jesus executed (v. 51). He boldly went into Pilate and asked for Jesus' body (v. 52; Mark 15:43). John tells us that another member of the Council, Nicodemus, the one who came to Jesus at night, went with Joseph to Pilate (John 19:39; 3:1–2).

After receiving permission from Pilate to take Jesus' body down, Joseph "wrapped it in linen cloth and placed it in a tomb cut in the rock, one in which no one had yet been laid" (v. 53). (Read also Isaiah 53:9 for the prophecy of this.) Luke noted the time was Preparation Day for the festival, and near sundown that would begin the Sabbath (v. 54).

The irony of Joseph and Nicodemus' actions was that, while they were secret followers of Jesus, they risked their position and persecution from their peers by openly identifying with Jesus. On the other hand, Peter and the other 10 disciples who followed Jesus openly for three or so years went secret when public ridicule and great risk were possible by identifying with Jesus.

What do the actions of Joseph and Nicodemus tell you about their faith? Write a prayer to God asking Him to give you that kind of risk-filled trust in Jesus.

_____

_____

_____

_____

_____

43.5 Witnessing Jesus' Burial

Jesus' burial is part of the details of the story of Jesus that cannot be overlooked. As with His death, His burial is at the core of the Jesus story. (Read 1 Corinthians 15:3–4 again.) The evangelistic writers recorded the certainty of His death and burial. Mark added the detail that Pilate refused to release the body of Jesus to Joseph until he confirmed Jesus' death with the centurion who oversaw the execution (Mark 15:44–45). In the same way, the writers provided witnesses beyond Joseph and Nicodemus to the place Jesus was buried.

Read Luke 23:55–56. List the actions of the women who followed Joseph as he took down the body of Jesus and laid it in the tomb.

Luke wrote, "The women who had come with Jesus from Galilee followed Joseph and saw the tomb and how his body was laid in it" (v. 55). Mark tells us "Mary Magdalene and Mary, the mother of Jesus," were those women (Mark 15:47). They witnessed the fact that Jesus was prepared for burial and His body was placed in a tomb. Their witness is important to confirm the witnesses of Joseph and Nicodemus that Jesus died and was buried. Matthew tells us Joseph "rolled a big stone in front of the entrance to the tomb" and that Pilate posted guards to secure the area (Matt. 27:60, 64–66). The number of people who could say they knew where Jesus was buried grew in size. If someone had either misplaced or stolen the body, one of the several witnesses would have known about it and reported it to the authorities. But that never happened.

After they made certain Jesus had been cared for, the women went to their home to prepare "spices and perfumes" for Jesus' body (v. 55). Since the Sabbath had begun, they rested and could not return to the tomb until the next day, at sunrise Sunday morning, which was the third day.

This chapter of the *Christos* is about Jesus' death and burial and those who put their trust in Him along the way. The criminal, centurion, Joseph, and Nicodemus were a motley crew of those who openly trusted Jesus and confessed their trust in some way. The Bible promises that "to all who received him, to those who believed in his name, he gave the right to become children of God" (John 1:12, the Memory Verse for this chapter). These became the "children of God" that day.

Review the death and burial of Jesus as you end this chapter. How would you describe your trust in Jesus now that you have witnessed His death for your sins? How has your trust in Him grown?

For further study:
- **Mark 15:39**
- **John 19:38–42**

44—Discovering God's Power: The Resurrection

The single, distinguishing mark of the Christian faith from all other religions is Jesus' Resurrection from the dead. All Jesus did was validated in God's powerful work of resurrection. Otherwise, Jesus would have been like every other world leader and would-be messiah who tried to set up a kingdom on earth only to have it all end with their deaths. Jesus' Resurrection vindicated His words and deeds, and validated His claim to be the *Christos*, the Son of the Living God. The Resurrection of Jesus stands as the lone event in history that confirms Jesus of Nazareth is the *Christos*.

After His bogus trial, cruel crucifixion, and burial, all was quiet the Sunday morning the women went to the tomb to put spices and perfume on Jesus' body. The disciples had huddled in their homes. All of Jerusalem returned to their daily, religious lives. Only this day would be different. When the women came to the

place Jesus had been buried, they noticed that the stone covering the opening had been rolled away. When they looked inside, all they saw were the grave clothes that had covered the One they loved. Thus began the Resurrection revolution that changed the hearts of those who first met the Risen *Christos* and those who meet Him today.

The Memory Verses for this chapter are 1 Corinthians 15:3–4. These verses contain the core message of the story of Jesus. To know it is to know the essence of the Christian faith. The heart of this message that has been told for centuries is the heart of what we believe.

Our question to consider for this chapter is "What is the significance of the Resurrection?" Observe the events of Resurrection Sunday in this chapter and then return to answer this question.

Christos—God's Transforming Touch

44.1 Spreading the News

The day my first child was born, I called as many people as I could to come and see her. When my wife and I bought our first house, we wanted all of our friends to see our new home. The day I held my first grandchild I posted pictures on the Internet and invited as many friends as I had email addresses for to view them. Good news travels fast. Bad news travels faster. The tragic death of a loved one or the news of a firing or indictment of a public figure hits news networks with more speed and volume than any pictures of a firstborn grandchild. Stunning turn of events must be told. Unexpected tragedies send people running to tell their friends.

What good news have you have communicated quickly and urgently to others? What unexpected or tragic pieces of information have you heard about and wanted your friends to know as soon as possible? Write your experiences here:

_____

_____

_____

Read John 20:1–2. Circle the names mentioned in the verses and underline Mary's message to Peter.

In the early morning hours on the first day of the week, the third day of Jesus' death and burial, Mary Magdalene and two other women went to the tomb where Joseph of Arimathea had prepared and laid the body of Jesus (Mark 16:1). "Just after sunrise," Mark noted, they arrived at the tomb and discovered it was empty (vv. 1–2). They had not mistaken where Jesus was laid. They had followed Joseph there Friday evening, and the sun was shining that morning. Peter and John later verified the women's story about the empty tomb.

Mary Magdalene has become famous of late by the resurgence of the myth that she married Jesus after His resuscitation from the grave and bore children to Him. The biblical record acknowledges her friendship with Jesus. However, her importance to the first Christians was not her relationship with Jesus but her witness to His empty tomb. Every evangelistic writer of the story of Jesus recorded her witness (Luke 8:2; Matt. 28:1; Mark 16:1; Luke 24:10).

When Mary Magdalene realized Jesus' body was not there, she ran to where Peter and John were staying and told them the shocking news: Someone had taken Jesus' body! Mary jumped to the conclusion any human under the same circumstances would conclude. No one had ever risen from the dead, so someone must have taken the body. This has been a claim since the day the empty tomb was discovered. Matthew warned that "this story has been widely circulated" until the day he wrote his story of Jesus (Matt. 28:11-15). But there is more to the story than first impressions.

Read the accounts from each story of Jesus when the women first discovered the empty tomb. What would have been your first thoughts? Who would you have run to and told about the empty tomb? Is there an answer to the claim someone stole Jesus' body? Write some of your feelings here:

_____

_____

_____

44.2 Witnessing the Empty Tomb

Verifiable evidence is essential to tell the true story when deciding a court case. Details are important to any witness' account of an event. The more authentic the details, the better a judgment can be made as to the person's innocence or guilt. In forensics every detail is weighed and examined to piece together the evidence to tell the true story. Fingerprints or DNA on an object become details that help write the truth of what happened and form the basis for how the judge and jury judge the case.

Have you ever been part of a trial in court where the detailed evidence made the difference? If not, what is your favorite film or television show that emphasizes these things? Write the details here:

_____

_____

_____

Read John 20:3–9. Circle the names of the two men who went to the tomb and underline the evidence they saw when they got there.

Simon Peter, the lead disciple, and "the other disciple" were the first to run to the tomb upon hearing Mary's report (v. 3; Luke 24:12). "The other disciple" or "the disciple Jesus loved" is John's cryptic name for himself in his story of Jesus (John 13:23; 19:26; 20:2; 21:7, 20). John made sure everyone knew that he outran Peter to the grave. When John looked in, he saw only "the strips of linen lying there" (vv. 4–5). Peter arrived after him but went immediately into the tomb. He not only saw the strips of linen Joseph had wrapped Jesus in but also

"the burial cloth that had been around Jesus' head." John took note that "the cloth was folded up by itself, separate from the linen" (v. 7). This did not appear to be the work of grave robbers. If it was, they took extra care to fold and arrange everything neatly in the tomb.

John then wrote that he witnessed what Peter had seen. He "saw and believed" (v. 8). Later when John wrote his story of Jesus, he added that they, too, did not know what to believe about the situation. Was Mary Magdalene right? Had someone stolen the body? What other explanation was there? After seeing Jesus, who had risen from the dead, John wrote, "They still did not understand from Scripture that Jesus had to rise from the dead" (v. 9).

John recorded the evidence he personally saw that day. Mary and Peter had seen the same thing, but they did not know the meaning of it yet. They came to the logical conclusion that without seeing Jesus walking around or without the evidence of His dead body someone must have stolen it. But why? But who? They were bewildered for the moment, but all this would soon change.

Put yourself in place of Mary, John, and Peter. What conclusions would you have drawn? Mary had been with Jesus at His death and burial on the first day. What emotions did she experience when she found His tomb empty? Write your thoughts here:

_____

_____

_____

_____

_____

Christos—God's Transforming Touch

44.3 Talking with the Angels

After the funeral of my grandfather on my mother's side, I stood outside the church building to face an open field at the edge of the small farming community. I can almost remember the smells and the feel of the warm wind blowing over the flat lands of the Texas Panhandle. He was my first grandparent to die. We had gone to see him and my relatives in the town of my parent's childhood since I was old enough to remember. I cried as I stood alone in the shade of the building. I cried because I felt like my childhood was being buried with my grandfather. I had already finished college and married. As long as my grandparents were alive, they were living memories of holidays and summers working on the farm. With his funeral, I buried the memories my grandfather held for me each time I saw him.

What did you feel when your grandparent(s) died? Did you feel like me? When did you sense that your childhood memories seemed to be lost with the one you buried? Write some of your feelings here:

_____

_____

_____

Read John 20:10–13. Circle the words that reveal Mary's emotions outside the tomb and underline the question of the two angels.

After Peter and John saw the empty tomb, they "went back to their homes" (v. 10). They wanted to tell their families and friends what they had seen. Mary, however, remained at the tomb crying. She had already told someone what had happened. Now she stood alone.

The One who had cast seven demons out of her, who had been her Leader, and who had died right before her eyes, was now gone. Memories and hopes flooded her heart; emotions rushed out. Through her tears she bent down and looked into the tomb to look at what Peter and John had seen (v. 11).

When Mary looked into the tomb, John wrote that she saw "two angels in white, seated where Jesus' body had been, one at the head and the other at the foot" (v. 12). John's witness fits with Luke's which stated, "two men in clothes that gleamed like lightning stood beside" the women (Luke 24:4, 23). The two angels wanted to know why she was crying. John gave us no other words from the two, but Luke added that they continued, "Why do you look for the living among the dead? He is not here; he has risen!" (Luke 24:5–6)

Mary shared her deep despair with the inquisitive messengers of God. She was still convinced someone had taken Jesus' body, and she did not know where they had taken it (v. 13). She had come to prepare His body for burial, and now He was nowhere to be found. Her emotions overwhelmed her.

Stand with Mary at the tomb. Remember the loss of a close loved one or friend. The sense of loss may have been more than you could stand. Where did you find the hope and strength to go on? Where would Mary find the same things she needed to go on?

_____

_____

_____

44.4 Holding on to Jesus

When Mary turned from the two men who had asked her why she was looking into an empty tomb, she saw a man standing nearby. It was Jesus, but she did not recognize Him (v. 14).

Based on what you know from the story of Jesus up to this point and any other references to the Resurrected *Christos*, why do you think Mary did not recognize Jesus when she first saw Him? Write your answer here:

_____

_____

_____

_____

Read John 20:15–16. Circle what Mary called Jesus after He said her name.

Jesus asked the same question as His messengers. He wanted her to share her confession of what she knew about the turn of events and why these events had upset her so. She thought He was the gardener who had come to work that morning and told him what she had told the angels. She wondered if he was the one who had taken the body (v. 15).

Jesus then said her name: "Mary." Upon hearing her name from the voice of her Leader, she turned back to Him. In her native language, she called Him by a title she had used many times before, "Rabboni," or "Teacher!" When Jesus spoke her name, she knew His voice and called Him by name (v. 16). Jesus told us that the sheep of the Good Shepherd would hear His voice, recognize it, and follow Him (John 10:3–4).

Read John 20:17. Underline what Jesus said to Mary and what He instructed her to go and do.

Mary must have embraced Jesus because He asked her not to "hold on" to Him for He had not "returned to the Father." We begin to get a glimpse of Jesus' Resurrection body from this encounter with Mary. She could hold on to Him—He was not ghost-like. She recognized Him when she saw Him after He spoke her name—His voice, figure, and face were similar to His pre-Resurrection body. But something was essentially different because He alluded to something else when He said He had "not yet returned to the Father."

Jesus instructed her to go and tell His "brothers," His disciples, that He would ascend to the Father as He had already explained to her (v. 17). "Go" and "tell" were Jesus' words to Mary. This is His message for us who follow Him today. Others will know what we have seen and who we have met only when we go and tell them.

Whom have you told about your meeting with the Resurrected Jesus? My hope is that, just as Mary saw and recognized Jesus, you have seen and recognized Him, too. If you were to tell someone about your meeting with Jesus, what would you say? Write your outline here:

_____

_____

_____

44.5 Being Obedient

Mary was obedient to Jesus' command. While she must have wanted to stay and ask many questions, she went to Jesus' disciples and reported, "I have seen the Lord!" She then went on to tell all that she had seen. Mary was the first witness to the Risen *Christos* (v. 18).

What feelings do you believe the disciples had when they first heard Mary's report? You have just heard her news again through John's witness to what she said. What feelings do you have about what you just read? Meditate on the setting and her message to get a sense of what the first disciples sensed when she came into their houses and told them the good news.

The Memory Verses for this chapter are 1 Corinthians 15:3–4. These verses contain the core message of the story of Jesus. To know them is to know the essence of the Christian faith and the heart of the message which has been told for centuries.

Read the Memory Verses again. What are the three essential parts of the message?

_____

_____

_____

Later, in that same letter, Paul explained that just as we have a "natural body" through Adam, we will have a "spiritual body" through Jesus (v. 44). Paul concluded, "Just as we have borne the likeness of the earthly man, so shall we bear the likeness of the man from heaven" (v. 49). The promise of Scripture is that we will have a resurrection body that bears the "likeness" of Jesus. Jesus showed Mary what that body looked like when He greeted her at the empty tomb. He was "the firstfruits of those who have fallen asleep" (1 Cor. 15:20). His resurrection body was living proof that those who are "in Christ" would join Him in this resurrection form (vv. 20–22).

Christianity alone proclaims a Risen Savior. The Risen *Christos* is the center of Christian faith and hope. His death and burial fulfilled the Old Agreement of God. His Resurrection verified His life and sacrifice and began the resurrection harvest for all people who trust Jesus. Review the biblical record about the Resurrection of Jesus. What is your own confession of this event and its importance to your trust in Jesus as the *Christos*? Follow Jesus' instructions and "go and tell" someone what you have seen.

For further study:
- **Matthew 28:1–10**
- **Luke 24:1–12**

45—Dealing with Failure: Jesus Reinstates Peter

After revealing Himself to Mary Magdalene outside the empty tomb, Jesus showed Himself to the other disciples. Jesus sought to encourage, instruct, and restore His followers to Himself. He wanted to prepare them to continue His mission after He ascended back into the Father's presence. He wanted to make sure they were free of guilt and confident His words were true and their assignments sure. Jesus ensured them of His love for them. His first call to follow Him remained valid.

John recorded Jesus' appearance to the disciples (John 20:19–20) and to Thomas (vv. 24–29). After Jesus appeared to Peter and the Twelve, He appeared to "more than five hundred of the brothers at the same time" (1 Cor. 15:6). Paul continued to chronicle Jesus' post-Resurrection visits by noting that Jesus went to "James, then to all the apostles," and "last of all" to Paul (1 Cor. 15:7–8). Jesus particularly sought out Peter as

He showed Himself to His followers. Peter had denied Jesus in public on the night of His betrayal after promising to follow Him to death. Jesus had invested a lot in Peter's leadership in the Kingdom movement, and He wanted to restore and assure His disciple of His love and confidence in him.

The Memory Verse for this chapter is James 4:10. James, the brother of Jesus, encouraged those he wrote to humble themselves before God, and He would lift them up. This principle was true with Peter and is true for all who desire to serve God and His purposes in their lives.

Our question to consider for this chapter is "Can we become unusable to God?" Observe Peter's denial of Jesus and Jesus' restoration of Peter to leadership among the disciples. Return to this question at the end.

45.1 Denying Jesus

My wife's birthday is Christmas Day. She does not like it being that day because her birthday celebration always gets lost in Jesus' birthday party. Some family and friends remember her birthday, but most are busy paying attention to their gift giving and family gatherings. They forget to call or write on that day. I feel it is up to me to be the first to wish her a happy birthday and have some form of party in the middle of all the Christmas activities. I usually do pretty well at this. But one year, she, her mother, our two daughters, and son-in-law were up early on Christmas Day to catch a plane for our shared Christmas vacation. About two hours into our preparation to get to the airport on time Kim said, "You forgot my birthday." No one had said a word about her birthday. I tried to cover up with something lame like, "I was going to say something, but we have been so busy getting ready that I was saving it for later." I was busted. I felt horrible and knew there was nothing I could do to make up for my failure to honor her on her birthday.

Have you ever disappointed or neglected to encourage or honor a loved one on a significant day like his or her birthday? How did you feel? What did you do to try and make up your lack of attention? Describe your experience here:

_____

_____

_____

_____

Read John 18:15–18, 25–27. Underline the three times Peter denied he knew Jesus.

Peter had promised that he would never fail Jesus even if it meant dying with Him. Yet, Jesus knew Peter's heart and had told him that he would deny Him three times before the rooster crowed to announce the new day (Matt. 26:31–35). Peter must have felt stunned at Jesus' words. Before the night ended, Peter had done exactly what Jesus said he would do.

Standing outside the proceedings that would convict Jesus and be the basis for His execution, Peter found himself among those directly connected to the trial of Jesus (John 18:15–18). When asked by a servant girl at the door of the high priest's house if he knew Jesus, Peter denied knowing Him. Later, while standing around a fire for warmth against the night air, two others asked if Peter had been with Jesus. Both times Peter denied knowing Him (vv. 25–27). Mark tells us that Peter became irritated and began to curse (Mark 14:71). When he heard the rooster crow, his heart was broken and he began to weep (v. 72).

Peter, who had confessed Jesus was the *Christos* and promised never to let Jesus down, openly denied even having been with Him. One of Jesus' closest friends deserted Him in His most trying time. Peter must have wondered if Jesus would ever forgive him.

Pray for God to show you the depth of Peter's hurt and the many ways we disappoint Him every day.

45.2 Catching Fish

A couple of questions get to me when someone I know well asks them. One is "How are you doing? Really."

That question means I have to tell the person the truth about how I am feeling, though I am not good at sharing my feelings with people—even my best friends. That question also makes me begin to wonder what I have done or said to signal that I am not OK. The other question is one my wife or daughters have never asked me: "Do you love me?" I hope they never do because when someone who is supposed to know you love them asks that question, you have not been doing and saying what is needed for them to know the answer to such a question. "Do you love me?" coming from someone who is supposed to know that means something more is at issue than the transfer of information.

How do those two questions make you feel? When was the last time someone close to you asked you one of them? How did you answer them?

_____

_____

_____

_____

Read John 21:15. Underline Jesus' question to Peter and His command to him.

Jesus had come to the Sea of Galilee to see His disciples after His Resurrection. When He arrived, He called out to His disciples who were fishing to cast their nets on the other side of the boat and they would catch something. They followed His instructions, and the catch almost sank their boat! Peter remembered Jesus had told him to do this when He called him to be His disciple (Luke 5:4–6), so he jumped out of the boat and joined Jesus on the shore. When the other disciples arrived on the shore, they all sat around a fire and ate the fish and the bread Jesus had prepared for them (John 21:1–14). This is the setting for the conversation that followed.

"When they had finished eating," John wrote that Jesus asked Peter if he truly loved Him "more than these" (v. 15). Jesus gave Peter a chance to declare his love for Him to His face and in front of his friends. Peter did not hesitate and answered, "Yes, Lord, you know that I love you." John recorded Jesus' use of the word love as *agape*, a love exemplified by God's love shown by sending Jesus (John 3:16). Peter answered with a different word for love, *phileo*, or warm friendship. While the words were used as synonyms in most cases, the difference here shows Jesus was pushing to something more than friendship with Peter. Jesus wanted Peter to move from a friend-like relationship to one in which Peter would be willing to lay down his life for Jesus.

Christos—God's Transforming Touch

Jesus did not comment on Peter's answer but told him to "feed my lambs," a pastoral picture of ministry (v. 15). Jesus gave Peter a job to do as the leader of His disciples: care for the "lambs" (new believers).

How would you answer if Jesus sat with you and asked you the question He asked Peter? Spend some time prayerfully to find your honest answer. Write some of your thoughts here:

_____

_____

_____

45.3 Reinstating Peter

The Christmas morning I forgot my wife's birthday began a long day of trying to make her day special. I sent her children and mother in to say "happy birthday" as she was getting ready. I kept telling her how sorry I felt that the day was not special for her and that it was my fault. We were going to Disney World, after all. Who would not want that for a birthday present? That did not matter. I had missed my chance to honor her, and I spent the next three days trying to make it up to her. She was kind about my efforts but finally told me to drop it. She stressed that whatever I said would not change the first misstep or the fact she has and always will have her birthday on Christmas Day. She said she loved me, and it was not a problem anymore. And if I brought it up again on the trip, she would hit me—figuratively speaking, of course.

Have you hurt someone before and then overcompensated for your mistake? How did the person respond to your efforts? Did it help or hurt the situation? Write your experience here:

_____

_____

_____

_____

Read John 21:16–17. In both verses, circle the word "love" and underline Jesus' instructions to Peter.

Jesus would not let Peter's first answer stand. He asked His denying disciple again, "Do you love me?" Again, Jesus used the word that meant the *Christos* kind of love Jesus demonstrated by dying on the cross for us. And a second time Peter answered His Leader with the same response, "Yes, Lord, you know that I love you." Peter either missed the intent of Jesus' word for love, or he hung on to the best word he knew for his commitment to Jesus. Again, Jesus responded with a command: "Take care of my sheep" (v. 16).

A third time Jesus asked Peter if he loved Him, but this time, Jesus addressed Peter by his given name, "Simon son of John," instead of the name Jesus had given him (v. 17; Matt. 16:17–18). Also, this time Jesus changed the word He used to inquire about Peter's love. Jesus switched to the word Peter had used to describe his love for his Rescuer and Leader. Why the change? Jesus may have wanted Peter to know He accepted his confession of commitment to Him by using his word. But John tells us, "Peter was hurt because Jesus asked him the third time" (v. 17). Did Jesus not hear him the other two times? Jesus did not respond to Peter's emotions, but a third time Jesus told Peter to "Feed my sheep."

Why did Jesus ask Peter three times if he loved Him? Why did Jesus give His disciple instructions to care for His sheep three times? Peter surely carried the guilt of denying Jesus three times. He must have wondered if Jesus would ever ask him to serve again. In one short, intentional conversation, Jesus allowed Peter to confess his love for Jesus as many times as he had denied Him. As many times, Jesus confirmed His disciple's usefulness to His mission.

Meditate on this conversation between Jesus and Peter by becoming Peter in the story. Sit and listen long enough to hear Jesus' question to you and your heart's true answer.

45.4 Warning Peter About His Death

At the time I am writing this chapter, my last living grandmother is 92 years old. She suffers from dementia, brittle bones, and overall weakness; but she still enjoys her life even though others have to help her do almost everything. When I think of her, I remember the days we spent at her house, weeks at a time in the summer and on holidays. I remember when she would behead, pluck, and clean chickens for Thanksgiving dinner and how she loved to paint. She even opened an art gallery and gave art lessons in her hometown of less than 400 people. She could get around and do a variety of things when she was younger. Now she is limited in what she can do by those who help her and the health of her weakening body.

Do do know someone who is along in years now whom you have memories of as much younger? Write his or her name and some of your memories in the space below. Ask God to let you be with the person today.

———————————————————————————

———————————————————————————

———————————————————————————

Read John 21:18–19. Underline in verse 19 why Jesus said what He did to Peter and His final instructions given to Peter.

Immediately after Simon Peter's final confession of loyalty and love to Jesus, Jesus offered a picture of what would happen to Peter. Jesus used the metaphor of youth and age and the mobility of both to paint the picture (v. 18). Jesus, however, did more than tell Peter he would get old and not be able to get around as well as he did as a youth. The purpose of Jesus' words was to show the disciple how his life would end. Peter's love for Jesus would cost him his life as did Jesus' love for Peter. Jesus told Peter, "you will stretch out your hands, and someone else will dress you and lead you where you do not want to go."

John explained, "Jesus said this to indicate the kind of death by which Peter would glorify God" (v. 19). We know from early Church history that Peter was crucified in Rome during the persecution of Christians by Nero, who was Caesar (about A.D. 67). Jesus' cryptic description about Peter's later years came true in history as Peter's martyrdom on behalf of Jesus demonstrated his confessed love.

Jesus repeated again the first words He said to Simon: "Follow me!" Jesus instructed Peter to continue following Him and to carry out the mission to "Feed

Christos—God's Transforming Touch

my sheep." Peter was now reconciled with the One he had denied and restored to his place of leadership on mission with Jesus.

How do you interpret Jesus' words to Peter for your own life as a disciple of Jesus? Write in the space below the words of Jesus that can give you direction for today. Read a Bible encyclopedia or commentary to learn more about Peter's death.

_____

_____

_____

45.5 Commissioning Peter

Our question to consider for this chapter is "Can we become unusable to God?" Many people fear that things they have done prevent them from being used by God to accomplish His purposes on earth. A decision to divorce, have an affair, get an abortion, or even to think about such things, must surely disqualify one to serve God and others in Jesus' name. Do you have anything in your life now or in the past that makes you think God cannot use you? Write about that issue here:

_____

_____

_____

We observed a conversation between Jesus and Peter that restored Peter to service with God, even after he had openly cursed and refused any allegiance to Jesus whatsoever. If Jesus might have ever said, "You are no longer worthy to represent Me," He would have said it to Peter. Jesus carefully and compassionately gave

Peter a chance to confess his love for Jesus. Then Jesus commissioned Peter to continue the mission Jesus had given him. Jesus feels the same about you if you will simply confess your love for Him and arrange your life around His mission for you.

The Memory Verse for this chapter is James 4:10. James, the brother of Jesus, encouraged those he wrote to humble themselves before God, and stressed that God would lift them up. This principle was true with Peter and is true for all who desire to serve God and His purposes in their lives. Humility begins with brokenness and results in usefulness by God. I wish there was another way to be useful to God, but there is not. Peter's brokenness led to his honest confession and gave Jesus an opportunity to restore him to his calling.

We will all fail. We will all disappoint our loved ones and God. But Jesus, the Risen *Christos*, will forgive and restore those of us who will humble ourselves before Him, confess our love for Him, and follow Him even if it results in laying down our lives for Him.

For further study:
- **Matthew 26:31–35**
- **Matthew 26:69–75**

46—Responding to the Call: The Great Commission

Mission is everything for a servant-leader. The mission is the purpose for his or her leadership and the benchmark for all he or she does. Mission, or purpose, is what you do when you wake up in the morning and why you live your life. If you feel your mission is to be a parent, that purpose in life will drive you morning and evening. If it is to make enough money to retire at age 55, that is what you will work to accomplish each day. On the other hand, if you make yourself a servant to God's mission call on your life, just as the first followers of Jesus did, then your relationship with Jesus and His way of life become why you do what you do.

Jesus lived a mission-driven life. He said, "I have come down from heaven not to do my will but to do the will of him who sent me" (John 6:38). Jesus had no reason to come to earth and clothe Himself in flesh but for His mission to be the Suffering Servant *Christos* for all people. Jesus modeled for us what a life submitted to the mission call of God looks like and the power of one life given fully to complete that mission. Before Jesus returned to the Father, He commissioned His apprentices to become servant-leaders on mission to make disciples of all people.

The Memory Verses for this chapter are Matthew 28:18–20. These words of Jesus before He ascended to heaven answer part of the question "What is God's will for my life?" While Jesus' command does not include the details, the direction and purpose for your life as Jesus' humble servant-leader is made crystal clear.

Our question to consider for this chapter is "What is my role as a Christian in a non-Christian world?" For an answer to this, let us walk through Jesus' last words to His disciples as recorded by Matthew.

Christos—God's Transforming Touch

46.1 Doubting Jesus

I would stake my life on the fact that Jesus was raised from the dead and now sits at the right hand of the Father, guiding history, and waiting for the moment to return to set up His Kingdom on earth. But I still have my doubts. My simple mind cannot get around all that goes on in my world, much less the world. I do not fully understand how my free will and God's sovereign rule mesh, or how God's love allows evil and suffering. So I instead focus on the things made clear by the words and actions of Jesus. This is what I know: love God, love others, and tell His story every day. These three things I know God wants me to do when I submit all that I am and all that I have to Him. One of the sources for these commands comes from Jesus' last words to His disciples before He returned to His Father. It is the reason for the "tell His story every day" part of what I know.

Read Matthew 28:16–17. Circle where the disciples went in verse 16, and underline their responses when they saw Jesus in verse 17.

After Judas hung himself, only 11 of Jesus' original disciples remained (Matt. 27:5). These 11 were bound by their shared experiences of following Jesus and seeing His resurrected body. They made the trek to Galilee from Jerusalem to hear their Leader's final instructions. Jesus had sent them word to go to Galilee through the women who encountered the Risen *Christos* the morning of His Resurrection (Matt. 28:7, 10). Matthew's story of Jesus has the disciples apparently going as soon as Jesus had told them to go. The other story writers fill in what happened in the time Jesus took to show Himself to many people.

Matthew recorded in his story of Jesus that when the 11 saw Jesus, "they worshiped him; but some doubted" (v. 17). Some of the disciples worshiped, showing honor to their Risen Leader. To see the One they knew had laid down His life for them and then rose again to defeat death must have called out true worship in their hearts. But Matthew also wrote "some doubted." We know that Thomas, the twin, had refused to trust Jesus was raised from the dead until he had seen and touched the Risen Leader (John 20:24–29). We can only guess the human men who followed Jesus had doubts about the mystery of Jesus' Resurrection.

Worship and doubt can dwell together in the hearts of Jesus' followers. Who Jesus is and what He does is too much for any of us to fully grasp. Those who trust Him worship Him for what they know about Him. Those who doubt Him can still be with Him because He will soon reveal who He is and His call upon their lives.

Which group of disciples do you identify with? Write your answer in the space below and explain why.

_____

_____

_____

46.2 Commissioning the Disciples

The person who commissions someone must have the authority to do so. I cannot decide this afternoon to fly to Russia and negotiate an arms deal with the Russian leaders. I have no authority, and no one with such authority has commissioned me on a mission to do that. If I were caught trying to make those deals, those with the authority would have me arrested and imprisoned for trying to do something I had no power to do. On the other hand, as a servant-leader under the authority of Christ, who is Head of the Church, I humbly use the authority given me to lead the people of Legacy on mission with Him. I can do this because God and the people, the church, have granted me the authority to act. Your mission in life is only valid if it comes from someone who has the authority to commission you to that mission. Some would argue that you alone have that authority. Jesus would argue otherwise.

What authority do you have in your life either through position or influence? How do you use that authority? List some ways here:

_____

_____

_____

Read Matthew 28:18. Circle the word "authority."

Jesus announced to His disciples, "all authority in heaven and on earth has been given to me" (v. 18). Jesus' death, burial, and Resurrection secured all authority over all things for Himself. His commission with the disciples was based on this authority.

Jesus had given His disciples "authority to drive out evil spirits and to heal every disease and sickness" when He sent them out the first time (Matt. 10:1). He also argued with the religious leaders about His authority to heal on the Sabbath (Matt. 9:5–7). And He marveled at the faith of a centurion who knew how to use the authority given him (Matt. 8:8–10). After Jesus completed His mission as the Suffering Servant *Christos,*

He was given all authority over all things created, physical and spiritual.

Read Ephesians 1:19–23. Underline the entities the Bible says Jesus has authority over as a result of His Resurrection and Ascension to the Father. How does this authority apply to Jesus' words to the disciples on the mountain? Write your answer here:

_____

_____

_____

Jesus shared His authority over all things with His disciples. This was the basis of His commission for them and the foundation of their power on mission. Without it they would have had no reason or power to continue.

What does Jesus' announcement about His authority mean to you today? How does it connect to what you will do today or the source of your confidence to live out His mission for your life? Write your thoughts here:

_____

_____

_____

46.3 Making Disciples

Every mission must be clear for those who receive it in order that they know what to do. A sergeant must have clear orders, or he will not know how to direct his men on the battlefield. A maestro must have precise plans for her orchestra or the orchestra will make noise, not music. Paul complained that one of the problems with disorderly speaking in tongues when the church gathered was that they sounded like a trumpet that does not sound a clear call. If that was the case, Paul asked, "Who will get ready for battle?" (1 Cor. 14:8) A mission is the trumpet call to action. It sets the course for those who become servants and leaders to it. Jesus was clear about what He commissioned His followers to accomplish.

Mission can include most anything from a directive from your boss to a wish by your child. What mission are you working on now? Step back from your current project and answer the question "What mission are you living for now?" Record some of your musings here:

_____

_____

_____

Read Matthew 28:19. Underline the verbs in the verse.

Jesus' mission for His followers began with "therefore." Jesus said, "Based on the fact I have authority in all heaven and earth, I now commission you to . . ." Most translations interpret the first word in the commission as "go," as if it were the command. It is actually a participle like "baptize" and "teach," which modify the main verb. It can be interpreted, "as you go" or "going." In other words, Jesus told them as they went about their lives they were to carry out His mission for their lives.

The main verb of the sentence is "make disciples." This concept is actually one word in the original language and is the process by which a teacher trained a student. To "disciple" people was to train them in the teacher's thinking and way of life. Jesus did this by His "follow me," training His disciples to live in the Kingdom of God until He returned.

If you transliterate (put an English letter in the place of an equivalent Greek letter) the word "nations," you get our word *ethnic*. We know from recent history that nations rise and fall, but ethnic groups cling together no matter who rules over them. Jesus' words can be interpreted to mean, "Train all ethnic groups to be Christ-followers."

How do you train others to be a follower of Jesus? Jesus' mission said to start by "baptizing them." Baptism is the outward sign of one's inward commitment to trust Jesus to be the *Christos*, the Rescuer and Leader. Baptism is the starting line of training to be a disciple of Jesus. It is the identifying act that you are with Jesus to learn from Him how to live like Him. Jesus began His public ministry by identifying with John's repentance movement. In the same way, a disciple of Jesus begins his or her public mission for Jesus by identifying with Jesus' redemption movement.

Apply Jesus' mission to your life as you now live it. What changes you would make if this truly were your mission in life?

_____

_____

_____

_____

46.4 Training the New Followers

Jesus commissioned the 11 disciples to train all people to be His disciples. The authority of that Great Commission was the *Christos*. The manner in which they were to go about their mission was as they lived their daily lives. The primary task of their mission was to invite and train others to be apprentices of Jesus like them. The scope of their mission included all ethnic groups. The public act of identification as an apprentice of Jesus was baptism "in the name of the Father and of the Son and of the Holy Spirit" (v. 19). This is Christ's mission for all of those who trust Him as the *Christos*.

If you profess to be a disciple-making disciple on mission with Jesus, evaluate your personal progress in completing this mission. How would you evaluate your fellow disciples together as you are the Church? Write some of your evaluation here:

_____

_____

_____

_____

Read Matthew 28:20. Circle the word "teaching" and underline the content of that teaching.

Making disciples of Jesus meant baptizing all people in order to publicly identify them with the Jesus movement. It also meant training Jesus' apprentices by "teaching them to obey everything" Jesus had commanded. Making disciples involved training those who trust Jesus as their Rescuer and Leader by teaching what He taught and how to live what He taught. To obey is to do what one is commanded to do. Therefore, disciple-making is teaching that results in doing what one is taught to do. Discipleship is training for a way of life. The result of the teaching is not completed workbooks but a new way of living, the Jesus way of life.

The Great Commission of Jesus for His followers then is this: As you go about each day, do something to invite or train someone you know or meet to trust Jesus. If they will trust Jesus as the *Christos*, baptize them so they can identify themselves as one of Christ's followers who now lives "in the name of the Father and of the Son and of the Holy Spirit." Train them to live like Jesus by teaching them how to do what Jesus taught all of His followers to do. This will take time. Be patient. You are not fully like Jesus yet either.

Jesus concluded His mission for His disciples with the promise, "And surely I am with you always, to the very end of the age" (v. 20). Jesus said He would go away but He would send "another Counselor" (John 14:16). This is how Jesus would be "with you always." When was the "end of the age"? This would be the time between Jesus' Ascension and His return. Jesus would empower and encourage His disciples while they are on mission with Him through the presence of the Holy Spirit until He returns to set up His Kingdom on earth.

Christos—God's Transforming Touch

Write Jesus' mission for your life in your own words in the space below. Again, as you grasp His clear call on your life, evaluate how you are doing.

_____

_____

_____

_____

_____

46.5 Rescuing All People

Some Christians debate which of Jesus' commands is most central to the life they live for Him. Some say that to glorify God like Jesus did is the most important thing we can do with our lives. Others want to emphasize our love for God alone as the hallmark of our lives. The biblical record supports these and other emphases. However, the Great Commission stands at the center of the Christian life and the church's purpose for being. Without the Great Commission, those who do not know who Jesus is or His way of life may never gain access to the things of God. The Kingdom of God advances as those who trust Jesus live like Jesus and share His story with friends and family in their world, one person at a time. Jesus commissioned 11 men to carry on His mission to rescue the hearts of all people. Look at what the result of their faithfulness to Jesus' call did in their lives.

Having reviewed Jesus' life and ministry, what would you place as the central theme of the Christian life? What role does the Great Commission have in the deci-

sions you make each day as you follow Jesus? Write your conclusions here:

_____

_____

_____

_____

The Memory Verses for this chapter is the passage we have just studied, Matthew 28:18–20. To know these words of Jesus is to know God's mission for your life. Set aside some time in the next week or so to become familiar with Jesus' mission call for your life. Meditate on it and apply it to the plans you have made. Make any adjustments you see as necessary.

Our question to consider for this chapter is "What is my role as a Christian in a non-Christian world?" Since your mission is to make disciples for Jesus as you go about your life, take some time to articulate that mission in an ever-changing culture in your own words. Compare the other story writers' versions of Jesus' words from the "For further study" section below.

For further study:
- **Matthew 28:16–20**
- **Luke 24:46–49**

47—Discovering God's Agenda: The Ascension

The story of Jesus did not end with His Resurrection and Ascension. Jesus and His mission to rescue all people continue in the lives of His disciples to this day. The story of the *Christos* coming as a baby and returning as Exalted Lord was a time in history that served as the touch point between the Old Agreement of God in the Law and the Prophets and the New Agreement of God in Jesus, the *Christos*. The Old was fulfilled in the New. When the Holy Spirit came upon the band of believers huddled in prayer at the Pentecost festival, the story of Jesus continued in the Church, or *ekklesia* (God's gathered people living out His mission call on their lives). Jesus' commission to His remaining 11 disciples is carried out today in the Church.

At Jesus' Ascension we learn from God's messengers, "This same Jesus, who has been taken from you into heaven, will come back in the same way you have seen him go into heaven" (Acts 1:11). Jesus' return to heaven marked the completion of His mission on earth. In the first chapter of the book titled the Acts of the Apostles, we observe Jesus' final words to His disciples, the scope of their mission, and His ascent into heaven, which is reminiscent of His mountain-top transfiguration.

The Memory Verse for this chapter is Acts 1:8. Jesus' final words to His disciples recorded by Luke are similar to those written down by Matthew. The distinguishing element in this account is the specific mention of the Holy Spirit and the widening circle of influence the witnesses to the *Christos* will have.

Our question to consider for this chapter is "When will the entire world hear about Jesus?" Take a shot at this question now and then answer it at the end of the chapter.

47.1 Promising the Holy Spirit

Luke tells us in volume 2 of his story of Jesus (Acts of the Apostles, the first volume being the Gospel of Luke) that Jesus appeared to the "apostles he had chosen . . . over a period of forty days and spoke about the kingdom of God" (Acts 1:1–3). During that time Jesus appeared to many of His disciples. We know He ate with several of them (John 21). Paul told of His appearance to over 500 people at once (1 Cor. 15:6). Matthew recorded that Jesus went to Galilee to a mountain and, while there, commissioned His disciples to "make disciples" (Matt. 28:18–20). And Luke recorded the unique encounter of two disciples with Jesus on the road to Emmaus as they returned home after Jesus' death and after resting on the Sabbath (Luke 24:13–35). Jesus spent the 40 days between His Resurrection and return to heaven connecting with, teaching, and encouraging those who trusted He was the *Christos*.

Take some extra time to read those accounts of Jesus' movements and activities during the time between His Resurrection and this time in history. Catalog some of those accounts here:

_____

_____

_____

_____

Read Acts 1:4–5. Underline Jesus' command to the apostles and what would happen "in a few days."

Luke introduced this conversation with the resurrected Jesus and His disciples with the indefinite phrase "on one occasion." Sometime in the 40 days of appearances Jesus sat and ate with the 11. Note here that Luke, the doctor (Col. 4:14), included the detail that Jesus in His resurrected state ate solid food like everyone else. Jesus was not a ghost but had a tangible body.

During the table conversation, Jesus told the disciples not to leave Jerusalem (v. 4). Jesus said to "wait for the gift my Father promised, which you have heard me speak about." To wait is a spiritual discipline few disciples master. But the 11 knew Jesus' words were true and did what He said to do.

Read John 14:16 and 26. What was Jesus' promise?

Jesus went on to describe the gift by explaining, "John baptized with water, but in a few days you will be baptized with the Holy Spirit" (v. 5). The promised Holy Spirit would come to them "in a few days." John the Baptist had prophesied at Jesus' baptism, "I baptize you with water, but he will baptize you with the Holy Spirit" (Mark 1:8). The gift of the Holy Spirit recorded in Acts 2 would be the fulfillment of John's prophecy and Jesus' promise.

Sit at the table with the 11 apostles. Hear Jesus' words to them as if they were to you. What did He say that would seem hard or confusing? Why do we have a hard time doing the clear things Jesus tells us to do?

_____

_____

_____

_____

_____

_____

47.2 Questioning Jesus

If Jesus appeared to you and you could ask Him one question before He returned to heaven, what would you ask? I would want the free will and rule of God thing explained or know why God appeared so mean in the Old Agreement. I would want to know if I was doing what He wanted me to do, and if my death would be sudden or if I could see it coming. I would ask Him to explain creation and how I could really know when He was coming back. Those concerns immediately come to my mind. But I said one, right? Then I would want to know if I was doing what He wanted me to do. All the others we could talk about in heaven.

You try it. What questions would you ask? What *one* questions would you ask? Write your list of questions in the space below and underline the crucial one.

_____

_____

_____

_____

Read Acts 1:6–7. Underline the disciples' question and Jesus' first response to them.

The disciples had the chance to ask Jesus many questions, but the last they asked was when He was "going to restore the kingdom to Israel?" (v. 6) The followers of Jesus still had hope He would set up His earthly Kingdom and restore Israel to its kingdom status among the nations. When they heard Jesus tell of the promised gift of the Spirit coming in a few days, they wanted to know if that would be the time they would see Jesus establish Himself as King of Israel.

Jesus reminded them that the timing of His Kingdom's ultimate manifestation would be unknown to them (v. 7; Mark 13:32). The Father had set the "times or dates," ticks of the clock and seasons of time, by His own authority. Jesus stayed consistent in His answer about when He would return.

Jesus seemed to ignore the part about restoring the kingdom to Israel in His answer. However, He did not so much ignore their question as He redirected their thinking from an earthly kingdom to the one in which they were to become witnesses. He would tell them that in the next breath, which Luke recorded in verse 8.

In what ways do Christians still confuse the physical Kingdom of God with its spiritual nature? For example, do you know of someone who puts his or her hope in a "Christian America" more than he or she seems to look

Christos—God's Transforming Touch

for the presence of God in all cultures? What examples show that some of us are still asking the disciples' question of Jesus? Write some of your thoughts here:

_____

_____

_____

_____

47.3 Making Disciples

We talk about "who is in your network of relationships" at my church. We ask the question so we will be aware of who God has put in our web of family members and friends. We are to be witnesses to people we live, work, and play with. I am convinced everyone in my nexus of relationships is there because they have something to do with the mission I am on to help people trust Jesus. Through these natural connections as I "go about" my daily life, I have the opportunity to live and act like an apprentice to Jesus. But how far does my network of relationships extend? That I will never know. If you see your relationships with others as the path of your witness to Jesus, you will soon realize you have connections around the globe.

To whom in your network of relationships can you be a witness for Jesus? List some names in the space below. You may want to draw a "web" of names to see the natural connection you have with people. That is your starting place for the mission call of God in your life.

_____

_____

_____

_____

Read Acts 1:8. Circle the word "witnesses." Underline the condition that will make them witnesses and the places where they would be witnesses.

Jesus offered His apprentices a more powerful mission than being leaders in an earthly kingdom. They did not understand the power they would need to carry out His call on their lives. Jesus told them He would empower them "when the Holy Spirit comes on you." Jesus commissioned His apostles with the authority of His name, and He empowered them with the presence of His Spirit (Matt. 28:19–20; Acts 1:8). What would they need His authority and presence to do?

_____

_____

_____

They, and those who followed them, would be "witnesses." We get our English word *martyr* from the Greek word that meant "witness." To be a witness is at the core of the mission of Jesus. Look ahead in the story of Jesus in Acts 2:32; 3:15; 5:32. You will see how Jesus' sent ones supported what they told people by the fact they were "witnesses" to Jesus. The Holy Spirit, the sent One by Jesus, would witness to who Jesus was and what He did.

Jesus told His disciples to "make disciples" of all ethnic groups (Matt. 28:19). Here He told them how the message and mission would spread. They would be His witnesses "in Jerusalem, and in all Judea and Samaria, and to the ends of the earth" (v. 8). You can follow the story of Jesus in Acts by Jesus' game plan for how their witness would grow. Their witness in Jerusalem is recorded in Acts 1–7. Their witness in Judea and all

Samaria is found in Acts 8–11:18. Acts 11:19 through the end of the story tells of their witness from Antioch to Rome.

Take a look ahead at the outline of Acts as laid out in Acts 1:8. Use a Bible atlas or map and draw concentric circles to mark where Jesus said His witnesses would go.

47.4 Watching the Ascension of Jesus

Our city hosts a balloon festival every year. More than 70,000 people attend the three-day event to see over 70 balloons float up from the city park into the fall Texas sky. Sometimes, the balloons' paths would come over our neighborhood. Some of the balloons float low enough to see the expressions on the faces of the pilot and riders. It is funny to see neighbors staring up into the sky to get a look at such a colorful and graceful balloon. We cannot help but wonder what it would feel like to soar over our houses with only the sound of our voices and an occasional flash of the burner.

Have you ever watched a hot air balloon fly? What other things have you watched fly or float past you and wondered what it would feel like to fly in or on them? Write some of your experiences here:

_____

_____

_____

_____

Read Acts 1:9. Underline the middle phrase of the sentence.

Jesus had given His servant-leaders their mission. His work on earth was done. When He had finished talking to the 11 disciples, Jesus was "taken up before their very eyes." This marks the Ascension of Jesus. Why is this event so important to the story of Jesus?

Jesus' Ascension meant He went to prepare a place for us (John 14:2). It meant He would send the Holy Spirit to empower His followers and convict the world of who He is (John 16:7–8). Jesus' return to heaven meant the establishment of the Church (Acts 2:1–4, 42–47) and the Holy Spirit's gifts to empower the people of the Church (1 Cor. 12). Jesus' Ascension meant the Father "seated him at his right hand in the heavenly realms, far above all rule and authority, power and dominion, and every title that can be given, not only in the present age but also in the one to come" (Eph. 1:20–21). Finally, although there are more, reasons Jesus would now serve as the disciples' High Priest (Heb. 4:14).

The Resurrection and Ascension of Jesus were His exaltation and glorification given for His humiliation of suffering and "obedience to . . . death on a cross" (Phil. 2:8). God, the Father, affirmed all Jesus had done through His glorious exaltation in His Ascension.

Write in your own words the meaning of Jesus' ascension in your confession of Him as the *Christos*. Look up the verses mentioned above or additional places where the Scriptures describe Jesus' work as the Second Person of the Trinity after His Ascension.

_____

_____

_____

_____

Christos—God's Transforming Touch

47.5 Going Back to Heaven

Many times my daughters have driven down our street, turned onto another street, and gone out of sight as I stood in the front yard and watched them leave. I always have mixed feelings about that experience. I first feel sad to see them go. We always have great experiences and build new memories when they are with us, and I am sad those have come to an end again. But I feel strangely excited because they are driving off into the next chapter of their stories, and we are always excited about what those might hold. Sometimes I get frozen between the grief of their leaving and the anticipation of their future, and just stand there no matter the weather or time of day or night.

When have you had a similar experience and sensed the grief and joy of leaving a loved one?

_____

_____

_____

Read Acts 1:10–11. Circle who spoke to the disciples and underline their message.

Frozen between the past and the future, the disciples only stared at the clouds into which Jesus had been taken up (v. 10). They had their orders, but no one had said, "March!" Like children gawking at a hot air balloon, they stood with their mouths hanging open wondering what to do.

While they looked into the sky, "two men dressed in white" (the same two men at Jesus' empty tomb?) suddenly stood beside them and said, "Men of Galilee."

The disciples must have been startled by the broken silence when the two addressed them. The messengers wanted to know why they still stared into the sky. Jesus was gone. They had work to do. The men reminded the disciples, "This same Jesus, who has been taken from you into heaven, will come back in the same way you have seen him go into heaven" (v. 11). In essence they said, "Quit looking for Jesus in the sky. The same One will return just as He said He would; now get on with what He told you to do."

Too many Christians are stuck between looking for Jesus in the sky and living out His mission for their lives now. Jesus saved us to serve His mission and others in His name. Too much sky gazing and not enough witnessing does little to help others trust Jesus is the *Christos*.

Where do your interests in Jesus lie? In the sky—when He is coming back? Or on mission—serving and loving others in the name of Jesus? Write your response here:

_____

_____

_____

Our question to consider for this chapter is "When will the entire world hear about Jesus?" What is the answer? When all of Jesus' disciples quit staring into the sky and go into the city to witness what they have seen in Jesus.

For further study:
* **Luke 24:50-52**
* **Revelation 1:9-18**

48—Coming Again: Jesus' Return

The Ascension of Jesus into heaven after His Resurrection is not the end to His-story. Jesus did not go to heaven never to return. Jesus now rules as the Exalted King over all creation. He will return to judge His enemies and bring the new heaven and new earth. The Kingdom of God brought to us by the *Christos* has begun to reveal itself through the Church, or *ekklesia*, but Christ's rule will not be complete until the King returns to destroy His enemies and rule from His throne on earth. His-story will not be finished until the King sits on the throne in His new creation.

God revealed His purposes in His-story through His Son, Jesus. After the Son's return to sit "at the right hand of God" (Mark 16:19), He sent the Holy Spirit to empower and guide *Christos'* body, the church. During the early years of the church, the Holy Spirit revealed how His-story would end to the disciple, John.

Exiled to the desolate island of Patmos as part of the persecution by the empire, John received a special revelation from God about the end of His-story. The Holy Spirit came to John and guided him to write down what he saw and heard so that the followers of Jesus would have hope when there seemed to be none.

The Memory Verse for this chapter is Matthew 24:42. Jesus central message about the end of this age was to "keep watch, because you do not know on what day your Lord will come." We are to watch for the King's return as we go about our lives and make disciples.

Our question to consider for this chapter is "What will Jesus look like when He returns at the end of history?" We will see an apocalyptic picture of Him.

Christos—God's Transforming Touch

48.1 Revealing the End of His-story

I like films like *The Matrix* and stories translated into film such as *The Lord of the Rings* and *The Chronicles of Narnia: The Lion, the Witch and the Wardrobe.* I like these type films because they tell the story behind the story. I enjoy the surface story because I know just underneath it lies a deeper meaning for me. While Neo and agents, Frodo and Gandalf, and Aslan and the White Witch are characters in the surface stories, we can find parallels and connections to deeper stories like the story of Jesus. The fictional images help me see real insights into life and matters of the heart. Do not get me wrong. I love factual depictions of Jesus' story, too. Few films have impacted me like *The Passion of the Christ* with its brutal clarity of Jesus' sacrifice on the cross.

What are your favorite films or stories like those I listed above? My wife does not like to look "behind" a story, so she prefers straight forward story lines and characters. You may be like her. If so, what are your favorite stories?

_____

_____

_____

Read Revelation 19. Underline some the images that seem curious to you. Mark those passages that give you a clearer picture of the things revealed to John.

Up to this point we have viewed the story of Jesus through narrative. The writers of His-story recorded the events and teachings of Jesus' life so that we would trust Him as the *Christos* (John 20:30–31). The Revelation of John is a kind of writing called apocalyptic literature. Apocalypse comes from the Greek word that means "to reveal or uncover." Books like Daniel and Revelation, or the Apocalypse of John, give two examples of this type literature in the Bible. Jesus' prophecies of the end times also serve as examples (Mark 13; Matthew 24–25). Through the person telling the story, God reveals the end of His-story. This is important to know as we interpret such a passage as the one we are about to study. This kind of biblical literature is no less true than that of history, wisdom, and prophetic writings. It is just sometimes harder to interpret to know its clearest meaning and find application to daily living. There is a story in the apocalypse, but it is intentionally veiled to provide hope for all generations until Jesus returns.

Look up apocalypse or apocalyptic literature in a Bible dictionary or encyclopedia. Read some of the biblical passages mentioned in the articles to become familiar with this type of literature. Anticipate the beauty and wonder of the passage we are about to study.

48.2 Considering the End of the Age

The Holy Spirit revealed to John, the apostle, how the end of the age would come. When we reach chapter 19, much has happened to describe the ending of His-story. Seven angels have blown seven trumpets that bring judgments on the earth (Rev. 8:–11). Seven angels pour out God's wrath from seven bowls that bring affliction to the earth (Rev. 15–16). A great prostitute rides a beast that rules over all other cities (Rev. 17). The city called Babylon is destroyed, and heaven rejoices over its fall (Rev. 18:1–19:10). This is part of the story line that leads up to the appearance of the first rider who comes in on the white horse in this episode of the apocalypse.

Read Revelation 19:11–13. Underline the names associated with the rider.

After the destruction of Babylon, heaven rejoices, and the "wedding supper of the Lamb" is celebrated (v. 7). Then John wrote, "I saw heaven standing open" (v. 11). God showed John the next episode in the final chapter of His-story. A rider on a white horse appeared, whom was called "Faithful and True." The rider brought with him justice and makes war with the rulers of the earth. John saw that "His eyes are like blazing fire," and he wore many crowns. He had both a name "no one knows but he himself" (v. 12) and the name " the Word of God" (v. 13). Clearly this is the exalted *Christos* ready to leave heaven and attack His enemies on the earth.

Compare this picture of Jesus with some of those you remember from the evangelistic stories of Jesus. For example, He held a child in His arms and wept at the funeral of a friend. John's revealed picture of Him here is nothing like those. What is different, and what do you believe the revelation of John is teaching you about the exalted Jesus? Write some of your thoughts here:

_____

_____

_____

48.3 Seeing Things through John's Eyes

The Roman Empire began to persecute Christians as they grew in numbers and influence. We know Peter wrote his first letter to the Christ-followers in Asia Minor. These Christians had begun to feel the heat of persecution and suffering due to their trust in Jesus

as the *Christos* (1 Peter 2:19–23). That persecution continued to grow to savage proportions in Rome under the rule of Nero (A.D. 37–68). The followers of Jesus on mission to make disciples of all people must have wondered if their suffering would ever end. John's letter would have given them hope no matter what they faced.

Read Revelation 19:14–15. Underline the metaphors that described the Returning Christ. How would these images encourage those who suffered for the sake of Jesus? Write your thoughts here:

_____

_____

_____

_____

_____

John saw "the armies of heaven" following behind the rider on the white horse, who was named "the Word of God" (v. 13–14; John 1:1–18). They, too, were dressed in clean, white linen. The armies of heaven followed their warrior King into battle against the enemies of God and His Church. John does not tell us if these were Christians who had died in Christ or angels. They are not armed. Only their leader has a weapon, and it was a "sharp sword" that came out of His mouth. This may be an image of the spoken Word of God that is "sharper than any double-edged sword" (Heb. 4:12). The Word of God need only speak to "strike down the nations." (Remember Jesus speaking and causing the guards in the garden to fall down? Read John 18:6 for this illustration.) The power of the spoken Word of God began creation (Gen. 1:1–3). It would be no surprise it could end creation, too.

It was revealed to John that the rider would rule the nations "with an iron scepter" (Ps. 2:9; Rev. 2:27; 12:5). He would also bring "the fury of the wrath of God Almighty" like one who treads in a winepress (v. 15; Isa. 63:3). This last image is the inspiration behind the famous Civil War song, "The Battle Hymn of the Republic."

What do these images of Christ's return do to help you trust Him? What hope do they bring to your expectations about the end of His-story? Record some of your thoughts here:

_____

_____

_____

_____

_____

Compare Jesus on the cross with Jesus in the passage we are studying. What is different? What is the importance of both in the scheme of God's plan to rescue all people? Write your thoughts here:

_____

_____

_____

_____

_____

48.4 Destroying God's Opponents

In the story of Jesus' crucifixion, we learned that Pilate ordered a notice to be nailed on the top of the cross upon which Jesus was executed that read "THIS IS JESUS, THE KING OF THE JEWS" (Matt. 27:37). The title was meant as a mockery of Jesus' claims to being King. The Jewish leaders did not like it, but Pilate said, "What I have written, I have written" and left the sign above the crucified King (John 19:20–22). This image of Jesus dying on the cross with the mocking title above Him may seem to be that of defeat. But as we read the rest of the story of Jesus we saw Him conquer death and the grave and return exalted to sit at the right hand of the Father until He would return (Mark 16:19). John's Revelation describes that return.

Read Revelation 19:16. Highlight the name that was written on the thigh of the rider.

John saw the rider on the white horse leading His armies to defeat the rulers on the earth. As the rider's robe flew back in the wind, John saw written on His thigh, "KING OF KINGS AND LORD OF LORDS" (v. 16; Rev. 17:14). There is no mistaking who the rider is and the rider's status among all so-called rulers on the earth or in heaven. The King of all kings and the Lord of all lords was returning to defeat all other rulers, governments, and powers to establish Himself once for all as the Supreme Ruler of the Universe.

This image can apply to both physical and spiritual rulers and powers. Paul wrote in his letter to the Christians in Ephesus that Jesus sits with the Father "far above all rule and authority, power and dominion, and every title that can be given, not only in the present age but also in the one to come" (Eph. 1:21). The revelation shown to John fulfills this reality for the age "to come." The Holy Spirit also revealed to Paul about the reality of this truth: "The end will come, when he hands over the kingdom to God the Father after he has destroyed all dominion, authority, and power. For he must reign until he has put all his enemies under his feet. The last enemy to be destroyed is death. For he 'has put everything under his feet'" (1 Cor. 15:24–27). This prophetic word is also fulfilled when the King of kings rides to earth to defeat all things that oppose Him. Jesus, the *Christos*, will be placed under the sovereignty of God and put in charge of all things (1 Cor. 15:28).

The punishment of crucifixion was the most degrading and humiliating experience a person could suffer. The Holy Spirit revealed that after Jesus' humiliation on the cross, God exalted Jesus. God exalted Jesus to the "highest place and gave him the name that is above every name, that at the name of Jesus every knee should bow, in heaven and on earth and under the earth, and every tongue confess that Jesus Christ is Lord, to the glory of God the Father" (Phil. 2:9–11).

How does the name on the thigh of the rider affirm the revelation of God to Paul? Combine all of the Scripture references in this section and write your confession of

who Jesus is and what He will do when He returns as He has promised.

_____

_____

_____

_____

_____

48.5 Returning to Reign

Jesus rose from the dead, ascended into heaven, and will return again as He promised. He conquered death, bought us salvation, and rules in heaven at the right hand of the Father. He awaits His signal to come to earth to judge His enemies and rescue His chosen ones. Jesus' return will bring an end to the fallen creation that has struggled since Adam and Eve, and He will bring with Him a new creation begun at His Resurrection. This is the hope of those who trust Him as the *Christos* and who have made themselves servants to His mission call on their lives. His-story will end when the exalted Christ returns to earth as the King of kings and Lord of lords. He will defeat all rulers, powers, and dominions with the sword of His Word. When He appears all will bow and worship Him for who He truly is. This is the end of His-story and the hope of His people.

The Memory Verse for this chapter is Matthew 24:42. Jesus' central message about the end of this age was to "keep watch, because you do not know on what day your Lord will come." We are to watch for the King's return as we daily go about our lives and continue to make disciples. As we keep watch, we diligently go about living out Jesus' mission call on our lives.

Christos—God's Transforming Touch

Reread Jesus' teachings about when the end will come in Mark 13 and Matthew 24–25. How do Jesus' words match with John's Revelation of Christ's return?

_____

_____

_____

Our question to consider for this chapter is "What will Jesus look like when He returns at the end of history?" John painted a graphic picture of the Returning *Christos*. How is his image different from what you expected? How does the image of a Returning Warrior-King leading armies to earth build your faith? What does the title King of kings and Lord of lords tell you about whom you love and serve?

_____

_____

_____

End this session by writing your confession of the Returning *Christos*. Include content from the stories of Jesus, the letters to the churches, and the Revelation of John. Tell someone who needs hope about what you have learned from the Bible today concerning the victorious returning King.

_____

_____

_____

_____

_____

_____

For further study:
* **Revelation 21:1–27**
* **Revelation 22:1–21**

Conclusion

His-story is not finished. Jesus, the *Christos*, began His public ministry on earth by calling us to change how we live "for the kingdom of heaven is near" (Matt. 4:17). Through His life and teachings, He challenged our self-centered way of life and taught us how to live as His Kingdom people. Through His death, burial, and Resurrection. He established the New Agreement of God. His new creation will be fully realized when He returns as the exalted King. Until then, we who trust Him to be the *Christos* and have made ourselves apprentices to Him, choose to live His way of life as His Kingdom people. We choose to be on mission with Him until "the very end of the age" (Matt. 28:20).

After Jesus' ascension back into heaven, He sent the Holy Spirit to empower His people to carry out His mission call on their lives. Their assignment? Make disciples of all ethnic groups until He returns. The Holy Spirit came upon the followers of Jesus during one of the Old Agreement festivals and formed the Church, the *ekklesia*. His-story continues in the *ekklesia* as God's chosen and gathered people serve on mission with Him. All He taught, modeled, and promised becomes evident in the fellowship of followers who band together to live out the *Christos'* mission call on their lives. This story is told in the New Agreement book known as the Acts of the Apostles. It is the next chapter in His-story and will be told through the Holy Spirit's work among and through the people called the *Ekkelsia*.

His-story will end with the *Christos'* return. Until then His followers must watch and carry out the work He has given us to do. We are the Body of Christ, the Church. I trust this study of the story of Jesus has brought you closer to the One who offers you the free gift of rescue if you will trust Him to be who He said He was and seek to live as He has taught and modeled for you to live.

Gene Wilkes
Ascension Day, 2008

A COMPLETELY
NEW APPROACH
TO ADULT BIBLE STUDY

NOW WITH 12 STUDIES TO CHOOSE FROM!

- Pick the right length course for you and your group. Choose from 4-6 week, 16-week or 48-week studies.
- Study guides available for each course allow for deeper personal study.
- Great lessons teach and affirm essential truth.
- Creatively developed.
- Additional supplemental resources also available.

YOUR TEACHERS' LESSON MATERIALS ARE ONLIN

- Access to everything in one place: lesson overviews, commentary, creative teaching plans, discussion questions, activities and so much more.
- Constant availability on the web.

CHOOSE YOUR NEXT STUDY
THROUGH THE **BIBLE**:
48-LESSON COURSES Great for Adult Sunday School and Bible Study!

YAHWEH: Divine Encounters in the Old Testament
We've all had moments that define our lives and change who we are forever. When we encounter God, everything changes. The Old Testament is a record of people who unmistakably encountered God. These encounters changed lives, shaped history and led to the redemption of the entire human race. And it all began by God revealing Himself to one person at a time.

CHRISTOS: God's Transforming Touch (Available June 2008)
For thousands of years before His birth, prophets spoke of His arrival. In the 2,000 years since, He has drawn people in with His love and transformed them through His Word. In 48 lessons, learners will encounter the central figure of history, Jesus Christ. They will be exposed to the prophetic messages concerning His coming, His birth, His three-year ministry of miracles and teaching and His death and resurrection. In each session learners will be challenged by His message of hope and invitation to abundant life.

EKKLESIA: The Unstoppable Movement of God (Available June 2009)
The word "relationship" may be the most important word in the English language. How we connect with others is second in importance only to how we connect with God. The community of believers, the Church, was created to equip those who have found life in Christ and to reach those who have not yet responded to His grace. This study explores the New Testament Church from its commission to its multiplication around the world. In Peter's preaching and Paul's journeys and letters, learners see what Christian community is intended to be.

THROUGH THE **BIBLE**
16-WEEK STUDIES Great for Adult Sunday School with a Semester Approach!

BEGIN, BELIEVE, BELONG

DEVOTE, DEPEND, DECLARE

REMEMBER, REPENT, RESTORE

TO US (Available June 2008)

AMONG US (Available October 2008)

FOR US (Available March 2009)

THE BODY (Available June 2009)

THE MISSION (Available October 2009)

CONFLICT & OPPOSITION (Available March 2010)

LIFE COURSES: 4-6 WEEK STUDIES Great Anytime!

COLLISIONS: My Expectations... God's Character / 4-week study

UNCOMMON: Compelled by God's Call / 6-week study

NO MATTER WHAT / 6-week study

JESUS: Image of the Invisible / 6-week study

FLAWED: Imperfect People Chosen by God / 6-week study

THE DARKEST HOURS: Seeking God in Desperation / 4-week study

life Bible Study

lifebiblestudy.com
877.265.1605